Y0-CDF-266

MASS MEDIA ISSUES

ANALYSIS AND DEBATE

GEORGE RODMAN

Brooklyn College

SCIENCE RESEARCH ASSOCIATES, INC.
Chicago, Palo Alto, Toronto, Henley-on-Thames, Sydney, Paris

A Subsidiary of IBM

To Karen

Acquisition Editors	**Michael Zamczyk** **Alan W. Lowe**	© 1981 Science Research Associates, Inc. All rights reserved. Printed in the United States of America.
Project Editor	**Gretchen Hargis**	**Library of Congress Cataloging in Publication Data**
Designer	**Barbara Ravizza**	Main entry under title: Mass media issues.
Photographers	**Lee Youngblood** **Terry Zabala**	Includes bibliographies and index. 1. Mass media—Addresses, essays, lectures—United States. I. Rodman, George R. P92.U5M29 302.2′3 80-20032 ISBN 0-574-22570-6
Compositor	**Interactive Composition Corporation**	10 9 8 7 6 5 4 3 2 1

Cover photo of camera lens courtesy of Nikon, Inc.

CONTENTS

PREFACE

This text is designed for college students in the introductory course in mass communication—a course that goes under a variety of titles, including "Introduction to Mass Communication," "Introduction to Mass Media," and "Mass Media and Society." The book may be used as a primary text when the course centers on media issues, or as an auxiliary text when the course is organized chronologically or by medium. All the articles expand on controversial issues that are mentioned in other texts. As one pre-publication reviewer pointed out, "An introductory text may suggest that certain arguments exist, but an anthology such as this can actually present those arguments."

Mass Media Issues: Analysis and Debate presents those arguments in such a way that students can debate them, either in class or on their own. The importance of presenting opposing viewpoints in this manner has become so apparent recently that at least one college has designed an entire curriculum around "verbal combat" between students.[1]

Many of the articles chosen for this anthology were originally direct debates between leading proponents for each side of the issues; other articles were originally published separately, but are now juxtaposed to form a debate. The rest of the readings are balanced articles that present an analysis of both sides of an issue.

I have selected materials from a wide range of sources: legal briefs, news clippings, editorials, interviews, press releases, and advertisements as well as magazine articles and excerpts from books. The result, I hope, will be an interesting, illuminating collection that will leave the student with the understanding that each issue has at least two sides, each with its merits, and ultimately one is left to decide the "correct" side for oneself.

I have tried to single out those issues that have received the most publicity and generated the most student interest in the last few years, as well as those that were required because of their inherent importance to this course. The articles selected are all current, but chosen at least in part because of a timeless quality that will keep them from becoming dated in the next few years.

The articles deal with issues that are relevant to all media, so there is no attempt to divide them "by media." Even without that division the issues are so interrelated that they are difficult to categorize at all. For convenience' sake, I have divided the book into four parts, and each part into several chapters. This division, like all organizational schemes, is to a certain extent arbitrary, but it has allowed me to group readings based on similarities and a more-or-less logical order. The index and the suggestions for further reading, however, should be consulted for a broader view of the way these issues fit together.

One final thought: Textbooks are mass media, and textbook writers are in some ways reporters, subject to the same pressures as other reporters. One group of authors point out one of those pressures as follows:

> Reporters are taught to "round out" their stories, to work at creating the impression that all relevant questions have been asked and answered, that the job (reporter's and audience's) is done. The result may be a redefinition of the obligations of a citizen. Instead of feeling obliged to do something about the world's problems, we may come to feel that it's enough just to know what the problems are. G. D. Wiebe calls this the syndrome of "well-informed futility." Most of us call it apathy.[2]

It is my hope that this book will be put to use to discourage apathy about these issues. Mass media issues may eventually affect many of the students in this course professionally. And they will certainly affect all of them personally, as members of American society.

I would like to thank the following reviewers for their many helpful suggestions: Mark Edelstein (Palomar College), Harry H. Griggs (University of Florida), Peter Longini (formerly of Brooklyn College), Don Pember (University of Washington), Rosalind Routt (Laramie County Community College), Donald E. Smith (Elizabethtown College), Kamil Winter (Southern Illinois University), and Morris M. Womack (Pepperdine University). Their help in shaping the manuscript is greatly appreciated.

NOTES

1. The college is William Penn College in Oskaloosa, Iowa, as cited in Jill Smolowe, "Debates Are Focus of College Curriculum," *New York Times* (February 26, 1980), p. C4.
2. Peter M. Sandman, David M. Rubin, and David B. Sachsman, *Media: An Introductory Analysis of American Mass Communications,* 2nd ed. (Englewood Cliffs, N.J.: Prentice-Hall, 1976), p. 20. The internal reference is to G. D. Wiebe, "Mass Media and Man's Relationship to His Environment," *Journalism Quarterly* (Autumn 1973), pp. 426–43, 446.

part I

SOME
PERENNIAL ISSUES

Some issues seem never to go away. We can expect
them to reappear each year, although they might be
wrapped in new rhetoric or put forth by new proponents or centered on new subissues. Perennial issues
in the mass media include (but are not, of course,
limited to) the concentration of ownership, the censorship of material that some consider offensive, the
ethics of advertising, and the ways in which media
practitioners choose what they will present to the
public.

The first chapter of this part of the book examines
the trend of more and more media falling into fewer
and fewer hands. The second chapter deals with the
classic arguments about censorship. Advertising
ethics are examined in the third chapter, and the
fourth chapter examines one of the most controversial devices ever used by a gatekeeper to decide
what to present to the public: the television ratings.

chapter 1

THE CONCENTRATION OF OWNERSHIP

As long as the media remain powerful in America, their ownership will be an important issue; and since there is no decline in media power expected in the foreseeable future, the issue of media ownership has to be classified as one of our "perennial" issues.

The first reading in this chapter is a general analysis of the problem of ownership concentration. It is written by Ben H. Bagdikian, who is a journalist, media critic, and professor in the Graduate School of Journalism at the University of California, Berkeley. Professor Bagdikian is one of the best-known critics of media concentration.

Bagdikian's article deals mostly with the newspaper industry, but concentration of ownership affects all media. The final three articles in this chapter examine the effects of big business on three other media industries: books, movies, and radio. "The razzle-dazzle world of today's book publishing" is discussed by Alvin P. Sanoff, associate editor of *U.S. News and World Report*. The equally razzle-dazzle world of Hollywood is examined by Michael Ruby, Martin Kasindorf, Pamela Lynn Abraham, and the staff of *Newsweek*. The radio business is discussed in an article from *Business Week*.

3

THE MEDIA MONOPOLIES

Ben H. Bagdikian

If the trend toward concentration of control in the news media is alarming, as I think it is, and if doing something about it is locking the barn door before the horse is stolen, I'm afraid I am writing about an empty barn. All media with routine access to mass markets are already controlled by too few people. If we are serious about preserving maximum practical access to the marketplace of ideas and information, we ought to be deeply concerned.

The 50 largest broadcast chains already have three-quarters of the audience. The 50 largest cable television companies have two-thirds of all subscribers. The 50 largest newspaper chains have more than two-thirds of all daily newspaper sales—and this is particularly troubling because concentration of control of daily newspapers has unique effects on all information media.

Our daily newspapers are still the dominant source for all news in the United States. I wish it were otherwise. I wish NBC, CBS, and ABC each had bureaus in all medium-sized and large cities, that all local radio and television stations spent 10 percent of their revenues on origination of news, and that the daily harvest was not limited to a dozen items. We would all benefit if we had a number of truly independent and comprehensive sources of daily news. But we do not.

Most news in all media comes overwhelm-ingly from two wire services, United Press International and the Associated Press. But UPI and AP do not originate most of their news; they pick it up from their local clients and members, the daily newspapers around the country. When there is a newspaper strike in New York City, not only the individual subscribers suffer: The national media—radio, television, *Time*, and *Newsweek*—originate a small amount of their own news but depend mainly on sitting down each morning and fearlessly reading the *New York Times*.

So when we talk about concentration of ownership of daily newspapers, we are talking about control of the only comprehensive and self-sufficient news system we have. There are more than 1500 cities in the United States with daily papers, but only 40 with competing newspaper managements. Of all cities with newspapers, 97.5 percent have newspaper monopolies.

The business trend among newspapers runs parallel to the trend in other industries. For example, there used to be more than 200 makers of automobiles in this country, and now there are only four. But even with this drastic concentration in the automobile industry, General Motors still competes with Ford, which competes with Chrysler, which competes with American Motors, and they all compete with Datsun, Toyota, Volkswagen, and other imports. But in concentration of ownership in daily newspapers, there is no competition even among the consolidated giants.

The Gannett chain, which had 76 papers the

Reprinted by permission from *The Progressive* (June 1978), 408 West Gorham St., Madison, Wisconsin 53703. Copyright © 1978, The Progressive, Inc.

last time I looked, does not compete with Lord Thomson's 56 papers or with Knight-Ridder's 32 papers or with Samuel Newhouse's 30 papers.* They are secure systems of local monopolies, effectively insulated from competition with each other. They are less like Ford and General Motors and more like AT&T, with its local operating subsidiaries, each an established monopoly in its own region.

This consolidation of monopolies is not something over the horizon; it is an accomplished fact. There are 1760 daily papers in the country—a number that has remained stable since World War II. Of these, 73 percent are owned by 170 corporations. And now these 170 corporations are consuming each other, with large chains buying small chains, so that control is gathering with disproportionate speed among the few at the top.

In 1950, 20 percent of all individual daily papers were owned by chains; by 1960, it was 31 percent; by 1970, 47 percent. Today it is 62 percent.

The same alarming concentration applies to total daily circulation. From 1950 to 1960, chain control of daily newspaper circulation remained at about 45 percent. But from 1960 to 1970, the percentage of papers sold each day owned by an absentee corporation rose from 46 percent to 61 percent. From 1970 to 1977, it went from 61 percent to its precent 73 percent. So almost three-quarters of all newspapers sold every day in this country are owned by a chain.

Some daily papers are so small—less than 5000 daily circulation—that their annual cash flow does not interest chains. For all practical purposes, there are 400 remaining independent daily papers with enough cash flow to interest outside corporations, and there are only 25 large chains that can effectively bid for them. Like beach-front property, independent daily papers are a disappearing commodity. So now

big chains are buying small chains, multiplying the rate of concentration. Since 1960, the 25 largest newspaper corporations have increased their control of daily national circulation from 38 percent to 53 percent. Ten corporations now publish 37 percent of all newspapers sold daily in the United States.

Newspapers have followed other industries in another form of concentration—the conglomerate. But as with chains, there is a qualitative difference in the social impact of media conglomerates as against companies that make plastics or musical instruments. If an ordinary conglomerate uses one of its companies to further the interests of another of its companies, it may be unfair competition but it is largely an economic matter. If a conglomerate uses its newspaper company to further the interests of another of its subsidiaries, that is dishonest news.

This subversion has happened in the past. William Randolph Hearst used his newspapers, magazines, and movie companies to urge us to declare war on Mexico to protect his mines in that country. The DuPonts owned, until recently, the major papers in Delaware, and used those papers to promote the financial and political interests of the parent company. The heirs of Jesse Jones in Houston used to do the same thing with their wholly owned subsidiary, the *Houston Chronicle*, ordering it not to run news that would discomfort its other properties, such as banks and real estate. The Florida East Coast Railroad owns papers in Jacksonville and has a history of using the news to promote or suppress information to suit the owners' other interests.

The growth of non-news investment in newspapers is not troublesome in itself; most original investment money in newspapers came from some other source. What is bothersome is that these are no longer single units in which the owner is locally based and recognized. And with chains, when contamination of the news occurs it can be on a massive scale. Atlantic Richfield recently bought the *London*

---

*Editor's note: As of late 1980, the Gannett chain owned 83 papers; the others have not changed substantially.

Observer. Mobil Oil says it is in the market to buy a daily newspaper. We might judge Mobil's dedication to independent journalism from its recent withdrawal of support from the Bagehot Fellowship for training business writers at Columbia University because the director of the program once wrote a book about the oil industry that Mobil disliked.

Blue Chip stamps now owns the *Buffalo Evening News* and 10 percent of the *Washington Post.* The biggest newspaper conglomerate, the Times-Mirror Corp., owner of the *Los Angeles Times,* also owns companies that publish most of the telephone directories in the West, produce maps for oil companies, and operate large agricultural and timber lands —all industries that are continuing issues in the news.

Some conglomerates seem to be focused on domination of national news. The Washington Post Company, in addition to its stable of newspapers, television and radio stations, owns *Newsweek* magazine. Time, Inc., another large publishing conglomerate, recently moved to match the *Post*'s position astride news out of the government by purchasing the only other Washington paper, *The Star.*

Finally, there is growing vertical control of information and cross-media ownership. not just between newspapers and broadcast stations, but among magazine and book publishers. RCA, for example, owns NBC and therefore has a lively interest in promoting books or magazine pieces that might make good television programming. A magazine article that leads to a book that leads to a TV series is considered ideal. So RCA also owns Random House book publishers and such subsidiaries as Ballantine Books, Alfred Knopf, Pantheon, Vintage, and Modern Library. CBS owns Holt, Rinehart and Winston, *Field & Stream* magazine, *Road & Track, World Tennis,* and *Cycle World,* plus the former Fawcett magazines. ABC has a big stake in the religious movement,

since it owns Word, Inc., a major producer of religious literature. And, of course, it owns Howard Cosell.

Music Corporation of America, in addition to large-scale control of entertainment, owns the G. P. Putnam book publishing firm, Paramount Pictures, and *New Times* magazine.

Concentration of ownership and acquisition by conglomerates sometimes happen in the business world when independent units begin to lose money and are, therefore, tempted to consolidate for survival. The opposite applies to newspapers: Chains are growing because individual newspapers and newspaper chains are making so much money that it is profitable to pay even exorbitant prices to buy up the few remaining independent entities.

Newspaper economics has always been a trade secret, but since 1963 major newspaper companies have begun to sell their stock to the public, and therefore must disclose their finances in accordance with requirements of the Securities and Exchange Commission. We know from brokers and others in the trade that the profits of publicly traded papers are comparable to those of privately held papers. Available data indicate that the newspaper industry is one of the most profitable: In 1976— not a banner year for the economy—the publicly traded newspaper companies, which collectively control 25 percent of all daily circulation, had pre-tax profit margins of 19.4 percent, after-tax profits of 10 percent, average return on stockholders' equity of 16 percent, and return on invested capital of 14 percent.

A journalist might rejoice at such fat figures. A logical assumption would be that the more money a newspaper makes and the better its chances of survival, the more it will invest in the paper and the community that provides its earnings. But the tendency is the opposite: The more money a paper makes, the more likely it is to attract a takeover or, if it is already in a chain, to use the profits to purchase other properties.

My own impression is that most papers were mediocre before they were bought by chains and remain mediocre after they are bought. With few exceptions, chain operators like to buy medium-size monopoly newspapers which require them to spend a minimum on the news. Newspapers are a multiple-appeal product—sports, stock reports, comics, news, fashions, supermarket prices, television listings—so it is usually not clear why people buy papers. Many publishers who issue daily junk as news find it easy to believe they are geniuses—but genius in publishing a daily paper consists of having a monopoly in a growing market.

No distinguished newspaper was ever created by a chain. I doubt that the *New York Times* would have been created by Adolph Ochs if the *Times* had been a wholly owned subsidiary of a Texas cement company. Or the *Washington Post* if Eugene Meyer had worked for Rupert Murdoch. Or the *Los Angeles Times* if Otis Chandler was a hired publisher sent from Rochester to keep the paper out of controversy and collect an annual bonus based on increased earnings.

But let us assume, for the sake of argument, that chain ownership actually makes newspapers better—that every property bought by a chain quickly becomes a first-rate paper. I don't think that eases the problems of narrow control.

At the present rate of concentration, we can expect that in less than 20 years almost every daily paper in the country will be owned by about 10 corporations. There is no assurance that the present trend will continue, but neither is there any reliable evidence that consolidation will stop.

One reason concentration in the media is dangerous is that media power is political power. There is no reason why newspaper publishers and broadcast operators should not promote their corporate welfare the way other industries do. But it would be naive not to recognize that for politicians there is a difference between being asked to support a corporate bill for the computer industry and being asked to support something wanted by the newspaper publishers and broadcast managers in the politician's home district. Remarkably many members of Congress believe that when a publisher or station manager comes to Washington to lobby a bill or fight some regulation, these are the people who will decide how to treat the politician in their media at the next election. And most of them preface their acknowledgment of this belief by saying it is strictly off the record.

I see no constitutional problem in establishing some limit on how many papers or how much circulation one corporation may control. At the same time, I believe that no one should be prevented from printing or saying anything, anytime, anywhere. If there were a legal limit to the existing media any one corporation could control, and Gannett, for example, wished to buy an existing paper in Peoria, it could do it by selling its paper in Pensacola. If it insisted, as it ought to, that it has a First Amendment right to print in both Peoria *and* Pensacola, then I would defend that right and insist that it could retain its paper in Pensacola and express its First Amendment right in Peoria by starting a *new* paper in Peoria.

I doubt that even the most energetic chain-builder in the business would insist that it is socially healthy to have one corporation control every daily paper in the country. We now have 25 chains that control a majority of all papers sold daily. If one corporation in control is bad and 25 is good, what is the proper number? At what point should someone—presumably the Department of Justice or Congress—step in and say no?

But I don't believe that the Department of Justice or Congress *will* step in. They have not so far, and the pace of concentration has increased in the last decade. And I believe the Department of Justice and Congress do not step in precisely because concentrated control of the media also represents concentrated political and economic power. But I can suggest more modest remedies.

One small gesture would be to end the meaningless ownership statement issued annually to the post office and printed as obscurely as possible each October. Instead, each paper using the second-class mailing privilege should be required to have available for public scrutiny at the local post office the names of all officers, directors, and major stockholders, the precise percentage of their ownership, and all their significant financial holdings. This is the same requirement of disclosure the SEC makes of officers, directors, and major stockholders of publicly traded companies. Local people should at least know who owns and controls their monopoly media and what other financial interests are held by those who make ultimate decisions about the news.

Another measure that would afford some insulation from potential subversion of news would be the election of editors by professional journalists on the staff of the paper. Obviously, this would require the consent of the owner, but one always dreams of owners with vision. Election of editors would also mean office politics, but office politics in the present methods are not unknown, and staffs as a whole could not make worse choices than managements as a whole. For those who insist this would make for mediocre papers, I suggest taking a look at *Le Monde*, one of the world's great newspapers, whose staff elects its editor.

An irrational decision of the tax courts that for years has fueled the growth of chains ought to be reversed. The Internal Revenue Code permits a newspaper to retain without normal taxation any undistributed earnings as a necessary cost of doing business if the purpose of this accumulation is to buy another newspaper. That makes neither social nor business sense.

Newspaper and broadcast editorials regularly warn against the potential danger of Big Government. They rightly fear uninhibited power, even in the hands of a wise and benevolent leader. But that fear should apply to corporate as well as to political power. We have 1700 daily papers, 8000 weeklies, 8000 radio stations, 900 television stations, and 10,000 periodicals. But we can no longer assume that these large numbers represent comparable diversity in control. We now must fear these numbers; most of our 215 million citizens are reached not by thousands of corporations in the media business but by the relative few that control consolidated organizations.

If we believe in the indispensability of a pluralistic marketplace of ideas and information, we cannot be complacent about a narrowly controlled management of that marketplace, whether it is governmental or corporate, benign or malicious. The greatest danger in control of the mass media is not, I think, the likelihood that government will take control, but that the public, seeing little difference between narrow corporate control and narrow governmental control, will be indifferent to which dominates the media.

RAZZLE-DAZZLE
WORLD OF TODAY'S
BOOK PUBLISHING

Alvin P. Sanoff

High-powered hucksterism is paying off with record profits for America's book publishers—but the approach is proving controversial. In an industry once known for its sedate marketing, aggressive promotion—including television advertisements featuring scantily clothed women—is now widespread.

The technique has proved particularly profitable for publishers of mass-market paperbacks. They chalked up a 24 percent increase in sales in 1977, with the number of paperbacks purchased jumping from 495 million to 531 million. Predictions are that 1978 also will be a good year.

PRINT POWER

Counting hard-cover books, industry sales leaped 10 percent last year to $4.6 billion. The sales proved in cold cash that Americans are still reading, despite the inroads of television.

But these encouraging figures have not diminished concern that the gains have come at the expense of quality. Authors worry that works of literary merit are being brushed aside in a search for the blockbuster—a book that can

Reprinted from *U.S. News & World Report* (June 5, 1978): 55–57.

be turned into a best seller through imaginative publicity.

Oscar Dystel, the president of Bantam Books, says that concentration on the "big book" keeps publishers from meeting their "cultural and social responsibilities" to provide the widest possible choice of books.

On the other hand, Michael Bessie, who is the senior vice-president of Harper & Row, argues: "We live in a time in which there is interplay among the media. The effect is to emphasize the supercommercial success. If I thought this detracted attention from less commercial books of higher quality, I would be seriously disturbed by it. It does detract a bit, but not an awful lot."

ERA OF THE GIANTS

In the view of some critics, emphasis on the big book is an inevitable result of the growing importance of conglomerates in publishing. They say the big combined companies seek high profits and are willing to spend vast sums buying and promoting a book in the hope of a large payoff.

Conglomerates first became active in the industry during the '60s when firms such as Raytheon and Xerox purchased textbook publishers. In recent years, conglomerates shifted their interest to trade publishing—acquiring firms which put out books with a broad general appeal. Such giants as RCA, CBS, Gulf & Western, and Time, Inc., now are active in the field.

QUALITY VS. QUANTITY

Critics say conglomerates pay little heed to the value of ideas and literature, placing profit above all other considerations. Consequently, according to many authors, it is harder to find publishers for scholarly works, and once such a book is printed it gets short shrift from publishers, who lavish their attention on potential best sellers.

The Authors Guild, which represents 5000 writers, wants the Justice Department and the Federal Trade Commission to halt what it views as a dangerous trend toward concentration of ownership in publishing.

The guild and several prominent authors, including Archibald MacLeish, also have spoken out against attempts by a New York-based conglomerate, Western Pacific Industries, to acquire control of Houghton Mifflin Company, a Boston publisher.

In a recent statement before a Senate subcommittee, the guild delivered the warning that "conglomeration and concentration endanger the country's most important social interest, the diverse and uninhibited marketplace of ideas."

THE PROFIT PICTURE

John Brooks, president of the Authors Guild, says that many worthwhile books are not printed in paperback editions because such works do not promise large profits to the conglomerates.

Comments Roger W. Straus, Jr., the president of Farrar, Straus & Giroux: "A lot of high-quality books that sell a few thousand copies a year go out of print permanently when a conglomerate takes over. That's not very good for literature."

The Association of American Publishers maintains that takeovers do not represent a threat to free expression, because there are more publishers in the U.S. today—over 1100—than 20 years ago, and more than 50 are major firms. The number of titles published in the past 20 years has climbed from 18,000 to about 35,000.

Publisher Straus, who resigned from the association because of its position on takeovers, says that the group ignores the fact that independent hard-cover publishers may be adversely affected by mergers taking place between hard-cover and mass-market paperback publishers. Straus points to such relationships as these:

CBS owns the paperback operations of Popular Library and Fawcett and the hard-cover publishing house of Holt, Rinehart and Winston. Doubleday operates Dell paperbacks. RCA is the owner of both the Random House hard-cover publishing complex and Ballantine paperbacks. Such firms have a competitive advantage over an independent hard-cover publisher when negotiating with a writer for both hard-cover and paperback rights.

THE CHAIN REACTION

Some book-publishing authorities also are concerned about developments in the retailing end of the business. Publisher George Braziller says that big chain bookstores, which now account for more than 20 percent of bookstore sales, have the same mentality as conglomerates and hence are not interested in works of literary merit unless extensive promotion of a book is planned.

Other publishers argue that the criticism of

conglomerates is unwarranted. Says Richard E. Snyder, president of Simon & Schuster, which is owned by Gulf & Western: "The larger the company, the more likely it will publish high-quality, marginal-sales books. We can afford the risk."

It costs publishers as little as $18,000 to $20,000 to print several thousand copies of a book by a little-known author who does not receive a large advance. But paperback rights to best-selling novels routinely sell for over $1 million.

Paperback organizations are willing to risk huge sums because they need a major seller almost every month to ensure that other books they put out will get adequate display space on supermarket and drugstore racks, where about 1700 new titles a year compete for attention.

LITERARY BLITZ

With vast sums riding on their success or failure, publishers use everything from television and radio advertisements to front-page newspaper stories to guest appearances by authors on television talk shows to stimulate interest in a book.

G. Roysce Smith, executive director of the American Booksellers Association, says that some writers are such adept television performers that they have been able to turn their books into best sellers. He says there is "so much demand for new faces, new talent, new ideas on television that authors are attractive as personalities."

The amount that is invested on promotion is usually proportionate to the investment in the book. Ballantine Books, which paid close to $1.4 million for the paperback rights to William Safire's political novel *Full Disclosure*, plans a major television and print advertising campaign and an eight-city tour by the author. A Ballantine official says, "We are pulling out all the stops on this one." Avon Books is mounting a $350,000 promotion campaign for *The Thorn Birds* to try to recoup its $1.9 million investment in the paperback, the largest sum ever paid in paperback rights.

The print media are an important part of publicity campaigns, with publishers selling book excerpts to newspapers and magazines to build interest in a work. The first chapter of a new paperback novel, *Jaws 2*, appeared in 22 newspapers in the U.S. and Canada.

Increasingly, publishers can count on works by controversial authors such as H. R. Haldeman and former President Nixon to make front-page headlines, and thus aid book sales. "The whole point is to whet people's appetites," says Irving Lazar, agent to Nixon and other writers. "Getting books onto the front pages of newspapers has become an accepted world of its own."

Not every book that receives reams of publicity becomes a best seller, however. A recent example: *Past Forgetting: My Love Affair with Dwight D. Eisenhower* by Kay Summersby, the former President's driver during World War II. Also, President Nixon's memoirs got off to a slow start.

Many publishers say that when high-powered publicity campaigns are successful, they not only spur sales but also make book buyers of people who normally aren't purchasers. The American Booksellers Association estimates that only 5 to 6 percent of the population are regular book buyers.

Gains in sales have been achieved despite rising costs that discourage purchases. Publishers note that people who used to walk out of a bookstore with three or four paperbacks now buy only one or two. Executives cite higher paper costs, inflation, and increased royalties that are paid to writers as reasons for the rise in prices.

But they add that the cost of books has not been going up as fast as inflation in general.

The American Booksellers Association estimates that publishers net only 25¢ on an average $10 hard-cover book. Commercial books
are sold to stores at discounts of 40 to 46 percent of the retail price.

PAPERBACK PUNCH

The average price of a paperback is creeping
up to $2, but that is still much less expensive
than a hard-cover book. Soft-bound editions
account for more than half the sales in America's approximately 7000 general bookstores.

Publishers of paperbacks increasingly are
looking to tie-ins with TV shows or movies to
help market books. Such television miniseries
as "Roots," "Rich Man, Poor Man," "Loose
Change," and "79 Park Avenue" aided sales of
the works on which they were based.

Serious literature also can profit from television. *I, Claudius* by Robert Graves rose to the
top of the trade-paperback best-seller list on the
strength of the television series aired by the
Public Broadcasting Service. "Anna Karenina,"
based on the Tolstoy novel, was recently on
PBS and this classic work also made the list.

Reversing the traditional process of turning a
book into a movie, paperback publishers find it
profitable to publish novels based on movie
and television scripts. *Jaws 2, Holocaust, Pretty
Baby, Casey's Shadow,* and *The Greek Tycoon*
are just a few of the current crop.

"A great many of these novelizations are
really slapped together," says Rollene Saal,
editorial director of the book-club division of
Doubleday. "Only once in a while do you get a
book that stands on its own." Others argue that
many of the novelizations are well written.

Whatever their merits, many of the books
find an enthusiastic audience. *Jaws 2*, first published April 19, 1978, already has been bought
by over 1.5 million customers. There are now
3.6 million copies in print, and it is at the top
of the paperback best-seller list.

THE SELLING OF *JAWS 2*

To help promote *Jaws 2*, Bantam Books sent
25,000 free copies to opinion makers, book reviewers, and booksellers in the belief that they
would spread the word about the novel.

At the same time, publishers are quick to say
that novelizations are a risky business because
their success depends less on the quality of the
books than on the popularity of the film or television production. Some writers find it ironic
that their success is closely tied to television
and films, often viewed as the enemy of the
printed word.

A factor in the emphasis on tie-ins: Many
conglomerates have interests in television,
movies, and book publishing. Thus multimedia
firms have the capacity to publish a novel in
both hard-cover and paperback, and then make
a movie production or television show out of it.

Simon & Schuster published *Looking for Mr.
Goodbar* in hard cover. Pocket Books put out
the paperback, and Paramount made the movie.
All are owned by Gulf & Western. The same
Gulf & Western subsidiaries are involved in the
book and movie *The Investigation*, and the
Paramount film *Grease* is being novelized by
Pocket Books. Despite these relationships, the
conglomerates say their hard-cover, paperback,
and movie divisions generally make their deals
independently of their huge overseers.

As a result of the attractiveness of the American market, foreign firms have entered the
field. Among them: the Bertelsmann Publishing Group of West Germany that recently acquired a controlling interest in Bantam Books.
Mayflower Books, Inc., subsidiary of a British
wholesaler and retailer, plans to import 110
book titles this fall, mostly of the self-help and
how-to variety that have proved to be popular
in the United States. Allan Lang, president of
Mayflower, maintains that "the book market in
the United States is nowhere near the saturation point."

For the most part, aggressive promotion has not yet been applied to the less glamorous fields of publishing—texts and professional books. These two areas account for more than 40 percent of the industry's earnings, and long have provided bread and butter for many organizations.

Sales of professional books were up about 12 percent last year over 1976, with elementary and secondary texts up 10 percent. Dan Lacy, who is the senior vice-president of McGraw-Hill, Inc., one of the nation's largest publishers of texts, says school systems were able to spend more on books than publishers expected. He speculates that declining school enrollments made money available that otherwise would have been spent on construction and maintenance.

"FOR THEIR SOULS"

Book clubs and the mail-order book business, with combined sales of about $750 million, also are doing well with promotions mainly along traditional lines of advertising in newspapers, magazines, and mailed brochures.

The way serious works are sold has not been much affected by the flamboyant methods used by many publishers. Most organizations continue to sell books such as histories and scientific treatises in a low-key way. According to one publisher: "Most people in this business are in it for their souls as well as their mortgage payments."

Over all, a cautious optimism has sprung up among industry executives about the future after many years of uncertainty. Observes Erwin A. Glikes, publisher of Harper & Row general adult books: "Television is not satisfying to many Americans. It cannot feed that part of their spirit that searches for meaning. Good books can do this, and the challenge for publishers is to find and encourage good writing and good thinking."

Copyright 1978 U.S. News & World Report, Inc.

INSIDE HOLLYWOOD

Newsweek Staff*

It is the best of times.

At Ma Maison, the chic restaurant currently favored by Hollywood's elite, sleek Rolls-Royces and Ferraris fill the parking lot as owner Patrick Tesrail greets the luncheon crowd with a deft combination of deference and familiarity.

From *Newsweek* (February 13, 1978): 70–76. Copyright 1978, by Newsweek, Inc. All Rights Reserved. Reprinted by Permission.

*Michael Ruby and Martin Kasindorf in Hollywood with Pamela Lynn Abraham in New York and bureau reports.

Along Rodeo Drive in Beverly Hills, the posh boutiques do blockbuster business—and in the famed Polo Lounge a mile away, the dealmakers "take a meeting" to cut contracts over coffee and English muffins for what they pray will be another *Star Wars*. In a seller's market, the major studios are richer than ever and the major stars, directors, and producers seemingly richer still. In the big-budget world of Hollywood 1978, says chairman Dennis Stanfill of Twentieth Century-Fox, "nobody is poor-mouthing."

It is the worst of times.

Variety calls Hollywood "shell-shock city" —and even in the nation's fountainhead of hyperbole, the description is painfully accurate. For what started with an isolated case of corporate embezzlement by Columbia Pictures executive David Begelman has suddenly escalated into a far-reaching examination of the ways Hollywood conducts its business. As never before, a public camera is probing the movie industry's arcane financial and accounting practices, its extravagant perquisites, its procedures for divvying up the take between superagent and star, distributor and theater, writer, producer, and outside financier.

Dozens of show-business figures—fed up with what they contend is a pattern of deceit and distrust—are breaking movieland's traditional code of silence to tell their stories about padded budgets, secret payoffs, and kickbacks. They have aroused the Securities and Exchange Commission, the Justice Department, and the Internal Revenue Service, and as a result, a Hollywood that tends to shrug off its intermittent scandals of sex and drugs is plainly running scared. "It is a crisis," says *Jaws* co-producer Richard D. Zanuck. "This has just got to be the tip of the iceberg when it comes to investigations."

Topic A, of course, is the Begelman affair. A former agent, Begelman was ousted as head of movie operations at Columbia Pictures last October, only days before the studio's superhit,

Close Encounters of the Third Kind, had its smash première. He eventually admitted forging and cashing three company checks and embezzling other funds totaling $61,000, repaid Columbia with interest and forfeited promised benefits worth $1.3 million; then, even though stripped of his officer's title and board membership, he was reinstated—to the astonishment even of Hollywood. Topic B—the recent mass resignation of United Artists's top five officers in a dispute with UA parent Transamerica Corp.—touches another raw nerve. "These men represented a certain type of integrity and the way a company should be run," says Max E. Youngstein, a respected independent consultant. "To lose those symbols when the business is so chaotic is truly shocking."

Still, Youngstein and other industry defenders discount the Begelman affair as an aberration and chafe at reports of financial gimmickry and payoffs. "By its overpublicizing, the movie business's warts look like mountains," argues president Jack Valenti of the Motion Picture Association of America. "I'm not suggesting that it's like the annual Cub Scout meeting. Some of the people in it are weird, but percentage-wise, it's probably got no more flaky characters than any other business." Paramount Pictures chairman Barry Diller, 36, says the studios' books are open: "Our key executives are under almost constant audit by our outside auditors in areas where there could be improprieties," Diller says. But that's the point, says accountant Sidney Finger, who for 15 years has been auditing books for Hollywood's creative talent. Finger's business is to prevent the studios from cheating his clients—and "If we didn't have findings," he says, "people wouldn't come back."

Such critics point to a fine line between outright illegality and questionable practices— and they charge that many people in the business frequently cross it. "Listen, this industry does attract a lot of unscrupulous people," says lawyer Kenneth Ziffren, one of a small army of attorneys serving stars, directors, and producers. When it comes to calculating the split between studio and stars, Ziffren adds, "the studio computers seem to be much more sophisticated about accruing costs than about accruing incomes."

Quid pro quos also tend to be a matter of interpretation. "What one man may consider bribery, another man considers clout," says 34-year old producer Peter Guber (*The Deep*). "An independent producer may say to a studio, 'If you take this, I'll give you my next project.'" In the end, nearly everyone is drawn into the rat race of comparative advantage—and in the self-serving pulling and hauling, mutual trust often breaks down. "The terrible thing is that you operate in a general atmosphere of distrust," says Youngstein. Adds screenwriter Josh Greenfeld (*Harry and Tonto*), "The movie business is at the moral level of the South Vietnamese Army."

It's not quite that bad: some studios play straighter than others, and individual agents, producers, and studio executives can be as proud of their word as any other businessman. But there is little doubt that Hollywood frequently trips over the narrow edge of probity. Among the games people play:

■ Big-name screenwriters called in for a fast rewrite sometimes forgo screen credits and cash fees in return for expensive gifts from a studio or producer. One such "body-and-fender man," in Hollywood's parlance, got a Rolls-Royce Corniche for his trouble, another a new $19,000 driveway. The studio buries such gifts in its overhead budget—and the screenwriters may neglect to report them to the IRS.

■ In New York, a grand jury was convened last month to hear allegations that Twentieth Century-Fox had demanded that theater owners take *The Other Side of Midnight*, a critical bomb with a questionable box office, if they wanted to show *Star Wars*. The practice, called block-booking, was outlawed in 1948 when the studios were forced to divest themselves of their theater chains. Fox denies the charge.

■ Producers Robert Chartoff and Irwin Winkler made *Rocky* and *New York, New York* for United Artists; the former soared, the latter sank. Under a complex contractual arrangement called cross-collateralization, UA has used black ink from *Rocky* to offset red ink on *New York, New York*—and thus, Chartoff and Winkler have not seen all of their "profit participation" from the hit.

■ During the filming of *The Missouri Breaks* in 1974, Marlon Brando convinced producer Elliott Kastner to give the star the new $30,000 motor home that had been purchased for location shooting in Montana. How? According to one account by Jack Grossberg, production manager on the film, Brando blew his lines for two days, and Kastner, worried after losing $25,000 in production costs, finally got the message. "Another day, another $10,000," Brando would say as he stepped from his new possession.

■ Director William Friedkin and author William Peter Blatty have sued Warner Bros., charging the studio with shortchanging them on the profits from the immensely successful *The Exorcist*. Similarly, actors Michael Caine and Sean Connery filed suit last month against Allied Artists Pictures, charging that the smallish distributor withheld $218,000 of their profits from *The Man Who Would Be King*.

GOING FOR THE BIG SCORE

That such charges are tossed about is hardly surprising, given the stakes involved. In Hollywood, each picture is, in effect, a separate business—and an expensive one at that. In addition to the normal price increases that affect all businesses, salaries of superstars are riding the same rocket as those of sports heroes. That kind of double inflation last year drove the average picture budget to $5.3 million, up 178 percent in just four years. To insure themselves against losses from box-office bombs, studios are promoting their films more aggressively than ever. "The marketing tail," says producer Peter Bart, "is now wagging the filmmaking dog." But advertising is no guarantee of a hit—and given the instant anonymity that financial failure often produces, each player involved generally goes for the big score each time out. Under such conditions, in a business where success hinges on the public whim, the long term is measured in months, and ethics, loyalty, and probity often take a back seat to profit.

But for those who stay on top. or near it, life in Hollywood brings riches that would make Croesus blush. To help executives keep up with the wealthy stars they must court, studios underwrite perks from a $200,000 home-screening room to the ubiquitous Rolls or Mercedes-Benz. There are so many Mercedeses in the MCA-Universal parking lot, chuckles David Brown, Dick Zanuck's co-producer, "you think you're in Stuttgart." Begelman, with a salary of $300,000, not only dipped into the till for $61,000 and piled up disputed "expenses" of $23,000, but also enjoyed still another perk: during its last fiscal year, Columbia picked up a "substantial" portion of his rent and "related costs." The annual tab: $66,000.

OLD WAYS DIE HARD

Since the sex scandals of the '20s, Hollywood has always leaned to personal excess as well—and the current scene is apparently no different. Last week, director Roman Polanski made front-page headlines by skipping the country rather than face a possible jail sentence for his peccadilloes with a 13-year-old girl. And by all accounts, drugs—particularly co-caine—are still getting a heavy play. "There are parties that are cast for that reason," says Zanuck. "Everybody knows certain people are on drugs, but that doesn't mean they're unreli-able."

Social engagements and business also com-mingle, more perhaps than in any other indus-try in America—and deals are struck, or at least discussed, at poolside and on tennis courts, at parties in Moorish-modern mansions and over lunch at Ma Maison. Friendship in Holly-wood? "If tomorrow I lost my three biggest clients, I'd like to believe that people I consider my friends would still be friends," says Sue

Mengers, one of the hottest agents in town. "But I sure wouldn't hear from them as often during the business day."

At the center of Hollywood's daily life is the deal—and at its epicenter, more often than not, is the studio company. Six familiar names dom-inate the business: United Artists, Twentieth Century-Fox, Columbia Pictures, Universal Studios, Paramount Pictures, and Warner Bros.[1] In the trade, each is known for its characteristic traits. UA, for instance, has gained a reputation for playing fairest when it comes time to distribute movie profits to the ac-tors, directors, and screenwriters eligible to share in them. Whether that changes with the departure of its highly respected top ex-ecutives—Arthur Krim, Robert S. Benjamin, Eric Pleskow, Mike Medavoy, and William Bernstein—remains to be seen. Universal, on the other hand, is notoriously tight-fisted, the result, its critics say, of the heavy overhead ex-penses required to support the company's huge studio lot. But all six do basically the same thing: drawing on their huge cash flows and bank credit lines, they finance film projects and then distribute the films to theaters.

BUSINESS IS BOOMING

Although there are scores of independent operators, the six majors account for 85 percent of the industry's $2.4 billion gross. And with box-office admissions rising, each is doing rea-sonably well—especially Fox, financier-dis-tributor of *Star Wars*. Last week the company reported record earnings of $50.8 million for 1977—an astonishing 474 percent increase over 1976.

But studios today are radically different from those of the golden age of Hollywood. Then the studios owned huge chains of theaters and churned out hundreds of movies each year to fill them. An antitrust consent decree in 1948 ended the studios' lock on the theaters, and then the advent of television freed the creative people. Without long-term contracts, the companies found themselves suddenly bidding for talent on the open market.

Since fewer movies are being made than in Hollywood's heyday, that's no boon to lesser talents, extras, and production crews, many of whom are unemployed in the midst of boom. But prices for the biggest stars are soaring beyond reason. According to one top agent, Burt Reynolds and Jack Nicholson command $2 million "up front"—in effect, their straight salaries for doing a single picture, not counting a share in the profits. Paul Newman, Robert Redford, and Steve McQueen get $3 million, and the word is that Marlon Brando received $2.5 million for twelve days shooting his part in *Superman*. Riskier, but sometimes more lucrative, is the "point" system—a percentage of a film's profits or gross rentals. Director George Lucas, for example, will collect 40 percent of the profits from *Star Wars*.

STAR FLIGHTS

In addition, the big names demand big perks of their own. Most require huge on-location expense accounts—as much as $2500 a week— and often their contracts stipulate that the studio bear the costs of budget fees for drivers, assorted sycophants, and services. During the location filming of *Lucky Lady*, for instance, million-dollar-man Gene Hackman got a contract clause requiring that all film and personnel fly from Guaymas, Mexico, to Los Angeles on one of his personal planes—for a fee. "The creative impetus is with the producers, the practical power is with the directors," says producer Tony Bill (*Hearts of the West*). "But the ultimate power is with the stars."

It takes all these powers, coupled with the financing-distribution clout of the studio, to make a deal go. Given the shifting mix of talent and mind-numbing financial ploys, there are endless permutations of any deal, but a standard scenario usually begins with a "property" —a screenplay or an idea for one. A producer buys the property or an option on it, and with or without specific stars in mind, he offers the property to a major studio.

Outright rejection can be costly for the producer who has paid as much as $500,000 for a leading screenwriter's script. But rejection can be costly for a studio, too. Universal, for instance, turned thumbs down on *Star Wars*—to the ultimate embarrassment of the studio's executive suite. If the studio gives a green light, the producer gets a fee—anywhere from $100,000 to $500,000 to top names these days—often payable in steps until the start of production. The script is massaged into final form, studio moneymen and producer budget the picture, director and cast are lined up—and at each step the studio can back out.

LAWYER LANGUAGE

If that sounds simple, it isn't. On the way to a final deal, legions of lawyers constantly bargain on behalf of their studio or clients, each attempting to maximize the personal take and minimize risk. Among those lawyers is Tom Pollock, who received 30 phone calls during a two-hour interview with *Newsweek*'s Dewey Gram. Five or six involved projects that had to be advanced right then, and what Gram heard was the unalloyed language of Hollywood dealmaking:

"Michael, how are you? . . . No, Joe is full of shit on that. He told me they got Carlton 50 points as producer and not just as actor. Mason got 250 [thousand dollars] and 100 deferred. My feeling is he's not as big a star as Mason and we should offer less than that. But that's up to you . . . Um, yes . . . No, no, nothing that's gone on at Paramount has any bearing. We have to say, 'Look, we can afford to pay 250 and five points. That's it, folks, that's it.' . . . Right, right,

OK. It's possible we could get him gross at break-even. It's essentially the same as net anyway . . . Yes, I can probably get him to go for that . . . ."

Thousands of such conversations move a property through its birth pains, and the resulting production-distribution-profit contracts can run the size of a big-city phone book—prompting a classic quip from director Billy Wilder that an Academy Award ought to be given for "best deal of the year." But the tactics are hardly a laughing matter. Studios, for instance, often prefer to grant stars, directors, and others profit shares rather than dilute the 30 percent distribution fee that they collect from their gross theater rentals. If the budget begins to mushroom, a nervous studio may also try to sell or "lay off" a piece of action to other investors; under Begelman's guidance, Columbia laid off $7 million of the ultimate $19.1 million budget for *Close Encounters*—a move that proved an embarrassment when the film turned out to be a blockbuster.

Independent producers Dino De Laurentiis and Joseph E. Levine use another ploy. Using his film's all-star American and British cast as bait, Levine sold off the foreign-distribution rights to *A Bridge Too Far* even before the $25 million movie went into production. His pre-production profit: $5 million. With *King Kong*, De Laurentiis did much the same.

The creative talents jockey for financial position just as aggressively. "No matter how strong the *artiste*," says novelist-screenwriter John Gregory Dunne, "they are all caught up in the narcosis of the deal." Some producers, for instance, usually try to make their money on fees rather than help finance a movie with a front-end investment. That posture can cost them points, but they assume the studio will swindle them on profit distribution anyway.

Other producers go for the quick score by staking a young screenwriter to a relatively small payment for an original script, then peddling the property to a studio for a handsome profit. Producer Mike Gruskoff, for in-

stance, paid writers Gloria and Willard Huyck $20,000 for the script to *Lucky Lady*—and sold it to Fox for $450,000. But perhaps the best deals come to producers with long-term contracts with a studio. In what is a typical arrangement, the David Brown–Richard Zanuck partnership brings properties to Universal. The studio generally accepts them, takes all the financial risks, and splits the profits 50-50, with the points of other participants coming out of the Brown-Zanuck share.

SIX FIGURES FOR THE POINTS

For all the contractual problems that arise before and during production, however, the real hassles begin after a film is released and the money rolls in. Despite rapidly increasing budgets, most movies distributed by the major companies make money these days, in part because of TV sales, product merchandising, and other ancillary income. In nearly every film, a few people, including the top stars, director, and screenwriter, have points—and given the stakes involved, especially with a blockbuster, they marshal teams of auditors and lawyers to pore over the picture's accounts and contracts to make sure the studio is playing fair. With standard profit-participation contracts running up to nine single-spaced pages and the more recondite becoming slim volumes, the lawyers earn their six-figure salaries. With a big movie, says lawyer Pollock, "each phrase can mean tens of thousands of dollars and each point can mean hundreds of thousands. That's why we're here."

There are almost as many types of profit-participation agreements as there are deals. The simplest—and plainly the most lucrative—is gross participation, which entitles the player to a fixed percentage of all rentals from the first ticket sold at the box office. Most major stars and directors now demand gross deals—and some work for less than their going rate up front to get the studio to go along. Jack Nichol-

HOW TO TALK HOLLYWOOD

What do you say to a body-and-fenders man in the Polo Lounge when you're taking a meeting? Herewith, some translations from the vernacular to help you *hondel* with the best of them:

Above the line: What it costs to make a movie even before the cameras roll: buying the rights to a play, book, or other "property," paying fees to directors and actors. Actual production costs are *below the line*.

Back-end money: A film's receipts after release. In a back-end deal, participants may have a piece of the net profits from distribution, television-resale rights, or even the sale of beer mugs and other promotional merchandise. The opposite of *front-end money*—fees paid before the movie hits the box office.

Body-and-fenders man: A facile screenwriter who can slap together a workable, if not always artistic, screenplay from a story idea.

Break (break-even): The magical point at which a distributor is declared to have covered expenses, so that others can start collecting their share of profits. Varies widely from contract to contract.

Distributors: The moguls in the middle, who often finance films for a producer, then peddle them to theater owners (exhibitors) for a percentage. Also known as studios, whether or not they still operate sound stages.

Four-walling: Paying an exhibitor a prearranged sum to take over a theater and all its operating costs for the duration of a run in exchange for all box-office receipts. A high-risk, high-stakes gamble.

Golden gater: A script that's so bad it's practically suicidal.

Gross: The total taken in at ticket windows is the "box office gross." After the exhibitor gets a cut, the distributor gets the rest, known as "theatrical rentals." An actor or director in a "gross position" owns a piece of the distributor's share, and is a "gross player." But only superstars command pure gross, "from the first dollar" with no deductions.

Hondel: Yiddish term for fancy haggling over a deal.

House nut: An exhibitor's operating and overhead expenses.

In the can: A film that's been shot, or "wrapped," but not edited or scored.

In turnaround: A property that's been dropped short of production and is in search of a new distributor. Upon divorcing his wife, one producer said: "I put her in turnaround."

Legs: Box-office longevity. *Star Wars* has great legs; *Jaws* was said to have "fins."

Majors: The six top U.S. distributors: Columbia, Paramount, United Artists, Twentieth Century-Fox, Universal, Warner Bros. The *mini-majors*, such as Allied Artists and Avco Embassy, are newer and smaller.

Most-favored-nation clause: A contractual promise to a star who signs early that no latecomer will get a better deal.

Negative cost: All above- and below-line costs of producing a finished film.

Net position: The right to a share in a movie's profits, after negative costs and assorted other controversial fees are deducted.

Play-or-pay: Ironclad agreement that an independent producer ("indie prod," in *Variety* jargon) will pay the star or other key figure in full, regardless of whether a movie package is bought by a distributor.

Points: Percentage of ownership in a movie.

Rolling break: Complex computation worked out by Columbia Pictures president David Begelman, and granted to big but not-quite-super stars. After deductions, the star gets a share of the profit in each accounting period, instead of having to wait for the break-even, as net players must.

Take a meeting: To get together to hondel, as in "Let's take a meeting on it next week at Ma Maison."

son took a "modest" salary of $750,000 to make *One Flew Over the Cuckoo's Nest*, but his 10 percent share of the gross has already returned him several million dollars. "From now on, I'll never take less than gross on anything," vows *Close Encounters* director Steven Spielberg, "because it's very hard to hide gross."

DARTH VADER'S PAYOFF

Others make big money on a film's ancillary rights. George Lucas settled for a low $50,000 for his *Star Wars* screenplay. His 40 percent net-profit position has returned millions, but Lucas is also cleaning up with what amounts to a *Star Wars* industry—everything from the movie's sound-track album and miniature Darth Vader characters to bed sheets and chewing gum. Producer Robert Stigwood could reap an estimated $20 million harvest in album sales from his film *Saturday Night Fever*. "The biggest change in the last four or five years has been the growth of all this ancillary-rights income," says Pollock. "It's been just huge and is now a major, major consideration in the making of any movie."

Still, the vast majority of a film's participants rarely get gross-position deals from the studios or rights to ancillary income. Instead, they are "net players" who take a share of the profits, rather than the gross, and they do so only when the studio declares the film a moneymaker. But despite the apparent success of most movies, getting a piece of that action is difficult. "You come out here and live for five years, ten years," sighs screenwriter Greenfeld. "They've been here for 70 years, knowing how to screw people. Like Bruce Jenner, they've been training all their lives."

The hassle begins with the studio's definition of "break-even"—the theoretical point where a movie's total cost is covered and the profits begin to flow. But it isn't quite that simple, for before a studio deems a film profitable, it deducts a bewildering number of costs and fees

from the gross. First comes the so-called negative cost—the total of all expenses associated with making a finished print, such as salaries, set construction, and equipment. To that the studios add a 30 percent distribution fee, and most include a 25 percent overhead charge to take care of such built-in costs as clerical expenses and utilities. They also deduct any interest charges on money borrowed to make the movie. Legal expenses and the cost of making photographic prints—$1.2 million on average—are deducted as well, the latter at retail even though the studio gets the work done at discount rates, often from a wholly owned subsidiary. In addition, foreign taxes are charged to the picture as a distribution expense even though a foreign tax credit is taken against U.S. taxes.

Advertising costs—which now sometimes run to 60 percent of negative cost—reduce the potential payout even further as studios try to squeeze the last bit of box office out of a picture. Once, the rule of thumb was that the break-even point would be reached when a movie grossed 2.5 times its negative cost. Now, says former United Artists production chief Mike Medavoy, the ratio even on an inexpensive picture may run 4 to 1.

HOW TO SHRINK PROFITS

More important, profit players and their accountants argue that many of the assorted costs amount to little more than padding by the studios to fatten their own take and reduce the payout. One studio device, they say, is charging one film the full cost of a purchase and then repeating the charge on the books of other films. The critics say the studios also pad ad budgets on successful movies, using the difference between what they declare and what they actually spend to cover losses on box-office duds. "The studio has the books and records, it interprets the contract, computes the profit, and decides how much should be paid out," says accountant Bennett Newman. "There's a certain amount of screwing going on all the time, but it's a mixed bag of inadvertent and intentional screwing."

Profit players with a piece of a TV sale believe the studios are shorting them by packaging several films in a network deal and assigning each picture a prorated share, thus diluting the return to the hottest movie in the bunch. Clint Eastwood's successful *Dirty Harry*, for instance, was sold to a network with fourteen other films, and profit participants were allocated only one-fifteenth of the total sale. Producer Paul Monash says the popular *Butch Cassidy and the Sundance Kid* was allocated only $900,000 when Fox sold it in a package deal to TV; after the participants threatened to sue, Fox raised the price to $2.2 million.

Not all profit participants are complaining, however. Producer Robert Evans, for one, says he has yet to see a penny on *Marathon Man* or *Black Sunday*—both otherwise considered profitable films—but believes Paramount's explanation of unexpected costs. Similarly, "point" men in *All the President's Men* accept Warner Bros.'s reasons for the lack of profit money despite the movie's estimated $40 million return on rentals.

'SUE ME, BABY'

Not surprisingly, the studios categorically deny that they cook the books. Calling the charges "a populist lie," Paramount chairman Diller cites company figures that show a five-year profit-participation payout of $90 million, with an "insignificant" $1 million added for disputed claims. Fox's Stanfill is equally adamant. "We keep an honest set of books and give everybody a fair break," he says. "Anyone who wants to audit our books can." But often, when the malcontents complain, the studios take a "sue me, baby" attitude, offering a choice between a small settlement or years of expensive litigation, and many participants hold their

fire. Still others are frightened even to call for an audit. "If you make demands, you'll never work that studio again," says screenwriter Eleanor Perry. "I certainly don't commission audits."

The film studios are also at odds with another segment of their industry: the owners of the nation's 15,000 movie theaters. "The love-hate relationship between exhibitor and distributor is astounding," marvels Gordon Stulberg, a Hollywood attorney and former president of Fox. "They don't trust each other from here to the corner." Both sides have good reason. Some distributors complain that theater owners regularly give them a short count on remittances—a charge that some exhibitors admit is true.

But the exhibitors counter that the real power in the relationship still resides with the studios, and they seem to have a case. In addition to allegations of block booking, exhibitors point to the system of "blind bidding" that requires them to lay out hard cash as a guarantee for movies they have never seen in order to secure a showing. "I don't know any industry in which a firm commitment is made without first seeing, feeling, or tasting," says Alan Friedberg, president of a 31-screen chain in Boston. "Blind bidding makes Vegas look like kid stuff. It's more akin to Russian roulette."

Even blind bidding wouldn't be so bad, exhibitors say, if the terms weren't so onerous. While conditions may vary, distributors normally get either 90 percent of box-office receipts, less a theater's operating expenses, or a straight cut of gross receipts that is scaled downward over the length of the run. Distributors demand the alternative—percentage or straight cut—that brings them the most, while exhibitors take what's left plus the concession money. And according to president Marvin Goldman of the National Association of Theater Owners (NATO), the popcorn-and-candy trade is about all that keeps the exhibitors above water. "Right now," he says, "theaters around the country are existing on supermarket profit levels of 1 to 1½ percent."

Tiny independent owners may be even worse off—victims, they charge, of collusion between the large chains and the distributors. At issue is the so-called five-o'clock see, the moment when distributors open exhibitors' bids on new films. As the independents tell it, distributors frequently permit chain owners with choice theater locations to take an early peek and improve their bids. If the bids from less desirable theaters come in too high, the distributor may simply renegotiate the terms of the bidding and place his picture in the preferred location. "We're looking at a conspiratorial arrangement," says president Tom Patterson of the National Independent Theater Exhibitors (NITE). Patterson also charges that the larger chains regularly make cash payments to executives in return for the most promising films—a charge the distributors flatly deny.

BRIGHT FUTURE AMID SCANDAL

For all the challenges to Hollywood's way of doing business, its corporate future looks bright. New markets for the industry's "software" are already opening up in video recorders, big-screen home-TV systems, and pay television—perhaps permitting a shift to lower-budget movies and giving more young talent an opportunity to work. More important,

the studios themselves will surely maintain their seller's market, both at home and overseas. "The international market is mostly American casts," says consultant Youngstein. "If you take the total world picture, America is still the place where most movies come from."

It is also the place where filmdom's scandals are born—and for the foreseeable future, the movie colony has to live with the waves set in motion by the Begelman case. They hardly seem likely to recede. All last week, for instance, a rumor swirled through Hollywood and New York that Columbia would bounce both Begelman and president Alan Hirschfield and hire the entire UA crew in their place. The SEC, *Newsweek* learned, has set up an unofficial "Hollywood task force" to explore the Byzantine world of movie moneymen and their studios. By its own lights, the movie industry should get a fairly clean bill of health once all the investigations are completed and the Begelman affair cools down. But then, Hollywood's stock in trade is fantasy, not cinéma vérité—and whether its current scenario is illusion or reality is very much an open question.

1.Two others could be included in the list, but Walt Disney Productions falls into a category all its own and M-G-M, once a giant, no longer distributes movies, concentrating instead on its hotel interests and rentals from its splendid film library.

STRIKING IT RICH IN RADIO

In the town of Moberly, Mo. (population 12,000), Jerrell A. Shepherd owns a radio sta-

Reprinted from the February 5, 1979 issue of *Business Week* by special permission, © 1979 by McGraw-Hill, Inc., New York, N.Y. 10020. All rights reserved.

tion operation so valuable that he claims "no one can afford to buy it." He charges advertisers only $5 to $10 for 30 seconds of time on KWIX, his AM station, and $6 to $12 per commercial on KRES-FM, but Shepherd's gross revenues are more than $800,000 a year. "A buyer today normally pays two to two and a half times the annual gross for a station," the broadcaster muses. "But if I wanted to sell, who's going to plunk down $2 million for a station in a town they've never heard of?"

The chances are, however, that if Shepherd put his property on the block, he would have no shortage of prospective purchasers. The business of radio is enjoying a prosperity undreamed of just five years ago, and a steady stream of new investors wants to share in it—at almost any price. When Storer Broadcasting Co. decided in December to take advantage of the seller's market and pick up some cash for cable-TV expansion, it received nearly 100 inquiries about the four radio stations it put up for sale, even though one station, WHN in New York, is priced at a record $17 million. "It's gotten to the point," says Richard A. Shaheen, a Chicago media broker, "where people are calling and saying, 'You've got to find a station for me to buy, right now!'"

In the world of advertising, radio as a viable medium is often ignored by anyone over 45, whose memories go back to the days of daytime soap operas—"Ma Perkins," "Our Gal Sunday," and "The Romance of Helen Trent"—and to nighttime broadcasts of "Fibber McGee and Molly," "The Shadow," and "Lux Radio Theater." That kind of radio, network radio, last year is estimated by Robert J. Coen, senior vice-president of McCann-Erickson Inc., to have attracted only $160 million in advertising expenditures out of a grand total of some $43 billion for all advertising.

But network radio, which peaked in billings in 1950, is a minor factor in the industry today. All radio this year will near the $3 billion mark in terms of ad expenditures, with local advertisers contributing more than $2 billion of that amount. Radio already takes in more ad dollars than does the magazine industry. And, still only one-third the size of the television industry and one-fourth as large as the newspaper industry, radio could outpace its rivals in growth in 1979 and beyond, say its proponents.

Because it is neither capital-intensive nor labor-intensive, radio is relatively free of the pressures that force repeated price increases in TV and in print, and advertisers can readily turn to it to stretch inflated media dollars by spending them where they will buy the most exposure.

Unlike television, it does not take a huge sum of money to buy a radio station. An FM station in Santa Fe, N.M., for instance, changed hands last month for $332,500, and one in Waco, Tex., was offered at $140,000. But as with TV, a radio station license is considered by many as "a license to print money." Says Alan R. Griffith, a vice-president at Bank of New York, whose office in the CBS Inc. headquarters building puts him in close proximity to numerous broadcasting executives: "Almost every day a sales or programming person wants to talk about financing a radio station purchase. 'I've made a fortune for my company,' they say. 'Now I want to do it for me.' " A well-managed station can throw off a lot of cash, he adds.

FUELING THE NEW INTEREST

The interest in radio as a flourishing industry has been heightened by several recent events. Among them:

■ The Federal Communications Commission at yearend released its figures on 1977 profits, showing that radio's pretax income climbed to $178.6 million, 37.8 percent over the 1976 figure, while revenues jumped 12.6 percent to a record $2.8 billion. Estimates from industry sources indicate that revenues climbed a further 12 percent in 1978, and a gain of 10 to 12 percent is predicted for this year.

■ In Washington, a movement toward almost total deregulation of radio is gathering momentum at both the FCC and in Congress. Although the nation now has some 4544 AM stations and 3993 FM stations on the air, the FCC is firmly in favor of more stations and greater competition. It is considering various plans that could make room for anywhere from 125 to several thousand new stations, many of which might be owned by minorities.

■ Stunning the entire industry, an FM station in New York City—a market with 43 AM outlets and 56 FM—began playing only disco music and virtually overnight jumped from near obscurity to become the country's No. 1 station. Capturing almost 16 percent of the total radio audience at times, WKTU supplanted WABC, a more powerful AM station that reigned for 16 years, and proved that the newer FM stations can have parity with the familiar AM ones.
■ On February 5, following an increasing number of tentative forays into radio by such TV-oriented national advertisers as General Foods Corp. (for Maxwell House) and Procter & Gamble Co. (for Ivory

Liquid), Sears, Roebuck & Co. begins an initial year of nightly sponsorship of "Sears Radio Theater." Emulating radio's heyday of the 1930s and 1940s, the one-hour series of drama, mysteries, and comedies will be fed by CBS to more than 200 affiliates. Many of them already carry network radio's only drama series, "CBS Radio Mystery Theater," that began its sixth year on January 8.

The CBS-Sears effort is only one of numerous new ideas at the radio networks, which recovered in 1977 from four straight years of losses to earn $25 million on $85.5 million in revenues.

HOW A STATION BECOMES A MONEY MACHINE

Edward L. Cossman does not look like a person who would be let in readily by the supercilious guardians of the gates at Studio 54, the famed New York City disco. Short, chunky, soberly attired, and with a fat cigar seemingly affixed permanently to his right hand, Cossman does not know his way around a disco dance floor at all—but he knows that a huge segment of the radio listeners in New York likes disco music. And, for a man interested in making money in radio, this is all he needs to know.

Cossman is currently overseeing WKTU-FM, the station that has the largest audience in the nation, and is executive vice-president of SJR Communications Inc., the broadcasting subsidiary of San Juan Racing Assn. Inc. A veteran broadcaster and sales executive, Cossman was brought in by Hyman N. Glickstein, president and chairman of the executive committee of the parent company, at the beginning of the decade to help it diversify into radio. Its principal asset at the time was the only racetrack in Puerto Rico. Cossman began buying individual radio stations and tinkering with their management and programming.

How well he has done is evident in the parent's annual report for fiscal 1978. The New El Commandante Race Track made less than $1 million on revenues of $24 million, the report says. The Washington Diplomats professional soccer team added $550,000 in revenues and chalked up a loss of $1.5 million. Cossman's group of 10 radio stations, however, made $2.6 million in pretax earnings on $13.2 million in revenues.

'Look what we did.' This month, while the company was buying another station, a Dallas FM outlet, for $4 million, it received a tentative offer of $66 million from a group interested in the track and the stations, which Cossman acquired over the last eight years for less than $10 million. "Let me show you why they're interested," says Cossman, riffling through a sheaf of computer printouts. "Look, in Cleveland, we bought a Storer FM station in 1971 for $700,000 when it was grossing—grossing, mind you—$802 a month. Look what we did this past October. On a gross of $234,000, we netted $105,000."

Similar figures for most of the other SJR stations lead him to exult, "It's a joy to be lucky 10 times in a row." But he readily admits that

Some of the money—which flows from four networks owned by American Broadcasting Co., two owned by Mutual Broadcasting System Inc., and one apiece by CBS and National Broadcasting Co.—is being poured back into new approaches in programming, research, and sales. At CBS, explains Sam Cooke Digges, the silver-haired president of the Radio Division, "people thought we were crazy when we bought the radio rights to the NFL's 'Monday Night Football.' After all, with 45 million people watching the games on ABC-TV, why would anybody want to tune in radio?" But audience research showed 10 million listeners tuned to the broadcasts each week—frequently watching TV at the same time, while tuning out TV announcer Howard Cosell.

At National Broadcasting Co., the media focus has been on the frenzied efforts of President and Chief Executive Officer Fred Silverman to shore up the TV network's ratings, but one of his first moves was to reorganize the company's radio operations. He followed the lead of ABC and CBS in appointing different

---

the huge success of WKTU came as a surprise. Cossman got his hands on the station three years ago when he spent $4 million to buy two New York City stations, WHOM and WHOM-FM. The AM station broadcast Spanish-language programs to a large part of the market, while the FM station played "continental music"— Greek, Latin, and East European selections.

Cossman cut the staff at both stations. "I've reduced the average to 14 at all our stations, going down from 29 or 30 people in some cases," he says. He retained the Spanish-program format at WHOM but gave the FM station new call letters, WKTU, and a new format of gentle rock music. With the aid of a promotion campaign costing several hundred thousand dollars, the "mellow sound" of the new WKTU began to attract listeners and advertisers.

Before the change, the station was drawing less than 0.3 percent of the area's total radio audience, far behind WABC, the powerful AM station that regularly gets 8 or 9 percent with its popular "top 40 songs" format. Slowly, the WKTU ratings edged upward, and the station, which lost $173,000 in fiscal 1976, made $184,000 the following year. In 1978 its earnings climbed to $325,000, and Cossman projected a profit of almost $1 million for fiscal 1979.

Throb. He saw a problem, however. The hard-hitting sound of disco music was becoming increasingly popular, but the "mellow" format of his station prevented the disc jockeys from playing the new records. Overruling a consulting team, Cossman ordered the format changed overnight to nothing but disco music, 24 hours a day. And he gave listeners a bonus: no commercials from 12:30 to 1:30 each afternoon, none from 11 p.m. to 5 a.m. at night, and only eight per hour at other times.

In just three months, the station's share of the listening audience leaped from 2 percent to 11 percent and more, and its distinctive throbbing sound could be heard in retail shops, luncheonettes, and record stores. Now, although advertising rates are quadruple the $60 per minute that the station first charged, advertisers, including some who defected when the format change was announced, are begging for air time. And Cossman has raised his profit projection to $5 million.

"I don't know how long disco will last," says Cossman. "But I know that when some stations began playing rock 'n' roll in the 1950s, others said it was just a fad. And I know that in this industry, you never have it made. Somebody else is always working to get your audience away. You have to think radio seven days a week to be successful."

executives to head the NBC network and the AM and FM station groups, and he put the former head of the combined radio division in a special slot to study the acquisition of more stations and the creation of additional radio networks.

Such a move is a radical change for a company which only a few years ago was interested in selling its radio stations and which lost an estimated $20 million with a faltering second network service that offered news around the clock. "We're spending money to make our programming more innovative," notes Richard P. Vern, the 39-year-old executive vice-president of the NBC Radio Division. "We're significantly more contemporary now, with features by Liz Smith, the gossip columnist, Mark Russell, the Washington satirist, and Joyce Brothers talking about kids and sex. During Christmas, we anchored our newscasts out of Bethlehem. For the first time, radio has its own sports unit, and this month we had the first convention of our radio affiliates in four years."

THE NEEDS OF LOCAL STATIONS

Less exuberant but equally bullish on the future of network radio is Harold L. Neal, Jr., the thoughtful president of ABC Radio, which pioneered the route to profits in 1968 by establishing four different networks. Each furnishes five minutes of news every hour to a different group of stations. (One group is "fed" at five minutes before the hour, a second on the hour, and so on.) In a single bound, ABC increased the number of affiliates carrying its news by 300 percent and greatly enlarged the number of advertising prospects on which it could draw a bead—offering makers of youth-oriented products a lineup of rock-music stations, for example, or giving the marketer of a high-ticket item a group of FM stations that appeal to upper-income listeners. The move also let ABC amortize the cost of its radio transmission lines, for

which the company pays about $3 million per year, over four separate five-minute periods per hour, rather than one or two.

Neal is convinced that "a network can succeed only by gearing its programming these days to the local station's needs." He sees radio at both the network and local level becoming "more and more like the magazine industry, where there are specialized publications with their own unique audiences and advertisers." To help impress on prospective clients that each of ABC's networks targets a different segment of the total radio audience, Neal announced on January 24 a reorganization of the network sales force. Where previously there was one group of salesmen for all four radio services, there are now separate groups of marketing specialists who determine the goals of advertisers in specific product areas and match them to the most suitable network.

The idea that radio today presents listeners in any large market with a number of specialized "magazines" is one of the industry's strengths, notes Miles David, president of the Radio Advertising Bureau (RAB). "We have research that shows the average listener tunes in regularly to 2.2 stations, no matter how many he can receive. That helps advertisers get a very specific fix on where their customers are."

Radio began to segment its audiences in the 1950s, after television had drawn off the listeners who once tuned in regularly. Some pioneer broadcasters—notably Gordon McLendon of Dallas and Todd Storz of Omaha—sought to cut costs by playing phonograph records all day and night. Perceiving that the typical jukebox of the time contained 40 records, they established a "top 40" format and played the same records in an appeal to music-buying youngsters. When the idea caught on, other stations began looking for variations. Some offered new forms of rock music, "soft" rock or "acid" rock; others offered hits of the past —"golden oldies"—or country-and-western music. A few stations hung onto the familiar blend of middle-of-the-road music, chattering "personalities," and sportscasts that typified the radio programs of the 1940s, much as *Reader's Digest* and *Parade* still survive for a general magazine audience today. Other formats—all-talk, all-news, and now, with the ascendancy of WKTU in New York, all-disco—were devised to lure different listener segments.

NEW SERVICES FOR BROADCASTERS

Segmentation of the radio audience has spurred the growth of new services in the industry. Stations that play nothing but a single kind of music all day can be almost entirely automated, and electronics manufacturers are busily selling computerized equipment to many of them. Consultants who specialize in determining a station's format —down to selecting music, network service, announcers, and how fast the announcers should talk—have flourished since the 1960s, but a new group of specialists has recently come on the scene. These are syndicators who provide taped "programs"—anything from a 90-second interview with "The Home Handyman" who talks about fixing a leaky pipe to a half-hour science-fiction drama, "Alien Worlds," or a weekend-long history of rock-and-roll music. Their customers are a growing list of stations that want to distinguish their programming—largely music—from that of their competitors, but do not want to spend money to produce their own programs. Providing shows at prices that range from $5 for a 60-second news feature to $15,000 for the 52-hour "History of Rock 'n' Roll," the syndicators have boosted annual volume from $5 million to $25 million in five years.

"Demand from stations is extremely high for this sort of thing," says Dwight Case, president of RKO Radio Group, which has 13 stations. In the past two years alone, at least two dozen new programs have been put on the market, and several scheduled to debut soon include "Odd Tracks," a 30-minute weekly program of recordings by major stars that were never released, and "The Other Side," a daily two-minute series providing alternative viewpoints on current issues. A big hit is a two-hour "Dr. Demento Show," a wacky potpourri of musical nostalgia distributed by Westwood One in Los Angeles.

Some of the shows have built-in appeal to advertisers. Cliff Barrett and Frank Gorin, two newscasters who were with NBC's failing all-news network, went into the syndication business two years ago as Barrett-Gorin Inc. "When NBC closed down the news service," says Frank Gorin, "they left a lot of stations that were committed to all-news out in the cold." BGI now distributes tapes of features on such subjects as photography, home repair, and personal finance—all of which can be sponsored by local camera shops, hardware stores, banks, and the like.

National advertisers also support the special features. Warner-Lambert now spends about 30 percent of its radio budget on five syndicated programs. "You're getting national coverage in programs appealing to the audience you're trying to reach on stations they listen to," says Robert A. Friedlander, manager of media planning and coordination for the company. Recently, Anheuser-Busch, Peter Paul, and International Harvester stepped up their syndication budgets. Many programs are given to the stations free in a barter arrangement that guarantees a national sponsor that the show will be aired and that he will get time for a commerical message.

The area of radio research also is prospering. With stations and ad agencies now clamoring for more data, two newcomers have begun issuing reports in a challenge to Arbitron Co., the subsidiary of Control Data Corp. that has held a near-monopoly position since it began radio audience measurement a dozen years ago.

Trac-7, the new service of Audits & Surveys, says it uses a larger sample of phone respondents than Arbitron. Burke Broadcast Research Inc., a subsidiary of a company that tests TV commercials for their selling power, thinks that its experience with ad agencies will help attract customers for its radio data.

"The availability of more research means that it's easier to measure radio audiences now," says Dawn Sibley, senior vice-president for media at Compton Advertising Inc. "Couple that with the tremendous cost increases that have taken place in the last few years in television and magazines, and you see why everyone's taking a new look at radio."

David of the RAB notes that while agencies such as Compton, which shifted some Procter & Gamble dollars from TV into a test of radio during the last quarter of 1978, are willing to study the medium, many others shy away from examining the research data of hundreds or even thousands of stations. Aware of this built-in liability, individual stations long have concentrated on selling their value to local advertisers: banks, retailers, restaurants, beauty shops, funeral homes, and the rest. Even the smallest local company could afford to spend a few dollars for a commercial, station salesmen argued, and there are no extra costs for typesetting, photography, plate-making, and the other requirements of print advertising. And even with their low rates, the bulk of the stations have grown solidly profitable, selling 18 commercial minutes per hour, as allowed by the FCC.

"It's the greediness of some AM stations that helped FM grow so dramatically," says J. Robert Cole, vice-president in charge of FM stations at CBS. "Not only can FM broadcast stereo music—which, after all, is the kind that people buy when they buy record albums—but it started out with much less advertising volume. People began tuning in because they knew that they would not be bombarded with a commercial every few minutes. We work to convince advertisers that they should pay more

for our minutes than they might pay elsewhere simply because they're in a less crowded environment." Adds Peter A. Lund, Cole's rival in charge of AM stations: "But one thing we don't do these days is sell against other radio stations by telling media buyers they made a poor selection. We point out to advertisers how they can add radio to TV and print schedules to increase their reach and frequency of impressions."

FM: "A GREAT NEW BUSINESS"

Although the 30-year-old FM broadcasting industry trails far behind the older AM service in total revenues, its profits are growing at a faster pace, and most radio executives think the day is not far off when the two services will be of equal size. The surge of FM radio was caused by government regulation, rather than in spite of it. "To think that we used to force applicants for an AM franchise to take an FM assignment as well!" exclaims Charles D. Ferris, chairman of the FCC. "Now, FM is on top in several markets and growing, simply because it really does provide a better signal." In addition to requiring would-be AM broadcasters to put an FM signal on the air, the FCC in 1968 ordered most owners of AM and FM stations in the same market to put different programming on each station, rather than merely play the same shows on both. The added expense angered some station owners, "but the commission dragged us kicking and screaming into a great new business," says Cole of CBS.

Helped once—albeit unwillingly—by the FCC, radio operators are now puzzling over the commission's latest ideas. One FCC proposal announced at yearend would reduce the power of the nation's 25 50,000-watt "clear channel" stations, which once were the only signals to serve rural areas. This proposal has drawn fire from the operators of the broadcasting giants, although one official privately concedes that his station would not lose much business if its

New York signal could no longer be picked up in remote areas of the Midwest at night. Still, the plan—which would allow 125 new stations to be built to serve the rural markets—"will be opposed strongly, as a matter of principle, and because we don't think that there will be a rush of applicants for a license in Appalachia," says the broadcaster. "People in areas like that may end up with no radio at all."

THE COSTS OF DEREGULATION

The FCC is considering two other proposals that could put more stations on the air, and Chairman Ferris says: "The need for more stations is simply self-evident. It springs from the new environment, particularly the recognition of diversity in communities and the profitability of serving parts of markets or specialized markets with news, popular and classical music, community information—you name it." Commissioner Tyrone Brown, a black who tends to be the magnet at the FCC for minority issues, agrees. "We have great evidence of scarcity," he says. "Radio station prices are exploding. That tells me there is a greater demand than supply."

With the strong probability of more stations on the dial and less burdensome regulatory paperwork, the industry may find itself with some new problems, says Ferris. "A lot of the regulatory detail came from the industry itself," he says, "because owners wanted specific rules they could obey to the letter and protect their license franchises. With less regulation, they may not feel so secure."

Now, however, radio executives feel secure that their medium will grow stronger in 1979 and will prosper even if there is a second-half recession. "No other medium is so flexible," says Robert J. Duffy, president of Christal Co., a sales representative for some 70 stations. "Nothing else lets you reach working women in such great numbers, or zero in on the millions who are light viewers of TV." That kind of optimism is expected to keep station prices climbing: Last month a Denver FM station went to an Ohio buyer for $6.7 million, a record for an FM outlet and $4 million more than an offer made a year earlier.

The FCC's actions to clear the way for new stations will have little impact on escalating prices, notes Ted Hepburn, a Cincinnati-based media broker. "I'll bet the expense of legal work and putting a new station on the air will surpass the cost of buying an existing one, even with prices soaring," he says.

chapter 2

PORNOGRAPHY, OBSCENITY, AND CENSORSHIP

The issue dealt with in this chapter revolves around some classic arguments. The arguments in favor of censorship are presented by Irving Kristol, a professor of urban values at New York University. Hollis Alpert, a film critic and contributing editor for *Saturday Review*, presents the opposing view.

These are more than philosophic arguments; censorship—and materials that some say should be censored—are all around us. The third article in this chapter points out the rise of censorship of public school reading materials. Author Jerzy Kosinski presents his view of this trend in the fourth article.

This debate continues to be a lively one, as can be seen in newspaper editorials nationwide whenever a case involving censorship comes up. This chapter concludes with four sample editorials on two recent obscenity cases. The first two editorials deal with George Carlin's "dirty words" case, in which the FCC warned a New York City radio station that playing Carlin's monologue, "Filthy Words," during daytime hours could be used against them at license-renewal time. The case went all the way to the Supreme Court, where the FCC ruling was upheld. The *Birmingham News* is one of the papers that came out in agreement with the court, and the *Des Moines Register* is one that came out against it.

The second set of editorials deals with the reaction of the press to Larry Flynt's conviction as a pornographer. The *Roanoke* (Va.) *Times* came out in favor of the conviction. The *Sacramento* (Ca.) *Bee* protested the same conviction.

PORNOGRAPHY, OBSCENITY, AND THE CASE FOR CENSORSHIP

Irving Kristol

Being frustrated is disagreeable, but the real disasters in life begin when you get what you want. For almost a century now, a great many intelligent, well-meaning, and articulate people—of a kind generally called liberal or intellectual, or both—have argued eloquently against any kind of censorship of art and/or entertainment. And within the past 10 years, the courts and the legislatures of most Western nations have found these arguments persuasive—so persuasive that hardly a man is now alive who clearly remembers what the answers to these arguments were. Today, in the United States and other democracies, censorship has to all intents and purposes ceased to exist.

Is there a sense of triumphant exhilaration in the land? Hardly. There is, on the contrary, a rapidly growing unease and disquiet. Somehow, things have not worked out as they were supposed to, and many notable civil libertarians have gone on record as saying this was not what they meant at all. They wanted a world in which *Desire under the Elms* could be produced, or *Ulysses* published, without interference by philistine busybodies holding public office. They have got that, of course; but they have also got a world in which homosexual rape takes place on the stage, in which the public flocks during lunch hours to witness varieties of professional fornication, in which Times Square has become little more than a hideous market for the sale and distribution of printed filth that panders to all known (and some fanciful) sexual perversions.

But disagreeable as this may be, does it really matter? Might not our unease and disquiet be merely a cultural hangover—a "hangup," as they say? What reason is there to think that anyone was ever corrupted by a book?

This last question, oddly enough, is asked by the very same people who seem convinced that advertisements in magazines or displays of violence on television do indeed have the power to corrupt. It is also asked, incredibly enough and in all sincerity, by people—e.g., university professors and school teachers—

From *The New York Times Magazine* (March 28, 1971): 24–25+. © 1971 by The New York Times Company. Reprinted by permission.

whose very lives provide all the answers one could want. After all, if you believe that no one was ever corrupted by a book, you have also to believe that no one was ever improved by a book (or a play or a movie). You have to believe, in other words, that all art is morally trivial and that, consequently, all education is morally irrelevant. No one, not even a university professor, really believes that.

To be sure, it is extremely difficult, as social scientists tell us, to trace the effects of any single book (or play or movie) on an individual reader or any class of readers. But we all know, and social scientists know it too, that the ways in which we use our minds and imaginations do shape our characters and help define us as persons. That those who certainly know this are nevertheless moved to deny it merely indicates how a dogmatic resistance to the idea of censorship can—like most dogmatism—result in a mindless insistence on the absurd.

I have used these harsh terms—"dogmatism" and "mindless"—advisedly. I might also have added "hypocritical." For the plain fact is that none of us is a complete civil libertarian. We all believe that there is some point at which the public authorities ought to step in to limit the "self-expression" of an individual or a group, even where this might be seriously intended as a form of artistic expression, and even where the artistic transaction is between consenting adults. A playwright or theatrical director might, in this crazy world of ours, find someone willing to commit suicide on the stage, as called for by the script. We would not allow that—any more than we would permit scenes of real physical torture on the stage, even if the victim were a willing masochist. And I know of no one, no matter how free in spirit, who argues that we ought to permit gladiatorial contests in Yankee Stadium, similar to those once performed in the Colosseum at Rome—even if only consenting adults were involved.

The basic point that emerges is one that Professor Walter Berns has powerfully argued: no society can be utterly indifferent to the ways its citizens publicly entertain themselves.[1] Bear-baiting and cockfighting are prohibited only in part out of compassion for the suffering animals; the main reason they were abolished was because it was felt that they debased and brutalized the citizenry who flocked to witness such spectacles. And the question we face with regard to pornography and obscenity is whether, now that they have such strong legal protection from the Supreme Court, they can or will brutalize and debase our citizenry. We are, after all, not dealing with one passing incident—one book, or one play, or one movie. We are dealing with a general tendency that is suffusing our entire culture.

I say pornography *and* obscenity because, though they have different dictionary definitions and are frequently distinguishable as "artistic" genres, they are nevertheless in the end identical in effect. Pornography is not objectionable simply because it arouses sexual desire or lust or prurience in the mind of the reader or spectator; this is a silly Victorian notion. A great many nonpornographic works—including some parts of the Bible—excite sexual desire very successfully. What is distinctive about pornography is that, in the words of D. H. Lawrence, it attempts "to do dirt on [sex] . . . [It is an] insult to a vital human relationship."

In other words, pornography differs from erotic art in that its whole purpose is to treat human beings obscenely, to deprive human beings of their specifically human dimension. That is what obscenity is all about. It is light years removed from any kind of carefree sensuality—there is no continuum between Fielding's *Tom Jones* and the Marquis de Sade's *Justine*. These works have quite opposite intentions. To quote Susan Sontag: "What pornographic literature does is precisely to drive a wedge between one's existence as a full human being and one's existence as a sexual being—while in ordinary life a healthy person is one who prevents such a gap from opening up." This definition occurs in an essay *defending* pornography—Miss Sontag is a candid as well as gifted critic—so the definition, which I accept, is neither tendentious nor censorious.

Along these same lines, one can point out—as C. S. Lewis pointed out some years back—that it is no accident that in the history of all literatures obscene words—the so-called "four-letter words"—have always been the vocabulary of farce or vituperation. The reason is clear; they reduce men and women to some of their mere bodily functions —they reduce man to his animal component, and such a reduction is an essential purpose of farce or vituperation.

Similarly, Lewis also suggested that it is not an accident that we have no offhand, colloquial, neutral terms—not in any Western European language at any rate—for our most private parts. The words we do use are either (a) nursery terms, (b) archaisms, (c) scientific terms, or (d) a term from the gutter (i.e., a demeaning term). Here I think the genius of language is telling us something important about man. It is telling us that man is an animal with a difference: he has a unique sense of privacy, and a unique capacity for shame when this privacy is violated. Our "private parts" are indeed private, and not merely because convention prescribes it. This particular convention is indigenous to the human race. In practically all primitive tribes, men and women cover their private parts; and in practically all primitive tribes, men and women do not copulate in public.

It may well be that Western society, in the latter half of the twentieth century, is experiencing a drastic change in sexual mores and sexual relationships. We have had many such "sexual revolutions" in the past—and the bourgeois family and bourgeois ideas of sexual propriety were themselves established in the course of a revolution against eighteenth century "licentiousness"—and we shall doubtless have others in the future. It is, however, highly improbable (to put it mildly) that what we are witnessing is the Final Revolution which will make sexual relations utterly unproblematic, permit us to dispense with any kind of ordered relationships between the sexes, and allow us freely to redefine the human condition. And so long as humanity has not reached that utopia, obscenity will remain a problem.

One of the reasons it will remain a problem is that obscenity is not merely about sex, any more than science fiction is about science. Science fiction, as every student of the genre knows, is a peculiar vision of power: what it is really about is politics. And obscenity is a peculiar vision of humanity: what it is really about is ethics and metaphysics.

Imagine a man—a well-known man, much in the public eye—in a hospital ward, dying an agonizing death. He is not in control of his bodily functions, so that his bladder and his bowels empty themselves of their own accord. His consciousness is overwhelmed and extinguished by pain, so that he cannot communicate with us, nor we with him. Now, it would be, technically, the easiest thing in the world to put a television camera in his hospital room and let the whole world witness this spectacle. We don't do it—at least we don't do it as yet—because we regard this as an *obscene* invasion of privacy. And what would make the spectacle obscene is that we would be witnessing the extinguishing of humanity in a human animal.

Incidentally, in the past our humanitarian crusaders against capital punishment understood this point very well. The abolitionist literature goes into great physical detail about what happens to a man when he is hanged or electrocuted or gassed. And their argument was—and is—that what happens is shockingly obscene, and that no civilized society should be responsible for perpetrating such obscenities, particularly since in the nature of the case there must be spectators to ascertain that this horror was indeed being perpetrated in fulfillment of the law.

Sex—like death—is an activity that is both animal and human. There are human sentiments and human ideals involved in this animal activity. But when sex is public, the viewer does not see—cannot see—the sentiments and the ideals. He can only see the animal coupling. And that is why, when men and women make love, as we say, they prefer to be alone— because it is only when you are alone that you can make love, as distinct from merely copulating in an animal and casual way. And that, too, is why those who are voyeurs, if they are not irredeemably sick, also feel ashamed at what they are witnessing. When sex is a public spectacle, a human relationship has been debased into a mere animal connection.

It is also worth noting that this making of sex into an obscenity is not a mutual and equal transaction, but is rather an act of exploitation by one of the partners—the male partner. I do not wish to get into the complicated question as to what, if any, are the essential differences— as distinct from conventional and cultural differences—between male and female. I do not claim to know the answer to that. But I do know—and I take it as a sign which has meaning—that pornography is, and always has been, a man's work; that women rarely write pornography; and that women tend to be indifferent consumers of pornography.[2] My own guess, by way of explanation, is that a woman's sexual experience is ordinarily more suffused with human emotion than is man's, that men are more easily satisfied with autoerotic activities, and that men can therefore more easily take a more "technocratic" view of sex and its pleasures. Perhaps this is not correct. But whatever the explanation, there can be no question that pornography is a form of "sexism," as the Women's Liberation Movement calls it, and that the instinct of Women's Lib has been unerring in perceiving that, when pornography is perpetrated, it is perpetrated against them, as part of a conspiracy to deprive them of their full humanity.

But even if all this is granted, it might be said—and doubtless will be said—that I really ought not to be unduly concerned. Free competition in the cultural marketplace—it is argued by people who have never otherwise had a kind word to say for laissez-faire—will au-

tomatically dispose of the problem. The present fad for pornography and obscenity, it will be asserted, is just that, a fad. It will spend itself in the course of time; people will get bored with it, will be able to take it or leave it alone in a casual way, in a "mature way," and, in sum, I am being unnecessarily distressed about the whole business. The *New York Times*, in an editorial, concludes hopefully in this vein:

In the end . . . the insensate pursuit of the urge to shock, carried from one excess to a more abysmal one, is bound to achieve its own antidote in total boredom. When there is no lower depth to descend to, ennui will erase the problem.

I would like to be able to go along with this line of reasoning, but I cannot. I think it is false, and for two reasons, the first psychological, the second political.

The basic psychological fact about pornography and obscenity is that it appeals to and provokes a kind of sexual regression. The sexual pleasure one gets from pornography and obscenity is autoerotic and infantile; put bluntly, it is a masturbatory exercise of the imagination, when it is not masturbation pure and simple. Now, people who masturbate do not get bored with masturbation, just as sadists don't get bored with sadism, and voyeurs don't get bored with voyeurism.

In other words, infantile sexuality is not only a permanent temptation for the adolescent or even the adult—it can quite easily become a permanent, self-reinforcing neurosis. It is because of an awareness of this possibility of regression toward the infantile condition, a regression which is always open to us, that all the codes of sexual conduct ever devised by the human race take such a dim view of autoerotic activities and try to discourage autoerotic fantasies. Masturbation is indeed a perfectly natural autoerotic activity, as so many sexologists blandly assure us today. And it is precisely because it is so perfectly natural that it can be so dangerous to the mature or maturing person, if it is not controlled or sublimated in some way. That is the true meaning of Portnoy's complaint. Portnoy, you will recall, grows up to be a man who is incapable of having an adult sexual relationship with a woman; his sexuality remains fixed in an infantile mode, the prison of his autoerotic fantasies. Inevitably, Portnoy comes to think, in a perfectly *infantile* way, that it was all his mother's fault.

It is true that, in our time, some quite brilliant minds have come to the conclusion that a reversion to infantile sexuality is the ultimate mission and secret destiny of the human race. I am thinking in particular of Norman O. Brown, for whose writings I have the deepest respect. One of the reasons I respect them so deeply is that Mr. Brown is a serious thinker who is unafraid to face up to the radical consequences of his radical theories. Thus, Mr. Brown knows and says that for his kind of salvation to be achieved, humanity must annul the civilization it has created—not merely the civilization we have today, but all civilization—so as to be able to make the long descent backward into animal innocence.

What is at stake is civilization and humanity, nothing less. The idea that "everything is permitted," as Nietzsche put it, rests on the premise of nihilism and has nihilistic implications. I will not pretend that the case against nihilism and for civilization is an easy one to make. We are here confronting the most fundamental of philosophical questions, on the deepest levels. But that is precisely my point—that the matter of pornography and obscenity is not a trivial one, and that only superficial minds can take a bland and untroubled view of it.

In this connection I might also point out those who are primarily against censorship on liberal grounds tell us not to take pornography or obscenity seriously, while those who are for pornography and obscenity, on radical grounds, take it very seriously indeed. I believe the radicals—writers like Susan Sontag, Herbert Marcuse, Norman O. Brown, and even

Jerry Rubin—are right, and the liberals are wrong. I also believe that those young radicals at Berkeley, some five years ago, who provoked a major confrontation over the public use of obscene words, showed a brilliant political instinct. Once the faculty and administration had capitulated on this issue—saying: "Oh, for God's sake, let's be adult: what difference does it make anyway?"—once they said that, they were bound to lose on every other issue. And once Mark Rudd could publicly ascribe to the president of Columbia a notoriously obscene relationship to his mother, without provoking any kind of reaction, the S.D.S. had already won the day. The occupation of Columbia's buildings merely ratified their victory. Men who show themselves unwilling to defend civilization against nihilism are not going to be either resolute or effective in defending the university against anything.

I am already touching upon a political aspect of pornography when I suggest that it is inherently and purposefully subversive of civilization and its institutions. But there is another and more specifically political aspect, which has to do with the relationship of pornography and/or obscenity to democracy, and especially to the quality of public life on which democratic government ultimately rests.

Though the phrase, "the quality of life," trips easily from so many lips these days, it tends to be one of those clichés with many trivial meanings and no large, serious one. Sometimes it merely refers to such externals as the enjoyment of cleaner air, cleaner water, cleaner streets. At other times it refers to the merely private enjoyment of music, painting, or literature. Rarely does it have anything to do with the way the citizen in a democracy views himself—his obligations, his intentions, his ultimate self-definition.

Instead, what I would call the "managerial" conception of democracy is the predominant opinion among political scientists, sociologists, and economists, and has, through the untiring efforts of these scholars, become the conventional journalistic opinion as well. The root idea behind this "managerial" conception is that democracy is a "political system" (as they say) which can be adequately defined in terms of—can be fully reduced to—its mechanical arrangements. Democracy is then seen as a set of rules and procedures, and *nothing but* a set of rules and procedures, whereby majority rule and minority rights are reconciled into a state of equilibrium. If everyone follows these rules and procedures, then a democracy is in working order. I think this is a fair description of the democratic idea that currently prevails in academia. One can also fairly say that it is now the liberal idea of democracy par excellence.

I cannot help but feel that there is something ridiculous about being this kind of a democrat, and I must further confess to having a sneaking sympathy for those of our young radicals who also find it ridiculous. The absurdity is the absurdity of idolatry—of taking the symbolic for the real, the means for the end. The purpose of democracy cannot possibly be the endless functioning of its own political machinery. The purpose of any political regime is to achieve some version of the good life and the good society. It is not at all difficult to imagine a perfectly functioning democracy which answers all questions except one—namely, why should anyone of intelligence and spirit care a fig for it?

There is, however, an older idea of democracy—one which was fairly common until about the beginning of this century—for which the conception of the quality of public life is absolutely crucial. This idea starts from the proposition that democracy is a form of self-government, and that if you want it to be a meritorious polity, you have to care about what kind of people govern it. Indeed, it puts the matter more strongly and declares that, if you want self-government, you are only entitled to it if that "self" is worthy of governing. There

is no inherent right to self-government if it means that such government is vicious, mean, squalid, and debased. Only a dogmatist and a fanatic, an idolater of democratic machinery, could approve of self-government under such conditions.

And because the desirability of self-government depends on the character of the people who govern, the older idea of democracy was very solicitous of the condition of this character. It was solicitous of the individual self, and felt an obligation to educate it into what used to be called "republican virtue." And it was solicitous of that collective self which we call public opinion and which, in a democracy, governs us collectively. Perhaps in some respects it was nervously over-solicitous—that would not be surprising. But the main thing is that it cared, cared not merely about the machinery of democracy but about the quality of life that this machinery might generate.

And because it cared, this older idea of democracy had no problem in principle with pornography and/or obscenity. It censored them—and it did so with a perfect clarity of mind and a perfectly clear conscience. It was not about to permit people capriciously to corrupt themselves. Or, to put it more precisely: in this version of democracy, the people took some care not to let themselves be governed by the more infantile and irrational parts of themselves.

I have, it may be noticed, uttered that dreadful word, "censorship." And I am not about to back away from it. If you think pornography and/or obscenity is a serious problem, you have to be for censorship. I'll go even further and say that if you want to prevent pornography and/or obscenity from becoming a problem, you have to be for censorship. And lest there be any misunderstanding as to what I am saying, I'll put it as bluntly as possible; if you care for the quality of life in our American democracy, then you have to be for censorship.

But can a liberal be for censorship? Unless one assumes that being a liberal *must* mean being indifferent to the quality of American life, then the answer has to be: yes, a liberal can be for censorship—but he ought to favor a liberal form of censorship.

Is that a contradiction in terms? I don't think so. We have no problem in contrasting *repressive* laws governing alcohol and drugs and tobacco with laws *regulating* (i.e., discouraging the sale of) alcohol and drugs and tobacco. Laws encouraging temperance are not the same thing as laws that have as their goal prohibition or abolition. We have not made the smoking of cigarettes a criminal offense. We have, however, and with good liberal conscience, prohibited cigarette advertising on television, and may yet, again with good liberal conscience, prohibit it in newspapers and magazines. The idea of restricting individual freedom, in a liberal way, is not at all unfamiliar to us.

I therefore see no reason why we should not be able to distinguish repressive censorship from liberal censorship of the written and spoken word. In Britain, until a few years ago, you could perform almost any play you wished—but certain plays, judged to be obscene, had to be performed in private theatrical clubs which were deemed to have a "serious" interest in theater. In the United States, all of us who grew up using public libraries are familiar with the circumstances under which certain books could be circulated only to adults, while still other books had to be read in the library reading room, under the librarian's skeptical eye. In both cases, a small minority that was willing to make a serious effort to see an obscene play or read an obscene book could do so. But the impact of obscenity was circumscribed and the quality of public life was only marginally affected.[3]

I am not saying it is easy in practice to sustain a distinction between liberal and repressive censorship, especially in the public realm of a democracy, where popular opinion is so vulnerable to demagoguery. Moreover, an acceptable system of liberal censorship is likely to be exceedingly difficult to devise in the United States today, because our educated classes, upon whose judgment a liberal censorship must rest, are so convinced that there is no such thing as a problem of obscenity, or even that there is no such thing as obscenity at all. But, to counterbalance this, there is the further, fortunate truth that the tolerable margin for error is quite large, and single mistakes or single injustices are not all that important.

This possibility, of course, occasions much distress among artists and academics. It is a fact, one that cannot and should not be denied, that any system of censorship is bound, upon occasion, to treat unjustly a particular work of art—to find pornography where there is only gentle eroticism, to find obscenity where none really exists, or to find both where its existence ought to be tolerated because it serves a larger moral purpose. Though most works of art are not obscene, and though most obscenity has nothing to do with art, there are some few works of art that are, at least in part, pornographic and/or obscene. There are also some few works of art that are in the special category of the comic-ironic "bawdy" (Boccaccio, Rabelais). It is such works of art that are likely to suffer at the hands of the censor. That is the price one has to be prepared to pay for censorship—even liberal censorship.

But just how high is this price? If you believe, as so many artists seem to believe today, that art is the only sacrosanct activity in our profane and vulgar world—that any man who designates himself an artist thereby acquires a sacred office—then obviously censorship is an intolerable form of sacrilege. But for those of us who do not subscribe to this religion of art, the costs of censorship do not seem so high at all.

If you look at the history of American or English literature, there is precious little damage you can point to as a consequence of the censorship that prevailed throughout most of that history. Very few works of literature—of real literary merit, I mean—ever were suppressed;

and those that were, were not suppressed for long. Nor have I noticed, now that censorship of the written word has to all intents and purposes ceased in this country, that hitherto suppressed or repressed masterpieces are flooding the market. Yes, we can now read *Fanny Hill* and the Marquis de Sade. Or, to be more exact, we can now openly purchase them, since many people were able to read them even though they were publicly banned, which is as it should be under a liberal censorship. So how much have literature and the arts gained from the fact that we can all now buy them over the counter, that, indeed, we are all now encouraged to buy them over the counter? They have not gained much that I can see.

And one might also ask a question that is almost never raised: how much has literature lost from the fact that everything is now permitted? It has lost quite a bit, I should say. In a free market, Gresham's law can work for books or theater as efficiently as it does for coinage—driving out the good, establishing the debased. The cultural market in the United States today is being pre-empted by dirty books, dirty movies, dirty theater. A pornographic novel has a far better chance of being published today than a non-pornographic one, and quite a few pretty good novels are not being published at all simply because they are not pornographic, and are therefore less likely to sell. Our cultural condition has not improved as a result of the new freedom. American cultural life wasn't much to brag about 20 years ago; today one feels ashamed for it.

Just one last point which I dare not leave untouched. If we start censoring pornography or obscenity, shall we not inevitably end up censoring political opinion? A lot of people seem to think this would be the case—which only shows the power of doctrinaire thinking over reality. We had censorship of pornography and obscenity for 150 years, until almost yesterday, and I am not aware that freedom of opinion in this country was in any way diminished as a

consequence of this fact. Fortunately for those of us who are liberal, freedom is not indivisible. If it were, the case for liberalism would be indistinguishable from the case for anarchy; and they are two very different things.

But I must repeat and emphasize: what kind of laws we pass governing pornography and obscenity, what kind of censorship—or, since we are still a Federal nation—what kinds of censorship we institute in our various localities may indeed be difficult matters to cope with; nevertheless the real issue is one of principle. I myself subscribe to a liberal view of the enforcement problem: I think that pornography should be illegal *and* available to anyone who wants it so badly as to make a pretty strenuous effort to get it. We have lived with under-the-counter pornography for centuries now, in a fairly comfortable way. But the issue of principle, of whether it should be over or under the counter, has to be settled before we can reflect on the advantages and disadvantages of alternative modes of censorship. I think the settlement we are living under now, in which obscenity and democracy are regarded as equals, is wrong; I believe it is inherently unstable; I think it will, in the long run, be incompatible with any authentic concern for the quality of life in our democracy.

---

1. This is as good a place as any to express my profound indebtedness to Walter Berns's superb essay, "Pornography vs. Democracy," in the winter 1971 issue of *The Public Interest*.

2. There are, of course, a few exceptions—but of a kind that prove the rule. *L'Histoire d'O*, for instance, written by a woman, is unquestionably the most *melancholy* work of pornography ever written. And its theme is precisely the dehumanization accomplished by obscenity.

3. It is fairly predictable that someone is going to object that this point of view is "elitist"—that, under a system of liberal censorship, the rich will have privileged access to pornography and obscenity. Yes, of course they will—just as, at present, the rich have privileged access to heroin if they want it. But one would have to be an egalitarian maniac to object to this state of affairs on the grounds of equality.

THE CASE AGAINST
CENSORSHIP

Hollis Alpert

The idea of censorship, particularly when it is aimed against pornography, has its attractions. What could be seemingly more wholesome than newsstands cleansed of those obnoxious little weekly sheets filled with gleeful celebrations of sexual acts, the more perverse the more gleeful? In what way would the community—any community—be harmed if stores purveying stacks of photographs, glossy magazines, and film strips devoted to illustrating what used to be known as private parts were closed down by police order? Or if cinema houses featuring acts of "love," natural and unnatural, were shuttered? Little would be lost, really.

Even so, I am against censorship.

Over the years, I have had occasion, for journalistic reasons, to examine the question of censorship. I have met and talked to censors; I have been called as an "expert" witness in court cases aimed at suppressing certain films. I have viewed a good part of the Kinsey Institute's collection of pornographic film material and talked to members of the staff. I have read a great many of the available works, legal, sociologic, and psychiatric, on the subject. Nothing I have encountered has changed the opinion stated above.

This is not to say that I, personally, have not been offended by some of what I have encountered. Pornography, according to the dictionary

on my desk, is "writings, pictures, etc., intended to arouse sexual desire." It is nonsense to claim, as some do, that there is no such thing as pornography, and that the use of the word indicates something suspicious about the mental and emotional state of the accuser. (There *can* be something suspicious, of course.) Pornography, simply, does intend to arouse sexual desire, and it fails as pornography if it doesn't. The problem is, for the habitual fancier of the stuff, that it takes more and more to arouse; and as a result, the tendency is for pornography to go farther and farther beyond the pale. Unfortunately, there are limits; and eventually, pornography, even for the addict, becomes dull and stale. The problem for the non-addict is that it becomes increasingly offensive.

What I dislike most about pornography is not the fact of its existence, but the level of its taste which, for the most part, is abysmal. Pornography represents a market—literary, jounalistic, and cinematic—for unimaginative clods, neurotics of many different persuasions, and the untalented everywhere. All such professional matters such as style, taste, craft, and artistry give way to the tasteless, the brainless, the mercenary, the scatological, the obscene. What is so annoying about obscenity, however it may be defined, is the mockery of human aspirations it essentially represents. I do not admire those who so proudly flaunt the banner of their sexual liberalism, for they mock what has meaning for me.

From *Censorship: For and Against* by Harold H. Hart, copyright 1971 Hart Publishing Company, Inc.

Therefore, I am not for pornography; I am merely against censoring it.

I do not regard pornography as an evil, but some of it I do regard as an abomination of sorts. I do not know if exposure to pornography harms either the young, the middle-aged, or the old, but this is not to say that it does not have its effects. It obviously increases the incidence (to use a Kinsey Institute term) of masturbation; but since we hear that masturbation is not harmful and that it is difficult to masturbate to excess, this would not seem to be necessarily a harmful effect.

I don't share the zeal of those who claim for pornography certain benefits for the repressed, the frustrated, the bewildered, and the confused; but I can see where, in certain cases, it might help overcome inhibitions, unwanted modesty, lack of ardor. Yet talking or a modicum of alcoholic drinking can achieve pretty much the same results. As an antidote for boredom and loneliness, pornography may well have some positive value. And by its very frankness, pornography may actually represent an improvement, educationally speaking, for the young who pick up their sexual knowledge on the street or even in some of those earnest sex education courses in schools.

But, again, its therapeutic value needs establishing far more than has been done up to now. In no country where the question has been studied has it yet been found that pornography increases crime. Where rape has been found to be on the rise, it is almost invariably due to social and economic conditions, not to the presence of pornography. While it probably does lead to more sexuality—conjugal and private—for those exposed and attracted to it, pornography does not seem to lead to much in the way of sexual abuse, and here I am speaking primarily of violent forms of sexuality.

In prisons, however, where pornography clearly is not present, sexual abuse, particularly of the homosexual kind, has become a matter of shocking public knowledge.

So I see very little reason to forbid pornography, except that I don't happen to like it.

On the other hand, the mentality of those censors I have met, and of those who advocate censorship, has often filled me with foreboding. All too frequently they have a way of equating pornography with "Godless un-American Communists," and the like. They cite religious tracts, even the Bible (generally overlooking the Song of Solomon) as "scientific" reason for their opposition to pornography and for the straitjackets they would impose on publishing and film making. The zeal with which they have attempted to counterattack against the glut of smut is worrisome in itself, revealing, perhaps, of a secret attraction to what they publicly proclaim as "sinful." Beware he of the impassioned rhetoric. All too often his voice, his words, his tone, remind of the righteous Goebbels.

But it is hardly news that there exists a tremendous amount of cant and hypocrisy among those who assume that a battle against pornography is a battle for law and order. While researching material for "History of Sex in Cinema," a lengthy series published by *Playboy Magazine,* I found that the very pillars of our society—veterans' groups, patriotic organizations, policemen and firemen—were the principal supporters of that hoary American institution, the "stag party." During these evenings one or two hours of a collection of stag reels would be shown to an all-male audience, and where did the evening's entertainment come from? Often enough from the local police or fire chief—confiscated, of course.

While testifying for the release of *I Am Curious—Yellow* and other cinematic works confiscated by U.S. Customs, I was interested to find that in conversation afterward with U.S. attorneys, a good many of them were not at all in agreement, personally, with the views they presented to the jurors. "Of course the film should be shown," said one young assistant district attorney, "it's really all a kind of infighting." Those twelve good men and true didn't exactly convince me either that the jury system was the best way to achieve a fair verdict.

In one case the attorneys for Customs didn't even bother to make a case for their point of view. They merely exhibited the film in question to the jurors, most of whom seldom left their television sets at night. They had no way of knowing precisely what was commonly shown in theaters across the country and around the world. The attorneys counted on only one thing: that they would be shocked by what they saw. They were, and they declared the film guilty. Of what? Of offensiveness to them, naturally.

And just as naturally, an appeals court overturned their verdict.

But of judges, too, I happen to be suspicious. One U.S. District judge, while upholding a Customs seizure of a film, presumably saw more of a sexually nefarious nature in it than I did; and the horrified language he used to describe those "unspeakable acts" was remarkably similar to what I once heard thundered from a pulpit. Too little separation of church and state, in other words.

Thus, I am inclined to think that pornography and what to do about it should be taken out of the legal sphere entirely. Lawyers and judges use terms like "indecent" without bothering to define "decency." Is killing a stranger in a strange land "decent"? Our decent soldiers do it every day, are encouraged to do it, and are not termed indecent except when they rape one or more of the local women. "Does the film appeal to the prurient interest. . . .?" I have long given up attempting to discover what "prurient interest" means—not even the dictionary is of much help here. "The average member of the community." Who is he? And where is this community? Times Square? Scarsdale? Spanish Harlem? Birmingham, Alabama?

The legal battle continues to be fought over a terrain that is inadequately defined, and

perhaps cannot be. It may not even exist any longer.

For look what we have: pornography shown in hundreds of theaters, openly; magazines of a crudity unimaginable just a few years ago; "revolutionary" newspapers filled with erotic junk.

In 1964, when my colleague (Arthur Knight) and I began to look into the erotic content of films, beginning with a clip of Fatima, who electrified Chicago's Columbian Exposition in 1893 with her "dance of the veils" and was subsequently immortalized on film in 1906, the stag film was very much underground, photographs showing male and female organs were still taboo, and movies were still obeying a set of restraints known as the Production Code. All that has changed in a mere half-dozen years.

Fatima, we discovered, was first victim of movie censorship. Peep show patrons had been vouchsafed a glimpse of her belly as she undulated, and the authorities of that day quickly stenciled picket fences over the offending portion of her anatomy. It was not more than ten years before the question of movie censorship reached the august halls of Congress; we very nearly had a national censorship statute. And the agitation for such a statute has not died down to this day.

What agitated censors in 1906, 1916, 1926, and 1936, would strike us as silly and laughable today. A bit of revealed nudity, for instance, as in *Ecstasy*, brought out the Comstockery in thousands across the land. Remember how long it took for one of the literary masterpieces of our century, *Ulysses*, to be sold publicly? It was not hard to reach a conclusion that standards of morality have varied, not to say gyrated, from period to period. Yesterday's obscenity is not necessarily today's. Would that all pornography were as gracefully written as, say, *Fanny Hill*.

But one thing has always existed and presumably always will: the urge to create pornography. And even more widespread is the curiosity it evokes and has evoked in untold millions. All efforts to suppress pornography have failed. If made illegal, it springs up illegally. If made legal, it springs up legally. Presumably, we will always have it. And in a measure never envisioned at a time when Victorian gentlemen took up their pens to relate their erotic experiences, real or imagined.

For technology has made pornography the realm of everyman. When it was discovered that the home movie camera could be employed to record bedroom activities in private, processing plants, in self-protection, refused to develop such intimate and illegal (then) goings-on. But there was always that unscrupulous employee who knew how to turn a buck by channeling furtive prints into the furtive stag market. Thus, in the Kinsey Institute collection and many private ones, are 8 mm and 16 mm films made by amateurs and employing amateurs who were mortified to discover (when, on occasion, the police knocked on their doors) that their private activities were being viewed by thousands.

Surcease came in the form of the Polaroid camera. Stills could be taken and developed instantly without recourse to a lab, and one wonders how much effect this "development" had on the stock of the corporation. More realism came with the Polaroid color camera. One reason, perhaps, that Americans were so ready for public pornography was that they had become so adept at producing it privately.

Then came the home video outfit, an expensive toy, surely, but its uses at home immediately evident for those with the insatiable urge to view the sexual behavior of themselves and sometimes intimate friends and sometimes intimate strangers.

Now, upon us, is the cassette and cartridge recorder, much cheaper, much simpler. Just as television brought havoc to the film industry, the home visual recording devices may wreck the public pornography industry. Instantly erasable, a record need never be there for prying officials.

That is why I strongly suspect that the legal terrain has all but vanished. Within another few years, there may be only one way of quelling the production of pornography and the voyeuristic habits it entails. And that is to bring on "Big Brother," which would amount to electronic surveillance and eavesdropping in every suspected home, in corn fields and on boats, in barns, garages, and garrets.

And that is the main reason I am so strongly opposed to the censorship of pornography, for it would require, sooner or later, a vast national (even international) effort, and *1984* would be here long before its time.

Must we live with it then?

Probably so. But should an actual community wish to control its availability, it does have a certain amount of legal leeway. The Supreme Court has already ruled that a community, a legally defined entity such as a township or a county, can "protect" its young by prosecuting those who purvey it to those under a certain age.

If sexual debasement has been ruled out of court, so to speak, as it has been by many, many "sexologists," psychiatrists, and so-called experts on the subject, surely the debasement of taste has not. And there are ways to make clear to the community why pornography usually represents a nadir level of taste. This judgment can be made on the theater owner who prefers to show "X" films over the less gamier kind because "it sells better." No reason not to let him know, through editorials and in community meetings, that his profit motive does not necessarily make him an admirable member of the community.

But censor him not, please, for the dangers in such action are too great.

The current flood of pornography may well be a symptom, but not with any certainty, of a moral decline. What *has* declined is the hold of religious faith, doctrine, and institutions over human impulses and desires. Even among the more devout, a demarcation now is being made between sexual and spiritual morality. With an increasing degree of scientific inquiry into the nature of human sexuality, sex has been taken out of the realm of the morally harmful and has been given literally a clean bill of health when practiced, so the legal language tells us, among consenting adults. Pre-adult sex is on the rise, too, according to gynecologists. For proof they simply cite the prescriptions for pills and other contraceptive methods dispensed to girls 14 and 15 years old. "The change," said one veteran woman gynecologist, "has been particularly striking during the past five years."

One aspect of the generational gap is the difference between how young people and their elders view the sex act. Among the older generation, there is still evidence of guilt and anxiety over sexual behavior that varies from what they assume to be the norm—and that norm being the sexual act practiced primarily for the purpose of procreation between females over 18 and males over 21. Taboos, though seldom spoken, still exist. The newer generation has tossed aside most of these taboos. Many among them practice experimental and communal forms of cohabitation. Sex is taken for granted, is thought of as natural, healthy, and an expression of a loving nature. Not by all young people, certainly, but by larger percentages than in previous generations. Community standards—by which censorship has traditionally justified itself—vary widely and extremely and often within the same community. No code of censorship could possibly do justice to the liberalized attitudes toward sex that exist today.

The day may not be far off when the commonly accepted standards of today may totally reverse themselves. In fact, right now the most commonly approved sexual activity—marital copulation aimed at producing an offspring—is being viewed with alarm by many. For the population explosion, long due, is now imminent. The population projections for 10, 20, and 30 years from now are eerily frightening. Already, in several states abortion has been legalized. But the awful pity of it is that the most economically and educationally blighted groups reproduce the most and perpetuate the problems that create the most stress in this society and others. A new sexual ethic—already existing in many groupings—that substitutes pleasure and release of tensions as its primary goals certainly makes more practical sense if the human race is to survive with any degree of comfort. For there would now seem to be a real need to channel sexual instincts so that they do not result in a cancerous surplus of population.

Perhaps today's pornography can even be regarded as a primitive expression of society's as yet inchoate recognition that sex, divorced from its procreative aspect and even from romantic and sentimental notions of love, can have its positive values. And it can also be regarded as evidence of the widespread frustration that exists in the sexual area, for pornography gets its appeal from its fantasy portrayal of sex. Fantasies arise when instincts are frustrated. In pornography females of any age and racial or ethnic coloration are ever-willing. Males are ever-potent. Thus, whether in the printed word, in photographs, or moving film images, pornography presents to the reader and the viewer fantasy situations that have something to tell us about the human sexual condition.

The artist, viewing his fellows through his personal vision, has through the ages attempted to portray what he sees and to present his understanding of it. Censorship in his case has perpetrated heavy and sometimes reprehensible blunders. Such recognized literary artists as Joyce and Lawrence were for many years relegated to pirated editions that were sold from beneath the counter. What untold artistic riches still reside, barred from the gaze of civilized man, in the Vatican's rumored collection of erotic treasures? The censor, when presented with this kind of evidence of artistic repression, usually has as his answer that a few geniuses may be deprived of their potential publics, but the many will benefit. But how? The censor, by hoping to bar all that he deems reprehensible, commits errors of taste at least equal to those committed by the most foul of pornographers. For each rules out a vast spectrum of gradations and distinctions.

Of the two dangers, restrictive censorship on the one hand and unrestrained pornography on the other, the latter would seem to be the lesser, by far. For the former can create real harm. The unscrupulous politician can take advantage of the emotional, hysterical, and neurotic attitudes toward pornography to incite the multitude toward approval of repressive measures that go far beyond the control of the printed word and the photographed image. Even with a report from a presidential commission that concluded that no societal or individual harm had resulted from the existence of pornography, highly placed officials still took the warpath against its dissemination. Since there seems to be no substantive base for the officials' stand, one must suspect other motives, the simplest one being, perhaps, that of corralling the votes of conservative elements of the population. Implicitly asking for censorship, they overlook the question of who should do the censoring. Whom shall we trust? Whom can we trust? How shall we agree on standards and criteria? Perhaps they don't really care.

I rather suspect that, left alone, the various media tend to regulate themselves. The largest mass medium, television, presents no pornography at all that I know of, unless it be that of violence which some would translate into fantasy sexual sadism and masochism. Thus disguised, much pornography finds its way into the most respectable channels.

Movies are regulated by their markets, and major film companies now espouse four main grades of entertainment which tend to take into account existing types of theatrical exhibition and audiences.

Radio has only the disguised kind of pornography—actually, no more than mild erotic stimulation—that comes from certain kinds of music and suggestive lyrics.

Magazines run a vast gamut; but no one is prevented from reading *Commentary* or *Harper's* by the fact that girlie publications are sold at the same corner newsstand.

Actually, the human mind is so various in its interests that its concentration on pornography takes but a minute portion of its attention. It is at worst a flea that bites an elephant. It requires little effort to overlook it entirely. It does take enormous effort to try to do something about it; and in the long run, it is no more productive than flailing at windmills.

CENSORSHIP OF TEXTBOOKS
IS FOUND ON RISE
IN SCHOOLS AROUND NATION

Wayne King

Parent and community groups across the country appear to have stepped up efforts to censor reading materials and course content in the public schools. The censors, in part reacting to the permissive attitudes that disturbed traditionalists in the late 1960s and early '70s, seem mainly concerned with language they

From *The New York Times* (March 27, 1979): B15. © 1979 by The New York Times Company. Reprinted by permission.

consider obscene or profane, and somewhat less so with sexual or erotic material.

But there is censorship of ideas, attitudes, and philosophy as well, as in the case of the Island Trees school district in Nassau County, where the school board removed 11 books from library shelves on the ground that they were "anti-American, anti-Christian, anti-Semitic, and just plain filthy." Two of the books had won the Pulitzer Prize. In other districts, material has been removed from student access because it was deemed unsupportive of free enterprise or other similar political values.

SIGNIFICANT INCREASE FOUND

The Committee Against Censorship of the National Council of Teachers of English found in a recent survey of secondary school teachers that censorship of books and other curriculum material, as well as of school newspapers, had increased significantly since a similar survey in 1966.

A check of school districts in a dozen states and localities across the country by the *New York Times* found none free of some censorship or controversy, although concerns over the suitability of reading matter varied widely. Censorship ranged from library review committees in most districts to the public burning of a high school English text in Warsaw, Indiana.

At Arcadia High School in Scottsdale, Arizona, a course called "Paperback Power" was renamed "Directed Reading and Literature" and stripped of graduation credit after parents complained about some of the 6000 books, which were purchased with student donations rather than school funds and made available in a reading room designed to encourage random reading. The school board ordered 20 of the books removed, including *Once Is Not Enough* by Jacqueline Susann, all books by Rosemary Rogers, and most books by Harold Robbins.

MATURE BUT EASY TO READ

"I used them because they were easy to read, but mature," said Robert A. Larabell, the instructor in the course, adding that he was no longer permitted to select the books. Counselors now suggest that the course no longer exists, Mr. Larabell said, and participation has declined so much that the number of sections of the class has been reduced from seven to two.

In Thatcher, Ariz., the town librarian returned from summer vacation last year to find all periodicals except *Arizona Highways* and the *National Geographic* removed from the shelves. The librarian, Emalee Philpott, was instructed, on the ground of limited space, to keep a list of each periodical she stocked and who read it. Earlier, an issue of *Sports Illustrated* was removed because of an article featuring women's swimsuits, and an issue of *Time* magazine was removed because of an illustrated article on fashion models.

In Louisiana, state legislators concerned by a rising teen-age pregnancy rate sought unsuccessfully to overturn the state's eight-year-old law forbidding "any courses specifically designated 'sex education' or a course by any other name in which instruction is given to the pupil at any grade level, primarily dealing with the human reproductive system as it pertains specifically to the act of sexual intercourse."

Most Louisiana teachers avoid entirely using the words "sexual intercourse" because of an opinion by the State Attorney General that such use would violate the law, and a standard biology text, *Action Biology*, has been banned because it dealt explicitly with the topic.

A study by Tulane University found that 30 percent of people from middle-class homes and 53 percent from lower-class homes had no knowledge of reproductive physiology. Louisiana has the fourth highest teen-age pregnancy rate in the country.

In the 33,000-student Union High School

District in Anaheim, California, the largest west of the Mississippi, the school board has established a list of 270 books that can be used in English class, and no others are permitted.

James Bonnell, president of the Anaheim school board, said: "The only effort to restrict comes from the content of basic grammar classes. If they teach grammar properly, they will have no need for further books. Nor will they have time for them."

Sharon Scott of the Anaheim Secondary Teachers Association said the district owned more than 200 titles that could no longer be used because they were not on the approved list. Efforts to have other books listed have been rebuffed, she said.

A COURSE ON CAPITALISM

Seniors are required to take a course called "Free Enterprise," which Miss Scott said contained such questions as "True or false: The Government spends too much money on the environment." The correct answer is "true," she added.

In the Island Trees district, the American Civil Liberties Union is representing parents and students in a lawsuit against the school board for removing 11 books from classrooms and library shelves in early 1976. The suit is pending in Federal District Court. Richard Emery of the ACLU said the case "brings more clearly to focus a new issue, that is, can books be banned for political, religious, and cultural reasons?"

Early in 1976, the school board removed 11 books from classrooms and libraries in the dis-

trict to review language and attitudes in them. The books removed were: *Go Ask Alice*, author anonymous; *A Reader for Writers*, by Jerome W. Archer and A. Schwartz; *A Hero Ain't Nothing but a Sandwich*, by Alice Childress; *Soul on Ice*, by Eldridge Cleaver; *Best Short Stories by Negro Writers*, edited by Langston Hughes; *The Fixer*, by Bernard Malamud; *The Naked Ape*, by Desmond Morris; *Laughing Boy*, by Oliver La Farge; *Black Boy*, by Richard Wright; *Down the Mean Streets*, by Piri Thomas; and *Slaughterhouse-Five*, by Kurt Vonnegut Jr.

TWO WON PULITZER PRIZES

Laughing Boy, which was later returned to the shelves, won the Pulitzer Prize for fiction in 1930, and *The Fixer* won the Pulitzer for fiction in 1967.

Of the 630 high school English teachers who responded to the Committee Against Censorship's survey, 30 percent reported pressure for book censorship, compared with 20 percent in the 1966 survey. The teachers reported that parents raised 78 percent of the objections, while 19 percent were from some member of the school staff—a dramatic shift from 1966, when 48 percent came from parents and 42 percent from the school staff.

"In a given year," said Lee A. Burress Jr., a member of the committee, "one out of five teachers hears objections to books. The result is that in approximately one-third of the cases, books are removed from libraries and recommended reading lists. Thus, one-third of the time censorship efforts are effective in getting books out of use."

AGAINST BOOK CENSORSHIP

Jerzy Kosinski

The impetus for Jerzy Kosinski's article on book censorship in the schools was a report that the Woodbridge, N.J. School District, under pressure from a local citizens' group, had banned his novel, Being There.

Media & Methods contacted the Woodbridge School District, and obtained the following information:

The Kosinski book was being used as a supplementary title in a high school course on mass media. A group of parents, claiming that Being There contained "objectionable passages," prevailed on the school officials to have the work removed from the reading list for the course. This was done, and Being There is no longer available in the Woodbridge schools.

While the Kosinski article obviously reflects the particulars of the Woodbridge action, its scope is much broader. At issue is the overall danger that school censorship of books poses and what educators can do when confronted by demands that a book be banned.

If properly learned, reading can prepare students to deal perceptively with the complexities of society. But it cannot be properly learned if self-appointed censors are permitted to force the exclusion from the schools of any literary work which they label as "objectionable." Such action, however lofty its stated motives, undermines one of the basic reasons for teaching contemporary literature: to present the students with hypothetical situations—

Reprinted from *Media & Methods* (January 1976): 22–24. © 1976, Jerzy Kosinski. Used by permission of the author.

emotional, moral, political, religious, sexual —which they are likely to face once they leave the protective structures of school, family, or community, or which they may be struggling to face already.

Zealots of the book-banning persuasion invariably confuse the literary work with the instructional manual, ascribing the same purpose to these two very different kinds of writing: to control the reader's behavior. Thus they see the reader reduced to a robot, destined to imitate the events portrayed in whatever book he or she happens to be reading.

Furthermore, the typical anti-literary mind perceives the student as an ideal, isolated being removed from the myriad influences that mass media, violence, social unrest, and commercialism bring to bear in contemporary society. Yet students today are anything but uncontaminated mentally. These forces reach them despite all attempts to sanitize the classroom (or the living room) and quarantine its occupants. Still, the zealot, locked in a past of fictitious purity, tends to see the student as inviolable, a perpetual child, and will stress his or her "immaturity," remaining oblivious to the student's need to understand the wider world and to grow socially and emotionally.

One source of this growth can be the confrontation between a student and a book. Exposure to various forms of fiction usually teaches students that they can (and *must* if they are to enjoy reading) re-create the text's situations within their own mind's eye. This ability to visualize, to know that one can shape and control images triggered by the printed word, is invaluable. Its presence or absence will color every aspect of an individual's life—as a member of the community, as a spouse or parent, as a participant in professional activities.

In this act of imaginative projection, readers remain aware that, however involved they may be in the act of reading, they nevertheless stand outside the depicted events. Such forced separation between reading and imagining can act as a catalyst for a formative realization: that the reader is a mediator, able to distinguish between false and true images, between appropriate and inappropriate responses. This goes beyond mental or aesthetic ability; it implies the power to judge, to see a novel's people and events in moral terms. And such judgment demands that the reader develop—or have already developed—a working ethical code. This is the irony of censorship, that it thwarts the very ethical development that its proponents see threatened by access to diverse literary works.

Of course, the actual process by which students come to terms with their complex role as reader is a highly personal, internal one that cannot be taught. But students can be led to read correctly, to appreciate unfamiliar literary terrain, and to choose books which will challenge their minds and continually demand new responses, new ethical judgments. As their reading skills develop, so too does their imagination—not to conjure up deviant spectacles and behaviors, but to project themselves into complexities of life which are yet beyond their present experiential perimeters.

Banning fiction of a certain type from the classroom is one of the surest ways to keep students from exercising and expanding their imaginations. Denied the opportunity to learn how to respond to all literature imaginatively—instead of simply accepting it—a student can lose the ability to handle real and potentially damaging events. The tragic outcome is that the myopia which characterizes the zealot's outlook may become reincarnated in the life of the student who is barred from a literary work because it contains an "objectionable passage."

Clearly, life in contemporary American society is not easy for most people, including the young. Suicide is the second most frequent cause of death among persons between the ages of 15 and 24. (The most frequent cause, accidental death, includes many drug-induced, de facto suicides.) A recent national survey of prosperous American business executives indicates that more than half of them feel too pressured to enjoy life; one third admit that the strain and tension of their jobs have hurt their health; over half say that their work is at best unrewarding; nearly half have changed or considered changing their professions; and about 70 percent admit they have been expected to compromise personal principles in order to conform to standards established by their superiors within the corporate structure.

One of the bulwarks against this increasing sense of personal frustration is a strengthening of the intellectual life. Yet Americans seem to be growing further and further away from such a life. And what is worse, they are abandoning the very tools upon which this life is built—a major one of which is reading. One-fifth of all Americans are known to be functionally illiterate. During the past few years the verbal aptitude of American high school graduates has consistently declined—hardly surprising since that same graduate has logged 18,000 hours of TV viewing, the equivalent of nine years of full-time employment. Only now are we recognizing the intellectual destruction that this unreflective pastime can produce. (See my comments in "A Nation of Videots," *Media & Methods*, April 1975.)

As this trend toward depression, passivity, and isolation becomes increasingly irreversible, schools are among the few remaining institutions that can help tomorrow's adults become thinking individuals, able to judge and function in a world of pressures, conflicting values, and moral ambiguities. The classroom experience in general, and the reading experience in particular, are two of the few demanding mental activities left in modern society. And both must be allowed to flourish freely—without arbitrary restrictions on what is taught and what is read—if we are to keep at least some small part of the student population from becoming emotionally and intellectually crippled.

Of course, ours is a free society and zealots are at liberty to suppress what they consider wrong and alien, just as teachers are at liberty to defend their authority and knowledge in the selection of material to be read. Yet there is a difference: professional training and the rights vested in teachers by the community should confer a special authority. But, at the hands of the small-minded traditionalists, teachers are often exposed to prejudice and attack. They are cast as scapegoats and forced to present time-consuming, humiliating defenses. They may be called upon to testify on behalf of a literary work they have selected for a course, or to justify such a choice as if *they* were the proponent of an outlandish vision of life, rather than being the victim of a handful of hysterical parents.

Since the specter of book censorship can emerge anywhere in America, a general play for counterattack must be drawn up. When the book-banners gather together, the teacher—in addition to alerting the teachers' association, the school, the library, and (if he or she is involved as an individual) the Civil Liberties Union—should promptly notify the novel's author, publishers, and regional and local book distributors. Some or all of these parties will no doubt be interested in providing assistance by furnishing materials (reviews from mass media and religious publications, scholarly analyses, and other pertinent opinions) that can assist the teacher in making a stand.

Teachers constrained from discharging their responsibilities must notify the community at large, and the larger the better. This is a national as well as a local issue; the entire country should be kept aware of every student's right to have access to all forms of art. So the national media should be alerted, in addition to local TV and radio stations, magazines, and newspapers.

Embattled teachers might also consider occasional visits to local magazine and newspaper stands where they can find materials which make the "objectionable passages" in school texts seem ridiculous. The students, whose protection is so earnestly invoked, have free access to these sources. A cursory review of local theaters will turn up films which portray violence and human destruction on a much more impressive scale than the "objectionable" passages in some school readings. Many a local supermarket offers boudoir confessional accounts in publications of questionable character, lubriciously illustrated, and placed conveniently near the check-outs for casual perusal if not actual purchase.

It is argued that such materials, though available, do not have any official sanction, that the schools are the guardians of public morals and thus should be more selective about what is approved for student use. This opinion undermines the more vital function of education, which is to help students cope with life by exploring with them the realities and ambiguities expressed in recognized literary works. The school offers one of the few structured forums for analyzing such situations—an opportunity to critically evaluate the human condition within the guidelines of literary value and human interchange. If students are exposed to a situation which departs from their ethical sense, better that this occur within the school context than behind some magazine rack. But the question is not one of exposure—that will occur no matter how protective the local citizenry might be. The question is rather one of analysis and evaluation—a function which the school is established to provide.

Finally, local boards of education as well as other community organizations would do well to recognize the importance of teachers who make their students aware of personal and world events, particularly at a time of political polarization, economic turmoil, and general unpredictability. These teachers, who want to prepare their students for various contingencies, deserve considerable respect. They are often attacked as "experimentalists," but they play a vital role in ensuring that schools will produce responsible individuals, men and women without fear of the world around them.

ON GEORGE CARLIN'S "DIRTY WORDS"

THE BIRMINGHAM NEWS

Birmingham, Alabama, July 12, 1978

The U.S. Supreme Court properly came down on the side of taste and good manners in ruling that the Federal Communications Commission did not abuse its regulatory powers when it warned a New York radio station to stop using "patently offensive material" on the air.

The case goes back to October 30, 1973, when so-called comic George Carlin used pigsty language in a monologue in an early afternoon broadcast by station WBAI. The 12-minute monologue consisted almost entirely of seven dirty words repeated over and over again. Carlin's idea was that dirty words are harmless and repeating them over and over removes their shock potential. But a listener disagreed violently: He complained to the FCC, and early in

Reprinted from *The Birmingham News* (July 12, 1978). Copyright 1978 The Birmingham News. Used by permission.

1975, that regulating body posted a warning to WBAI.

In its opinion on the use of the dirty words, the FCC cited the legal doctrine of "public nuisance." In his opinion for the majority, U. S. Supreme Court Justice John P. Stevens cited the same doctrine. Stevens said, in effect, that a pig in a pigsty is to be expected and appropriate, but a pig in the parlor is certainly a pig out of place. In other words, such language might be acceptable in a nightclub or on a radio program aired at two in the morning.

In explanation, Stevens went on to say that "of all forms of communication, it is broadcasting that has received the most limited First Amendment protection," because . . . "broadcasting is uniquely accessible to children, even those too young to read."

In knee-jerk lock-step, the New York radio station was joined by the National Association of Broadcasters and the U.S. Justice Department in appealing the case, arguing that the FCC lacked the power to ban the seven filthy words, even during hours when children are listening. The NAB claimed that the ban amounted to censorship in violation of the First Amendment, and the Justice Department said the FCC rule was too broad, because it was impossible to know when children are listening.

The positions of both the NAB and the Justice Department were simply silly. No freedom of speech or freedom to express ideas or freedom to pass on information was abridged. And as a practical matter, one can safely assume that only a fraction of a fraction of children are listening to radio late at night. On the other hand,

the vast majority of the public has a right to expect language on the public's airwaves that is in keeping with public standards for information and entertainment.

The case was simply another one of those instances that tend to make the media seem neurotic, if not paranoid, silly and irresponsible in the eyes of the public which has no problem in discerning violations of the First Amendment and the necessary protections for free speech and a free press. One would hope that the media someday develops the maturity to recognize that public tastes and standards should not be flouted unless the case is of overriding importance to all.

THE DES MOINES REGISTER

Des Moines, Iowa, July 12, 1978

The irony of the U.S. Supreme Court's ruling in the "dirty words" case is that it reflects precisely the kind of attitude—shocked and punitive—that continues to give such words their potency.

If no one paid much attention to "dirty words," they would, eventually, lose their capacity to offend. It is a lesser irony in this case that the George Carlin monologue at issue was intended to demonstrate just this point. By repeating seven familiar "dirty words" at length, Carlin showed how immature and silly it is to let them offend.

The Federal Communications Commission declared that the broadcast violated a federal law prohibiting "any obscene, indecent or profane language by means of radio communica-

tion." It did not revoke the license of the station, WBAI-FM in New York City, but the small nonprofit station was put on notice that the incident would be considered at license-renewal time.

Because there was no prior restraint, the Court said, the FCC did not violate the Communications Act of 1934, which forbids the agency from censoring content or issuing any regulation interfering with "free speech by means of radio communication."

If the FCC's ruling did not discourage WBAI from further broadcasts that might be considered offensive, there would have been no reason to issue it. As Justice William Brennan Jr. observed in dissent, "the visage of the censor is all too discernible here."

The majority opinion rests on radio's pervasiveness—the fact that it can be turned on in practically any home, anytime, by nearly anyone. Because of that, the majority said,

Reprinted from *The Des Moines Register* (July 12, 1978). Copyright 1978 The Des Moines Register. Used by permission.

radio listeners—especially children—are virtually defenseless against onslaughts of indecency and have a right to be protected, even if someone else's First Amendment rights are slightly bruised.

The court's decision turned on the definition of "indecent." The four-man minority held that it means the same as "obscene," and that Carlin's monologue was not obscene (or indecent) because it had no prurient appeal. The majority upheld the FCC's contention that "indecent" has a broader meaning: "nonconformance with accepted standards of morality"—a yardstick too slippery for almost any application. Because the monologue violated those "standards," it was "indecent" and thus broke the law.

The majority recognized that the radio can be turned off, or the station changed, but it called this insufficient protection. We find the reverse—that turning off the radio, even after an offending word or two has slipped past an unguarded ear, is far simpler than restoring the right to listen once the right has been diminished.

The Constitution protects the print media in their use of "dirty words," but few publications of general circulation avail themselves of the right. The words are shunned as a matter of taste, not because a government official might act in reprisal. It's hard to see why broadcasters should not be allowed to exercise the same discretion in their choice of language.

The Court said it wished to strengthen parental rights with its decision; it actually is supplanting parental authority and establishing itself as parents of all adults as well. The case gives censorship an ominously freer hand.

ON THE CONVICTION OF LARRY FLYNT, PORNOGRAPHER

THE ROANOKE TIMES

Roanoke, Virginia, February 11, 1977

The conviction of the publisher of *Hustler* magazine, the corporation itself, and assorted individuals connected with it may give at least momentary encouragement that society can prevail over the freaks hiding behind the First

Reprinted from *The Roanoke Times* (February 11, 1977). Copyright 1977 Roanoke Times & World-News. Used by permission.

Amendment. The conviction hits where the motive is: money-making. To imagine these people are interested in "art," etc., is to be deluded.

The word "momentary" is used because victories like these are so often short-lived. The day before the Ohio conviction, a raid in New York City brought indictments against 14 people charged with distributing pornography including children as young as six years engaged in sexual acts! Even the most abstract, automatic liberal is shocked by that. But will he or she be shocked 20 years from now? Generation by generation, the standards have lowered and someday, except for an intransigent rear guard, nobody will be left to be shocked by anything.

Among those arrested in the Times Square, New York, raid was a man identified in 1960 by the Manhattan district attorney as "the largest known producer and distributor of pornographic material in the United States." And what happened to the gentleman? Last December he was convicted of wholesale distribution of obscene film, fined $2000, and ordered to spend weekends in jail for six months. Victories in the war against pornography indeed tend to be momentary.

What the American Civil Liberties Union (ACLU) thinks of the New York cases we do not know; a practical sense might suggest it should wait 20 years before defending even the use of children in pornographic material; the time has not yet come for the final defense by the doctrinaire. But in Ohio a spokesman for the ACLU has snickered at the conviction, called it laughable, and pledged the ACLU to the defense of *Hustler's* rights. Since the ACLU is doing what it has the right to do, Ohio should assemble the requisite legal talent to present the other side with equal sophistication and vigor.

THE SACRAMENTO BEE

Sacramento, California, February 17, 1977

Hustler magazine is tasteless and understandably offensive to many people. But we would be blind to the implications if we remained silent and failed to protest the conviction of its publisher, Larry Flynt.

Flynt was found guilty by a county common pleas court in Cincinnati and sentenced to 7 to 25 years for publishing obscene material and engaging in organized crime, the latter because more than five people participated in what was found to be an illegal act under state law.

It is disturbing that a local court, not satisfied merely to keep such a crude magazine off local newsstands can attempt to impose its standards of obscenity on the nation. Allowed to stand, this concept threatens freedom of expression in

Reprinted from *The Sacramento Bee* (February 17, 1977). Copyright 1977 The Sacramento Bee. Used by permission.

America guaranteed by the First Amendment. Left unchallenged, it would force publishers, and movie distributors as well, to tailor their material to tastes of small and conservative communities which do not necessarily reflect the tastes of the entire population.

The biggest problem in dealing with the pornography issue is the legal definition of obscenity itself. The U.S. Supreme Court has revised its tests for obscenity several times. Its last ruling empowered each community to determine its own standards. But it is still considered vague and elusive.

The Court at the time acknowledged the application of local community standards could prevent dissemination of materials in some places. It did not define exactly what it meant by "community" or "local." The dissenting justices warned the opinion would make it possible to "ban any paper or any journal or magazine in some benighted place." And they were proved right when such a place turned up in the *Hustler* prosecution.

Matters of taste are difficult to circumscribe. It is proper to try to keep hard-core pornography away from those too young to decide for themselves, just as restrictions are clamped on cigarettes and alcohol. But censorship is a greater evil than the right of adults to choose what they care to read and see.

Other cases being appealed ask the Supreme Court to clarify its interpretation of obscenity. The questions raised by the *Hustler* publisher's conviction underscore the need for the Court to rethink the entire issue of how far government can go in dictating the kind of literature or entertainment consenting adults may enjoy.

chapter 3

ISSUES IN ADVERTISING

Some of the practices that have brought the advertising industry the most criticism include fake "scientific" claims, phony demonstrations, phony secret ingredients, manipulated statistics, meaningless testimonials, meaningless comparisons, exaggerations, and out-and-out lies. The first two readings in this chapter take up the basic issue of whether advertising is inherently dishonest. The ad run by the National Advertising Review Board advances the idea that advertising is basically honest. The second blurb, from the book *The Vulnerable Americans* by Curt Gentry, takes the opposite view: that advertising is "wordsmithing," which is, as far as Gentry is concerned, inherently dishonest.

Every few years, new subissues within the general issue of advertising ethics surface. In fact, more of these subissues surface than we can reasonably deal with here, and so I've chosen four areas that have prompted the most questions from my own students: comparative ads, TV ads aimed at children, ads by doctors and lawyers, and subliminal ads.

In the article about comparative advertising, *New York Times* reporter Edwin McDowell looks back fondly on the days when "brand X" was the only product used for advertising comparisons. Today's use of comparative ads, according to McDowell, increases confusion for everyone.

The question I receive most often from my students about comparative advertising is "How can they get away with that?" The answer, as seen in McDowell's article, is that "they" sometimes don't, because of industry and government controls, and lawsuits brought by competitors.

I'm seldom asked *why* the industry uses comparative ads in the first place. McDowell's argument is that the FTC insists on them. This may or may not be true, but remember that the issue here is comparative ads that are *deceptive*, and the FTC has never asked for those.

The comparative ad issue is mostly an industry controversy. Of more general concern is the protest against children's television ads, which is perhaps the hottest issue to surface recently in the world of advertising. In the fourth reading in this section, Ernest Holsendolph of the *New York Times* analyzes both sides of the issue, as well as its background and outlook. In the fifth article, Peggy Charren (president of Action for Children's Television) and Kitty Broman (chairman, TV Board of Directors) expand on the pro and con arguments of children's television ads.

The question my students usually raise about professionals (doctors, lawyers, and dentists) advertising their services is, "What's the issue? Why shouldn't professionals be allowed to advertise?" These students are usually surprised to find that until a few years ago commercial speech had been denied First Amendment protection; it is only in the last few years that the Supreme Court has developed its "commercial speech doctrine," which has encouraged advertising by professionals.[1] This has led to the debate which is summarized in the sixth article in this section, by Barbara Slavin of the *New York Times*.

The final issue dealt with in this section might be one of the biggest pseudoissues of all time: subliminal advertising. Each semester I have a number of students who dig up a copy of Wilson Bryan Key's *Subliminal Seduction* (1973) or *Media Sexploitation* (1976) and ask, incredulously, "Do advertisers really *do* that?"

I've read recently that Key has a new book (*The Clam-Plate Orgy*, 1980), and so I am sure the question of subliminal advertising will continue to raise its head. My students are seldom satisfied with the answer I give them, which is based on the available research:

> There is no scientific evidence that subliminal stimulation can initiate subsequent action, to say nothing of commercially or politically significant action. And there is nothing to suggest that such action can be produced "against the subject's will," or more effectively than through normal, recognized messages.[2]

But my students still say, "Yeah—but do they (the ad people) really *do* that stuff?"

The answer, of course, is that it depends on whom you talk to. But a problem arises in getting both sides of this issue because it is difficult to find articles that take a serious look at Key's ideas. As one of my pre-publication reviewers pointed out, "I rank subliminal advertising in a category with material about visits to earth by ancient astronauts, the Bermuda Triangle, and Bigfoot. I don't even allude to it in my course."

Unfortunately, the topic keeps coming up. So I've included here an article by Jerry Goodis, an advertising professional, which takes an analytical look at subliminal advertising.

NOTES

1. The commercial speech doctrine has also encouraged corporate advertising on public issues. The Gannett Company ad in Chapter 10 (Part III) is an example of this type of ad. Corporate advertising on public issues has led to one type of access issue; see, for example, Herbert Schmertz's comments in the final reading in Chapter 16 (Part IV).
2. Bernard Berelson and Gary A. Steiner, *Human Behavior: An Inventory of Scientific Findings* (New York, Harcourt, Brace and World, Inc., 1964), p. 95. Cited in S. Watson Dunn, *Advertising: Its Role in Modern Marketing* (New York: Holt, Rinehart and Winston, 1969).

"I think that ad is lying."

If you think that an advertisement is misleading or untruthful, here's what you can do about it.

Most advertisers work very hard to make sure their advertising is completely honest and truthful. But if you ever see an advertisement or a commercial that you think takes liberties with the truth or makes questionable claims, there's something you can do about it.

Write to the National Advertising Review Board.

If truth or accuracy in a national ad or commercial is your concern (not matters of taste or matters of editorial or program content), the advertiser will be asked for substantiation of the claims made.

Where justified, advertisers will be requested to modify or discontinue any claim for which there is not adequate support.

You will be notified of the results of the investigation and they will be reported in a monthly press release.

NARB IS SELF-REGULATION

The NARB was formed in 1971 out of the conviction that self-regulation of advertising is preferable to government regulation. It is faster. No tax dollars are required to support it.

The NARB is sponsored by four leading advertising and business organizations: The American Association of Advertising Agencies, the American Advertising Federation, the Association of National Advertisers, and the Council of Better Business Bureaus. Its board of directors consists of representatives of advertiser companies, advertising agencies, and members representing the public sector.

Since its inception, more than 1,300 inquiries regarding national advertising have been reviewed.

Advertisers have cooperated in providing substantiation of the advertising in question.

More important, not one advertiser has refused to modify or discontinue advertising found to be misleading.

NARB is self-regulation that works.

If you would like further information or if you see advertising that you feel is untruthful...

**write to:
National Advertising Review Board,
845 Third Avenue,
New York, New York
10022.**

Courtesy of the National Advertising Review Board. This ad appeared in the January 29, 1979 issue of *Time*.

OF COURSE
THAT AD IS LYING

Curt Gentry

The object of advertisers is to capture the trust of consumers and, in so doing, make them spend their money. This is done through *wordsmithing*—arranging words and phrases in such a way that they (1) make a true statement and (2) at the same time convey, or, better still, *suggest* a meaning which they don't actually possess. For example, take this TV commercial of a few seasons ago:

ARRID IS ONE-AND-ONE-HALF TIMES
AS EFFECTIVE AS ANY OTHER
LEADING DEODORANT TESTED.

We can assume this statement is true, and that Arrid's makers and advertising agency undoubtedly have evidence to support it if challenged. Nor are they to be blamed if the public chooses to misinterpret it. Yet, unless one were listening carefully—and who listens carefully to commercials?—he just might come away with the impression that Arrid is one-and-one-half times more effective than any other leading deodorant. The catcher here, of course, is that word "tested." Giving it some thought, one might come up with a number of questions: How many other leading deodorants were tested? One? All? Who conducted the test or tests? How representative were they? Were they conducted scientifically, in a manner free from bias? The real catch is that few of us would give it that much thought.

Another:

THREE OUT OF FOUR DOCTORS
RECOMMEND THE MAJOR INGREDIENT
IN ANACIN FOR THE RELIEF
OF SIMPLE HEADACHE PAIN

Once in a critical mood, this seems easy. How many doctors were interviewed? Were four doctors picked whose opinions were already known? Or were a number of doctors questioned, in sets of four, until three in one set so recommended? If your reasoning has followed this pattern you've been misled, for this part of the statement means exactly what it implies—if all the doctors in this country were questioned, at least 75 percent would make this representation. The catcher here is "major ingredient." Three out of four doctors *would* and *do* recommend the major ingredient in Anacin—but by the generic name by which that ingredient is best known: *aspirin*.

Reprinted from *The Vulnerable Americans* by Curt Gentry (New York: Doubleday, 1966), p. 22. Copyright 1966 Curt Gentry. Used by permission of Paul R. Reynolds, Inc.

OH, FOR THE GOOD
OLD DAYS OF BRAND X

Edwin McDowell

There was a time when the average advertising executive would sooner be caught with ring around his buttondown collar than mention a competitive product in a client's ad. If it were absolutely necessary to trumpet the superiority of one's own product, it could always be compared with that ubiquitous scapegoat, Brand X.

But the Federal Trade Commission argued that comparative advertising could increase competition and serve to educate the public, and in 1972, the TV network ban on ads that mention the competition by name was ended at the FTC's urging. The field exploded, taking over 8 to 10 percent of the advertising market overall, and perhaps twice that proportion of television commercials, and then—like many an ad fad before it—comparative advertising lost its glamour and settled down for a long but no-growth, undramatic run.

Now, suddenly, the field is exploding again—not in terms of revenues but in terms of controversy. There are indications that the advertising community is losing patience. Earlier objections on grounds of taste and ethics have been broadened to include attacks on comparative advertising's value to consumers. Ad men have complained that the FTC has been "pushing" the technique, and in fact Michael Pertschuk, the commission's chairman, has recently warned advertisers against "no-comparative-advertising" agreements and urged the use of the technique for alcoholic beverages. Moreover, two contretemps—both involving the Gilette Company—have set the industry on its ear.

Last month, Gillette and the J. Walter Thompson advertising agency agreed to pay the Alberto-Culver Company $4.25 million to settle a lawsuit over a television comparative ad that Alberto-Culver claimed "disparaged and destroyed" its Alberto Balsam hair conditioner. On the other hand, Gillette is a complainant as regards comparative ads run by the Bic Pen Corporation, claiming they are based on faulty research.

Such developments are not calculated to increase enthusiasm for the technique. The Alberto-Culver settlement, for example, "will certainly make people think twice about comparative advertising, I won't deny that," said Mitch Paul, a staff attorney in the commission's bureau of consumer protection.

Yet even before the settlement, comparative advertising appeared to have peaked. "It gained rapidly in the beginning, but now it's about where it has been for a couple of years,"

From *The New York Times* (April 22, 1979): Cl. © 1979 by The New York Times Company. Reprinted by permission.

said Ralph Daniels, vice-president of broadcast standards for NBC, to which some 47,000 separate advertisements were submitted last year.

Even some of comparative advertising's longtime champions wonder what went wrong. "It's not growing, there's no bandwagon for it, that's for sure," admitted Stanley I. Tannenbaum, vice-chairman of Kenyon & Eckhardt Enterprises, a longtime supporter of the concept.

Why? "I have a lot of theories, but no proof," said Mr. Tannenbaum. "I think some people just don't know how to use it. Other people are afraid of the law. Maybe there isn't a clear-cut product difference. Maybe agencies aren't digging hard enough to find ways to apply it."

Moreover, even the benefits to consumers appear to be fewer than had been expected. Ogilvy & Mather, one of four U.S. ad agencies that billed over $1 billion last year, conducted three separate investigations into the effects of comparative advertising. Each time it concluded that the method failed to heighten consumer discrimination or lessen confusion.

"If it were effective, there'd be a lot more of it being used, and I think its use is decreasing," said Philip Levine, Ogilvy & Mather's executive director of research.

Most advertising is comparative to some degree. And even when advertisers compared the virtues of their products to that despicable, imperfect, or undesirable Brand X, most consumers had little doubt who or what Brand X represented. Even now, according to Mr. Daniels, NBC defines comparative advertising as that where the identity of the competitive product is implicit as well as explicit.

Moreover, even those who regard such advertising as unseemly or unethical admit that— regardless of the legal perils, and regardless of what research studies indicate—it will always have a certain amount of appeal to advertisers who are trying to overtake the leader.

"It's not the kind of advertising that everybody is going to do," said the FTC's Mr. Paul. "Why should your Procter & Gamble, which

spends millions and millions of dollars on advertising its products, give free mention to its competitors? But it's probably the most effective advertising technique for also-rans and for the new entrants. It's a good way to tell people, 'Look, I'm the new boy on the block.'"

Mr. Tannenbaum agrees. "One of my principles is that the leader, the person who's No. 1 in the marketplace, shouldn't ever use it." His agency created the ads favorably comparing the Mercury Monarch to the Mercedes-Benz.

While enthusiasts and disparagers often disagree about the effects of comparative advertising, there is general agreement that it has sometimes helped users to increase sales or market share.

The Vivitar Corporation's ads in 1975, with Arthur Godfrey comparing the less expensive Vivitar 600 pocket camera with the Kodak 28, are credited with helping to sharply increase Vivitar's sales and expand its market share. Opel doubled its share of the American imported car market in 1977 with the help of an estimated $4 million ad campaign comparing it with the VW Rabbit, the Toyota Corolla, the Datsun B-210, and the Subaru DL.

Others cite the success of ads for Dynamo liquid detergent (comparing it with Tide), Louis Sherry ice cream (comparing it with Breyer's), and Carefree Sugarless Gum (comparing it with Trident).

In most cases, companies whose products are compared unfavorably tend to shrug off such ads, as though disparagement is a small price to endure for the sake of industry leadership.

But turning the other cheek has its limits, and there are signs that those limits are being reached sooner than ever before. For example, about 20 percent of the advertisements reviewed in 1977 by the National Advertising Review Board involved comparative advertising. Last year's comparable figure was 36 percent.

The review board was established in 1971 by the Council of Better Business Bureaus and three advertising groups. Its five-member panels adjudicate questions of truth and accuracy in specific advertisements, after they have been reviewed and investigated by the Council's National Advertising Division, and only after that division is unable to resolve them.

Although the board has no enforcement powers, it publishes the panel reports, favorable or unfavorable. If an advertiser is found guilty and refuses to cooperate, usually by halting the offending ads, the board's chairman publicly refers the matter to the appropriate regulatory agency. The threat of adverse publicity is usually an inducement for compliance.

In one of the earliest tests of comparative advertising, the review board ruled in 1973 that the campaign for the Schick Flexamatic electric shaver, which was touted as superior to shavers made by Norelco, Remington, and Sunbeam, was "false in some details and misleading in its overall implications." It ordered Schick to stop running the ads.

The company said that although it disagreed with the panel, in the interest of industry self-regulation any future advertising created on the basis of its tests would be "guided by the recommendations of the panel."

But some companies have been so enraged by a competitor's comparative ads that they have raced straight to the courts, bypassing the industry review panel. The most notable case: that of Gillette and Alberto-Culver.

The first commercial was broadcast in May 1974. Two months later, after failing to get a preliminary injunction to stop the commercial, Alberto Balsam sued Gillette and J. Walter Thompson, saying the ad violated federal antitrust laws and Illinois deceptive trade practices, consumer fraud, and trade libel law. It demanded that Gillette be forced to run ads to correct what it said was an effort to show that Alberto Balsam "left an oily, greasy residue on the hair . . . ."

According to testimony developed during the eight-day trial in United States District Court in Chicago, when the comparative ad campaign began Alberto Balsam commanded almost 12 percent of the market (compared with Tame's 17 percent). By September 1974 that share had fallen to about 6 percent and by 1976—even though the company spent $2 million in advertising in 1975 and 1976—it was below 3 percent. Finally, after sales sank 75 percent below previous levels, the product was taken off the market.

Alberto-Culver originally sought $23.5 million in lost profits, actual and potential, but it settled for $4.25 million. Neither Gillette nor J. Walter Thompson would give details except to say that the settlement is not an admission of guilt, that they expect to recover their share of the settlement from insurance, and that the payment will not affect their financial results.

But one highly placed Gillette source spoke bitterly about comparative advertising and the fact that the FTC had "pushed" companies to use it. Last November, Michael Pertschuk, the commission's chairman, warned advertisers that if they agree "expressly or tacitly" not to resort to comparative advertising they are liable to be talking to the commission.

The FTC has been moving on another front as well, recently urging the Bureau of Alcohol, Tobacco and Firearms to support comparative advertising for the alcohol beverage industry—something to which the bureau has been strongly opposed.

Gillette has long been ambivalent about the virtues of comparative advertising. Recently it complained to the National Advertising Review Board about Bic commercials asserting that the Bic throwaway shaver is as good as the more expensive Gillette Trac II. Gillette charged that the Bic claim is based on "contrived and artificial research," but the review board has not yet investigated.

Gillette also asked the television networks not to run the 30-second Bic commercials and requested them to demand greater substantiation from Bic. "We are going to require some changes in the Bic advertising," said Richard Gitter, ABC vice-president of broadcast standards and practices.

Gillette is comfortably ahead with some 58 percent of the market share of disposable razors, which account for about 15 percent of the $425 million blade market. Bic claims that they will eventually represent about 40 percent, but Gillette views the disposable market as only about half that. Yet it has no intention of surrendering its lead without a fight— particularly since, like Alberto-Culver, it considers itself the victim of unfair advertising.

Similarly, several years ago, after complaining that its Right Guard deodorant was being put at a competitive disadvantage by other antiperspirant deodorants, Gillette asked the networks to declare a moratorium on comparative advertising as "confusing and misleading." But before long its ads were favorably comparing its pump-spray version of Right Guard to Ban Basic, the industry leader.

How, given the industry's system of checks and balances, do misleading or false comparisons ever appear on television or in print?

The big companies have huge testing facilities or access to independent testing labs. The big advertising agencies review the results of those tests before developing the ad campaigns. And the television networks have detailed guidelines to ensure that ads adhere to their own stringent policies, as well as the policies and codes of the Federal Communications Commission, the FTC, the National Association of Broadcasters, the Civil Aeronautics Board (if they involve airlines), state agencies (insurance ads), and a host of other agencies.

Throughout this entire process, test results, theoretically at least, are analyzed by a battery of vice-presidents, product managers, editors, lawyers, and copywriters down to the least detail. When Gillette set out to prove the superiority of its twin blade some years ago, it built a high-speed movie camera that would film 1400 feet in three seconds.

So how then did that controversial Gillette ad get on the air? Gillette won't say, and those who don't hide behind "no comment" are not able to provide a terribly satisfactory explanation beyond the catch-phrase "human error."

"We made numerous changes in the advertising before it was submitted. We spent a great deal of time examining the substantiation and in reviewing the challenge," said Richard Gitter, vice-president of broadcast standards and practices at ABC. He added that of some 50,000 individual ads submitted to the network last year, 5 percent were rejected outright, some 30 percent were accepted without modification, and the remainder accepted only after modification and substantiation.

An anonymous Gillette official had a different explanation of the expensive contretemps. "The case hinged on the question of disparagement," he said. "Some judges might think that comparative advertising is disparagement per se."

But for the most part, friends and foes of comparative advertising were at a loss to explain how the fail-safe system upon which the advertising industry prides itself could have failed to sound the necessary alarm. "Gillette wasn't found guilty," said a source close to the case, "But from the second day, the judge urged the defendants to settle, so he must have thought Alberto-Culver had a good case. And remember, that represents the first big cash settlement of any kind in those matters."

"I can't explain that case," said Mr. Tannenbaum. "I really don't know how it happened."

Mr. Tannenbaum is quick to say, however, that one of the principal tenets of comparative advertising is not to disparage a competitor or be condescending. "You're basically challenging the judgment of the person who uses the other guy's product, and he's likely to get his back up if you put down that product too much," he said.

He added: "You need to develop points of superiority that are important to consumers—

the ride of a car, the taste or durability of a product—something that people care about. You should say that the other guy has a great box of cereal, but we have 32 raisins and they only have 14. By pointing out these real differences, you can force the other guy to improve his product. That's really what comparative advertising is all about.''

TV ADS AIMED AT CHILDREN: SHOULD THE FTC STEP IN?

Ernest Holsendolph

Regulation of children's television, a long-simmering issue among broadcasters, advertisers, and producers of goods for the young, appears to be approaching the boiling point.

For nearly a decade the Federal Communications Commission and the Federal Trade Commission have circled the issue, poking it gingerly, then moving on to something else. But this year, the trade commission appears ready to face it head on, and the communications panel too has revived its interest.

To broadcasters the quest for regulation is a red flag, an attack on free speech. To Peggy Charren and Robert Choate, two New Englanders who have fought children's ads for years, our children's health, if not their lives, is at stake.

The complex issues will be thrashed out here beginning tomorrow in a month-long hearing before a Federal Trade Commission administrative law judge. In brief, what is being considered by the trade commission and more than 130 witnessess scheduled to appear is a series of proposals by the commission staff based on the premise that industry self-regulation has not worked.

One staff proposal under consideration would ban all televised advertising of children's items where the advertising was aimed at young children. A second would ban the advertising of certain sugared foods for children.

A third staff proposal would require advertisers of sugared foods to balance their commercials with statements about the proper nutritional use of the food.

THE BACKGROUND

The first moves against children's advertising occurred when Action for Children's Television, a group based near Boston, asked the Federal Communications Commission to limit advertising practices.

ACT, which now claims 12,000 dues-paying members and operates on a $500,000 yearly budget, asked the commission to prohibit ''host-selling,'' in which the star of the chil-

From *The New York Times* (March 5, 1979): B6. © 1979 by The New York Times Company. Reprinted by permission.

dren's show would make a personal pitch for the product. The industry voluntarily stopped this before the government moved.

The group also sought a general prohibition of commercials on children's shows and a requirement that broadcasters put on the air a minimum of 14 hours of shows a week keyed to specific age groups among children.

The government demurred, but the industry, on its own, cut the maximum volume of advertising to children from 16 minutes to 9.5 minutes per hour on weekends and 12 minutes per hour on weekdays.

Mrs. Charren, ACT's president, and Robert Choate, head of the Washington-based Council on Children, Media and Merchandising, joined in filing a flurry of petitions with the Federal Trade Commission.

They asked that advertising for children's vitamins, toys, and certain foods be curtailed. The action prompted a number of voluntary controls by pharmaceutical companies and voluntary agreements between the trade commission and drug companies and between the commission and toy manufacturers to address some of ACT's complaints.

However, the commission never made the comprehensive changes that were sought by the private groups.

Now, with the energetic support of its chairman, Michael Pertschuk, the commission has undertaken a comprehensive examination of the issues.

The debate, however, has been joined by a host of industries that have billions of dollars of business at stake, and an estimated $600 million a year in children's advertising alone. They include interests as varied as the National Association of Broadcasters, which represents stations and networks, as well as cereal manufacturers, the Association of American Advertising Agencies, the Grocery Manufacturers of America, the Chocolate Manufacturers Association, and the Toy Manufacturers of America.

FOR REGULATION

Mrs. Charren and Mr. Choate assert that they are fighting for the children's rights. They say that children, especially young children, do not understand the world around them, have no comprehension of health implications of foods, and do not understand the consequences of handling potentially dangerous toys.

Thus, they argue, children are easily sold on the fantastic and the spectacular and are easy game for the savvy and creative resources of the merchandisers.

"We just say that the advertising subjects youngsters to harmful deception," Mrs. Charren said, "and the child, as a citizen, has the right not to be deceived."

Critics of the ads say the nation has a history of giving special protection to youths, with examples being age limits on drinking, child labor laws, and protection against pornography.

Even though parents clearly hold the purse strings and thus have the final say on purchases in the case of young children, the youngster nonetheless has much to say about which products to buy. Children's ads often lead to unnecessary confrontations between parents and children, harming the peace and harmony of the families, those favoring regulation say.

Rather than set son and daughter against parents, advertisers should instead help educate both children and parents about nutrition in their ads, warning about overindulgence, and cautioning consumers against careless handling of toys.

AGAINST REGULATION

Broadcasters and the advertising industry say that the forces favoring regulation simply do not prove their assertions that either the products or the advertising is dangerous.

Arthur R. Schulze, a group vice-president at General Mills, said at a meeting with reporters last week that "nobody" would contend that sugar cannot be harmful to teeth. "But we have studies," he said, "that show that other carbohydrates that stick to the teeth, such as bread, may be even more likely to cause cavities." Those studies are scheduled to be presented to the trade commission on Tuesday.

The industry defenders say that their opponents commit unwarranted intellectual leaps in making their case. Brenda Fox, attorney for the broadcast association, said, "We are told to regulate because of untold, unquantified harm to children—and without even proving that advertising creates the craving for sugar."

She said that, if the products were bad and harmful, then they should be regulated or labeled and that this task is more likely the job of the Food and Drug Administration, not the Federal Trade Commission.

Creators of programs and commercials assert that their freedom of speech would be limited by curbs on children's advertising.

THE OUTLOOK

The outlook is for no clear government action that will change regulation in the near term.* The proceeding before the trade commission is preliminary, and there is even the slim chance that it may be sidetracked on a technicality.

At the moment only two members of the commission are qualified to vote on the issue. Elizabeth Hanford Dole resigned, Robert Pitofsky withdrew voluntarily because he had been associated with some of the participants in the debate before joining the commission, and Mr. Pertschuk was barred by a federal court from taking part because he appeared to have decided in advance that children's advertising might be harmful.

If a third voting commissioner is not appointed by President Carter before the proceeding comes up from the administrative law judge, the case could run into legal problems.

*Editor's note: Recent actions by Congress have precluded the FTC from legislating in the area of children's television commercials.

BAN TV ADS AIMED AT CHILDREN?

YES—"THEY EXPLOIT AMERICA'S MOST VULNERABLE POPULATION"

NO—"THE PARENT, NOT THE TELEVISION SET," SHOULD CONTROL WHAT KIDS SEE

Interview with Peggy Charren

Interview with Kitty Broman

Q: Mrs. Charren, why should the government ban television commercials aimed at children?

A: Television ads for children are an inappropriate use of the public air waves. They exploit America's most vulnerable population.

Q: Mrs. Broman, why are you in opposition to Government regulations that would prohibit television advertising directed to children?

A: Children get a lot of great things from television, and advertising is one way that some of these marvelous programs are paid for.

Reprinted from *U.S. News & World Report* (January 16, 1978): 47–48.

Interview with Mrs. Charren continued

Because children are inexperienced and lack consumer sophistication, they deserve the highest standard of protection from the unconscionable, hard-sell commercials manufacturers now use on TV.

Q: What do you consider the most harmful children's ads on television?

A: I'm especially concerned about food commercials. Only 2 percent of these ads are for fruit, vegetables, or dairy products—the kinds of food that people who care about children want them to eat. The rest of the food ads are for highly sugared foods, such as candy and sugar-coated cereal.

And these foods are advertised for all the wrong reasons. A candy bar is promoted because it lasts a long time—but its long-lasting quality is precisely what causes cavities. With $4.2 billion being spent for dental bills in this country, it's not rational to keep reminding children to eat something that is a health hazard.

Q: What about toy ads?

A: The toys now being promoted to children on television are the most underdesigned, overpriced toys ever put together. Toys are now designed to make a good commercial instead of a good plaything. That's why the dolls walk, talk, blow bubbles, burp, and write their names. A rag doll, by comparison, looks dead on television.

Although the National Association of Broadcasters has made some rules that have eliminated some of the more obvious manipulative practices in toy commercials, many ads are still deceptive—even for adults who are sophisticated commercial watchers. They promote more than what really comes with the toy.

Q: Aren't children smart enough to know when a commercial is misleading?

A: No. The young child—the 2-to-8-year-

Interview with Mrs. Broman continued

I think only a small minority—although a vocal one—is concerned about TV commercials for children. According to a 1976 Roper study, 66 percent of the parents surveyed said they could see nothing wrong with advertising on children's programs.

I think television is damned for a lot of things that it shouldn't be damned for.

Q: Aren't children so vulnerable to TV advertising that they need special protection?

A: What you're saying is that television is talking directly to a child and that nobody else is around to educate him.

I absolutely disagree with that argument. Television is not teaching the child everything. If that were true, then the parent would have abdicated his responsibility to educate his own child.

The final authority has to rest with the parent, not the television set. There is a knob that turns on and off, and if you don't like the program, you can always flip to another—or turn the set off. If a parent doesn't accept this responsibility, then I think he or she is a very bad parent.

Q: Isn't it nearly impossible for parents to compete with the 30-second commercial, even if they are watching television with their children?

A: No. If that were true, then the parent has no control over his child.

And I wouldn't want anyone to tell me that I hadn't had control over my children. I can remember sitting down with my own children and telling them candy is fine at certain times, but you can't eat it at eight in the morning.

Q: Some critics say that commercials for candy and sugar-coated cereals are so powerful and so frequently seen that it becomes difficult for parents to teach their children about proper eating habits.

Interview with Mrs. Charren continued

old—mixes up the commercial message with a program's content. He cannot appreciate the commercial motives behind advertising or make discriminating choices.

And even the older child who can recognize a misleading commercial is still gullible. Parents can tell him, "That toy's going to break when you get it home." Having had that experience with other toys, he will say, "Yes, I know—but I want it anyway."

I want to make it clear that ACT (Action for Children's Television) doesn't think there shouldn't be any television commercials, but only that there shouldn't be any commercials specifically geared to children. The commercial should be directed to adults who have the experience and intelligence to know if, when, and how a product should be used. You gear a candy-bar message to an adult who will know what place that candy bar should take in a balanced diet. You let the adult beware.

Q: Shouldn't it be the responsibility of parents—not of the federal government—to be aware of and control what their children see on television?

A: You can't expect every parent to watch TV with his or her children. You can't set up a system that's going to work only for committed parents who manage to have the time to spend with their children. There are many homes where parents have to work.

But even if parents watch TV with their children, it is difficult to compete with the hard-sell commercials. As one parent who watched programs with her children, I know that the 30-second messages are the most persuasive kind of message you can give to a child.

Q: Advertisers and broadcasters say that they themselves can regulate the commercials to keep them from being misleading or deceptive—

A: The networks, the local stations, the ad-

Interview with Mrs. Broman continued

A: There is never an ad for sugar-coated cereal that isn't accompanied by an audio and video statement indicating that cereal is just part of a balanced diet and shouldn't be the only thing a child eats for breakfast. I don't consider a cereal shown in that context as a bad or misleading ad.

Have you ever had a child who wouldn't eat? I would suspect that there are some mothers who are very happy to have those sugared cereals. At least they get cereal into their children. And if you can get them to take that cereal—even though sugar-coated—with the orange juice and milk and banana, then I think you're well on the road to starting a child on a better-balanced meal than he would otherwise eat.

Q: Don't children—especially younger ones—lack the experience and intelligence to differentiate between the usual puff in a commercial and the truth?

A: I don't think you see much puff in commercials any more. I think the National Association of Broadcasters Television Code has done an excellent job of making sure that there is no puff. The Code does not allow manufacturers to advertise something that is not true. Advertisers can't take a toy and make it look like it's doing something it can't possibly do.

Q: Why are advertisements addressed to a market that has no direct purchasing power?

A: In many cases, advertising has always been geared to children.

You look at magazines and you'll see a little girl playing with a doll or a doll house. That picture isn't geared to the parent any more than the commercial on television is geared to the parent. It's showing the child what the product will do. Then the parents can make the choice on whether or not they'll buy it.

Q: Don't commercials aimed at children create an unwarranted strain on parents if

Interview with Mrs. Charren continued

vertising industry, and the National Association of Broadcasters all have censors that look at advertising messages. Why then is there a need for a group like Action for Children's Television to say: "Don't do this; don't do that"? Because these censors are not protecting the consumer.

A perfect example is what happened to children's vitamins. When ACT began in 1971, almost one-third of the advertising directed to children was for sugar-coated vitamin pills. These vitamins were being sold like candy, even though half of them had iron in them and were so dangerous in overdose that the law required they be bottled with the warning label: "Keep out of the reach of children." It took ACT until 1976 to make sure there would be no more vitamin advertising for children. Now, if the self-regulatory mechanisms had been operating properly we should never have had to deal with that problem.

Q: Would a ban on ads aimed at children be unconstitutional?

A: Absolutely not. We protect children in all kinds of ways in this country. We don't let them work in factories, sign contracts, vote until a certain age or drive a car. This is just one more area where ACT believes that children deserve special protection.

Q: Won't restrictions on children's advertising bring about an end to television programs for children?

A: No. Fortunately, the air waves in this country are public. Commercial television stations have promised that in return for using the air waves for profit they will serve the public interest.

We believe that commitment means serving the broadcast audience that is 2 to 11 years old. If a station tried to stay on the air with no

Interview with Mrs. Broman continued

children pester them for the products they see advertised on TV?

A: Hasn't there always been a strain between parents and children when they wanted something? I have yet to see a child at any age who didn't want everything he saw.

Long before television, children would want everything that they saw in a store. I, myself, wanted every doll that I saw. I don't think television has changed that situation one bit.

Q: Doesn't television advertising influence the toys that are being made today? Anything that doesn't sell well on TV, such as rag dolls, isn't made anymore.

A: I don't think so. How does a Model T [Ford] look today to you when you're looking at one of the new sports cars? Times have changed, so consequently toys have changed —just as everything else in life has changed. The rag doll of 50 years ago might have been the doll for the child at that time, but not today's child.

Q: What would happen to children's programs if there were no commercials to pay for them?

A: I don't think the programs would go off the air, but I think there might be fewer of them, and their quality might suffer a bit. I would *not* like to see that happen.

Q: Do you regard any restriction on TV advertising as an impingement on the freedom of speech?

A: Yes, I do. I think that TV is being unfairly singled out if a product can't be advertised there but can be in a magazine, newspaper, or on radio. I don't agree with the argument that television is such a powerful medium that it needs to be restricted more than a newspaper or magazine.

Interview with Mrs. Charren continued

programming for that audience, we think an aroused public would see to it that that station would lose its license.

Q: But wouldn't the quality of the programs suffer without the financial help of commercials?

A: That certainly is a rational problem to consider. But if you read what TV critics now say about children's television, you realize that the system we now have is not providing children with enough high-quality programs.

Copyright 1978 U.S. News & World Report, Inc.

Interview with Mrs. Broman continued

Q: Why would a restriction on advertising directed to children be unconstitutional? After all, the United States already has laws restricting the rights of children.

A: I look on any restriction, no matter how limited, as unconstitutional.

You don't have to let children watch television. Nobody says that you have to put a child in front of the television, turn it on, and make the child sit there. You always have a choice.

RIGHT OF PROFESSIONALS TO ADVERTISE THEIR SERVICES

Barbara Slavin

In the Middle Ages, professional people were walking advertisements. You could tell them by their clothes. Doctors, wrote Barbara Tuchman, in *A Distant Mirror*, wore purple or red gowns with furred hoods, silver belts, embroidered gloves, and golden spurs. Boccac-

cio's Doctor Simon, she recalled, went further, advertising his specialty—proctology—by having a chamber pot painted over his door.

Costume and custom have changed considerably over the years. In the United States, advertising by most professionals was restricted from the early 1900s until just a few years ago. Supreme Court decisions, Federal Trade Commission rulings, and unilateral action by professional associations, often in anticipation of

From *The New York Times* (March 17, 1979): 17. © 1979 by The New York Times Company. Reprinted by permission.

legal challenges, have combined to knock down the prohibitions one by one.

Yet many professionals remain uneasy about the use of commercial advertising. Some view it as inappropriate, seeing themselves as businessmen second and servants of the public first. There is also uncertainty about whether advertising will lower the price of professional services by enhancing competition and whether the quality of service will decline in proportion to the price. And there are questions about the enforcement of guidelines to prevent deceptive and misleading claims.

THE BACKGROUND

Professional associations' proscriptions against advertising are almost as old as professional associations themselves. Such groups as the American Medical Association and the American Bar Association were founded largely because doctors and lawyers felt that they needed a set of rules to work by; one of those rules invariably restricted advertising.

The medical association restrictions, which are 75 years old, came in response to rampant hucksterism in the days when newspapers were filled with promises of sure-fire cures for every ailment from impotence to lumbago. The bar association ban, introduced in 1908, reflected the gentlemanly traditions of the English bar. Newer professional associations, among them the American Institute of Certified Public Accountants, emulated the ethical codes of lawyers and doctors, along with their privileged social status.

The first major blow against these codes and a range of other practices long considered professional prerogatives was struck in June 1975 when the Supreme Court ruled that lawyers could no longer set uniform minimum fees because the "learned professions" were not exempt from federal antitrust laws. Two years later, in a case brought by two young Phoenix lawyers, John R. Bates and Van O'Steen, the Court struck down state and bar association restrictions on advertising as a violation of lawyers' right to free speech.

Since then, other professional associations, notably architects and accountants, have voluntarily revised their antiadvertising codes. The medical association and the American Dental Association have not. The Federal Trade Commission, taking its cue from the 1975 Supreme Court decision, sued both groups, charging that they were acting in restraint of trade.

The suit against the dental association was settled out of court in February. Next month, the trade commission will hear an appeal by the medical association on a December ruling against the association's advertising restrictions. The medical association has promised to fight the case through the courts, a process that could take several years. But even its lawyers concede that it will probably lose.

FOR ADVERTISING

The main argument in favor of advertising by professionals is that it will spur competition and lower prices, making professional services more accessible to lower- and middle-class people.

Charles Corddry, Deputy Assistant Director of the Trade Commission's Bureau of Competition, noted that fees for routine legal services had dropped markedly with the advent of advertising, which permitted low-cost legal clinics to mushroom around the country. He saw an analogous relationship between advertising and health maintenance organizations, the so-called HMOs, in which one pays an overall fee for health care, and anticipated a similar effect on private physicians' fees.

For legal clinics, the assertion of cost-cutting has been generally borne out. Jacoby & Meyers, the most successful of the clinics, with 22 offices in California and 12 that opened in mid-January in New York, quoted a price of $245 plus $30 to $60 in court costs for an uncontested divorce—a third to half the going rate. The Baltimore-based clinics of Cawley and Schmidt charge $150, excluding court costs, which average $135 in Maryland.

Proponents of advertising also assert that it will help to demystify the professions. The public will begin to see professionals as businessmen with special skills and will be more apt and able to question whether all the services they recommend are really necessary.

AGAINST ADVERTISING

Opponents of advertising focus on its potential for abuse. Many physicians, in particular, say that medical advertising is bound to be misleading because it is impossible to define routine services and set a standard price.

"The trouble is, what is routine?" asked Dr. Drummond Rennie, deputy editor of the *New England Journal of Medicine*. "Do you clock an office visit? Suppose you see Mrs. X and she bursts into tears and tells you that her husband beats her. At the end of the session, do you write up the notes, make a few calls, and unclick the meter?"

Some officials involved in the enforcement of advertising guidelines are concerned about its effect on the quality of care. Robert Asher, who as director of the Division of Professional Conduct of New York's Education Department, has handled complaints about professional ads since they were permitted in the state in 1977, had a highly pessimistic view. Dentists, he suggested, might use base metals, instead of

more durable procelain or gold. "Professionals in this society have come to expect a certain income," he said, "and they will lower the quality of service if necessary to retain that income."

Mr. Asher also said that professionals, in an ad man's version of synecdoche, were apt to advertise a price for a part of a service that the lay public could easily mistake for the whole.

David T. Link, dean of the Notre Dame law school and a member of the bar association's Commission on Advertising, suggested an alternative to advertising: lawyer referral services maintained by local bar associations.

THE OUTLOOK

In the law books, professional advertising's time has come, but in the minds of most professionals it has not. Dr. Rennie summed up the feelings of many of them: "When I see F. Lee Bailey advertising on the front page of the *New York Times*, nobody could say it was obscene, nobody could say it was tasteless, but somehow it seems wrong."

According to a survey conducted by the *Journal of the American Bar Association*, only 3 percent of the nation's lawyers have put their shingle on a newspaper page or television screen since 1977.

Yet for legal clinics and health maintenance organizations, advertising is both crucial and successful. "Clinics is where all or a substantial part of the action will be," said Jerold Auerbach, a professor of American history at Wellesley and author of *Unequal Justice*.

"It's easy enough for the fat cats to say that advertising is something professionals don't do because they don't need it," he said. "They went to Yale and Harvard and are members of all the clubs."

HELP! THERE'S SEX IN MY SOUP

A SMALL PLEA FOR AN END TO SUBLIMINAL SILLINESS

Jerry Goodis

When I was a schoolkid in Toronto, there was a joke going around about a psychologist who was testing a subject by holding up ordinary geometric figures and asking what they made him think of. Each figure—square, oblong, or rectangle—apparently made his subject think of only one thing: sex. Finally the psychologist could take no more. "Good God," he cried. "Does *everything* make you think of sex?" "You should talk," his subject retorted scornfully, "you're the one who keeps showing me all those dirty pictures!"

For years, every time I thought of that story, I believed it would take a very disturbed person or, conversely, some marvelously zany bunch like Monty Python's Flying Circus to see sex in such ordinary things. But, when I first read Wilson Bryan Key's book, *Subliminal Seduction,* subtitled "Ad Media's Manipulation of a Not So Innocent America," (New American Library paperback, $1.95) I realized that here was someone who *did* see sex, or at least *said* he did (in the understandable interest of selling more of his books), in virtually every picture, every illustration, and every advertisement in magazines, newspapers, films, TV shows, and other entertainment and communication media.

And Key didn't mean only suggested or subtly implied sex. Key saw the actual word *sex* spelled out in bold letters on whisky glasses, on the faces and arms of infants, on Ritz crackers, in clouds, grass, and trees, in every curve and indent of pneumatic *Playboy* cuties, and of course, even on his own portrait adorning the dust jacket of his book. But this astounding discovery was mild compared to the utter maelstroms of depravity and deception Key could readily find worked into your average, run-of-the-fridge *ice cube,* in some of the most prestigious and expensive advertisements for soft drinks and liquor.

"The right side of the ice cube above the lime slice," Key points out on page 100 of the paperback edition of *Subliminal Seduction,* as part of his clinical dissection of a Sprite ad which appeared in *Esquire* magazine, "forms the back of a large shaggy dog with a pointed nose, or quite possibly a polar bear."

The animal's legs are extended outward to the left, parallel with the top of the lime. The animal's arms (or legs, as you will) appear to be holding another figure which is human with long, feminine hair. Her face is located just above the animal's head.

The two figures, animal and human, are in what can only be described as a sexual intercourse position. The polar bear, dog, or whatever, is in sexual embrace with a nude woman.

Bestiality may be illegal throughout most of the world, but, at the symbolic level, it appears to have sold a lot of Sprite. The Coca-Cola/Sprite advertisement was designed to sell around a subliminal theme of highly taboo sex.

Reprinted from the article of the same name by Jerry Goodis, Chairman and President, The Jerry Goodis Agency Inc., Toronto, Ontario, in Quest (February–March 1979): 57–58. Used by permission.

This incredibly ludicrous excursion into the utterly absurd sent a chill up my spine. If it wasn't all so appallingly perverted, it might be mildly humorous.

My mind was still reeling when, a few pages later, Key claimed to have found, in a *fake* ice cube, something much more sinister:

> The primary symbolic device, subliminally perceived in the Bacardi ad, appears at first to be an ice cube in the centre bottom of the glass. Look more carefully. The ice cube is a golden skull with a flattened nose, large eye sockets and jagged teeth.... The thematic implication ... implies that one might richly enjoy dying if well fortified with Bacardi rum ....

On page 115 Key declares, in the authoritative, straight-from-heaven style he employs throughout his book:

> There is not even an outside chance, however, that major U.S. media embeds [Key's own term for hidden messages] inadvertently or without full knowledge of what they were doing.

What malicious effrontery!

Though Key specifically refers to American advertising agencies in his convoluted indictment, he is damning all advertising agencies, Canadian as well, as he later confirmed. And since I've spent most of my life in advertising and am fiercely proud of the work my agencies have done, I consider Key's allegations a *personal* insult.

Also, I have another cogent reason for leaving the sidelines and jumping head-first into the controversy Key precipitated with his ridiculous, disturbed fantasies. For some years I have been traveling to Canadian universities and community colleges (at their invitations), talking to students about what I do for a living and how I sincerely believe advertising benefits society. And I've had some rip-snorting, knock-down, drag-out arguments in many a college bear-pit.

The connection between these collegiate confrontations and Wilson Bryan Key is that by the time I got around to perusing his first book—he's since done another one containing even more bizarre claims of alleged media malpractices and misdirections called *Media Sexploitation* (New American Library paperback, $1.95)—he was snugly ensconced as professor of journalism at the University of Western Ontario in London.

His inauspicious term at that institution lasted only one year, at the end of which its administrators undoubtedly heaved a collective sigh of intense relief as he headed back to California. But even in that relatively brief interval, Key's fantastic theories, and the bland certainty with which he spouted them, infected a good number of impressionable young people. He convinced them that there really was a deep, dark plot to poison people's subconscious minds with all sorts of unspeakable messages and suggestions, and that large advertising agencies like mine were only the evil front-men for "the merchandisers and the culture controlled by merchandisers."

I first found it incredible that anyone would swallow the Key brand of foolishness, except possibly as basic training for a career with the CIA. But I had to face the fact that hundreds of Canadian post-secondary students, bemused perhaps by Key's undeniable gift for high-flown rhetoric, had accepted his maniacal meanderings as valid research.

While Key was on staff at Western, he swore there was a secret room at the local daily paper, the highly respected *London Free Press*. Here, Key claimed, unknown even to the publisher himself, expert retouching artists allegedly earned the tainted money supplied by big advertising agencies, by superimposing or cunningly inserting their sordid, hidden commands or scenes of debauchery, bestiality, and other orgies on any photograph or illustration they could lay their filthy paws upon.

Further, on Key's own office wall, emphasized by its own special spotlight, was a *Time* magazine cover of Queen Elizabeth, on whose face and hair Key revealed he'd located the common, explicit word for fornication—not only once, but literally dozens of times.

But beyond these instances of Key's personal obsession as recorded by responsible people who knew him at Western, I think a statement of my own credo may help convince students and others that neither I nor my confrères could possibly be a party to such devilish plots against the public.

I am an advertising practitioner—a salesman, if you will—a man who does his damndest to persuade Canadians to buy the products people pay me to promote—Speedy Muffler, Hiram Walker, Alcan, London Life, The Permanent, Scotiabank, and Molson's, to name only a few.

All the time I've been in advertising, we've tried to produce *tasteful* ads, whether they were slated for magazines, television, newspapers, radio, kids' balloons, shopping bags, mountainsides, fireworks displays, or to be towed behind low-flying aircraft. And if possible, not only tasteful ads, but often ads with a bit of humor added for good measure.

A lot of people who had read David Ogilvy's book, *Confessions of an Advertising Man*, published in 1963, firmly believed this last whim of ours would be the downfall of our little Toronto firm, because David, senior partner in a very successful American advertising agency, had decreed that though humor undoubtedly had its place in the cosmic scheme of things, that place was definitely not the advertising business. Wrong, David.

In every ad campaign we launch, we know what segment of the public we are aiming at, and how we should go about reaching them, usually because we've done exhaustive market research beforehand—or as much research as the client's budget will stand. Even so, we're sometimes wrong. But not too often. Every word in the copy block, every illustration, the precise positioning of the text in relation to the

illustrations, the choice of colors, models, and typefaces, the media to be employed, the amount of money to be allocated to each medium—these and a host of other details are all deliberately chosen to strike a balance between artistry and salesmanship. And always with good taste.

If anyone in my organization was "embedding" secret messages in our ads, I would certainly be aware of it. But what I must ask is this: what could possibly be the point of anyone inserting words like *sex*, death's-heads, earthy verbs, euphemisms for female fixtures, or artfully concocted scenes of wanton bestiality into their ads? What particular section of the consuming public would they be trying to reach with such messages? What possible financial gain would any sponsor hope to glean from the exhortation alleged by Key to be embedded in *Time's* portrait of Queen Elizabeth, urging everyone to rush out and fornicate?

And who is paying for all this? As I read Key, the art of "embedding" is a very complicated one, requiring experts to do the job properly. Experts cost money—piles of it. We use them only in dire necessity. Just arranging for the word *sex* to be embedded randomly a dozen-odd times across each Christie Ritz cracker, as Key claims, would cost thousands of dollars for the molds used by the bakeries alone. And has Key's own market research proved conclusively that you can slip a Ritz under ham or a Ritz under jam much more easily and tastily if it happens to be slathered with the word *sex*?

Our ads, besides being in what we consider to be good taste, are usually subtle, requiring a little thought on the part of the viewer/reader to grasp their full significance, but often rewarding this cerebral exercise on our client's behalf with a chuckle. But however we do it, everything we want to get across to the public is right out there for them to see. Why? Because otherwise they might not get the message at all, even after thinking about it. And that would mean we've failed miserably at our job and should lose the account and our franchise to operate.

Unlike Key's ads, which, to detect their full significance, usually have to be held upside down or sideways, viewed through the paper onto the next page—or at the very least, examined under a magnifying glass (according to his directions)—we liberally estimate that we have about 10 seconds at the very outside to get our message across. If we have to instruct our audience how to hold the page or watch the screen, then we've lost before we've even begun.

It is noteworthy that Key is usually the only person able to see all these hidden messages. And even then, if I understand him, he is only able to do so by relaxing and letting his subconscious take command. The rest of us are obviously just too uptight and repressed, too brainwashed by the Machiavellian media and their lackeys, to see what to Key is exceedingly clear.

It astounds me that it has taken this long for someone to throw down the gauntlet to Wilson Bryan Key and expose his sick, perverted ideas.

What is even more disturbing than Key's infatuation with these ludicrous theories is that some misguided cynics actually believe them. And that *really* scares me.

chapter 4

TELEVISION RATINGS

The debate surrounding the TV ratings system began with the advent of commercial television and will continue as long as commercial television exists. Although the main debate is whether the ratings exert an unfair influence on what the public sees, a debate-within-the-debate takes up the question of whether another system—one based on quality of programming, rather than just number of people watching—might not better serve the public's needs. In the first article in this chapter, Les Brown of the *New York Times* presents an overview of the general question. In the second reading, Martin Mayer of *American Film* offers his opinion of ratings based on program quality.

DOES THE TV RATINGS SYSTEM EXERT AN UNFAIR INFLUENCE?

Les Brown

Audience ratings have been commercial television's demon almost from the medium's beginnings. The Nielsen popularity digits have caused the demise of hundreds of weekly series over the years, and they have been blamed also for causing a common-denominator approach to programming that has favored mediocrity. But in the view of some, they foster a cultural democracy.

In the current season alone, more than two-thirds of the series the networks introduced in September, including some that were well received by critics, have vanished because of inadequate ratings. Not only do programs rise and fall by the ratings, but so also do network administrations and the careers of news anchormen and Hollywood producers, writers, and actors.

The ratings, which are actually percentage figures for the number of television households that have tuned in to a program, are at the center of virtually every decision made in the television industry. Because they represent the estimated size of the audience, they govern how much an advertiser will pay for air time and thus how large a network's or station's profits will be.

The ratings bear on the market value of television stations and on the loyalty of affiliates to their networks. More significantly, the trends of the Nielsen averages from week to week are reflected in the fluctuating stock prices for the network's parent companies.

So much rides on the Nielsen ratings that inevitably they become a focus of criticism of the American commerical television system.

THE BACKGROUND

In adopting the program and business structure of commercial radio in the late '40s, television also adopted the means of counting heads in the audience. The A. C. Nielsen Company, having already developed a methodology for radio audience research employing a mechanical device that was attached to receivers in the home, became the principal scorekeeper for national television and one of two—Arbitron the other—for local television.

The national ratings are projected from a sample of approximately 1200 households equipped with a device known as the Audimeter, which records the set-on, set-off information and the channel tuned to. This information is carried over special telephone lines to a computer center, where it is collated with material gathered from viewing diaries kept by a smaller sample of households.

From the two sources, projections are made not only of the total audience but also of its breakdown for each program by age and sex.

Several hundred companies subscribe to the Nielsen ratings, but the networks are the largest

From The New York Times (January 17, 1980): 22+. © 1980 by The New York Times Company. Reprinted by permission.

customers in terms of the rates they pay for the service. Each spends $1.5 million to $2 million a year for the ratings.

The networks' interests as sellers of air time are counterbalanced by those of advertisers, the buyers of air time and the largest group of Nielsen subscribers. A number of production companies also subscribe. Nielsen's annual revenues for its television research services, national and local, come to around $35 million.

An industry organization known as the Broadcast Rating Council, made up of research executives from the networks and advertising agencies, keeps watch on the Nielsen operations and methodology.

The British Broadcasting Corporation uses two rating services, one to measure the number of viewers, the other to gauge appreciation. At least two organizations in the United States, the John and Mary R. Markle Foundation, which specializes in communications, and the National Citizens Committee for Broadcasting, a consumer-oriented group, are working separately toward establishing a second ratings service here that would measure viewer appreciation and satisfaction.

FOR THE RATINGS SYSTEM

Annoyed by its reputation as a killer of shows, the Nielsen Company maintains that it makes no judgments but merely provides the raw data that are analyzed and interpreted by the broadcasters and advertisers who subscribe to its service. Its traditional response to those who question the small sample used to measure a vast audience is expressed in an analogy to medical blood tests: "When a doctor wants to count your red corpuscles, he doesn't drain the body but merely takes a small sample of blood."

There is an acknowledged 3 percent margin of error in Nielsen's methodology with the present sample size. "There is always talk of increasing the size of the sample," said William Behanna, vice-president of public information for the Nielsen television division. "But to decrease the margin of error by 50 percent would mean increasing the sample four times, and that would involve astronomical costs the industry isn't willing to meet."

Audience-research specialists at the networks and at advertising agencies are generally satisfied with the Nielsen standards and vouch for the validity of its methodology. A second national ratings service, they say, would only duplicate what Nielsen provides while doubling the expense of counting audience.

In the view of Marvin Mord, vice-president of research for ABC Television, the Nielsens have been a positive, rather than negative, influence on commercial television. "They serve to stimulate programmers to perform better all the time," he asserted. "We're no different from any other business; all businesses need to know their markets."

Network research executives point out that, internally, their companies do use various forms of qualitative research—such as TvQ and special studies by the R. H. Bruskin research concern—in making programming decisions.

"We're continually looking for information on tastes and trends, and what people enjoy." Mr. Mord said. "The Nielsens are not our only criteria."

AGAINST THE RATINGS

Criticism of the broadcast industry's obsession with ratings dates back even before the public outcry in the early '50s when the critically admired "Fred Allen Show" was cut down by a quiz-giveaway show on a competing network. Over the years, the ratings system has been assailed by television producers, writers, performers, intellectuals, politicans, and members of religious, minority, and cultural groups, all of whom have felt disfranchised or otherwise victimized by the tyranny of the numbers.

There has been a widely held view over the years that commercial television would be able to raise its standards and broaden its scope if somehow it could be liberated from its dependency on audience ratings.

The Rev. Everett C. Parker, head of the Office of Communication of the United Church of Christ and one of the leading activists for broadcast reform, contends that the ratings system violates the public-interest provision of the Communications Act because it does not serve the entire public. "The ratings that count most," he says, "are those that involve people in the 18 to 49 age range, the group advertisers consider the prime customers for their products. The networks have no interest in programming for people over 50. This deprives the society of important cultural forms."

Another activist, Sam Simon, executive director of the National Citizens Committee for Broadcasting, asserts that the present ratings system makes viewers the merchandise that television sells, because advertisers buy Nielsen numbers, and the numbers represent people. "We believe the viewer should have the role of consumer and not be treated as the product of television," he says. "That's what we think a second ratings service could accomplish, a service that tells how people feel about programs."

THE OUTLOOK

The financial support for a qualitative ratings service would have to come from the same companies that need, and subscribe to, the Nielsen service. At present, there is no manifest demand either on the advertising or the network side for ratings that reflect appreciation and enjoyment, since these are not factors in the business transactions between advertisers and broadcasters.

However, as Lloyd N. Morrisett, president of the Markle Foundation, points out: "If it can be demonstrated that people have better retention of commercials that air in programs they enjoy than in programs they don't enjoy, or if it can be shown that people are more likely to buy products advertised in programs that are most satisfying to them, then ratings that measure subjective reactions will matter greatly."

Until that can be determined conclusively, the Nielsens are likely to remain the lone axis on which commercial television turns.

THE NIELSENS VERSUS QUALITY

Martin Mayer

It's open season again on the ratings, that root of all evil that takes the reason prisoner. The Markle Foundation, ever busy doing good,

Reprinted from *American Film* (March 1979): 11–12. Copyright © 1979 The American Film Institute. Reprinted by permission of Curtis Brown, Ltd.

is sponsoring a push toward "Q" ratings, measuring people's approval of what they're watching, to diminish our servitude to the brute audience totals of Nielsen and Arbitron. The foundation's consultant on these matters recently warned in a piece in the *New York Times* that "it will probably take some outside business threat to convert the networks to the use of qualitative ratings." Providentially, and just in time, Ralph Nader has taken over the National Citizens Committee for Broadcasting. (Is there no antitrust law to prevent this sort of blatant, competition-destroying conglomeration of public interest groups?) So we can count on lots of threats, and bluster, too.

The Corporation for Public Broadcasting likes Q ratings because the audience for PBS shows tends to be loyal and often proud of itself for watching something by definition "better" than the pap on the networks. And program producers like them (at least in theory) because they offer a kind of reward for extra effort, which is painfully lacking in television as conventionally measured. Best of all, there's no open opposition: Nobody can be *against* "quality."

Nor can anyone say that quality is unmeasurable. Shakespeare, Mozart, Rembrandt, Château Latour, Rolls Royce, Secretariat (the horse)—all these, I think, would be universally conceded to have quality. Yet even here, if you were doing approval measurements by public opinion poll—asking the personal reactions of a representative sample to the direct experience of this quality—you might get some results that were hard to handle. Lots of people would be quite negative about watching Shakespeare or listening to Mozart; Lambrusco drinkers would find the Latour sour; and all the people who bet against Secretariat would be displeased with the race. Pleasure with the telecast of the Super Bowl is always much lower in the hometown of the losing team.

Television ratings à la Nielsen are feasible because there really is one "public" out there, defined by the national borders. Virtually all the population Nielsen covers watches television, and the only way it can do that is by being in front of a television set that has been turned on and tuned to a station. Under these circumstances, measurements of a thousand or so randomly selected homes can indeed, to known levels of statistical reliability, give approximate audience figures for a universe of 70 million households (or 1 million households—the size of the universe is unimportant to the accuracy of measurement by sample, provided the sample is truly random).

When you start measuring qualitative reactions, you get into both practical and theoretical trouble. The sample shrinks (with a show's rating of 20, for example, the thousand Nielsen respondents drop to 200 viewers who can be queried about their reactions), which greatly decreases reliability. And you vastly increase the complexity of what you are measuring when you change from Nielsen's set of yes-no questions about whether the set is on a given channel to something even so simple as an individual's like or dislike on a five-point scale. Thus, samples must be larger to give anything like the same, if I may, "quality." The homogeneous universe Nielsen measures becomes a helter-skelter of separate "publics" once you start quantifying the Qs.

(It's interesting to note that commentators who cannot restrain their doubts about the adequacy of a sample of a thousand to measure viewing habits will insist that everybody take seriously the results of Q surveys measuring the attitudes of a sample of about 200. One of the really nice things about working for a foundation in America is that you can look out on a snowy landscape and, just because you want to drive somewhere today, God will vacuum all the snow and make the roads dry. This never happens to people who don't work for foundations.)

The Markle Foundation consultant, writing in the *Times*, noted that British and French television make efforts at supplementary quality ratings, but somehow forgot (it's hard to believe she didn't know) that such ratings have been attempted on and off in this country for a quarter of a century. There was a demand for them because well into the '60s some advertisers believed strongly in what was called a "gratitude factor" in the pulling power of commercials. Texaco still goes a distance out of its way to identify Bob Hope with its products (having done the same years ago with Milton Berle), and NBC salesmen peddling the "Today" show always stress the values of having the show's personalities sell the sponsors' goodies.

Partly because television shows became too expensive to be supported by single advertisers (even companies with many brands), advertising theoreticians stopped supporting the idea of the gratitude factor. At least as important as the economic logic, however, was the inability of researchers to find any statistically credible justification for it. The research firms that had specialized in measuring Q factors in the '50s and '60s folded their tents and crept away.

Instead of measuring the quality of shows, advertisers and their agencies now seek to discover the qualities of audiences. Demography reigns: Advertisers want to know what proportion of the audience Nielsen rates is women 18 to 49, who spend all that money in the supermarkets. Beyond that, they want to know the proportion of dog or cat owners in the rated audience. Beyond *that* (and now our statistical reliabilities are no better than those of the Q services), they want to know what proportion of the audience buys their brand. The tyranny of numbers is more complicated than critics think and has been for a long time: twenty years have passed since Philip Morris dropped its sponsorship of "I Love Lucy," then the most popular show on television, because there were too many nonsmokers in the audience—and among the smokers, too many who did *not* smoke Philip Morris.

By far the most profitable recipient of an advertising message is the extant customer, whose habits can be reinforced. As Norton Garfinkle of Brand Ratings Index liked to say, "It isn't people who use products. People who use products use products." That's a Great Truth, so if you need a minute to figure it out, I urge you to invest the minute: Great Truths take time to grasp.

Actually, considerable Q research is done by the networks, not on a continuing basis but be-

fore a series goes on the air. For 40 years, CBS has been playing around with the Stanton-Lazarsfeld Program Analyzer, dragging people off street corners to come to conference rooms and watch pilot programs with a "like" button in one hand and a "dislike" button in the other. Audience Studies, Inc., does something similar in a large theater for the other networks and for program producers. Reactions to promos for shows not yet made are put through the social science equivalent of the electron microscope to discover whether or not these characters and plot ideas are likely to stimulate curiosity and loyalty in the great public out there.

If, in fact, a continuing Q survey of what's on the air could produce useful data, the networks would gladly spend the money for it—not to justify the simple go–no go decision, which is what the newspapers report, but to improve casting, character, or story typology for a failing show that represents a large investment of money, time, and bureaucratic blood.

And, of course, the go–no go decisions *are* influenced by perceptions of quality. A spectacular recent example is "Lou Grant," which bombed in the ratings in its first year and was retained because significant persons at CBS had a high regard for the cast and the producers, who were urged to make future story lines less fantastic, less like other television. "The Waltons" did poorly in the program analyzer and made its start in the apparently hopeless slot opposite Flip Wilson, then the ratings champ; it was maintained essentially at the insistence of Lou Dorfsman, head of promotion at CBS, who loved it and demanded a budget to sell it to the public.

"All in the Family" also got off to a weak start, and Fred Silverman thought so little of it that he initially scheduled it for its second season in the dry gulch opposite the roaring success of "Monday Night Football"; only the persistence of Robert Wood, then CBS-TV president, got it a more valuable slot and a full chance. The general contempt for ABC among television professionals derives from the feeling that this sort of respect for programs never interferes with ratings-based judgments at what is now the number one but always the junior network. ("All in the Family," incidentally, was made for ABC, but refused a time slot on the basis of tryout Q ratings.)

Nothing in American life—certainly not politics—is so democratic, so permeated with egalitarianism, as the use of television ratings to influence program decisions. Whatever the failings of Nielsen ratings, they do assert the equality of souls. What television's critics from the foundations are trying to say without saying it is that this sort of democracy is no good: *Real* democracy demands consideration of intensities of feeling as well as brute numbers. The critics don't want to say that, because in their circles these intensities equate to "special interests" and "pressure groups," which are presumed bad. But in the end, only individual judgment—political leadership, if you will; "elitism," if you insist—can give intelligent attention to intensities. What is wrong with television is the lack of leadership, of sense, or of pride of purpose—and Q ratings won't help.

At that, frankly, I'd rather trust the network executives than most of the critics. "Lou Grant" is now doing well enough to be fair game, and in a recent issue of the *Columbia Journalism Review*, it was denounced for failing to tell viewers where good men and true should stand on the often real issues raised by this year's story lines. But this presentation of complexity is what makes the program unusual and valuable—God knows we have enough idolatry of crusading in our mass media. No doubt the show finds sugary conclusions to coat its intelligent irresolution. But if viewers are going to be left in the air (as they were, for example, in a quite brilliant recent presentation of the influence of friends and personal interests on journalists' work), they're entitled to an upbeat gesture at the end.

The critic said scornfully that the failure to take positions in "Lou Grant" was the result of its nature as an (ugh) entertainment program. To the contrary: Entertainment usually takes a position, directly or by inference. It's education that avoids easy answers. A successful education creates tolerance of ambiguity. (The success ratio, admittedly, is low—almost as low as the quality ratio on television.) What makes "Lou Grant" an important show is that at its best it is authentically educational. But you'd never learn that from Q ratings.

SUGGESTIONS FOR FURTHER READING

Chapter 1 The Concentration of Media Ownership
Peter Drier and Steve Weinberg, "Interlocking Directorates," *Columbia Journalism Review* (November–December 1979): 51. Discusses the implications of the fact that most of the directors of the 25 largest newspaper companies are tied to institutions the papers cover.

"After a Rash of Take-Overs, New Worries about Press Lords," *U.S. News and World Report* (January 24, 1977): 54. Some of the information in this article is now dated, but the trends and concerns expressed are still valid.

Chapter 2 The Censorship of Pornography and Obscenity
Harold H. Hart (ed.), *Censorship: For and Against* (New York: Hart Publishing Co., 1971). Twelve essays from authorities on both sides of the issue. One of them, the article by Hollis Alpert, is included in Chapter 2 of this text.

Chapter 3 Advertising Ethics
Carl P. Wrighter, *I Can Sell You Anything* (New York: Ballantine, 1972). An interesting account of manipulative advertising techniques, including what Wrighter calls "weasel words," which are qualifiers (such as "virtually") used in advertising to mislead.

Chapter 4 Television Ratings
Eugene S. Foster, *Understanding Broadcasting* (Reading, Mass.: Addison-Wesley, 1978). See especially Chapter 10, "Ratings," for a discussion on how ratings work and how broadcasters use them.

part II

MASS MEDIA AND AMERICA'S PERCEPTION OF REALITY

It has become axiomatic to point out that we live in a media-saturated age, surrounded by messages that change our perception of the world. Changing our perceptions is, after all, what mass media are supposed to do. The process of changing the way people look at things underlies the often cited functions of informing, entertaining, serving the economic system, and influencing public opinion. So the issue here is not *whether* the mass media help mold America's perception of reality. They do. The issue is *how* they mold that perception, and whether that molding is beneficial to American society.

The first chapter in this part of the book deals with the manipulation of truth by journalists. The second chapter extends that examination to television news. The third chapter looks at television entertainment. The fourth chapter presents some pro-and-con arguments about the way media depict minorities and women. The final chapter presents analyses and debates on the depiction of sex and violence.

chapter 5

JOURNALISM
AND THE TRUTH

In recent years a credibility gap has arisen between newspapers and the public. Newspapers have been accused of slanting news, ignoring news, and sensationalizing news more than at any time since "objective reporting" became the standard for American journalism. Most of the arguments that arise over bias in reporting are simplistic, and hinge around the idea of whether the newspaper intentionally misled its readers. However, as seen in the first reading in this section, the differences between "news" and "truth" are more complex than that.

"Journalism and Truth" is written by Edward Jay Epstein, a media critic who has experience both as a journalist and as a political scientist. This reading comes from his book *Between Fact and Fiction: The Problem of Journalism*. Epstein is also the author of *News from Nowhere*, an examination of television news.

If news reporting is one way that a newspaper could intentionally alter the public's perception of reality, there are other ways that might happen accidentally, such as through mistakes or unintentional double entendres in headlines, pictures, captions, and news copy. Although there is ample evidence that headlines and pictures have been used intentionally to slant news stories,[1] I suspect that most of this type of distortion occurs accidentally. Consider, for example, the story about the person who read the headline "Government to Cut Fallout" and called the local newspaper office to ask, "Does that mean we're going to go right from summer to winter from now on?" The story is probably apocryphal, but it is almost believable because we do have a tendency to leaf through newspapers, glancing mostly at headlines, pictures, and captions. Imagine some of the misconceptions that might be caused by some of the items in the second reading in this section. These appear every month in "The Lower Case," a section in the *Columbia Journalism Review.*

NOTE

1. See, for example, Robert Cirino, *Power to Persuade: Mass Media and the News* (New York: Bantam, 1974).

JOURNALISM AND TRUTH

Edward Jay Epstein

The problem of journalism in America proceeds from a simple but inescapable bind: journalists are rarely, if ever, in a position to establish the truth about an issue for themselves, and they are therefore almost entirely dependent on self-interested "sources" for the version of reality that they report.

Walter Lippmann pointed to the root of the problem more than 50 years ago when he made a painful distinction between "news" and truth. "The function of news is to signalize an event; the function of truth is to bring to light the hidden facts, to set them into relation with each other, and make a picture of reality on which men can act." Because news-reporting and truth-seeking have different ultimate purposes, Lippmann postulated that "news" could be expected to coincide with truth in only a few

From *Between Fact and Fiction: The Problem of Journalism,* by Edward Jay Epstein. Copyright © 1975 by Edward Jay Epstein. Reprinted by permission of Random House, Inc.

limited areas, such as the scores of baseball games or elections, where the results are definite and measurable. In the more complex and ambiguous recesses of political life, where the outcome is almost always in doubt or dispute, news reports could not be expected to exhaust, or perhaps even indicate, the truth of the matter. This divergence between news and truth stemmed not from the inadequacies of newsmen but from the exigencies of the news business, which limited the time, space, and resources that could be allotted to any single story. Lippmann concluded pessimistically that if the public required a more truthful interpretation of the world they lived in, they would have to depend on institutions other than the press.

Contemporary journalists would have some difficulty accepting such a distinction between news and truth. Indeed, newsmen now almost invariably depict themselves not merely as reporters of the fragments of information that come their way, but as active pursuers of the truth. In the current rhetoric of journalism, "stenographic reporting," where the reporter simply but accurately repeats what he has been told, is a pejorative term used to describe inadequate journalism; "investigative reporting," on the other hand, where the reporter supposedly ferrets out a hidden truth, is an honorific enterprise to which all journalists are supposed to aspire. In the post-Watergate era, moreover, even critics of the press attribute to it powers of discovery that go well beyond reporting new developments.

Yet despite the energetic claims of the press, the limits of journalism described by Lippmann still persist in basically the same form. Individual journalists may be better educated and motivated today than they were 50 years ago, but newspapers still have strict deadlines, which limit the time that can be spent investigating a story; a restricted number of news "holes," which limit the space that can be devoted to elucidating the details of an event; and fixed budgets, which limit the resources that can be used on any single piece of reportage. Today, as when Lippmann wrote, "The final page is of a definite size [and] must be ready at a precise moment."

Under these conditions, it would be unreasonable to expect even the most resourceful journalist to produce anything more than a truncated version of reality. Beyond this, however, even if such restraints were somehow suspended, and journalists had unlimited time, space, and financial resources at their disposal, they would still lack the forensic means and authority to establish the truth about a matter in serious dispute. Grand juries, prosecutors, judges, and legislative committees can compel witnesses to testify before them—offering the inducement of immunity to reluctant witnesses and the threat of perjury and contempt actions to inconsistent witnesses; they can subpoena records and other evidence, and test it all through cross-examination and other rigorous processes. Similarly, scientists, doctors, and other experts can establish facts in a disputed area, especially when there is unanimous agreement on the results of a particular test or analysis, because their authority and technical expertise are accepted in their distinct spheres of competency. Such authority derives from the individual reputation of the expert, certification of his *bona fides* by a professional group which is presumed to have a virtual monopoly of knowledge over the field, and a clearly articulated fact-finding procedure (such as was used, for instance, in establishing the erasures on the Nixon tapes). Even in more problematic areas, such as the social sciences, academic researchers can resolve disputed issues. Acceptance of such an academic verdict, however, will depend heavily on the qualifications of the researcher, the degree to which his sources are satisfactorily documented, and the process of review by other scholars in the field through which, presumably, objections to the thesis are articulated and errors corrected. In all cases, a necessary (though not sufficient) condition for establishing the truth is the use of an acceptable procedure for examining, testing, and evaluating evidence.

Reporters possess no such wherewithal for dealing with evidence. Unlike the judicial officer, journalists cannot compel a witness to furnish them an account of an event. Witnesses need only tell reporters what they deem is in their own self-interest, and then they can lie or fashion their story to fit a particular purpose without risking any legal penalty. Nor can a journalist test an account by hostile cross-examination without jeopardizing the future cooperation of the witness. Indeed, given the voluntary nature of the relationship between a reporter and his source, a continued flow of information can only be assured if the journalist's stories promise to serve the interest of the witness (which precludes impeaching the latter's credibility). In recent years, journalists have cogently argued that if they are forced to testify before grand juries about their sources, they will be cut off from further information. The same logic applies with equal force to criticizing harshly or casting doubts on the activities of these sources. The misreporting of a series of violent incidents involving the Black Panthers in 1969 is a case in point: the reporters closest to the Black Panthers could not dispute their public claim that an organized campaign of genocide was being waged against them without jeopardizing the special access they had to Panther spokesmen.

Moreover, since journalists generally lack the technical competence to evaluate evidence with any authority, they must also rely on the reports of authoritative institutions for their "facts." A reporter cannot establish the existence of an influenza epidemic, for instance, by conducting medical examinations himself; he must rely on the pronouncement of the Department of Health. (A journalist may of course become a doctor, but then his authority for reporting a fact rests on his scientific rather than journalistic credentials.) Whenever a journalist attempts to establish a factual proposition on his own authority, his conclusion must be open to question. For example, following the overthrow of the Allende government in Chile in 1973, *Newsweek* carried a dramatic report by a correspondent who claimed to have gained entrance to the Santiago morgue and personally examined the bodies of those killed after the coup. By inspecting the hands of the corpses, and the nature of their wounds, the correspondent concluded that these were workers with callused hands who had been brutally executed. When the *Wall Street Journal* challenged these findings (on the basis of inconsistencies in the description of the morgue), the reporter acknowledged that he personally had spent only two minutes on the scene, and *Newsweek* fell back on an earlier unpublished report of a UN observer who claimed to have witnessed something similar in the Santiago morgue at some different time. While the dispute remained unsettled, the burden of proof

was shifted from *Newsweek*'s own reporter to an outside "authority."

Finally, journalists cannot even claim the modicum of authority granted to academic researchers because they cannot fulfill the requirement of always identifying their sources, let alone documenting their claims. Protecting (and concealing) the identity of their informants is a real concern for journalists, and one on which their livelihood might well depend, but it also distinguishes the journalistic from the academic product. Without identifiable sources the account cannot be reviewed or corroborated by others with specialized knowledge of the subject. Even the most egregious errors may thus remain uncorrected. For instance, in what purported to be an interview with John W. Dean III, the President's former counsel, *Newsweek* reported that Dean would reveal in his public testimony that some White House officials had planned to assassinate Panama's head of government, but that the plan was aborted at the last minute. This *Newsweek* "exclusive" was circulated to thousands of newspapers in an advance press release, and widely published. When it turned out that the story was untrue—Dean did not testify about any such assassination plot, and denied under oath that he had discussed any substantial aspects of his testimony with *Newsweek* reporters—*Newsweek* did not correct or explain the discrepancy. Presumably, Dean was not the source for the putative "Dean interview," and the unidentified source had misled *Newsweek* on what Dean was planning to say in his public testimony. Since the error was that of an unidentified source, *Newsweek* did not feel obligated to correct it in future editions.

It is not necessary to belabor the point that gathering news is a very different enterprise from establishing truth, with different standards and objectives. Journalists readily admit that they are dependent on others for privileged information and the ascertainment of facts in a controversial issue (although some might argue that the sphere of measurable and noncontroversial issues is larger than I suggest). Indeed, many of the most eminent journalists in America submitted affidavits in the Pentagon Papers case attesting that "leaks" and confidential sources are indispensable elements in the reporting of national news. And despite the more heroic public claims of the news media, daily journalism is largely concerned with finding and retaining profitable sources of prepackaged stories (whether it be the Weather Bureau, the Dow Jones financial wire service, public relations agencies, or a confidential source within the government). What is now called "investigative reporting" is merely the development of sources within the counter-elite or other dissidents in the government, while "stenographic reporting" refers to the development of sources among official spokesmen for the government. There is no difference in the basic method of reporting.

Even in the case of Watergate, which has become synonymous with "investigative reporting," it was the investigative agencies of the government and not the members of the press who assembled the evidence, which was then deliberately leaked to receptive reporters at the *Washington Post*, the *Los Angeles Times*, *Time*, and other journals. Within a week after the burglars were caught in Watergate in June 1972, FBI agents had identified the leaders of the break-in as employees of the Committee for the Reelection of the President (and former employees of the White House), traced the hundred-dollar bills found in their possession to funds contributed to President Nixon's reelection campaign, and interviewed one of the key conspirators, Alfred Baldwin, who in effect turned state's evidence, describing the wire-tapping operation in great detail and revealing that the transcripts had been delivered directly to CRP headquarters.

This evidence, which was presented to the grand jury (and eventually in open court), was systematically leaked by investigative agents in the case. (Why members of the FBI and the Department of Justice had become dissidents is another question.) The crucial evidence which the FBI investigation did not turn up—such as the earlier burglary of Ellsberg's psychiatrist, the offers of executive clemency, the intervention with the CIA, the suborning of perjury, the cash payoffs made from campaign contributions, the "enemies list," and the 1970 subversion control plan—came out not through "investigative reporting," but only when one of the burglars, James McCord, revealed his role in the cover-up to Judge John Sirica and when John Dean virtually defected to the U.S. prosecutor and disclosed the White House "horror stories." Indeed, it was John Dean, not the enterprising reporters of the Washington press corps, who was the real author of most of the revelations that were at the heart of the present federal conspiracy indictments and the impeachment inquest. (And it was Ralph Nader, another non-journalist, who unearthed the contributions from the milk industry.) To be sure, by serving as conduits for the interested parties who wanted to release information about Watergate and other White House abuses of power, journalists played an extremely important role in the political process—but not as investigators or establishers of the truth.

The reliance on "leaks" or "authoritative" sources might not be an insoluble problem for journalism if reporters had some means of evaluating them in advance and publishing only those portions which did not distort reality by being either untrue or out of context. Unfortunately, however, the inherent pressures of daily journalism severely reduce the possibility of verifying a leak or disclosure in advance of publication. Reporters can of course seek out more than one source on an issue, but there is no satisfactory way available, other than intuition, to choose among conflicting accounts. The democratic criterion of adding up confirming and disconfirming interviews, as if they were votes, produces no decisive result, as even total agreement might simply mean that a false account had been widely circulated, while total disagreement might mean that only the original source was privy to the truth about an event.

"Plausibility" is also an unsatisfactory criterion for evaluating leaks, since the liar is always capable of fashioning his account to fit the predispositions of the journalist to whom he is disclosing it, and thereby to make it appear plausible. Nor can a reporter simply give weight to the source that is most intimately involved with the issue, since those closest to a dispute might have the greatest interest in distorting or neglecting aspects of it, and might well be the least impartial. In certain instances, leaks, if publication were delayed, could be tested by the direction of unfolding events—for example, the advance disclosure of John Dean's testimony could have been refuted if *Newsweek* had delayed its story until Dean actually testified—but such a procedure would undercut the far more basic journalistic value of signaling the probable direction of events before they fully unfold. Given these circumstances, a journalist has little basis for choosing among conflicting sources. The *New York Times* thus carried two completely contradictory reports of the same insurrection in the Philippines in different sections of the same Sunday edition (February 17, 1974). The "News of the Week" section placed the casualties at 10,000 dead or missing, while the general news section refuted this higher figure and placed the total casualties at 276. Both accounts were based on sources within the Philippine government, and the editor of each section simply chose the account he preferred.

When journalists are presented with secret information about issues of great import, they become, in a very real sense, agents for the surreptitious source. Even if the disclosure is supported by authoritative documents, the journalist cannot know whether the information has been altered, edited, or selected out of con-text. Nor can he be certain what interest he is serving or what will be the eventual outcome of the leak.

Consider, for example, the disclosures by the columnist Jack Anderson of the minutes of a secret National Security Council meeting on the 1971 Indo-Pakistani war for which he was awarded the Pulitzer Prize for national reporting. Anderson claimed that the blunt orders by Dr. Henry Kissinger in these private meetings to "tilt" toward Pakistan contradicted Kissinger's public professions of neutrality; this claim received wide circulation, and sharply undermined Kissinger's credibility (although the *Wall Street Journal* demonstrated by printing the public statements to which Anderson referred that Kissinger was in fact consistent in both his private and public statements in expressing opposition to the Indian military incursion into East Pakistan). At the time it was generally presumed that the leak came from a dissident within the administration who favored India or, at least, opposed the administration's policy in the subcontinent. Only two years afterward, as a by-product of the Watergate investigation, was some light cast on the source of the leak. A White House investigation identified Charles E. Radford, a Navy yeoman, who was working at the time as a stenographer, as the proximate source of the National Security Council minutes supplied to Anderson. But the investigation further revealed that Yeoman Radford was also copying and transmitting to members of the Joint Chiefs of Staff highly classified documents in a "surreptitious operation" apparently designed to keep them aware of Kissinger's (and the President's) negotiations. And Yeoman Radford has testified that he acted only on the express orders of the Joint Chiefs of Staff, and not on his own initiative, in passing documents. If this is indeed the case, it would appear that members of the Joint Chiefs of Staff authored the Anderson leak in order to undermine the authority of Henry Kissinger (who was involved in developing the détente with China and Russia at that time). In this case, Anderson was used as an instrument in a power struggle he probably was unaware of—and which might have had nothing to do with the Indo-Pakistani war he was reporting on.

The important question is not whether journalists are deviously manipulated by their sources, but whether they can exert any real control over disclosures wrenched from contexts to which they do not have access or with which they are unfamiliar. In most circumstances, the logic of daily journalism impels immediate publication which, though it might result in a prized "scoop," divorces the journalist from responsibility for the veracity or consequences of the disclosure. Jack Anderson was thus able to explain a blatantly false report he published about the arrest for drunken driving of Senator Thomas Eagleton, then the vice-presidential nominee of the Democratic party, by saying that if he had delayed publication to check the allegation he would have risked being scooped by competitors.

But even in rare cases in which newspapers allot time and manpower to study a leak, as the New York Times did in the case of the Pentagon Papers, the information still must be revised into a form and format which will maintain the interest of the readers (as well as the editors). Since the Times decided not to print the entire study of the Vietnam war—which ran to more than 7000 pages and covered a 25-year period—or even substantial parts of the narrative, which was complex and academic, sections of the material had to be reorganized and rewritten along a theme that would be comprehensible to its audience. The theme chosen was duplicity: the difference between what the leaders of America said about the Vietnam war in private and in public. The Pentagon study, however, was not written in line with this theme: it was an official Department of Defense analysis of decision making and, more precisely, of how policy preferences crystallized within the department. To convert this bureaucratic study into a journalistic exposé of duplicity required taking certain liberties with the original history: outside material had to be added and assertions from the actual study had to be omitted. For example, to show that the Tonkin Gulf resolution (by which in effect Congress authorized the escalation of the war, and which was editorially endorsed at the time by most major newspapers, including the New York Times and the Washington Post) resulted from duplicity, the Times had to omit the conclusion of the Pentagon Papers that the Johnson administration had tried to avoid the fatal clash in the Tonkin Gulf, and had to add evidence of possible American provocations in Laos, which were not actually referred to in the Pentagon Papers themselves.

Journalists, then, are caught in a dilemma. They can either serve as faithful messengers for some subterranean interest, or they can recast the message into their own version of the story by adding, deleting, or altering material. The first alternative assures that the message will be accurately relayed to the intended audience, although the message itself might be false or misleading. The latter alternative, while lessening the source's control over the message, increases the risk of further distortion, since the journalist cannot be aware of the full context and circumstances surrounding the disclosure. In neither case can journalists be certain of either the truth or the intended purpose of what they publish. Such a dilemma cannot be remedied by superior newsmen or more intensive journalistic training. It arises not out of defects in the practice of journalism, but out of the source-reporter relationship which is part and parcel of the structure of modern journalism.

To some degree, the tension in the dilemma could be alleviated if journalists gave up the pretense of being establishers of truth, recognized themselves as agents for others who desired to disclose information, and clearly labeled the circumstances and interests behind the information they reported so that it could be intelligently evaluated. By concealing the machinations and politics behind a leak, journalists suppress part of the truth surrounding the story. Thus the means by which the medical records of Senator Thomas Eagleton were acquired and passed on to the Knight newspapers (which won the 1973 Pulitzer Prize for disclosing information contained in these records) seem no less important than the senator's medical history itself, especially since copies of the presumably illegally obtained records were later found in the White House safe of John Ehrlichman. (In rifling through Larry O'Brien's personal files, the Watergate burglars were probably looking for material damaging to O'Brien and the Democrats; if they had succeeded, such material would no doubt have found its way into print by being leaked to "investigative journalists.") Similarly, the motives and circumstances behind the well-timed leaks to the press by elements in the Nixon administration which ultimately forced Justice Abe Fortas from the

Supreme Court do not necessarily make a less important part of the story than any of the alleged improprieties committed by Fortas. And the leaks provided by senior executives in the FBI and other investigative agencies in an attempt to resist White House domination still remain the unreported part of the Watergate story.

Since journalists cannot expose these hidden aspects of a story without damaging the sources they are dependent on for information (and honors), they cannot realistically be expected to label the interest behind any disclosure. (Indeed, it is a practice among journalists to mislead their readers by explicitly denying as occasion arises that they received information from their real source.) Under these conditions, journalism can serve as an important institution for conveying and circulating information, and signaling changes in the direction of public policy and discourse, but it cannot serve as a credible investigator of the "hidden facts" or the elusive truths which determine them.

The Lower case

In an emotional speech, Mayor Lawrence W. Lorensen told aldermen that Smaha had received telephone death threats warning him that he and the mayor would be shot if he took the job.

The council then approved the appointment of Smaha, 42, by a 7-6 vote.

Quad-City Times 8/14/79

Boston, Oct 1, Reuter--Pope John Paul II at the start of his seven-day visit to the United States urged young Americans tonight to seek escape from responsibility through selfishness, sex, drugs, violence or indifference.

Middle-Aged Men Get New Fun From Organs

The Daily Yomiuri (Tokyo) 8/28/79

Thanks to God
New Miss America was crippled

Democrat and Chronicle (Rochester, N.Y.) 9/10/79

Nofziger to Advise Curb on the Media

SACRAMENTO—Lt. Gov. Mike Curb, whose relations with the press have been at best marginal, plans to hire as a media adviser veteran political consultant Lyn Nofziger, a longtime strategist for Ronald Reagan.

Los Angeles Times 9/27/79

Even in the Yankee bastion of Hartford, Conn., the National Association for the Advancement of Colorado People, reports a notable increase in Klan activity over the past six months.

Rocky Mountain News 8/26/79

Defective show unofficially starts new TV season

Toronto Star 8/24/79

G.A.O. STUDY ASSERTS THAT OIL COMPANIES WORSENED SHORTAGE

The New York Times 9/14/79

GAO Says Oil Firms Aren't to Be Blamed For Recent Shortage

The Wall Street Journal 9/14/79

School homecoming queer a former football player

The Frederick (Md) Post 10/16/79

Piqua Man Peddles Self Into Health

The Columbus Dispatch 8/17/79

Nicaragua sets goal to wipe out literacy

The Boston Globe 10/1/79

Two innings later, Jefferson was beaned in the back of the head by a line drive off the redhot bat of Mariner all-star Bruce Bochte. Jefferson was not injured on the play; the baseball, which ricocheted all the way to right field, was taken to hospital for X-rays.

Toronto Globe and Mail 8/21/79

The Lower case

Two Soviet ships collide, one dies

The Blackfoot, Idaho, News 11/1/79

Teachers Strike Annoying Students

Palm Beach (Fla.) Post 11/21/79

Deficit goal met, but budget is 'fair to poor,' Carter says

Chicago Tribune 1/18/79

Iran executes 7 more, cancels scholarships

Chicago Tribune 7/27/79

More bad mushrooms

NEW BRITAIN, Conn. (AP) — Five more persons were charged Wednesday in the mushrooming investigation of alleged corruption in New Britain's city government, state police reported.

Greenwich Time 11/15/79

Democrats in Empire State Building for 1980 Senate Race

The Washington Post 8/19/79

LONDON—Zimbabwe Rhodesian guerrilla leaders demanded Monday that a Commonwealth peacekeeping force of several thousand armed men—one with teeth—be set up to enforce a cease-fire in the war between their forces and white-led troops of the government of Prime Minister Abel Muzorewa.

Los Angeles Times 11/20/79

PM-VIRGINIA NEWS ADVISORY, Wire Desks:
Upcoming within 15 minutes will be an explosion damaging the Greene County government building.

The AP 10/24/79

No Permit Needed For Accidents

The Times Argus (Barre-Montpelier, Vt.) 11/5/79

Obituaries
Area
Ms. Michelle O'Brien, 39, of Wistar Village Drive, a tired employee of Richmond Newspapers Inc.

Richmond Times-Dispatch 11/25/79

Police seek woman's Id

The Highland Parker (Highland Park, Mich.) 10/18/79

Pages 97–98: Reprinted from *Columbia Journalism Review* (November/December 1979 and January/February 1980). Excerpts from *Dog Helps Squad Bite Victim* by The Trustees of Columbia University. Copyright © 1965, 1966, 1967, 1970, 1971, 1972, 1973, 1974, 1975, 1976, 1977, 1978, 1979 by Graduate School of Journalism, Columbia University. Copyright © 1980 by Trustees of Columbia University, the City of New York. Reprinted by permission of Doubleday & Company, Inc.

chapter 6

ON
TELEVISION
NEWS

As seen in the readings in Chapter 5, newspapers can distort reality. Distortion, when it occurs, can be purposeful (as when journalists shield their sources) or accidental (as in the case of a flubbed headline).

Newspapers have received their share of criticism for distortion, but not nearly as much as television news programs. TV news is criticized mostly because of distortion caused by superficiality, and the print media have been the loudest critics. In the first reading in this chapter Eric Sevareid, the retired CBS news anchorman and commentator, strikes out against the print media for their criticism of television news.

Sevareid manages to turn many of the standard criticisms of television into praise, including its effect on conversation, reading, and the English language in general. In doing so, he gives us a good introduction to the issues that arise out of the differences between print and broadcast journalism. In the second reading, David Brinkley builds on those differences to argue that TV news ought to present only news that is interesting to its audience. In the final reading J. M. Sullivan, a teacher, editor, and freelance writer, reacts directly to Brinkley's ideas.

WHAT'S RIGHT WITH
SIGHT-AND-SOUND JOURNALISM

Eric Sevareid

A kind of adversary relationship between print journalism and electronic journalism exists and has existed for many years. As someone who has toiled in both vineyards, I am troubled by much of the criticism I read. Innumerable newspaper critics seem to insist that broadcast journalism be like *their* journalism and measured by their standards. It cannot be. The two are more complementary than competitive, but they *are* different.

The journalism of sight and sound is the only truly new form of journalism to come along. It is a *mass* medium, a universal medium; as the American public-education system is the world's first effort to teach everyone, so far as that is possible. It has serious built-in limitations as well as advantages, compared with print. Broadcast news operates in linear time, newspapers in lateral space. This means that a newspaper or magazine reader can be his own editor in a vital sense. He can glance over it and decide what to read, what to pass by. The TV viewer is a restless prisoner, obliged to sit through what does not interest him to get to what may interest him. While it is being shown, a bus accident at Fourth and Main has as much impact, seems as important, as an outbreak of a big war. We can do little about this, little about the viewer's unconscious resentments.

Reprinted from *Saturday Review* (October 2, 1976): 18–21. Copyright 1976 Saturday Review. Used by permission.

Everybody watches television to some degree, including most of those who pretend they don't. Felix Frankfurter was right; he said there is no highbrow in any lowbrow, but there is a fair amount of lowbrow in every highbrow. Television is a combination mostly of lowbrow and middlebrow, but there is more highbrow offered than highbrows will admit or even seek to know about. They will make plans, go to trouble and expense, when they buy a book or reserve a seat in the theater. They will not study the week's offerings of music or drama or serious documentation in the radio- and TV-program pages of their newspaper and then schedule themselves to be present. They want to come home, eat dinner, twist the dial, and find something agreeable ready, accommodating to *their* schedule.

For TV, the demand-supply equation is monstrously distorted. After a few years' experience with it in Louisville, Mark Ethridge said that television is a voracious monster that consumes Shakespeare, talent, and money at a voracious rate. As a station manager once said to a critic, "Hell, there isn't even enough mediocrity to go around."

TV programming consumes 18 to 24 hours a day, 365 days of the year. No other medium of information or entertainment ever tried anything like that. How many good new plays appear in the theaters of this country each year? How many fine new motion pictures? Add it all together and perhaps you could fill 20 evenings out of the 365. As for music, including the finest music, it is there for a twist of the dial on any radio set in any big city of the land. It was radio, in fact, that created the audiences for music, good and bad, as nothing ever had before it.

Every new development in mass communications has been opposed by intellectuals of a certain stripe. I am sure that Gutenberg was denounced by the elite of his time—his device would spread dangerous ideas among the God-fearing, obedient masses. The typewriter was denounced by intellectuals of the more elfin variety—its clacking would drive away the muses. The first motion pictures were denounced—they would destroy the legitimate theater. Then the sound motion picture was denounced—it would destroy the true art of the film, which was pantomime.

To such critics, of course, television is destroying everything.

It is destroying conversation, they tell us. Nonsense. Nonconversing families were always that way. TV has, in fact, stimulated billions of conversations that otherwise would not have occurred.

It is destroying the habit of reading, they say. This is nonsense. Book sales in this country during the lifetime of general television have greatly increased and well beyond the increase in the population. At the end of a program with Hugo Black, we announced that if viewers wanted one of those little red copies of the Constitution such as he had held in his hand, they had only to write to us. We received about 150,000 requests—mostly, I suspect, from people who didn't know the Constitution was actually down on paper, who thought it was written in the skies or on a bronze tablet somewhere. After my first TV conversation with Eric Hoffer, his books sold out in nearly every bookstore in America—the next day.

TV is debasing the use of the English language, they tell us. My friend Alistair Cooke, for one. Nonsense. Until radio and then TV,

tens of millions of people living in sharecropper cabins, in small villages on the plains and in the mountains, in the great city slums, had never heard good English diction in their lives. If anything, this medium has improved the general level of diction.

The print-electronic adversary relationship is a one-way street. Print scrutinizes, analyzes, criticizes us every day; we do not return the favor. We have tried now and then, particularly in radio days with "CBS Views the Press," but not enough. On a network basis it's almost impossible because we have no real national newspapers—papers read everywhere—to criticize for the benefit of the national audience. Our greatest failure is in not criticizing ourselves, at least through the mechanism of viewers' rebuttals. Here and there, now and then, we have done it. It should have been a regular part of TV from the beginning. The Achilles heel of TV is that people can't talk back to that little box. If they had been able to, over the years, perhaps the gas of resentment could have escaped from the boiler in a normal way; it took Agnew with his hatchet to explode it, some years ago. The obstacle has not been policy; it has been the practical problem of programming inflexibilities—we don't have the 15-minute program anymore, for example. If we could extend the evening news programs to an hour, as we have wished to do for years, we could do many things, including a rebuttal period from viewers. It is not the supposedly huckster-minded monopolistic networks that prevent this; it is the local affiliates. It was tough enough to get the half-hour news; apparently it's impossible to get an hour version.

I have seen innumerable sociological and psychological studies of TV programming and its effects. I have never seen a study of the quality—and the effect—of professional TV criticism in the printed press.

TV critics in the papers tell us, day in and day out, what is wrong with us. Let me return the favor by suggesting that they stop trying to be Renaissance men. They function as critics of everything on the screen—drama, soap operas, science programs, musical shows, sociological documentaries, our political coverage—the works. Let the papers assign their science writers to our science programs, their political writers to our political coverage, their drama critics to the TV dramas.

Let me suggest also that they add a second measurement to their critiques. It is proper that they judge works of fiction—dramas, for example—entirely on the basis of what they see on the little screen because in that area the producers, writers, and performers have total control of the material. If the result is wrong, *they* are wrong. News and documentaries are something else—especially live events, like a political convention. Here we do not have total control of the material or anything like it. On these occasions, it seems to me, the newspaper critic must also be a reporter; he must, if he can, go behind the scenes and find out why we do certain things and do not do other things; there is usually a reason. In the early days such critics as John Crosby and Marya Mannes would do that. A few—Unger on the *Christian Science Monitor*, for example—still do that, but very few.

Let me suggest to their publishers that a little less hypocrisy would become them. Don't publish lofty editorials and critiques berating the culturally low common denominator of TV entertainment programming and then feature on the cover of your weekly TV supplements, most weeks of the year, the latest TV rock star or gang-buster character. Or be honest enough to admit that you do this, that you play to mass tastes for the same reason the networks do—because it is profitable. Don't lecture the networks for the excess of violence—and it *is* excessive—on the screen and then publish huge ads for the most violent motion pictures in town, ads for the most pornographic films and plays, as broadcasting does not.

Now, at this point the reader must be thinking, what's this fellow beefing about? He's had an unusually long ride on the crest of the wave; he's highly paid. He's generally accepted as an honest practitioner of his trade. All true. I have indeed been far more blessed than cursed in my own lifework.

But I am saying what I am saying here—I am finally violating Ed Murrow's old precept that one never, but never, replies to critics—because it has seemed to me that someone must. Because the criticism exchange between print and broadcasting is a one-way street. Because a mythology is being slowly, steadily, set in concrete.

Why this intense preoccupation of the print press with the broadcast press and its personae? Three reasons at least: broadcasting, inescapably, is the most personal form of journalism ever, so there is a premium on personalities. The networks are the only true national news organs we have. And, third, competition between them and between local stations is intense, as real as it used to be between newspapers.

So the searchlight of scrutiny penetrates to our innards. Today we can scarcely make a normal organizational move without considering the press reaction. Networks, and even some stations, cannot reassign a reporter or anchorman, suspend anyone, discharge anyone, without a severe monitoring in the newspapers. Papers, magazines, wire services, don't have to live with that and would very much resent it if they did.

We live with myths, some going far back but now revived. The myth that William L. Shirer was fired by Ed Murrow and fired because he was politically too liberal. He wasn't fired at all; but even so good a historian as Barbara Tuchman fell for that one. The myth that Ed Murrow was forced out of CBS. At that point in his great career, President Kennedy's offer to Ed to join the government, at cabinet level, was probably the best thing that could have happened to him. The myth that Fred Friendly resigned over an issue of high principle involving some public-service air time. There are other such myths, and a new generation of writers are perpetuating them in their books, which are read and believed by a new generation of students and practitioners of journalism.

We have had the experience of people leaving, freely or under pressure, then playing their case in the papers to a fare-thee-well; they are believed because of that preconceived image of the networks in the minds of the writers. What does a big corporation do? Slug it out with the complainant, point by point, in the papers? Can it speak out at all when the real issue is the personal character and behavior of the complainant, which has been the truth in a few other cases? It can't. So it takes another beating in the press.

There is the myth that the CBS News Division —I am talking about CBS, of course, because it is the place I know and because it is the network most written about these days—has been somehow shoved out to the periphery of the parent corporation, becoming more and more isolated. What has happened is that it has achieved, and been allowed, more and more autonomy because it is fundamentally different from any other corporate branch. Therefore it is more and more independent.

There is the myth that the corporation is gradually de-emphasizing news and public affairs. In the last 16 years since CBS News became a separate division, its budget has increased 600 percent, its personnel more than 100 percent. It does *not* make money for the company; it is a loss leader, year after year. I would guess it spends more money to cover the news than any other news organization in the world today. This is done because network news servicing has become a public trust and need.

There is the myth that since the pioneering, groundbreaking TV programs of Murrow and Friendly, CBS News has been less daring, done fewer programs of a hard-hitting kind. The Murrow programs are immortal in this business because they were the *first*. Since then we have dealt, forthrightly, with every conceivable

controversial issue one can think of—drugs, homosexuality, government corruption, business corruption, TV commercials, gun control, pesticides, tax frauds, military waste, abortion, the secrets of the Vietnam War—everything. What shortage has occurred has been on the side of the materials, not on the side of our willingness to tackle them.

In case I had missed something myself, I have recently inquired of other CBS News veterans if they can recall a single case of a proposed news story or a documentary that was killed by executives of the parent organization. Not one comes to anyone's mind. Some programs have been anathema to the top executive level, but they were not stopped. Some have caused severe heartburn at that level when they went on the air. Never has there been a case of people at that level saying to the News Division, "Don't ever do anything like that again."

For 13 years I have done commentary—personal opinion inescapably involved—most nights of the week on the evening news. In that time exactly three scripts of mine were killed because of their substance by CBS News executives. Each one by a different executive, and none of them ever did it again. Three—out of more than 2000 scripts. How many newspaper editorialists or columnists, how many magazine writers, have had their copy so respected by their editors?

There is the perennial myth that sponsors influence, positively or negatively, what we put on the air. They play no role whatever. No public-affairs program has ever been canceled because of sponsor objection. Years ago, they played indirect roles. When I started doing a 6:00 P.M. radio program, nearly 30 years ago, Ed Murrow, then a vice-president, felt it necessary to take me to lunch with executives of the Metropolitan Insurance Company, the sponsors. About 14 years ago, when I was doing the Sunday-night TV news, a representative of the advertising agency handling the commercials would appear in the studio, though he never tried to change anything. Today one never sees a sponsor or an agency man, on the premises or off.

There is the myth, which seems to be one of the flawed premises of so successful a reporter as David Halberstam, that increased corporate profitability has meant a diminished emphasis on news and public affairs. The reverse, of course, is the truth.

There is the new myth, creeping into print as writers rewrite one another, that an ogre sits at the remote top of CBS Incorporated, discouraging idealistic talents down the line, keeping the newspeople nervous, if not cowardly. His name is William S. Paley, and the thesis seems to be that the tremendous growth of CBS News in size and effectiveness, its unmatched record of innovation and boldness in dealing with public issues, its repeated wars with the most powerful figures of government and business, have all taken place over these 40 years or more in spite of this man's reluctance or downright opposition. The reverse is much closer to the truth. *Only* with a man of his stripe could all this have been done. Think what it is to sit up there all those years, whipped by gales of pressures from every public cause group, politicians, Presidents, newspapers, congressional committees, the FCC, affiliates, stockholders, and employees, individually and organized. To sit up there under unrelenting pressures of an intensity, a massiveness, rarely endured by any print publisher and still keep the apparatus free and independent and steady on its long course. After all, in this country networking might at its inception have become an appendage and apparatus of government; it might have gone completely Hollywood. It did neither. It grimly held to every freedom the law allows, and it fights for more. This has not been accomplished by weak or frightened men at the top.

I am no appointed spokesman for William Paley. We are not intimates. I owe him nothing; I have earned my keep. I have not got rich. I have had my differences with him, once or twice acutely. I have been a thorn in his side a number of times. But we had our differences out, and never once was his treatment of me less than candid and honorable. He is now in the evening of his career; I am now pretty much the graybeard of CBS News. I must soon go gently into that good night of retirement. But I shan't go so gently that I shall not say what I think of the mythologists who now surround us, what I think of these ignorant assaults on Paley. It would be cowardly of me not to say that many of these critics are simply wrong—wrong in their attitude, wrong in their premises, repeatedly wrong in their facts.

We are not the worst people in the land, we who work as journalists. Our product in print or on the air is a lot better, more educated, and more responsible than it was when I began, some 45 years ago, as a cub reporter. This has been the best generation of all in which to have lived as a journalist in this country. We are no longer starvelings, and we sit above the salt. We have affected our times.

It has been a particular stroke of fortune to have been a journalist in Washington these years. There has not been a center of world news to compare with this capital city since ancient Rome. We have done the job better, I think, than our predecessors, and our successors will do it better than we. I see remarkable young talents all around.

That's the way it should be. I will watch them come on, maybe with a little envy, but with few regrets for the past. For myself, I wouldn't have spent my working life much differently had I been able to.

A QUESTION FOR TELEVISION NEWSMEN: DOES ANYONE CARE?

David Brinkley

Television is a mature and serious news medium, and it is time we who work in it had our own standards of news judgment, instead of those handed down to us from the newspapers.

It is time to do things our own way, to meet the needs of our audiences and the strengths and the weaknesses of the medium we work in.

Why should we develop our own standards? Those we inherited are pretty good. They've served the newspapers well for a long time, and the public is used to them.

And, if it is news in a newspaper, is it not also news on radio and television? No.

No, it is not, and for a basic reason we all know but tend to forget. The basic reason we are different is that in a newspaper you can skip around, read what is interesting to you, and ignore the rest. While on a news broadcast you have to take it as it comes, in order.

A newspaper can print items most of its readers don't care about, because those who don't care about them can skip them, and go on to something else. We can't.

So, what does that mean? In my opinion, it means we should not put a story on the air unless we believe it is interesting to at least 10

Reprinted with permission from *TV Guide*® Magazine. Copyright © 1977 by Triangle Publications, Inc. Radnor, Pennsylvania.

percent of the audience. Preferably more. But at least 10 percent.

For example, one night last summer we put on the "NBC Nightly News" a two-minute story about the Lebanese civil war. There was a little military skirmish on the front line, and we ran two minutes on it with great confidence and assurance that this was important news.

But was it? That night I spent a little time thinking about it. Why did we put that on the air? Who, in this country, really cared about it?

Who really cared about it? Lebanese living in the United States? Even if they do, they're a tiny fraction of 1 percent of our population. Americans who have business or other interests in Lebanon? How many can that be? A fraction of 1 percent? Foreign-policy specialists, government and private? How many can that be? A fraction of 1 percent?

Ordinary working Americans like the rest of us? A fraction of 1 percent? That is not enough.

The Middle East is of great interest to Americans, but Lebanon is peripheral to the area we're concerned about. It has very little effect on the lives, hopes, problems, needs, fears, or future security of Americans sitting at home looking at television. In my judgment, 99.9 percent of them did not give a damn.

What I concluded in thinking about it that night was that practically nobody was interested in our story from Lebanon and that the two minutes we devoted to it were an utter waste of effort, money, and air time.

So why did we put it on? Because nobody stopped to ask all these questions. Because the decision was made by habit, by rote, unthinkingly. Wars are always news, aren't they?

Well, no, they aren't. It depends on who's fighting whom and what they're fighting about and what the consequences are likely to be.

We couldn't even use the excuse that the story was easy to get. It wasn't. It was hard, dangerous work for a correspondent and a camera crew and it was sent to the United States by satellite, which is expensive.

And in the end, after all the work, danger, time, and money, who really wanted to see it? In my opinion, almost nobody.

But even so, we do that kind of thing frequently, if not every day.

Because we continue—in radio and television—making news judgments by habit, by rote and formula developed over the years by the newspapers and inherited by us.

This is not to be critical of the newspapers. I enjoy reading them, have worked on them, and may sometime do so again. The good ones do their job very well.

But their structure and format are so totally different from ours that very few of their rules and habits are relevant to broadcasting. We follow them, nevertheless. We really ought to stop it.

The Lebanon story is only one example. We could all think of many more.

If news is something worth knowing that we did not know already—as it is—then the appropriate test is: Worth knowing to whom? And to how many? The right question to ask is:

Who really cares about this? Does anyone care and should anyone care?

It's a question we often forget to ask ourselves. If we did, and built our programs accordingly, we'd have bigger audiences, better served . . . which is supposed to be our job.

Obviously, applying this little test would not eliminate foreign news and shouldn't. It would not eliminate any particular kind of news. It would not eliminate news our viewers are not informed about but which they would find interesting if we did inform them.

But it would eliminate a lot of stuff, like the Lebanon story, that we put on without really thinking about it because it sort of looks like news, or sounds like it, even though when you get down to it, it is not.

Of course, there are days, as we all know, when material of any kind is scarce, and we have to use what we can get, including some we know is not great, but air time is air time and it has to be filled.

On those days we all just do the best we can.

But on the days when we have a choice, I don't want to see a news program filled with jokes and laughs and light stories about children and cats and dogs and the reporters elbowing each other in the ribs and laughing it up. We have more than enough of that.

I do not suggest more light or frivolous news or more laughs. What I do suggest is that the news judgments the newspapers and wire services have developed over the generations may be fine for them, but not for us. We should stop using their habits and practices and develop our own.

We should not bore the audience any more than necessary.

TV NEWSMEN
—STOP CHEATING MY
CHILDREN!

James Michael Sullivan

For some time now, David Brinkley, the NBC newsman who spends a half-hour each night in many of our homes, has been writing and lecturing on a particular media issue. It is an issue which demands a strange kind of professionalism from his colleagues. Brinkley is claiming that news stories should not be broadcast which do not "interest" 10 percent of the audience.

Thus does Brinkley plea for the final cop-out of his news industry. We already have the glamorous and golden-tongued, making the TV newscaster the consummate cosmetic image. Now, we are to reach even greater professional depths and present only that news which lends itself to the same cosmetic appeal. Let us not, Brinkley has decided, involve ourselves in that complicated, yet critical, area of values and social judgment. Let us pretend that the only news there is is the news we want—a clear value judgment to be sure.

Brinkley's notion will probably receive wide support, however. It fits hand in glove with the contemporary American social philosophy— whatever turns you on is good and deserves to be propagandized; whatever does not make you thrill should be ignored as if it did not exist.

Reprinted from *Intellect* (April 1978). Copyright 1978 by Society for the Advancement of Education.

As Brinkley has mentioned, and quite correctly, a civil war in Lebanon is probably of interest to only a fraction of 1 percent of the population. He goes on to draw the logical, if simplistic, conclusion given our social norms today—forget it. It does not interest people, therefore it is not worth reporting. Let the newspapers handle it.

A quarter-century ago, that argument, given the competition between the media for their shares of the American audience, was defensible. Profit, after all, is still the name of the game when you are running a business.

Two important factors have come into play in recent years, however, which poke a few holes in this argument. First, television is not simply a business anymore. It is a powerful social force which has yet to define or have defined limits for itself. Second, if people did, indeed, supplement their news intake from other media, TV could surely make some case for determining what, for it, is newsworthy. Yet, polls consistently show that the great majority of people, if they do take in news at all, take it in from TV and not from newspapers, magazines, or the radio, as they did in yesteryear.

Brinkley may look at this as a chance to narrow his sights and his responsibilities. It may, on the other hand, be regarded as fantastic opportunity and challenge.

Television is in the values business, like it or not. Network presidents may not intend it to be so, and their networks are run as if it were not so, but the evidence is too overwhelming to deny that, regardless of intent or actual management, the effects of television on an individual and on a society must be considered in full and frightening range.

I want my children to have, as part of their TV diet, as many issues and opinions as can possibly be presented to them. Children believe that little machine far more than they should. However, as long as it is there and unavoidable in its social scope, I want television to do a job parallel to its influence. Yes, I want them to know of a tiny, forgotten civil war in a tiny, forgotten country—so that they'll turn and ask me what it is all about and so that their father, in turn, will feel put upon enough to try and find out the answer.

The TV newsman represents a business and a tradition greater than television. I don't care what *medium* Joseph Pulitzer or Walter Lippmann or Edward R. Murrow worked in. Theirs was not a tradition of radio or TV or magazine or paper—it is a tradition of *news-reporting* and it is a tradition that has a right and a responsibility to endure.

SUPERFICIALITY

Television news today suffers from much more than a "tell them what they want to hear" syndrome, however. The narrowing scope of news coverage has been quickly followed by an easy superficiality. Network bosses argue that, in the average 22 minutes per broadcast in which they have to deliver the news, full justice cannot possibly be done to each story, feature, or issue. Expand the broadcast? The idea has been toyed with, yet the conclusion is always the same—the *people* won't stand for it. They want their news fast and simple. Thus, in

yet another way, do network "leaders" jettison their responsibility to that cornerstone of audiovisual communication—creativity. Where is the experimentation, the studies, the pilot projects, the trial and error incorporating all different possibilities which might offer some proof that more than 22 minutes of an evening news show is completely unworkable? It is such failure of creativity in areas where it counts the most that poses a serious threat to our children's understanding of their world and contributes to our own superficiality as a people.

There isn't enough time in a few minutes of nightly news to address the causes of specific issues. The complex fabric of social, political, and economic factors which create a race riot or a religious war or a Third World revolutionary movement is not explored—not because it is impossible, but because it is not expedient for network management. It is this continual insistence on controlling and manipulating the news so that it might be neatly packaged into two-minute presentations that is so dangerous. Content with the illusion of control such news packaging gives us, we are unchallenged to probe deeper into the problems of our day, searching meaningfully for a solution or at least some grounds for hope. Our politicians, moreover, have sensed our contentment with the superficial and have responded to it in kind.

The newsbroadcaster's lack of sensitivity to root causes, then, has implications which echo through our social and political system. When no parallels are drawn, when no context is established, we may as well be watching "I Love Lucy" reruns, for, although information is imparted, it does not challenge us with the consequences of the history we are a part of. We are not learning or growing or understanding. Even that video violence of the century, the Vietnam War, seems to have taught us little about war or history or ourselves. What TV news coverage of that war did do was confirm that even violence at its most hideous could lull us into apathy.

At its most simplistic, television consecrates competition of opposites—success or failure, Democrat or Republican, win or lose, guilty or innocent, yes or no. As Harris has noted, "A conflict must always be established, a race, a contest; and, whenever possible, someone must be drawn into the trap saying something provocative about someone else. Addicts of the media become confined to limited alternatives. No third, no fourth, no limitless possibilities exist, nor even shades of those we have. There isn't time."[1]

Thus does television news remain part of our contemporary problems, rather than part of our solutions. In its refusal to challenge and upset, it feeds existing prejudices. The very criteria it uses for judging a story newsworthy necessarily coincide with a predetermined value system and a particular view of economics and social philosophy. Let us not forget that it is network sponsors, with their own particular value systems and world views, who pay the bills.

We must never overlook the fact that television news considers itself bound to values only of its own choosing. Of course, the values of honesty, fair play, etc. are first in line and taken for granted—television fortunately inherited what consumers had traditionally demanded of other media—but sponsors measure a program's "effectiveness" in dollars and cents, and it is the overriding value of profit which can cause great harm to any so-called "unbiased" and "impartial" reporting. As Harris notes: "During the months of Watergate, thousands of people suffered starvation; the world was progressively endangered by military expansion and ecological neglect. By what corruption of values were the crises of Richard Nixon a million times as newsworthy as the facts of human starvation? . . . Starving people are bad box-office."[2]

We have demanded little of television or its newscasting in the nearly three decades of its history. It has, in turn, demanded little of us. Too often, it assures for us only a measuring up to our least common social denominators, hindering our maturity as individuals and as a society. It cannot be denied that some attempt to raise reporting standards and coverage has been in evidence (documentaries and specials on the oil industry, energy crisis, forced bussing, etc.). These deserve praise as far as they go—which, unfortunately, is not far enough. Included in this number is not the pseudo-documentaries on pornography and violence —sensationalism masquerading as journalism. Nor is intensive television coverage to be confused with the reporter who crassly jams a microphone into the face of a grieving widow or a terminally ill cancer patient. This too appeals to the more base dimensions of our psyches, distracting us from the more vital issues of our day.

We have not, in this brief article, touched on all the dangers and disappointments of television journalism. Hopefully, we have focused on a few core issues that point out what is keeping TV news from becoming the positive social force that it has the potential to become. We could write whole other articles on the news reporting of other media which have long neglected their commitment to the public. Yet, until a more powerful medium comes along, this is the day of television. It is an extremely difficult and demanding enterprise. What we ask of the Brinkleys and the Cronkites, the Chancellors and the Walters, and the host of "news consultants" who so critically influence the industry is a sense of responsibility. On behalf of our children and their futures, we seek from these people an accountability proportionate to television's all-pervasive influence.

1. Mark Harris, "The Last Article," *New York Times Magazine* (October 6, 1974).
2. *Ibid.*

chapter 7

ON TELEVISION ENTERTAINMENT

As we move deeper into Part II, we move into media genres that have been subjected to harsher and harsher criticism for their misrepresentation of reality. Criticism of newspapers has been light compared to criticism of television news, and criticism of television news has in turn been light compared to the criticism of television entertainment. It seems as though every person who has learned to write has written at least one essay decrying the low state of television entertainment and the way it is warping us as individuals. The readings that follow are admittedly a small sample of this body of literature, but I have tried to make it a representative sample.

The first reading, by professor/scriptwriter Joan Vail Thorne, examines television's distortion of family life. The second reading, by Benjamin Stein, author of *The View from Sunset Boulevard*, gives some of the reasons television tends to distort everyday life. The third reading examines yet another type of distortion: the distortion of history through "docudramas." In the fourth reading philosophy professor Paul Kurtz of the State University of New York (Buffalo) discusses some of the possible implications of this type of distortion. Finally, Richard Hawley, a high school dean, takes a look at how television influences his students' norms of behavior and taste.

THE TUBULAR FAMILY

ANY RESEMBLANCE TO PERSONS LIVING
OR DEAD IS PURELY COINCIDENTAL

Joan Vail Thorne

Once upon a Sunday, an extraterrestrial being beamed his infinitudinal antennae toward the planet Earth, and began to pick up vaguely intelligible signals from the southwestern coast of the continent of North America. Quite by chance, the Being had intercepted a video telecast of the vastly popular family drama, "All in the Family." Being a computer by nature, and a "panthropologist" by trade, IT immediately embarked on the first interplanetary surveillance of the institution of the family as seen through the tube of a television receiver, and IT's first printout bore the title "The Tubular Family." When the complete report was discovered by earthly explorers of outer space light years later, it was promptly classified "Science Fiction," and filed in the archives of interplanetary documents with the following warning: "Any resemblance to persons living or dead is purely coincidental." However, because the contents may prove interesting to students of the family, the society, and the leading entertainment medium of the late twentieth century in America, they have been summarized and analyzed in the following article.

Reprinted from *New Catholic World* (March–April 1978): 57–60. Copyright 1978 New Catholic World. Used by permission.

End of fairytale! To the author of which Archie Bunker, of "All in the Family" fame, would undoubtedly say, "So what are *youse*? Some kind of *subvoisive prevert*, or *sumump*? *Toining* out that *peeseudo* science *friction.*"

"Hope not, Archie," I'd have to answer. "But as much an alien to family television drama as any Martian could be. Having never before this month of November 1977 watched a single episode of any of the shows mentioned here, I came to them as unspoiled as any extraterrestrial creature. But being entirely terrestrial, I brought human experience to compare them with. And I have to say that I was dismayed and deluded."

"Don't talk *doity!*"

"I won't, Arch. Just personally, honestly, and openly."

Any advocate of the ten dramas that are explored and deplored, commended and condemned can justifiably argue that this commentary is misleading, and not representative of the ongoing process of television, for my "surveillance" lasted only ten days (from November 6 through November 16, 1977). It therefore brings no indictment against a whole season's offerings or an overall producing philosophy. It simply makes observations and records impressions. Unfortunately, judgments are often the offspring of the instant.

"But I like *you*, Archie, the best! You're my favorite."

"Don't you cotton-mouth me, you weirdo. I'm a *foist* class citizen of the U.S. *of* A."

The Bunkers *are* my favorite television family, and fast becoming the most famous family in America. However, it still can be said that Archie bears no resemblance to any *one* American, living or dead, because he is the collective portrait, or caricature, of so many Americans. In his arrogance, self-righteousness, simplicity, selfishness, insensitivity, stubbornness, downright ignorance, and inexplicably redeeming vulnerability, Archie is an archetype, a collection of clichés given life by art. Yes, art—the most popular folk art of the twentieth century, television.

The Commedia dell' Arte would have welcomed Archie Bunker. Ben Jonson and Molière would have tipped their hats to him. He is brother to their children, a creature of comedy in that he exposes society's scandals and sacrileges in satire and in laughter. He and Lucy are the two television characters that surely have the life blood of comedy in their veins. It is interesting that both of them are as much the creations of their performers as of their creators.

In two connected episodes of "All in the Family" in early November, contemporary society's drug dilemma became Archie's and Edith's temporary undoing. And in a rerun of the same period, recession and unemployment were the plagues on their house.

Archie is also the only decent competition Mrs. Malaprop has had in all these years, and when he lets go with "Harper's Brassiere" or "Jan Fierce" or "Ralph Noodle" or "Lazarus rising from the bed" or "prostate server," Richard Brinsley Sheridan must turn green with envy in his grave.

Despite their indiscretions, Archie, Edith (who deserves attention all her own that time prohibits), Gloria, and Mike offer the most consistently high quality family comedy to be seen on television. Like all archetypes, they afford the audience recognition *and* removal: "It takes one to know one," *and* "He's worse than I am."

In the Bunkers we *recognize* our nuclear families with their traditional male-female roles, subservient offspring, and unwelcome in-laws. But, with all our secret predispositions and prejudices, we can *remove* ourselves from the errant bigotry, chauvinism, and self-indulgence of which Archie Bunker is a master. His wise-fool wife Edith bears with him, and so do we. Society wouldn't suffer the social ills it does if there weren't Ediths to the Archies in us all.

In spite of themselves, there appears to be an unmistakable strength in the Bunker family. They fret together, they endure together, they even fight together. In the drug episode of November, when Archie was at the pit of his post-drug depression and had taken to his bed and set the alarm for 1997, Edith insists on lying by his side "until death do us part." Then Gloria and Michael join them, and the bed breaks down. It may seem singularly simpleminded on paper, but it made true farce on the tube. The family is alive and well, not exactly heroic, but let's risk "archetypal" in "All in the Family."

The Tubular Family sadly deteriorates from here on down; as its content softens, so does its form suffer. Enter the canned laughter, or the liquid saccharine. Having begun with "the best," we now begin the irreversible descent to "the banal."

The first step is seldom a leap, and we slip gently down to two more entirely "bearable" family dramas, "The Fitzpatricks" and "Eight Is Enough," more alike than dissimilar, even in their differences. Both are "too good to be true," "too true to be good," and too numerous to be typical. The Fitzpatricks have six children, and widowed Tom Bradford has eight. Neither of these families is an archetype. Both are American stereotypes—domestic moralities with Sunday school themes, Home Sweet Home samplers, beguiling as the youngest children in them. One of these, young Nicholas Bradford in "Eight Is Enough," is played by perhaps the most appealing child actor to have graced the Great Grey Tube in all the years of its existence. I should have liked the opportunity of watching these two programs in the company of a small child, for despite their usual sentimentality, they are capable of sentiment, and it takes only a child to tell the difference.

Any abhorrer of the violence on television must be vastly relieved to have these options. The Fitzpatricks and the Bradfords are pleasant, sometimes poignant alternatives. They can even be honest. Tom Bradford, the father of the Eight, is actually balding, and the actor, Dick Van Patten, has the courage, in this hirsute culture, to play him that way. I only regret that his thinning hair is always so perfectly combed. Do you ever wonder where the wind went in Hollywood? Then there are those early morning lines for the bathroom. Didn't anyone ever go to bed? There doesn't seem to be a rumpled nightgown or a tousled head or a bad breath among them.

Contrast this with the opening scene of a recent Carlo Ponti movie entitled *A Special Day*, wherein a family is seen, better scrutinized, getting up in the morning, and you will weep at the transparent dishonesty of the usual use of a medium that may have, above all others, eyes fit for the truth—microscopic or telescopic upon command.

If the dishonesty is obvious, so is the interaction of these two families with their cultures. In the several episodes I saw, the institution of the church figured in both: a wedding for the Bradfords, beautifully Protestant and pure, and a First Communion for the Fitzpatricks—no liturgical comment. The secular rituals of society were also featured in both: the Olympics to which a young Fitzpatrick lost his young love, and a local beauty contest in which a young

Bradford honed her ego by losing. Both fathers are observed in their economic roles—Fitzpatrick's blue collar, and Bradford's white. And both families sing their hymns to the cultural god of togetherness. The lambs are allowed to stray, but they are always found, *if* the actor renews his contract. It's a shame: the family problems are sometimes real, but the resolutions of them are always fabricated, tailored to the last five minutes of the strict half-hour, and ultimately unreal and phony.

The second stage of descent is far more precipitous. It takes us from "the bearable," always acceptable, sometimes delightful "Eight Is Enough" and "The Fitzpatricks" to the utterly "banal" "Happy Days" and "Good Times." In the episodes I saw, "Happy Days" was an affront to the nuclear family, and "Good Times" was as vapid and synthetic as any "white" hypocrisy, sufficient indeed to set the civil rights movement back to Birmingham.

In both, the poor old family—phony as it seems to be—serves only as a setting, a handle, an umbrella for other inanities. In "Happy Days" the Cunninghams are a flimsy excuse for 1950s nostalgia. Even the star performer, the famous Fonz, is but an upstairs boarder who behaves like nothing human I've ever encountered. What an unlikely guru for the conventional wisdoms of middle-class morality: be yourself, go to college, don't let reform school get you down! How a nation could become enamored of such an anomaly must be evident in the episodes I've never seen. Elvis Presley's immortal hips and Tom Jones' immortal chest may be erased from the American consciousness by the Fonz's cool-cat hands and feet. I found it frightening to consider that this creation is the role model for modern American youth. The Cunningham family is but fodder for contrast—their conventionality against this anti-hero's aberration.

In "Good Times" the family is a poor excuse for "ethnicity," as the programmers are wont to call it. But the sample I saw of it was so adolescent and silly as to be a disgrace to the people it presumably dignifies. For anyone who stores either *A Raisin in the Sun* or *For Colored Girls Who've Considered Suicide When the Rainbow Is Enough* in the treasures of his or her memory, "Good Times" is an anthology of one-liners performed by poor actors looking for laughs.

If the three categories of "Martian" criticism have up to this point gracefully eluded the reader's comprehension, it is time they be owned up to. In the top category of "the best" there is only one entry, "All in the Family"—an admittedly ironic choice since it is its own indictment of the institution of the family and the American social structure it spawns and buttresses. But it is forthright, funny, and unashamed, and it is, at its best, folk art of the finest comic quality.

In the middle bracket of "the bearable"—and sometimes better—are "The Fitzpatricks" and "Eight Is Enough." And in the bottom barrel of "the banal" are "Happy Days" and "Good Times." It is important to note that the industry's designation for these last two shows is not "family drama" but "situation comedy." When viewed from that perspective, they are partially acquitted of their aesthetic and thematic crimes. If they are designed for canned laughter, they get what they deserve. But the poor family they pretend to portray suffers from acute plasticity all the same!

Now for the exceptions that beg, if not break, the rule. First, the show that bears the name of the whole category, where the family is, ironically, still only a backdrop, this time for "melodrama." In one episode of that show, "Family," the Lawrence's son, Willie, a young man in his early twenties, has become inordinately attached to a homeless black boy, and in another the 14-year-old daughter, Buddy, is confronted, alienated, and ultimately saddened by an equally young girl friend's alcoholism. Although the mother and father participate indirectly in the drama and counsel their children about the handling of their respective problems, it is evident that the plots could quite easily have excluded them, and that their on-screen time is telltalingly minimal. The redeeming feature of this program lies in the thoroughly professional and restrained performances of James Broderick and Sada Thompson as the father and mother. But the fact remains that this family drama is a menu of far-ranging melodramas in disguise.

Two more exceptions to the triple categories of family television drama are "the bizarre" shows, "Maude" and "Soap." "Maude" is hardly a family drama; indeed it is not billed by the industry as such, but as another situation comedy. And what family conflicts and crises are in it are exploited, understandably, for laughs. There is a genuinely funny update of the successful best friend-and-neighbor syndrome of "I Love Lucy." But it is the strength of the actress Beatrice Arthur, who plays Maude, that puts this program in a class by itself—one we might clearly classify as "matriarchy" drama.

Far more bizarre than "Maude" is "Soap," the most sensational and controversial newcomer of this season. Perhaps it's the Martian in me, and I'm a bit embarrassed by it, but I cannot report any outrage or shock from either of the two episodes I saw. The show is certainly *not* appropriate for general audiences, and is quite likely to offend some, but there is an "absurdist" dimension to it that intrigues one, and incites a very rare brand of satirical laughter. ("Soap" is clearly indebted to Ionesco and Albee, even if it doesn't know it—a poor relation, the purists would say, but a relation all the same.) The cutting irony here is that those devotees of the traditional soap opera, who feed on a diet of the most deplorable sexual and social ills, would be most likely to deplore "Soap"'s irreverent treatment of the very same material. It is as if the organ (or organlike) accompaniment of the morning and afternoon soaps turned the most secular, hedonist, libertine subjects into sacred fare.

With impotence and sex change and infidelity as staples of the plot, the evening "Soap" blatantly seeks to shock us into laughter, or to laugh us into shock, which paradox bears echoes even of Aristophanes, if you please. After all, *The Sun Also Rises* has been with us for a very long while, Renée Richards *did* play at Forest Hills this September, and infidelity has been Hollywood's lodestone since forever. "Soap" simply says the unspeakable words out loud, instead of only insinuating the secret, silent horrors. Many an artist has been there before it. As one of "Soap"'s characters sums up her personal experience, "That's not life, that's something out of Tennessee Williams."

Two final exceptions—one with deep regret, the other with fiendish delight. For all its historical accuracy, and all its catch-up-with-the-British-courage, CTW's "The Best of Families" is, in short, a bore. Pity! But any Elizabethan could tell you that verisimilitude has nothing to do with art. As for fiendish delight, "The Little House on the Prairie" is absolutely hopeless in every department—as family, as drama, as entertainment, as art—except perhaps as a filler of time that some kind of glorification of violence might otherwise take up.

Is it not ultimately and profoundly ironic that the best known, most shared, and most intimately experienced institution in any society makes its way through the tube in "emperor's clothes"? Any real resemblance of the tubular family, in all its categories, to families living or dead *is* purely coincidental. Why? Why is the largest audience in history, of the most popular art forms in history, willing to accept such counterfeits? In the mornings and afternoons they wallow in traumas that are worse than their own problems—to enjoy the other man's misery? In the evenings they tolerate tinsel incidents that are less than their own lives—to avoid their own misery? Why? Why is escape more desirable than identification? Is the audience getting the drama it wants and deserves, or are the merchants of tubular dreams selling seconds? Is the revelation of art no longer salable, or is it simply no longer available? On a weekly schedule! There's the rub! Can there ever be mass produced, prefabricated, short order art?

There are some amazing family dramas floating around. *Oedipus* is a family drama, *Lear* is a family drama, *The Cherry Orchard, The Glass Menagerie, Death of a Salesman.* It's not the form that's fragile. And it may not be the television medium either. Perhaps it's the weekly turnstile system of production. None of the above masterpieces was wrought in a week, a month, or even a single television season. Once again it's the old American dilemma—quantity versus everything.

Whatever the answers or the explanations, the fact remains that if an extraterrestrial observer *did* monitor the family dramas on American television for ten days in November, IT's idea of the American family would be as mythical as IT's pointed head. However "best," "bearable," or "banal" the tubular families may be, they bear little resemblance to the reality of family life in late twentieth-century America. Reality requires revelation—the discovery of the known but not understood.

EPILOGUE

Once upon two Thursdays, the extraterrestrial being's infinitudinal antennae malfunctioned, and IT never saw "The Waltons." Well, everyone's human . . .

HERE'S WHY LIFE ON TV
IS SO DIFFERENT FROM REALITY

Benjamin Stein

There is, on prime-time television, a unified picture of life in these United States that is an alternate reality. For hours each day, people can leave the lives they are compelled to lead, lives whose limitations and frustrations hardly need to be detailed, and enter a different world that is more pleasant and less difficult in almost every way—life on television.

Most TV shows are set in the present or in a time within the memory of the viewers. Their characters are supposed to be types we are familiar with. While that familiarity may be more imaginary than real, we do see a world on television with which it is not difficult to feel a distant kinship. More than that, we see a world that is extremely appealing in a whole variety of ways. These ways have to do largely with simplification.

The alternate reality that television creates is not a coincidence or a result of random chance. It is the product of the thinking of TV producers and writers about life. We can see reflected on our video screens the attitudes of TV creators. More than that, we can sense the experience and "feel" of a city replicated on television. For what we see on prime-time television is nothing less than the apotheosizing of Los Angeles, and the spreading of the Los Angeles experience across the TV screens of America.

No show displays a kind of life that is anything but immaculately clean and neat, in which people are anything but well-groomed and hygienic and their motivations anything but straightforward.

Today's television is purer, in terms of backdrop and story endings, than the lines of a Mercedes convertible. Every day's shows bring fresh examples. A while ago, I saw an episode of "Charlie's Angels" about massage parlors that were really houses of prostitution. The three beautiful "angels" of the show were compelled to pretend they worked at massage parlors in seamy areas. Anyone who has ever passed by a massage parlor knows that they are invariably dirty, shabby places, with pitiful and degraded denizens. On "Charlie's Angels," the Paradise Massage Parlor compared favorably in terms of cleanliness with the surgical theater at Massachusetts General Hospital. The girls were immaculate and well-groomed, soft of speech and clear of eye and skin.

On "The Waltons", we are supposed to believe that we are in a Depression-era farming town in backwoods Virginia. Anyone who has been to a backwoods farming town in the South knows that, whatever else may be said about them, they are invariably dirty and bedraggled. On "The Waltons," even the barnyard is immaculate. Marie Antoinette could not have asked for more agreeable play-farm quarters.

The grittiest TV show, when it was on, was generally believed to be "Baretta." Yet even there, the supposedly shabby boardinghouses

Reprinted from *The View from Sunset Boulevard* by Benjamin Stein (Basic Books, 1979). Copyright © 1979 Benjamin Stein. Used by permission of the author.

are neat, bright, and cheery. Even the junkies wear fresh clothing and sport recent haircuts.

Why is television so clean? The answer is simple. TV writers and producers replicate the world in which they live in their art, and the world they live in is the superclean, superbright world of Los Angeles, where even the slums are spotless and have palm trees in front.

Until I moved to Los Angeles, I had no idea where the images of television came from. Where on Earth, I wondered, were pastel drugstores, low stucco apartments with balconies overlooking artificial waterfalls in the poor neighborhoods and bars with almost pitch-black interiors, opening onto glaringly bright sidewalks, utterly without litter or refuse? Drive along any boulevard in Los Angeles. There is block after block of pastel drugstores and apartment houses with balconies and artificial waterfalls. Close by are the bars with pitch-black interiors.

When I lived in Washington and in New York, I wondered where in America were all cars bright and shiny, unspattered by mud, with their original colors gleaming in the sun. Where did people have new cars even if they were secretaries or rookie policemen?

In Los Angeles, where everyone spends a few hours a day in a car, everyone has a shiny new auto, even if it is a financial sacrifice. In Los Angeles, where the sun shines every day and rain never falls, cars never get muddy.

Where are policemen handsome, thin, neatly dressed, and polite? They certainly were not in New York or Washington or New Haven or Santa Cruz or anywhere else except in Los Angeles. In Los Angeles, the policemen look like male models, except that they do not look effeminate. They are the models for the ruggedly modish cops on a dozen TV shows.

Among the TV writers and producers I interviewed, whenever people spoke of Los Angeles they spoke of a "fantasy land," "plastic paradise," "wonderland," "sterile concrete," "lotus land," and similar hackneyed phrases that are nevertheless accurate. The writers and producers see and experience a life of cleanness and emphasis on good appearance that would be unbelievable to anyone who did not live in Los Angeles. That has become their image of life, so that when a world is re-created on television, the Los Angeles world, the one in the creators' minds, is the one that comes out. However much the writers and producers may mock and decry the sterility and cleanliness of Los Angeles, it is Los Angeles they are broadcasting around the world as the model environment. The faces, clothes, haircuts, and cars of people on television are the faces, clothes, haircuts, and cars of people walking down Rodeo Drive in Beverly Hills.

But this applies only to the question of appearance. There is also a moral and philosophical world on television, and that, too, has to come from somewhere.

Beyond the physical and visual cleanliness on television is an attitude appealing far beyond most of what real life has to offer. On television, everything ends happily, which might be a way of summarizing the TV climate. There is far more, however. Every problem that comes up on television is cured before the show is over. No one suffers from existential terrors. They are not even hinted at.

On a smaller scale, people on television are not small-minded, nasty folks. No shopping-bag ladies, reeking of urine, stalk a traveler in a crowded subway. No snarling teenagers threaten and mock on a deserted sidewalk. Instead, people move along rapidly on highways and byways. Impediments are cleared out of the way, both visually and psychologically. At the end of 60 minutes, at the most, everything has come up roses, even if there were a few minor thorns along the way.

On television, people get things done. No one spends all day in a windowless office going over musty volumes of figures and regulations, seeking to comply with guidelines and plans laid out by persons long since dead. No one on television spends all day in bed, too lethargic or depressed to get up. On television, in fact, there is no such thing as depression. That most widespread of modern psychic ailments simply does not exist in the alternate world of television. Everyone, good or bad, is charged with energy. If someone wants to do something, he or she simply goes out and does it.

Further, people on television think big. They are no longer concerned with telling Ricky Ricardo how much they spent on a hat. Instead, they think about making a million by selling heroin, or about ridding Los Angeles of the most vicious killer of the decade. In a comedy, a poor family thinks of getting rich. A middle-class family thinks of getting into the upper class. A black family thinks of overcoming racism.

"Out there," for the folks on television, is a big world, full of possibilities. Here, a sharp distinction needs to be made between social activism and personal ambition. The people on television are never interested in social movements. They want money and happiness. They want to be great sleuths or great criminals. They have big plans and hopes for themselves, but not for society.

This entire psychic galaxy is, as far as I can tell, a reflection of the psychic makeup of the Hollywood TV producer and writer. Before I came to the world of TV production I never would have imagined that a group of people as psychologically successful and liberated as TV writers and producers existed. It is their mental world that is up there on the TV screen.

In the world of television are people who are financially successful, creative, living in comfortable surroundings, and generally quite happy. Around a successful TV production company (and the unsuccessful ones quickly vanish), there is an air of confidence and self-satisfaction that is rarely encountered anywhere else.

Those people are highly unusual folk, operating in a highly unusual milieu, and it shows. In the eighth decade of American life in the twentieth century, the working situation of Americans has become steadily more bureaucratized.

Almost everyone coming out of school goes to work for a large enterprise of some kind, finding a spot on a bureaucratic ladder. The worker must flatter everyone over him and worry about everyone under him. His real rewards come not from producing anything, but from pleasing those above him on the ladder.

Workers derive their security and status from the bureaucratic structure in which they find themselves. They are cogs in a vast machinery. There is little or no creativity in their daily lives. Advancement comes with infuriating slowness. To reach a position of financial independence or modest wealth is impossible. Getting that extra few thousand a year in wages becomes the key goal, and few see further than that.

On the other hand, the bureaucratic structure provides a protection against having to actually produce anything. Simply serving one's time at the office is all that is required to get by. Eventually, however, that too takes its toll. The realization that one is doing nothing but serving out a life sentence results in devastating blows to one's self-esteem.

The whole process of the engorgement of institutions and the swallowing up of the individual into large enterprises leads, in my experience, to a smallness of mind. Bitterness and pettiness are generated by the unmixed frustration that is each day's portion.

Imagine, on the other hand, the world of Hollywood. It is a throwback to the world of individual entrepreneurs. Each writer sinks or swims on the basis of his product. Those people do not have to wait in a bureaucratic holding pattern all of their lives. If their product is good, they become successful and important immediately. They are not judged by how well they can accommodate themselves to a paranoid boss's suspicions. Rather, they move along or fall out depending on what they get done. They are immediately able to make themselves independent by having a skill that is in great demand and correspondingly highly paid. They float from contract to contract. Each time they begin a project, they have the opportunity to become millionaires, and many of them do.

A story about Bob Dylan comes to mind. When Dylan started out, he wrote about depressed, crazy people suffering daily crises. After a few years, when his income had risen to eight figures left of the decimal point, he started to write only about happy, cheerful subjects. When asked about the change, he is reported to have said, "It's hard to be a bitter millionaire."

So it is with the people in television. They have many firm and negative opinions about various groups within the society, but they are basically fairly satisfied with life. There may be, and probably are, starving would-be TV writers in North Hollywood and Studio City who are filled with rage and anger. But the ones who have made it, the ones who are working regularly for many thousands a week, are quite content for the most part.

The successful TV writer and producer is a person who gets things done and who feels good about it. After spending years in bureaucracies of various kinds, I found it staggering to see how much each individual writer and producer got done each day. In Norman Lear's T.A.T. Communications, there is a full-time staff of fewer than 50 to get out hundreds of millions of dollars' worth of TV product. If the government had a department of TV comedy, there would be at least 75,000 employees—and they would do nothing. Naturally, each of those few people who are producing so much feels good about it and about himself. The opposite of small-mindedness is generated.

No one is completely or even mostly happy, but the Hollywood TV writers and producers that I met went a long way along that line. They were, and are, people who take risks and live successfully. Their horizons are broad. The small annoyances of life do not faze them unduly. They see life not as a prison sentence but as a garden of rich potentialities.

TV writers and producers are not starving in garrets. They lead fulfilled, productive lives, by most standards. They live those lives in an attractive, uncluttered world of immaculate sidewalks and gleaming new cars, pastel storefronts and artificial waterfalls. They have been a party to striving and success in their own lives, and they have not missed the lesson of the possibilities of life. And it is this way of life that has been translated into the flickering colorful images on hundreds of millions of TV screens.

DO TV "DOCU-DRAMAS" DISTORT HISTORY?

A new wave of television shows and movies mixing fact with fiction is stirring widespread controversy about the role of truth in entertainment.

Reprinted from *U.S. News & World Report* (May 21, 1979): 51–52.

Presentations at the center of the debate include "Ike," a made-for-TV program based on the wartime career of Dwight D. Eisenhower; *The China Syndrome*, a film about an accident at a nuclear power plant, and "Blind Ambition," a TV treatment of the Nixon administration from the viewpoint of John Dean, a disillusioned onetime aide to the former President. Some comedies and dramas, entirely fictional in nature but reflecting real-life situations and values, also have been attacked for alleged distortions.

Much of the criticism is aimed at "docudramas," which scholars say often twist the truth by failing to make a clear distinction between actual events and a writer's imagination. The danger, historians say, is that fact and fiction will be linked forever in the minds of millions of viewers who seldom read much or are rarely presented with serious information from sources other than TV and films. Many scholars fear that distortions of reality may make it harder for democracy to function well in the future.

Observes Richard B. Morris, a leading American historian: "It is very serious when these programs depart from the facts. Even if only 5 percent of the facts are wrong, that could be the crucial part, and much of the public would always have it wrong. Misapprehensions about important events could have serious national consequences."

WARPING HISTORY?

Objections to recent presentations range from claims that some programs unfairly damaged personal reputations to charges that history was warped to accommodate a fictional story line. Members of the Eisenhower family, for example, contested a major theme of "Ike"— that the general and his aide, the late Kay Summersby, were romantically involved.

Attacks also have been leveled at the docudrama "Blind Ambition," even before its May 20 premiere, as well as the dramatic series "Washington: Behind Closed Doors," based on a work by a former Nixon aide, John Ehrlichman. Critics say both programs offer one-sided views of national politics.

Controversy also has engulfed the movie *The China Syndrome*, which opponents say greatly exaggerates the dangers involved in operation of nuclear power plants. Defenders, however, claim that the Three Mile Island reactor accident in Pennsylvania proved that makers of the film were right.

WHAT VIEWERS PERCEIVE

Few, if any, scientific surveys have been made of how much the public's perceptions have been changed by the electronic media. But many scholars are worried about the cumulative effects.

William M. Young, an Illinois educator who studied television violence for the National PTA, observes that misleading TV shows have altered many Americans' perception of the truth. "Both adults and children have been affected," he asserts. "Their misconceptions have put great strains on our society."

Some critics say that many distortions stem from the personal views—not always shared by the general public—of a relatively small number of writers whose works dominate TV and film screens. Ben Stein, a columnist who interviewed dozens of Hollywood writers, says "the homogeneity of the views of television's creative people is almost uncanny." Stein's new book, *The View from Sunset Boulevard*, concludes: "The supermedium of television is spewing out the messages of a few writers and producers (literally in the low hundreds), almost all of whom live in Los Angeles. Television is not necessarily a mirror of anything besides what those few people think."

Among the basic concepts that Stein says are propagated by many of these writers: "Businessmen are bad, evil people." "Military men are either irrelevant or bad." "The typical TV murder involves a well-to-do white person killing another well-to-do white person," although in real life, the perpetrators and victims of such crime "are usually poor, minority-group people."

MISUNDERSTOOD AUTHORS?

Writers themselves acknowledge problems in mixing fact with fiction, especially in stories openly based on history. TV author David W. Rintels notes that writers since Homer have faced similar problems, but concedes that responsibilities are greater on TV because that medium has a "potentially enormous social and political impact" beyond any other form of mass communication. Much of the difficulty, writers say, is that they are widely misunderstood outside the television industry.

"It is wrong to conclude that we all speak with one voice," asserts Melville Shavelson, writer and co-director of "Ike" and former president of the Writers Guild of America. "We have 5000 members in the guild, and we come from every kind of background—conservative, liberal, Easterners, Westerners—and stories on television reflect this diversity."

Shavelson insists that most authors are faithful to the facts, and cites his own experience in creating "Ike." The research and production took two years—a long period for television—

and hundreds of sources, including military files and film archives, were consulted in the process. The author is proud that the series was watched by millions of young people and adults.

"Many kids had incredible notions about the war—even about the role of Hitler," Shavelson notes. "Now, as the result of watching this show, they understand considerably more about that period."

Authors widely concede that some recent presentations have fallen short of the facts, but industry officials insist there is little to be done except to try harder for accuracy the next time. Concludes Rintels: "With foreknowledge that the whole story is never there, that we are at the mercy of incomplete and biased sources, that we are required to condense and telescope to fit program times, that we have to guess at what was said in the bedroom and what was not said, that some participants will exaggerate or minimize their roles in self-serving accounts—we set out to do the best we can."

Copyright 1979 U.S. News & World Report, Inc.

"SOME PEOPLE BELIEVE ANYTHING THEY SEE" ON TV

INTERVIEW WITH PROFESSOR PAUL KURTZ OF THE STATE UNIVERSITY OF NEW YORK

Q: Professor Kurtz, is the American public increasingly mixing fact with fiction as a result of stories on TV and in films?

A: Yes, regretfully. I say "regretfully" because we are the most advanced scientific and technological society in the world and we face very complex problems that require the use of critical intelligence. Yet a whole new generation of people are being confused and overwhelmed by the electronic media and are finding it increasingly difficult to distinguish fiction from reality.

Reprinted from *U.S. News & World Report* (May 21, 1979): 52, 54.

Q: Can you give some examples of what you're talking about?

A: A number of scientists I've been associated with in the last few years are especially concerned about the growth of belief in the paranormal and the occult.

One example is the "Bermuda Triangle," which has been packaged and sold on TV and in books and magazines as true. There are millions of people who believe that there's something mysterious south of Bermuda—that more ships and planes go under or disappear there than anywhere else. But that's not true. If you do a careful scientific analysis, you find that it's largely science fiction at work. No greater number of ships and planes go down, proportionately, south of Bermuda than any other area of heavy traffic, and all that have can be given natural explanations.

The revival of the belief in exorcism, demonic possession, and reincarnation also is incredible. I've taught in universities for 30 years, and until five years ago almost no student would have expressed a belief in reincarnation or devil possession. But now I find that as many as 30 percent of the students, as I lecture around, claim that they believe in this.

When you ask them what their source of information is, they often cite TV shows called "docu-dramas" that mix fact with fiction—sometimes very, very loosely, but so cleverly that it is hard for the layman raised in the television age to sort things out. He thinks it's all true.

Q: Do drama and comedy alter a viewer's ideas of reality?

A: Definitely. Many scriptwriters warp reality by portraying the world from their own personal points of view. The abuses of scientific technology are exaggerated, but its bountiful contributions to modern life are rarely extolled. The bad guy is often the big businessman and never the poor kid from the slums. In real life, of course, there are some good businessmen and some bad guys from the slums, but you'd

hardly know it if you only watched movies and television.

These shows don't indicate that the writers are committed to any particular political ideology. It's more that their stories reflect the thinking of a primitive social romanticism. They have helped to create in the media a general atmosphere of antitechnology and antiscience and a lack of appreciation for traditions such as the free-enterprise system.

Q: Which shows, specifically, have contributed to this?

A: People have been so inundated by movies such as *The Exorcist* or *Audrey Rose* that they tend to believe in prior lives or the operation of mysterious and demonic forces in the universe.

Q: Might this reflect a deep need to believe in something that these people don't find elsewhere?

A: Perhaps to some degree, although it may be nothing more than a fad. What really happens is that fashions and moods develop, and these are furthered by the skillful use of propaganda—conscious or unconscious. These beliefs are something like the ideological religions that were popular in the '20s, '30s, and '40s in many parts of the world. We're witnessing a growth of occultism, and this is being sold to the gullible public. People are fascinated by it. It strikes their imagination and fancy.

It may very well be that the breakdown of certain aspects of traditional religion is more than some people can bear, and so they slide to this new belief in the paranormal.

Q: What sort of belief?

A: There was the case of a rumor that an unidentified flying object had landed and that its occupants were ravaging the countryside. The "proof" offered was that cattle were being mutilated by these creatures—that they were removing the eyes from the cattle and leaving them dead. The truth was that cattle die of diseases in the open fields, and their carcasses are eaten by predators such as rodents. It's a very natural process, but nobody could dissuade the believers in UFOs, fed by the movies and TV.

Cases like that show that some people who need meaning and purpose in this rapidly changing technological world are getting their answers in the wrong places. For millions of Americans, the electronic media have replaced the university as a revered institution for learning. Now the media are also replacing the church. The media have become sacred because they deal with the realm of imagination.

Q: How dangerous would you say this trend is?

A: Very dangerous. When people watch TV for entertainment, that's fine. But it's more than that now; it's the main source of information and education for the American people. The average child spends approximately 50 to 60 hours a week before the tube, and the adult isn't far behind. This is the only kind of knowledge that they get: imagery in color, with sound, shock, horror. If it's not situation comedies and violence on the one hand, it's the paranormal and science fiction on the other.

That's all right if it's labeled and people can make distinctions. What bothers me is that critical judgment is being perverted and polluted. Watching the tube is replacing analysis. Imagery is replacing language and symbols. That is dangerous to a society because it means people can't tell what the truth is. That can be carried over to religion and politics.

Q: What do you mean?

A: The danger is that some people will believe anything they see and that they will buy political or ideological positions the same way. I am afraid of what may happen if there is a further decline in objective or critical thinking—if people are not willing to be skeptical about what they hear or read.

A notable example is the tragic case of the

Rev. Jim Jones and his followers in Guyana. He claimed to be a faith healer, and he used paranormal tricks. He performed psychic surgery—supposedly performing an operation without cutting. What he actually did on the stage before his gawking onlookers was to put his fingers in somebody's throat and pull out chicken gizzards dipped in Mercurochrome—which he had palmed—and then say, "Look, I've cured him of cancer!"

Look at all the gullible people who fell for him. What would happen if a new Reverend Jones comes along on a white horse and assumes political power? That is a possibility that we should not discount, especially since the media are changing our perceptions of the truth.

Q: Why do you think these problems are more serious on TV and in the movies than in books, newspapers, and magazines?

A: Today, books and magazines are aping television. Unfortunately, television is leading the way. The electronic media are far more powerful in intensity; they can really seize a person and capture him. Reading skills are declining. We know how poorly students are doing in the schools and the colleges. People read less and watch more, and it's undermining their ability to judge ideas.

It doesn't have to be this way. Television could be used for constructive means, and the electronic media have the potential for this. It's the abuses that cause so much concern.

Here is an example: I lecture in various universities throughout the country, and many students tell me that they go to fortunetellers or that they believe in psychic detection. About 80 percent of the students I have met believe in extrasensory perception—receiving information outside the ordinary senses. Something like 56 percent believe that unidentified flying objects come from outside the earth. And most of these students base their beliefs on what they have seen on TV and in the movies.

Q: How should we combat media-induced misconceptions?

A: The only solution, I think, is to encourage more diversity, to have more give-and-take of ideas, especially on TV and radio. Now we don't have sufficient debate. The electronic media, for example, do not present sufficient conservative or radical opinion; most of what is presented is lukewarm liberalism. We really don't have—as we should have—a wide range of ideas. We need more dialogue, more debate, more criticism. The segment of the public that is still sophisticated and educated is surely entitled to it. Television is talking down; it should be talking up to the people.

The great difficulty here is that it's almost impossible to deal with this concentration of power in the electronic media. I'm afraid that the fairness doctrine—which is supposed to guarantee that opposing points of view are presented equally on the air—has failed and is not being applied by the Federal Communications Commission. We're not getting balance in the presentation of controversial ideas. Conservative as well as liberal ideas have to be expressed, and at present they're not very often.

Q: How do you think that should be changed?

A: Cable TV, which will open up thousands of channels nationwide, will help to provide alternative voices. Maybe when cable TV is more widespread, we will get more hard-hitting, in-depth treatments of issues, which will enable people to make rational judgments. We need to encourage people to read more and watch less.

Q: Have you sensed in your visits around the country that any particular area is especially willing to accept fiction as fact?

A: One place stands out above all others: Southern California.

Q: Why?

A: I don't know, except that maybe that's where the people go who most believe in these things. The trend is nationwide now, but there seems to be a greater concentration in California than anywhere else.

I was in San Diego last year, and I was taken to a meeting hall which had been rented to a group of believers. Here were 300 people, many of whom were holders of advanced college degrees, who believed in UFOs and creatures from outer space. A woman walked in who was dressed in a very strange costume and told everybody she was from Venus and that she communicated with our "space brothers" on outer-space ships. This was soon after the films *Close Encounters of the Third Kind* and *Star Wars* had appeared, and belief in spacemen was very current.

I asked some of her disciples: "You don't really believe in this, do you? You know, the temperature is at least 800 degrees on Venus. Don't you think she'd burn?" They said: "No, no, no. You don't understand. She's on an ethereal plane." I was floored!

That's what the electronic media are doing to us—making it possible for anyone to believe anything. Indeed, unfortunately this is becoming the age of believing the unbelievable.

Copyright 1979 U.S. News & World Report, Inc.

TELEVISION AND ADOLESCENTS:
A TEACHER'S VIEW

Richard A. Hawley

Ever since its novelty wore off in the fifties, we have all known, really, that television in its commercial form wasn't up to much good. This isn't to say that millions of people don't still depend on it, but dependency is hardly a sign of virtue. Except for Marshall McLuhan's grab-bag theoretics, few claims have been advanced for the improving effects of television. In fact, recently there has been a flurry of publishing activity, most notably Marie Winn's *The Plug-in Drug*, about television as a cause of downright mental erosion. But what I think Marie Winn and others need is a concrete, closely observed, and intensely felt illustration of the larger thesis. That's what I offer here.

Television has a way of intruding into our lives, and last year it intruded into my life and into the life of the school where I work in a way that many of us there will never forget. We had all taken our seats for morning assembly. The usual announcements were read, after which the morning's senior speaker was introduced. Like many independent schools, ours requires each senior to address the student body in some manner before he graduates. Since public speaking is not a widely distributed gift these days, the senior speeches are infrequently a source of much interest or intentional amusement.

Reprinted from *American Film* (October 1978): 52–56. Copyright © 1978 The American Film Institute.

As the curtains parted, we could see that the speaker had opted for a skit. On the stage were a covered table and a number of cooking implements. Out stepped the speaker wearing an apron and chef's hat, which very quickly established that he was going to satirize one of my colleagues who has a national reputation as a gourmet chef. Since this colleague is also a man who can take a joke, the prospects for the skit seemed bright. But not for long.

At first, I think almost all of us pretended that we didn't hear, that we were making too much of certain, possibly accidental, double entendres. But then came the direct statements and a few blatant physical gestures. Then it was clear! This boy was standing before 500 of us making fun of what he suggested at some length was the deviant sexual nature of one of his teachers. The response to this was at first stupefaction, then some outbursts of laughter (the groaning kind of laughter that says, "I don't believe you said that"), then a quieting, as the speech progressed, to periodic oohs (the kind that say, "You *did* say that, and you're in for it").

When he had finished, there was a nearly nauseating level of tension afloat. As the students filed off to class, I made my way backstage to find the speaker. It had by now dawned on him that he had done something wrong, even seriously wrong. We met in my office.

He expressed remorse at having offended a teacher whom he said he particularly liked. (Before the conference I had checked briefly with the teacher and found him badly flustered and deeply hurt.) The remorse was, I felt, genuine. But something was decidedly missing in the boy's explanation of how he came to think that such a presentation might, under any circumstances, have been appropriate. He hadn't, he admitted, really thought about it, and some of his friends thought the idea was funny, and, well, he didn't know. When it occurred to him that serious school action was in the offing, he protested that in no way had he intended the sexual references to be taken sexually—they were, you know, a joke.

I pointed out to him that the objects of such jokes have no way to respond: To ignore the insinuation might affirm its validity; on the other hand, to object vigorously would draw additional attention to the offense and sustain the embarrassment connected with it. I pointed out further that sometimes innocent parties *never* regain their stature after being offended in this manner, and that the injured party was, at the very least, in for a terrible day of school.

The boy became reflective and said, "Was it *that* bad? You can see worse on 'Saturday Night Live.'" I told him I doubted this, but if it were true, and were I in a position to judge, I would be in favor of expelling "Saturday Night Live" from the air. He left the office, and subsequently endured the appropriate consequences.

For my part, I resolved to turn on "Saturday Night Live," and when I did, I realized the student had spoken truly. The show's quick-succession, absurdist comedy spots depended for their appeal on establishing an almost dangerous sense of inappropriateness: exactly that sense created by our senior speaker. To me, for some years a lapsed viewer, it seemed that both the variety and specificity of sexual innuendo had developed considerably since, say, the once daring Smothers Brothers show of the

sixties. What struck me more, however, was how many punch lines and visual gags depended on suddenly introducing the idea of injury or violent death.

I happened to tune in the night a funny caption was put over the documentary shot of Middle Eastern political partisans being dragged to death behind an automobile. Was this funny? I asked my students. They said it was "sick" and laughed. Does this kind of fun trivialize crisis? Trivialize cruelty? Inure us to both? Or is it, you know, a joke?

The right things were said, I think, to our students about the boy's speech. But I can't say the situation improved. Not more than a couple of weeks later, a speaker garbed in a woman's tennis dress took the podium and began to talk humorously about the transsexual tennis player Renee Richards. I can't think of a subject harder for an adolescent to discuss before an adolescent audience. Rarely noted for their confidence and breadth of vision in matters of human sexuality, adolescents are unlikely to be objective, sympathetic, or (let me tell you) funny about so disturbing a phenomenon as sex change. This particular boy, whose inflection is very flat and whose normal countenance is especially stony, managed to convey almost a sense of bitterness in making his string of insulting and, in his references to genitals and to menstruation, awfully tasteless cracks.

So there it was again: the inappropriateness, the tension. This time the injured party was remote from our particular world, so the hastily arranged conference with the boy turned on general considerations of taste and judgment. This time, however, the speaker was recalcitrant: We could disapprove of his speech and discipline him if we chose, but we ought to know that we could hear the same thing on television.

At that moment something clicked for me. Not only did my brief exposure to "Saturday Night Live" convince me that, yes, I would hear the same thing on television, but I was suddenly struck with the realization that he was using television as an arbiter of taste—that is, *as an arbiter of good taste.* I began to see in this premise a common ground upon which he and I could at least argue. Both of us were in agreement that what is broadcast over television ought to be acceptable; our point of disagreement was his feeling that broadcasting something over television *made* it acceptable. Alarming as such a feeling is to me, it is not hard to see how it has developed over the past few decades.

Until the middle sixties, with the exception of the very earthiest plays and novels, the values of home and school and the values of the popular culture were fairly continuous; if anything, radio, television, and motion pictures were more staid than real life. Of course, all this would change very quickly—not because change was requested or even consented to, but because it wasn't, perhaps couldn't be, resisted. And suddenly there it all was at once: the most embarrassing expletives as common speech; every imaginable kind of sexual coupling depicted in ever increasing candor; obsessively specific wounds, mutilations.

These formerly unacceptable kinds of stimulation made their way more easily into the relatively insulated world of print and film than they did into the more communal world of the television set. Television is typically viewed in homes, and what is communally seen and heard must be communally integrated, or there will be friction. Since American households— set-holds?—share this communal experience for an estimated two to seven hours per day, the potential for friction is considerable. This is why, on grounds of taste, criticism of television programming tends to be more bitter and more relentless than criticism of books and films.

Television foes and partisans alike continue to advise, with some reason, that those who object to certain programs ought not to watch them. But given the impossibility of monitor-

ing the set at all hours, control over the amount and quality of viewing is difficult to maintain even in principled, surveillant households. Too, some viewers will insist on being their brother's keeper. Not everyone who is convinced that what is beaming over the national airwaves is inhumane, unscrupulous, or scurrilous is going to fight to the death for the networks' right to be so.

For many people, television is no longer on the polite side of real life. This is an obvious observation about a novel development, one whose consequences are only just dawning on us. A realist or an existentialist may argue that the unflappably suburban world of "Father Knows Best" revealed none of the complex, ambivalent, and often irrational forces at work in real families: But it is hard to argue that "Father Knows Best" in any way *contributed* to those dark forces. On the contrary, it is possible to argue—although one hesitates to carry it too far—that the theme of Father Knowing Best serves as a psychologically soothing backdrop to the prickly dynamics of real family life. And while today's most highly rated shows suggest that the prevailing seventies' theme is Nobody Knows Anything, there are still apparently enough viewers who like Father Knowing Best to support series like "The Waltons" and "Little House on the Prairie."

Sometimes the theme is compromised in a typical seventies' manner, of which "James at 16" provides a good example: The parents are cast very much in the Robert Young–Jane Wyatt mold, but their son James is, to borrow a phrase, kind of now. By far the most interesting thing he did was to lose his virginity on prime time. The 15-going-on-16-year-old boys I work with, many of them at least as sophisticated as James, typically hold on to their virginity a bit longer, until the disposition of their sexual feelings is under surer control. The best clinical evidence maintains that the process of bringing newly emergent sexuality under control is *in-*

herently delicate and troublesome. James's television plunge planted the anxiety-provoking notion in the mind of the adolescent viewer that he was sexually lagging behind not only the precocious kid down the block, but the Average American Boy character of James. (One was allowed to be less anxious when Father Knew Best.)

Why shouldn't television make people anxious? say the producers of programs that make people anxious. After all, the *world* is anxious. (An awfully self-serving position: Programs that arouse anxiety are relevant; those that don't are enjoyable.) Before long, this line of argument begins to lay claim that programs which bring up irritating subjects in an irritating manner are performing a valuable social mission. Norman Lear, the producer of comedies such as "All in the Family" and "Maude," makes such a claim. According to the Lear formula, a controversial topic will be raised, tossed around for laughs, then either discarded or resolved. Resolution occurs when one of the characters tolerates or forgives the controversial person or practice, while some other character, usually a combination of lovable old coot and ass, does not.

As many critics have pointed out, this is only apparent resolution. Nothing much really happens to a racial or sexual conflict when it is laughed at (a device that is supposed to soften outright slurring and stereotyping), discarded, tolerated, or forgiven. The idea that "if we can joke about it this way, we have taken a humanitarian stride" is mistaken. There is plenty of evidence, particularly among the student population, that, for one thing, race relations are more strained today than they were a decade ago. No one would want to claim that racism among youth disappeared during the politically active sixties; however, a claim can be made that when a student was confronted then with having made a racial slur, he seemed to be aware of having violated a standard.

Who is to say that Archie Bunker hath no sting? More and more television comedians, in the manner of Don Rickles, seek *only* to sting. It is really an empirical question, not a matter of taste, whether or not it is harmless, much less healing, to denigrate everybody, including oneself. A hit song by Randy Newman insults small people; this is no parody of unkindness or bigotry, but the real thing. My students understand it perfectly and parrot it enthusiastically. Rebuked, they grimace in exasperation. Nothing in their youthful experience tells them that bigotry is a sign of cultural regression ("It isn't bigotry; it's, you know, a joke"). They prefer to see whatever wicked delights crop up in the media as a progressive casting off of prudish inhibitions. According to such a view, progress is whatever happens next.

Toleration of the intolerable is always worrying, but it is especially so when it takes place among the young, in whom we want to invest so much hope. Tolerating the intolerable is part of a dynamic, not a static, process; the intolerable, when it is nurtured, grows.

Which brings me back to the senior speeches. Two so thoroughly inappropriate presentations in a single year represented a high count for us, so we were not ready, at least I wasn't, for the third.

This time the talk was about a summer spent working on a ranch, and the format was that of a commentary with slides. No apparent harm in this, but there were a number of factors working against the speech's success. The first was that the speaker was renowned for being a card, a reputation the welcoming ovation insisted he live up to. Second, he had not adequately rehearsed the projection of the slides, so that they tended to appear out of order and askew, the effect of which was to provide a subtextual comedy of visual nonsequiturs. Third, he chose to capitalize on the audience's nearly unrestrained hilarity by playing up certain questionable references.

The speaker made a fairly good, not too inappropriate crack about a slide which depicted a bull mounting a cow—"Sometimes the corrals get so crowded we have to stack the cattle on top of one another." But he chose to exploit his references to the gelding of bulls. There were, in all, four jokey and brutal evocations of this process which served to keep the image of bull genitalia before our minds for quite a few minutes. Since laughter had already been spent, the castration jokes were met with a kind of nervous applause. Bolstered by this, the speaker closed with a coda to the effect that he would be available after assembly to anybody who wanted tips on "cutting meat."

Since I happened to be in charge that day, I sent him home. It seemed to me, in light of the various reprisals and forewarnings connected with the previous speeches, that this particular performance, though perhaps less offensive in its specific references than the other two, ought to be the last straw. The speaker had clearly exceeded anything required by either schoolboy or cowboy saltiness. He had created an anything-goes atmosphere, and then he had let it go—for which he was applauded. "That was great!" said the boy next to me on the way out of the auditorium.

That morning and afterward scores of students, most, but not all, of them civil, hastened to let me know that they felt it was unfair to have sent the speaker home. Not one of them failed to remind me that I could see worse on television. Had I never seen "Saturday Night Live"? That afternoon an opinion poll went up requesting signatures from those who disapproved of the action I had taken and, in an opposing column, those who approved. Within the hour, hundreds expressed disapproval, only one approved.

For a day or two at school there was an animated atmosphere of martyrdom (the speaker's, not mine), but it dissipated rapidly, possibly because the right to make castration jokes from the stage was not, as a cause, very catalytic. The banished speaker, a very likable boy, returned, was received warmly, and apologized not at all cringingly.

In the calm that has followed, my colleagues and I have taken pains to stress to our students, especially at the commencement of the new school year, that whenever somebody addresses an assembly, it is a special occasion. Speakers are expected to observe definite standards when they speak or perform; audiences are expected to be courteous and restrained. Humor at someone else's expense is out, unless it is prearranged with the party lampooned, and even then it ought not to be inhumane. Excretory and copulatory humor is out; it's too easy. Preparation is important. Being persuasive is important. Being controversial is important. Being funny is a delight to all, though it is harder than it looks.

Perhaps these expectations are high. However, schools, especially parochial and independent schools, are gloriously unencumbered in setting such standards: Schools are often *chosen* for the standards they set, the difference they represent. One of the things schools have an opportunity to be different from is television, for although we are all wired into it and it feels public, like the law, it is actually private, like a door-to-door salesman. We don't have to buy the goods.

Since children who watch a fair amount of television will quite naturally assume they are being told and shown the truth, it seems to me crucial that they are exposed to models who view it selectively and critically, who judge it by criteria other than its potential to engage. My own experience has been that students are surprised, but not hostile, when television programming is harshly judged. I think they may even come to like the idea that they themselves, at their discriminating best, are in the process of becoming people television ought to measure up to.

chapter 8

ON MINORITIES AND WOMEN

The media's distortion of reality can be particularly troublesome when it relates to the depiction of minorities and women. TV is the most common culprit in this issue; since it doesn't do an accurate job of portraying life-in-general, there is little hope that it will do so for minority life. Still, the battle rages as each minority—racial, religious, occupational, or sexual—tries to get television and the other media to depict its members the way they would like to be seen.

The next four readings take sides on our two biggest minority issues: the representation of blacks and the representation of women. These arguments may be considered representative of those concerning most minorities. One side will say the minority is unfairly represented; the other side will say that the media are doing the best they can or that the situation is improving or, as one of the readings suggests, that the media are being *too* fair.

In the first reading in this section Roscoe C. Brown, Jr., the president of Bronx Community College, argues that television presents mostly negative images of blacks. In the second reading John J.

O'Connor, the television critic for the *New York Times*, suggests that television actually goes overboard presenting positive images of blacks—which, to him, is "only distortion in another direction."

In the third reading E. Simson, a writer with a Ph.D. in sociology, points out the evidence and consequences of stereotyping women on television. The final reading in this chapter is by Linda Bird Francke and Lisa Whitman, two *Newsweek* staffers. It tells how the stereotyping of women is lessening, at least in the world of advertising (which was one of the offending areas pointed out by Simson).

LET'S UPROOT TV'S IMAGE
OF BLACKS

Roscoe C. Brown, Jr.

During an eight-day period in January 1977, 130 million Americans tuned their television sets to ABC and, in so doing, contributed to a media phenomenon: "Rootsmania." A record-breaking 85 percent of the viewing public watched at least one episode of this dramatization of Alex Haley's best seller *Roots*. Consistent with the television programming reflex of building on past successes, "Roots: The Next Generations" will have its premiere tonight at 8 on ABC-TV. . . .* The commercial and artistic merits of these TV miniseries aside, the question arises as to whether television's "Roots" made a significant difference in racial attitudes in this country and, more particularly, in the way in which blacks are commonly portrayed on the medium.

A recent U.S. Civil Rights Commission study reported that blacks as portrayed on television continue to be seen in a "disproportionately high number of immature, demeaning, and comical roles." It further stated that minorities, especially black men, were most often portrayed as teen-agers, service workers, or students, particularly during prime time when TV viewing is heaviest. Certainly the portrayal of blacks in such situation-comedies as "Good Times," "What's Happening," and "The Jeffersons" is evidence of this. The comical buffoon "J.J." on "Good Times," the bossy sister on "What's Happening," and the boastful nouveau-riche husband on "The Jeffersons" all reinforce widely held stereotypical beliefs about black people. Each of these characters is a prototype of what some whites would like blacks to be like: "J.J." is the all-knowing black teen-age male whose bravado and self-confidence all too often crumble into a kind of modern-day Uncle Tomism. Dee, the sister in "What's Happening," reinforces the commonly held idea of the woman controlling the males in black families, and George Jefferson of "The

---

*Editor's note: "Roots: The Next Generations" attracted 110 million viewers.

From *The New York Times* (February 18, 1979): B35. © 1979 by The New York Times Company. Reprinted by permission.

Jeffersons" portrays what some whites predict successful blacks would be like—superficial and braggadocious.

The situation is not much better when the action/adventure/detective series that include black characters are examined. Although Bill Cosby was acclaimed for his performances in the "I Spy" series, the character he portrayed could just as readily have been played as a hip white detective; there was little or no distinctive "blackness" to the character other than the fact that a handsome, winning black actor was cast in it. The black detective in the "Tenafly" series of a couple of seasons ago reinforced the idea that today's black male is a tough woman-chaser.

Even when TV a few seasons back tried to "blacken up" its semiserious portrayals of middle-class America, the best it could produce was "Julia," a sepia version of Jane Doe, R.N.

The respectable ratings for such serious TV productions as "The Autobiography of Miss Jane Pittman," "A Woman Called Moses" (the story of Harriet Tubman, the "conductor" of the Underground Railroad), and the recent biographical account of Detroit Tiger baseball star Ron LaFleur (featuring LaVar Burton of "Roots" fame) attest to the fact that the television audience will respond favorably to meaningful portrayals of the black experience. But occasional specials are just not enough when it comes to giving a picture of the lives, hopes, fears, and joys of black Americans. The mere fact that television must conjure up a "special" to tell about the real situation of blacks is an indication of how short-sighted the decision makers of the industry are in their attempts to include blacks as a part of the TV world.

Even dramatic programs that do not focus specifically on the black experience but that have significant black characters often tend to perpetuate the familiar stereotypes. Consider, for example, NBC's miniseries "Backstairs at the White House," the fourth and final install-

ment of which will be shown tomorrow evening. Although faithful in its retelling of the real-life story of Lillian Rogers Parks and her mother, who were maids to Presidents from Taft through Eisenhower, the roles of the "backstairs" blacks—the maids and butlers—perpetuate the stereotype of the loyal, dutiful, all-knowing servant.

Black viewers might watch programs with black characters as a welcome variation from white-only programming, but television's decision makers should visit a supermarket or a beauty shop or a church center in a black community to eavesdrop on what blacks really think about some of these shows. These programs invariably present a white man's imaginings of what a black man's existence, his life, is like. One probable explanation for this is that the decision makers in television are mostly white males, which also accounts for the fact that women, too, as cited in the Civil Rights Commission study, are so often portrayed in stereotypic roles.

Public television's fare with such programs as "Black Perspective on the News," produced in large measure with actual input for blacks, is often commendable; yet, in light of public television's relatively small audiences in comparison with the vast numbers of viewers of commercial programming, the impact is minimal. Some of the local public-affairs programming by commercial stations, such as WABC-TV's "Like It Is," produced by Gil Noble, present a valid picture of black concerns; however, these programs are all too often relegated to unpopular hours in the TV schedule, the aptly nicknamed "Sunday morning ghetto."

Even though the vast majority of Americans saw the first telecast of "Roots," a Lou Harris poll published in April 1977 indicated that the miniseries had little impact on their racial attitudes. Eighty-two percent of those polled felt that "Roots" was "beautifully produced and acted—a real work of art," as opposed to 12 percent who felt it was not. But fewer, 55 percent of the total surveyed, felt that "Roots" was a "highly accurate history of how blacks were treated in slavery." Blacks predictably responded more favorably (76 percent) than whites (52 percent) in the sample. The survey's inquiry as to beliefs held by whites about discrimination against blacks revealed that a majority of white viewers (73 percent) still believed that blacks were not victims of discrimination in obtaining a quality public education as compared with 75 percent of the year before.

The general reaction to "Roots" was certainly favorable and, in the context of what a specific program could do, undoubtedly created a positive climate for discussions of black/white relations. Given the depth of racial attitudes in this country, however, it is probably unrealistic to expect a single TV series to have a lasting and significant influence on race relations.

Television has a lot more to do if it is to portray the black experience with any real honesty. It is possible to portray black family life on television without making every family member a caricature. There have been a few recent efforts along these lines, such as the NBC pilot last spring called "Love Is Not Enough," starring Bernie Casey as a black father raising his children alone. The network, I am told, is preparing a series based on that pilot, which it expects to put on its schedule later this season.

There are any number of dramatic and important factual stories that could show black Americans as strong personalities with commitments to human justice and dignity. One such portrayal could be a televised biography of Dr. Charles Drew, the black doctor who developed the procedure for producing blood plasma. (It is ironic that Dr. Drew died after an automobile accident in a Southern town when he was not given blood transfusions because he was black.) A source that has all the dramatic potential of anything that has been done on television about World War II is a story of the 33rd Fighter Group (of which this writer was a member), which was stationed in southern Italy and flew fighter escort and straffing missions throughout southern Europe. Many of the pilots and support personnel of this group of men are leaders in today's society, including Coleman Young, the Mayor of Detroit; Percy Sutton, the former Manhattan Borough President; Otis Smith, the general counsel of General Motors; William Coleman, the former Secretary of Transportation; Lee Archer, Jr., president of North Street Capitol Corporation; and scores of physicians, lawyers, and Ph.D.'s.

One of the most culturally sensitive epochs in this country's history is part of the story of James Weldon Johnson, the first black Executive Secretary of the NAACP and the co-composer of what has become known as the black national anthem, "Lift Every Voice and Sing." Johnson was one of the most universal men of his time, an ambassador to Latin American countries, a Broadway composer of note, and one of the leaders in the Harlem Renaissance.

If life at the White House is to be dramatized, why not tell the story of the relationship between Franklin Roosevelt's wife, Eleanor, and Mark McLeod Bethune, a member of F.D.R.'s "Black Cabinet," who with Mrs. Roosevelt shattered many of the racist traditions at the White House.

These accounts and others like them could provide sorely needed role models for young people—black and white—on TV screens all across the country.

TOWARD BALANCING
THE BLACK IMAGE

John J. O'Connor

In "Harris and Company," a weekly series currently on a trial run on NBC, the widowed father is noble and saintly enough to make Daddy in "Father Knows Best" look like an insensitive meanie. Normally, this kind of phenomenon might be allowed to pass quietly into the electronic night of failed projects. But, in this case, the father, played by Bernie Casey with his usual stately dignity, is black. And this provides an example, in perfect miniature, of the sensitive question of the portrayal of minorities on television.

Blacks are hardly the only segment of the public to be concerned with the question. Just about all minorities—religious, ethnic, racial, social—harbor factions whose strategy is almost painfully simple: If you don't have anything good to say about them, don't say anything. There are Jews who come out fighting at the slightest criticism of Israel, justified or not. There are Irish who don't like to be reminded of their humble beginnings in this country. NBC's recent dramatization of "Studs Lonigan" drew strong protest from some Irish-Americans, because they found insulting the use of crude language or the scenes of sexual promiscuity or a hundred other details. The fact that these things may have been portrayed accurately is totally beside the point for these Defenders of

From *The New York Times* (March 25, 1979): B33. © 1979 by The New York Times Company. Reprinted by permission.

the Image. For consumption by outsiders, they are content to limit perceptions of the Irish to the lovable slyness of a Barry Fitzgerald in "Going My Way."

The black experience, of course, has been different in several respects. For years, blacks were almost invisible on television, just as they are curiously absent today from so many science fiction films offering visions of the future. Even in the 1960s, it was still possible to generate national headlines when white Petula Clark placed her hand on the shoulder of black Harry Belafonte. In the '70s, blacks made it to the national forum of the situation comedy—"The Jeffersons," "Good Times," "What's Happening." In one sense, this merely proved that blacks had won the opportunity to be as silly as their white sit-com counterparts. But that achievement should not be dismissed lightly. Black audiences began to get regularly scheduled reflections, no matter how superficial, of their own existence on the most pervasive of communications media. At the same time, the black presence became a fixed part of white America's psyche. The very process of television exposure implies acceptance.

The theory persisted, however, that blacks were not likely to be accepted in noncomedy formats. Every time a dramatic series starring black actors failed to get solid audience ratings, network executives would retreat behind I-told-you-so facades. It was rarely noticed that the vast majority of failed dramatic series had no blacks in them, but no one was about to argue that whites be restricted to situation comedies. Ironically, the most popular and acclaimed programs of the past decade have featured black talent and black themes: "The Autobiography of Miss Jane Pittman," "Roots," "Backstairs at the White House," "Roots: The Next Generations." The old theory about blacks not being accepted in noncomedy formats simply won't hold.

Meanwhile, black professionals, in increasing numbers, are understandably pushing for further television gains in both exposure and prestige. And, again understandably, part of that push is concerned with positive images. For one representative example, there is the evolution of "Tony Brown's Journal." Now in syndication to commercial stations, the program began on public television several years ago as "Black Journal." In the beginning, it was militant in espousing such causes as the rights of blacks in prisons. Later, entering what was called a "sophisticated suite" stage, it became a black version of the Johnny Carson show, with Mr. Brown in tuxedo interviewing a broad variety of achievers. Now, the show is more consciously positive. One recent episode, "In the Black," examined the economic clout of American blacks (56 percent own their homes, 52 percent have credit cards) while stressing that there is "too much emphasis on the image of blacks as a disadvantaged community." Interestingly enough, the show's most positive moments are found in the commercials for PepsiCo, sponsor of the series. In those sparkling, lyrical kinds of productions that soft-drink makers favor, several generations of upwardly mobile black families are seen gathering for joyful family reunions. It would be difficult to overestimate the impact of carefully packaged commercials on mass public perceptions.

But accenting the positive can create problems, especially when excesses lead to an outright censoring of the negative. Such an attempt was made a month or so ago at WNET/13

when minority employees at the station objected strenuously to the presentation of "Street Corner Stories," a documentary by Warrington Hudlin. Black working men were shown congregating for several mornings at a corner store in New Haven. Mr. Hudlin, himself black and a former student at the Yale Film School, sought to capture something of the American black storytelling tradition. He explained: "The oral tradition is preserved, very much alive. The guy who can speak well is respected, a sort of secular minister. He has dramatic flair, movement, a very sophisticated body language—and those standing around will comment on the speaker's performance as well as on his story." The storytellers in Mr. Hudlin's documentary spoke of daily survival with compassion and bitter humor, spiked constantly with vivid street language in which obscenities are used like commas and semicolons. Apparently, the images were not positive enough for some of WNET's employees. Protests were registered and the machinery for a well-organized attack on the production began to be set in motion. However, the protesters were unable to mount a full-scale campaign, primarily because there was not enough time to do so before the broadcast date. For himself, Mr. Hudlin maintains that he is, first and last, a filmmaker. He is not interested in the positive and negative aspects of images; he is not a propagandist.

The argument is made that after decades of invisibility or essentially negative projections, the black community is owed compensation in the form of positive images. The point is certainly legitimate. The danger, though, is in overcompensation, which is only distortion in another direction. On the admittedly minor level of "Harris and Company," that is part of the nagging problem. Developed from a well-done television movie called "Love Is Not Enough," the limited series revolves around Mike Harris, who has moved his five children from Detroit to Los Angeles following the death of his wife. Working in a gas station owned by a white couple, Mike's sensitivity is so fine-tuned that he can listen to the engine of a custom-made car and announce that "the sixth cylinder is off a bit." The children are models of unreal decorum. The oldest daughter not only can whip up a Brazilian stew for dinner, but she receives warm compliments from the rest of the family for her culinary adventurousness. Grace is said before meals. When Daddy gets up from the table, he carefully asks the children, "Will you all excuse me, please?"

The white employers are placed on similarly lofty planes, at one point offering to put up the equity of their house to help Mike pay for a required hospital stay of his youngest son. This is all very comforting, of course, but unfortunately, it is also slightly boring. Transforming everybody into a goody two-shoes results in a curiously lifeless product. Clearly, in the quest for positive images, a balance must be struck. A world of lovable Barry Fitzgerald types, no matter what their color, would be singularly dull.

STEREOTYPING OF WOMEN
ON TELEVISION

E. Simson

While millions of Americans contentedly turn on their favorite TV programs day after day, growing numbers among the population have come to believe that there is a sinister side to the medium. They maintain that watching TV is not a harmless pastime, but can have a detrimental impact. Their concerns range over such diverse issues as possible brain damage to young viewers, dehumanization of social interaction, low quality of programs, inaccuracies in the data presented, the promoting of promiscuity, and the glorification of violence. Many studies have given support to these accusations, although much regarding the extent and direction of the impact of TV remains still controversial.

Reprinted from *USA Today* (September 1978). Copyright 1978 by Society for the Advancement of Education.

One issue that has not received as much public attention as I feel it deserves is how are women portrayed on TV and what consequences does this portrayal have. A number of years ago, criticisms of the portrayal of women were beginning to surface. In response, TV executives promised improvements for the forthcoming seasons. To delineate what kind of image of women has emerged, I began to view first-run serialized TV crime dramas for the 1976–77 season.

WOMEN IN CRIME DRAMAS

Having surveyed 157 programs, I found that women in crime dramas were typically pretty, but not unique, young, and resided in California. Of those over 20 years of age, 45 percent were estimated to be in the 20–29 age category—about twice the rate found in the American population. In contrast, women 40 and older were notably underrepresented.

The most prevalent occupation was prostitution. Of women shown earning a living, the modal source of income was prostitution. This was true for all three of the major networks and involved 16 percent of the women who worked, reaching 47 percent on one series. The other popular occupations were secretary (8 percent), policewoman (7 percent), nurse (5 percent), waitress (5 percent), airline hostess (4 percent), singer (4 percent), landlady (3 percent), clerk (3 percent), receptionist (3 percent), and night-club dancer or stripper (3 percent).

In the infrequent cases when professional career women were actually a real part of the story (and not simply tokens, minor consultants, etc.), they were treated none too charitably. They were often failures as wives and/or mothers or they hated men. At times, they were overly dependent on men or chased after men. Occasionally, they were depicted in a tongue-in-cheek or highly unrealistic manner.

In general, women were present less frequently than men. When present, they were more incompetent, silly, dependent, and passive—much less likely to be either the heroine or the villain. Of those criminals who were pursued by the hero, 13 percent were women (nationally, approximately 16 percent of those arrested are women). In at least 28 cases, women were depicted as irrelevant—as a decorative object or padding for a weak story. They had lines, but absolutely no relevance to the plot. If their roles had been deleted, they would not have been missed.

Over and over again, women were depicted as morally, mentally, and physically weak. They were seen as mindless sex objects, as ridiculous beings, or as slavishly devoting themselves to men or children. They were patronized, used, and humiliated. Men had to rescue them not only from the clutches of the evil villain, but also from the mess they made of their own lives. The following are just a few samples taken at random:

On one program, the plot centered on how a woman cannot be expected to raise a child without the presence of a man. In her efforts to cope with her situation, the woman repeatedly turned to the hero for advice, even on such matters as whom she should date. Also, prostitution was given a positive boost. On another program, the heroine, although loving her ex-husband and vice versa, had to obtain a divorce because, as she explained, a working wife and marriage are incompatible. On a third program, the point was made in the case of a junior account executive that, if a woman wants to pursue a professional career, she had better be prepared to provide male associates with sexual favors. On still another program, the hero woke up another "good guy," a minor character, in the middle of the night and ordered him immediately to get rid of whoever else was in the apartment with him because he wanted to hold a brief discussion on an important topic. With the tacit approval of the hero, a partially dressed, sleepy woman was forcibly evicted. It was never made clear who she was—wife, sister, girlfriend, hooker—as her role involved only the one incident of being thrown out of bed.

OTHER FINDINGS

Women on Words and Images studied prime-time TV programs—the majority of them situation comedies—for the 1973–74 season. They found that more men than women were shown. The men worked at nearly twice as many different occupations as women. All adult characters exhibited more negative than positive characteristics, but the behavior of women was even more negative than that of men. Men were shown as dominant, authoritative, and competent, while women were shown as stereotyped housewives, sex objects, or otherwise dependent on or subservient to men.[1]

Soap operas have been observed to project men as independent, rational, advice-giving professionals. In contrast, women were emotional, dependent, inept, and subservient wives, mothers, and girlfriends. Even successful professional women would get themselves into predicaments from which they had to be saved by men.[2]

In cartoons, more males than females were shown, and males were shown in a greater variety of occupations. Males were depicted as more stable and intelligent than females and even mechanized robots took on sex-stereotyped mannerisms.[3]

Commercials have been repeatedly criticized by women and concerted efforts have been made to institute changes. One study of their content found that women were central figures in 43 percent of the cases, although they made up 51 percent of the population and an estimated 75 percent of the consumer purchasers. During prime-time commercials, men constituted 70 percent of the central figures. Men were also more likely to be the authority on the product advertised, while women tended to be the product users. Women were less likely to have either their own independent identity or to be shown in occupational settings.[4]

Pat Brandin of the National Organization for Women (NOW) stated that among the reasons why she objected to the commercials is that they tend to belittle women—to show them as frivolous, docile, stupid, and incompetent; preoccupied with efforts to catch a man; or possessing an insane obsession with cleanliness.[5] While several commercials have been modified in response to pressures, during the 1976–1977 season, I saw far too many that were simply atrocious. Although many viewers have become cynical regarding the commercials, this cynicism seems to apply to the product sold, not to values portrayed.[6]

A trend of increased degradation of women in the motion pictures, many of which eventually end up on TV or are made specially for TV, has been noted. The height of positive images of women in movies was reached back in the 1930s, with women not infrequently holding rewarding professional careers and exhibiting strong, individualistic, and unique personalities. Since then, the image has declined steadily, reaching a particularly low point presently in the 1970s, with the ideal woman being not a woman, but a bland, inarticulate, and amoral girl who is pushed around by men.[7] Rape and other violence towards women have not only increased, but conscious efforts are being made to glorify rape and perpetuate the myth that women are masochistic by nature— that they enjoy being raped, beaten, and otherwise abused.[8]

CONSEQUENCES

With nearly every family, regardless of socio-economic class, having at least one TV set and the average set being turned on 6.3 hours per day, TV has emerged as an important source for promulgating attitudes, values, and customs. For some viewers, it is the only major contact with outside "reality," including how to relate to women. Thus, not only is TV's sexism insulting, but it is also detrimental to the status of women.

That traditional sex stereotypes are strengthened by TV has been supported by several studies. Evidence indicates that TV can affect our attitudes toward certain characteristics exhibited by men and women by virtue of exposing us to some types more often than others.[9] High amounts of TV watching (25 or more hours per week) among children have been found to be distinctly associated with a stronger internalization of traditional sex roles than among those who spend less time with TV (10 or fewer hours per week). This held equally for boys and girls and did not change with increased age.[10] Girls who were heavy TV watchers, however, were much less likely to aspire to attend college than were boys who watched as much TV. This difference was greater for children with college-educated parents, indicating that the cause was TV and not social class.[11] Furthermore, a lack of occupational role models for women exists on TV, promoting a more limited view of opportunities than reality warrants. Those programs I surveyed did not include among the main characters even one professional woman who was worthy of serious emulating. Rather, these women tended to alienate viewers. The message was that career women are caustic individuals who have little chance at finding personal happiness. Thus, TV watching can have a negative impact on the occupational interests and aspirations of girls and women.

It has been alleged that the sexist stereotypes on TV have become a major source of prejudice and lead to job discrimination and a growing hatred of women, manifesting in extreme situations in rape and other physical violence. That the increased prevalence on TV of prostitutes with the heart of gold, as one example, may well have deleterious effects can be ascertained from Susan Brownmiller's arguments that men will not accept women as equals until prostitution has been eliminated. She has attributed the acceptance of prostitutes, pornography, glorification of rape, and other anti-female propaganda in the mass media as promoting a climate in which acts of sexual hostility against women are not only tolerated, but ideologically encouraged and the belief in man's right to the female body is given legitimacy.[12]

Whatever the reason—as a backlash to the growing women's movement or greed regarding the ratings battle—the 1976–77 season was probably the most sexist in TV history, with women being relegated largely to children, kitchen, and the bed. An exceptionally offensive treatment of women emerged on the series "Baretta," one that had not been present in that show during previous seasons, or certainly not to that extreme degree.

The prevailing negative stereotypes can have the effect of a self-fulfilling prophecy and hinder self-realization among women. NOW's Task Force on the Media has been trying to change some of the stereotypes, but much more support is needed. Women have to become more assertive and start mass complaints to sponsors and organize boycotts of products and programs. They should also pressure organizations such as the National Citizens Committee for Broadcasting, the National Congress of Parents and Teachers, and others to become concerned with the "psychological violence" done to women. These organizations have demonstrated in their successful fight against televising of physical violence that the values promoted by the TV industry can be altered.

1. Women on Words and Images, *Channeling Children: Sex Stereotypes on Prime Time TV* (Princeton, N.J., 1975).

2. "The Television Image of Women," *Intellect* 103 April 1975): 424–25.

3. Richard M. Levinson, "From Olive Oyl to Sweet Polly Purebread: Sex Role Stereotypes and Televised Cartoons," *Journal of Popular Culture* 9 (Winter 1975): 561–72.

4. Leslie Zebrowitz McArthur and Beth Gabrielle Resko, "The Portrayal of Men and Women in American Television Commercials," *Journal of Social Psychology* 97 (December 1975): 209–220.

5. Lynn Taylor, "How Ads Slight Women," *Chicago Tribune* (September 21, 1971): 21.

6. "The Television Image of Women," op. cit.

7. Molly Haskell, *From Reverence to Rape: The Treatment of Women in the Movies* (New York: Holt, Rinehart & Winston, 1973); and Molly Haskell, "Tatum O'Neal and Jodie Foster: Their Combined Age Is 27—What Is Hollywood Trying to Tell Us?," *Ms Magazine* 5 (April 1977): 49–51.

8. Susan Brownmiller, *Against Our Will: Men, Women and Rape* (New York: Simon & Schuster, 1975).

9. McArthur and Resko, op. cit.

10. Terry Frueh and Paul E. McGhee, "Traditional Sex Role Development and Amount of Time Spent Watching Television," *Developmental Psychology* 11 (Jan. 1975): 109.

11. Gaye Tuchman, "Mass Media Values," *Society* 14 (November–December 1976): 51–54.

12. Brownmiller, op. cit.

ADVERTISING GROWS UP

Newsweek Staff*

The commercial opens on an imposing executive office. Behind the huge oak desk, the leather chair swings around to face the camera, revealing a no-nonsense woman in horn rims, her blond hair sensibly caught back in a ponytail. "If you work, you know how tough it is to go home and start cooking," she sighs. Now comes the pitch, in this case for Stouffer's frozen foods: "I've worked hard today, but thanks to Stouffer's, I'm not cooking tonight." Then, whoosh, Madam Executive Consumer slides some papers into her briefcase, clicks off the light and heads home, presumably to an empathetic chorus of "Right on!" from all her time-squeezed, work-burdened sisters in the audience.

BELIEVABLE

Advertisers and their agencies are finally beginning to raise the consciousness of their commercials out of the cupboard and into the real world. Going—but not yet gone—are the baby-faced actresses and models whose youth, beauty, and vacuity traditionally supplied the plastic for the sponsors' pitch. Coming on strong are believable, attractive women in their 30s, whose appeal is based on character and experience. "Eight years ago, the 33-year-old was virtually all through," says Wilhelmina, the director of the Wilhelmina Model Agency in New York. "Now advertisers are realizing that the experienced thirtyish model not only has an ageless quality about her but a kind of wisdom which the consumer instantly recognizes."

Even the traditionally youth-obsessed cosmetic companies, whose love affair with the dewy-eyed nymphet once seemed eternal, are now turning to older models. Oil of Olay's "international beauty" TV spot ends with the slogan, "So every age can be the best you've ever looked." And N. W. Ayer vice-president Sally Kandle has just cast a 35-year-old woman for an Avon cosmetic commercial. "There's much more acceptance now that being older isn't a terrible thing," explains Kandle. "The trend now is to emulate someone real instead of an illusion on a pedestal."

The move to maturity is motivated by some highly practical considerations. Due to longer life spans, the median age of the female consumer rose from 29.3 in 1970 to 30.6 in 1977 and is expected to hit 32.7 in 1985. In addition, many women are now spending more time outside the home than in it. All this, plus the feminist-inspired drive to dispel the youth-is-all myth, has finally forced the ad industry to do some growing up. "Models my age project a kind of womanliness," says commercial actress Karen Howard, a 39-year-old mother of two, who has been hawking such products as Grecian Formula and Pepperidge Farm cakes. "Many of the products I advertise are ones

From *Newsweek* (March 19, 1979): 59–60. Copyright 1979, by Newsweek, Inc. All Rights Reserved. Reprinted by Permission.

*Linda Bird Francke with Lisa Whitman in New York.

which require somebody who's had some experience in life, who projects a certain maturity and authority without suggesting someone who's middle-aged.''

The retreat from the youth cult may also be due to the aging of the ad people themselves. "All the Madison Avenue people who were in their twenties during the '60s are now in their late thirties," says actress Linda Watkins, 32, who has worked for Gentle Touch, Clairol, and Winston cigarettes.

PLAYBACK

Besides hiring older models, advertisers have begun upgrading the usual roles assigned to their female media representatives. Leading the way up the consciousness path are such once stodgy institutions as the Chase Manhattan Bank, which is pitching for female customers by portraying a woman who has just been made a corporate vice-president. "The playback from strangers on the street has been fantastic," says Chase Manhattan's "VP," Carla Meyer, 32. "People are so relieved to see a woman as a money earner rather than always in a secondary role." Reaction has been just as enthusiastic for Gayle Pope, 35, who plays Stouffer's working woman: "Even stewardesses come up to me after they've seen my commercial and say it's wonderful we're all out there working together."

Inevitably, perhaps, the recent shift to women who are "with it" has given birth to yet another stereotype. Women may soon sense that they haven't made it unless they are corporate vice-presidents or crack journalists. "There are lots of calls for a Mary Tyler Moore type," says commercial actress Nina Mann, 35. "Female reporters have become the role models for women of intelligence and ability. It's no longer just Miss Diddle Brain."

SARCASM

Commercial male-female relationships have also come a long way from the days when a Geritol spot ended with the husband smugly announcing: "My wife . . . I think I'll keep her." In the current TV commercials for Polaroid's OneStep camera, actor James Garner and actress Mariette Hartley banter with good-natured sarcasm. Garner: "Polaroid's OneStep is the world's simplest camera; even a woman can use it." Hartley: "How'd that go again?" Garner (smirking): "I thought that would get her attention." Hartley (with mock outrage): "I could have 1000 women here in half an hour . . . all marching with big signs."

The 38-year-old Hartley, who has previously pitched Nestlé's chocolate chips and Jif peanut butter, relishes her new role. "It's so refreshing," she says. "Now I can use all of me instead of having to give myself a lobotomy before I go on a set." There's only one problem: the Polaroid commercials have worked so well that Hartley has taken to wearing a T shirt that reads: "No, I'm not Mrs. James Garner."

chapter 9

ON SEX
AND VIOLENCE

Protests against sexual content in all media are common in the United States. It would be redundant to include here articles protesting or defending sex in print, in film, or on the radio, because the arguments are so similar to those against sex on TV; they are, in fact, similar to the arguments for censorship in general (see Chapter 2).

The first reading in this chapter, by Harry Waters and the staff of *Newsweek*, outlines the controversy on both sides of the sex and TV issue. It is interesting to note that although this article appeared in the February 20, 1978 issue of *Newsweek*, all but one of the TV series it mentions as offenders are still on the air—and high in the ratings—as this anthology goes to press. It is also interesting to note that this article itself illustrates some of the points discussed within it; it is itself an exploitation of sex, highlighted (in the original) with sexy plot summaries and color pictures.

Before sex on TV, the major protests were against violence on TV (and once again, protests occurred against violence in the other media also). Since sex effectively replaced violence, there is always the chance that the pendulum will swing back and violence will replace sex as TV's staple. In the mean-

143

time, many media critics believe that TV entertainment is still too violent for children. The second and third readings in this chapter look at two sides of this issue. In the second reading Harry J. Skornia, Professor Emeritus at the University of Illinois (Chicago), explains why he thinks televised violence is dangerous. In the third reading psychologist Jerome J. Lopiparo explains why he thinks television violence might be a beneficial "safety valve" that helps reduce societal aggression.

An interesting subissue to the violence issue arose a few years ago in what has come to be called the "Born Innocent" case, in which NBC was sued because of violence that was allegedly incited by a television movie of that name. The final reading in this chapter, a sample of newspaper editorials, gives the details of the case, along with some of its implications. The *Deseret News* (Salt Lake City, Utah) believes that NBC should have been held responsible for the effects of its violent programming. The *St. Petersburg (Florida) Times* presents the other side of the argument. The case was eventually thrown out of court (which was considered a victory for NBC), but the issue is still with us.

SEX AND TV

Newsweek Staff*

Chrissy is a busty, born-innocent blonde who has erotic dreams about unicorns, chocolate-chip cookies, and appearing at a dance wearing blue shoes. So? "Just blue shoes," she giggles. Chrissy shares a Santa Monica apartment with Janet, who is noticeably less pneumatic and not at all happy about it. Janet contemplates cosmetic surgery, but abandons the idea after being told she's "making mountains out of molehills." Chrissy and Janet also room with Jack, who must pretend he is a homosexual so that Mr. Roper, their uptight, downstairs landlord, will allow the three to split the rent. When a female visitor admiringly refers to Jack as "a man's man," Roper disgustedly replies: "I know what you mean." The landlord's sex-starved wife, meanwhile, needles her husband about his lack of virility. "There goes that banging again," he sighs, glaring up at the ceiling. "Oh, c'mon," leers Mrs. Roper. "A little of that never hurt anybody."

Chrissy, Janet, Jack, and the Ropers, of course, all live together in the libidinous little world of ABC's "Three's Company," a confection of one-liners and double entendres about a ménage à trois. Only five years ago, so sex obsessed a series would have had about as much chance of becoming a prime-time hit as a Russ Meyer adaptation of the Kama Sutra. Yet almost from the moment it first tittered through the tube last spring, "Three's Company" has become a permanent fixture in Nielsen's Top Five.

From *Newsweek* (February 20, 1978): 54–61. Copyright 1978, by Newsweek, Inc. All Rights Reserved. Reprinted by Permission.

*Harry F. Waters with Martin Kasindorf in Los Angeles, Betsy Carter in New York and bureau reports.

By all appearances, the sexual revolution has finally seeped through the looking glass. And while the result is a far cry from *Deep Throat* or even *Network*, a whole lot of viewers are mad as hell—and vowing they're not going to take it any more. The most widespread suspicion is that prime time's new blue hue is a carefully calculated replacement for the old blood-red one. Now that all the pressure groups have toned down video violence, the theory goes, the networks are turning to risqué material as the next best lure for the viewers. "TV is hydraulic," says Ben Logan, head of one media-watchdog group. "You push down violence and up pops exploitative sex." Network officials publicly scoff at that suggestion, but at least one insider sees it otherwise. Concedes CBS censor Donn O'Brien: "With the mix of programming today, sexuality has taken the place of violence."

When compared with what's available on movie screens, stages, and newsstands, today's vidsex stacks up as pretty tame stuff. But prime-time entertainment is at least mentioning the heretofore unmentionable. Remember when the CBS censor forbade the star of "I Love Lucy" to tell her husband she was "pregnant"? A female character in ABC's "Soap" was described as "in heat" after an apparent assignation in an airplane lavatory. Remember when Jack Parr got in trouble for attempting to tell a joke about a water closet? On the made-for-NBC movie "The Dark Secret of Harvest Home," the leader of a kinky fertility cult seduced the hero's wife while head witch Bette Davis cheered him on by chanting: "Plow the furrow . . . plant the corn." Remember when My Little Margie's father brandished a shotgun when she and her beau came home late from a date? Julia, the bachelor girl on CBS's "On Our Own," recently tried to talk a handsome disk jockey into shacking up.

Just this season, Edith Bunker survived a rape attempt and discovered that her deceased spinster cousin was a lesbian. "Baretta" ex-plored the sleazy world of male prostitution, while "Police Woman" exposed a white-slave ring specializing in teen-agers. NBC dealt with an incest fantasy ("Sharon: Portrait of a Mistress"), the seduction of a gigolo by a 15-year-old girl ("Aspen"), and nymphomania and female frigidity ("What Really Happened to the Class of '65?"). In two weeks, NBC will test just how far television can go when it presents a six-hour, three-part adaptation of "Loose Change," Sara Davidson's let-it-all-hang-out memoir of the '60s counter-culture. The miniseries offers up two deflowerings, a teacher exposing himself to his class, and a woman finally achieving her first climactic orgasm—out of wedlock, of course—after ten years of failure.

Still, today's vidsex remains almost exclusively verbal rather than visual. Nudity and explicit portrayals of sexual acts are still taboo. Frank Price, president of Universal Television, goes so far as to propose that "the sexual breakthrough in TV has probably taken us to where the movies were in 1935." The problem is that television, as the Federal Communications Commission recently described it, is a medium with "uniquely intrusive qualities." Mike Shapiro, overseer of ABC's Dallas affiliate, puts it more plainly. "If you go out to the theater for sexual material, that's one thing," says Shapiro. "But if you bring it into the home unannounced, that's a totally different thing. I listen to my viewers' bitches. And all I've gotten since September is 'too much sex'."

Complaints to the FCC about obscenity, indecency, and profanity on the airwaves have leaped from 6143 to 20,146 in just one year. In a recent survey by the Doyle Dane Bernbach advertising agency, 54 percent of the 400 adults polled voiced general dissatisfaction with TV's handling of sex-related themes.

The complaints may be reminiscent of the public protests against TV violence, but there is a major difference between the two issues. Hardly anyone seemed to be willing to make a case for more video mayhem. And there was sufficient evidence pointing to the damaging effects of televised violence on adolescent psyches to bolster the case for reform. But, at least so far, there is almost no available evidence as to just how much influence vidsex may have on children or, for that matter, on adults.

As a result, there is not—and there probably never can be—a public consensus about how much sex television should serve up and in what manner. For the networks, the problem may well be unsolvable. How can a mass, family medium manage to appear both modern to the more sexually adventurous audience and moral to the traditionalists? "We're highly divided in this country about sexuality," observes psychologist Robert M. Liebert, one of the most respected analysts of television. "To get the most viewers, the networks must stay neutral. But who is to define for them what are neutral positions? TV is being caught in the cross fire of a moral war."

In the front lines of the assault are religious groups, who are fighting from a moral position; gay activists, who object to TV's swishy stereotypes, and parents, who don't want to entrust their children's sex education to a commercial medium ruled by ratings. Each faction has a legitimate argument, and certainly all have the right to sound off. The industry's own position—that TV is hardly sexually permissive—is equally valid. Yet as a medium licensed to operate on the public airwaves, and one that is as much a part of the American family as the living-room furniture, television must learn to live with all manner of public pressure.

The angriest and most sustained protest comes from religious groups. The Southern Baptist Convention, America's largest Protestant denomination, has mailed "Help for Television Viewers" packets to more than 50,000 pastors and lay leaders. Included in the kits are suggested criteria for judging a TV show, survey forms so viewers can log incidences of immoral programming, and postcards pre-addressed to the three networks. During the past year, a coalition of Lutheran, Methodist, and Church of the Brethren activists has conducted a series of highly sophisticated, antividsex workshops throughout the nation. The 16-hour courses, called "Television Awareness Training," teach participants all manner of tactics to use in pressuring the networks into cleaning up their acts.

Last month, the National Religious Broadcasters, which includes the operators of 24 religious TV stations, launched an equally ambitious mail-and-phone campaign to sanitize the tube. As part of the NRB's self-proclaimed "blitz," Christians of every denomination will be exhorted to contact local stations and corporate sponsors involved in programs they deem objectionable. "It is not that we're against sex," explains NRB spokesman Carl Richardson. "What we are concerned about is gratuitous, excessive, and perverted sexuality being depicted on the screen. I don't think homosexuality and impotency are matters to joke about."

In response network officials contend that, while any citizen or group has the right to criticize their product, such protest becomes repressive when it threatens the viewing rights of others. Says ABC-TV president Fred Pierce: "The issue is whether special-interest groups should usurp the program judgments of broadcasters, advertisers, and the creative production community." Others maintain that the robust ratings of the more risqué programs indicate that they are in tune with society's newly liberated tastes. "The viewers speak with forked tongue," claims A.R. Van Cantfort, program manager of NBC's Atlanta affiliate. "They say, 'Gosh, there's too much flesh shown on "Charlie's Angels".' Then they go home, kick off their shoes, turn on the set, and ogle those three broads on what is probably the poorest written show on television."

If ABC is doing kiddie porn, NBC will give the audience adult porn.

—An NBC programming executive

By common industry consensus, ABC owns the trophy for titillation—but NBC is beginning to breathe hard on its neck. The programming tactic employed by the No. 1 network to lure its teen-age following is known in the trade as "jiggly." The writers of "Charlie's Angels," for instance, use any pretext to get the buxom trio into an equatorial clime, then into wet T shirts and finally into whatever run-and-jump situation that best displays their unfettered charms. ABC's "The Love Boat" is almost equally single-minded. In one segment, the ubiquitous Charo played a stage-struck Mexican stowaway who, thanks to a series of wildly improbable events, was allowed to perform a sizzling bump-and-grind number for the cruise ship's passengers.

The queen of jiggly, however, is "Three's Company." In 29-year-old Suzanne Somers, who plays the dishy Chrissy, ABC has produced the heiress apparent to the departed Farrah as TV's most dazzling celestial body. Somers is currently doing for the towel—not to mention shorty pajamas and lingerie—what Lana Turner once did for the sweater. The actress, who played the blonde in the Thunderbird in *American Graffiti*, is not exactly offended about finding herself in déshabille each week. "I enjoy it," Somers says with a chuckle. "If you've got it, bump it with a trumpet."

Over at NBC, meanwhile, programming head Paul Klein reports that the network has decided to concentrate its courtship on women between the ages of 18 and 49 (a highly prized target for advertisers). And what will NBC use as bait? "Sex themes attract more female viewers than male ones," claims Klein, who recently grabbed up a Norman Lear proposal for a series about a cohabiting unwed couple without even asking to look at a pilot show. Klein also thinks that "even jiggly shows attract women more than men."

In Hollywood, NBC vice-president Deanne Barkley is enthusiastically applying Klein's strategy to the novels-for-television genre. One of her projects is adapting Taylor Caldwell's "The Glory and the Lightning," set in ancient Greece. "The women wore little togas, like mini-skirts," muses Barkley. Another selection is "Child of the Morning," a novel about a female Egyptian pharaoh. "I imagine the Egyptians exposed more of their bodies," says Barkley. NBC's skin game, of course, must eventually be approved by Fred Silverman, the ABC programming defector who will take command of the network later this year. But no one expects Silverman to be scandalized. As "Three's Company" co-producer Don Nicholl recalls it, Silverman instructed the show's architects to make it "the same kind of breakthrough in sexiness that 'All in the Family' was in bigotry."

Network censors have always applied different standards to different time periods. In the daytime, when the kids presumably are in school, the soap folk are allowed to come and go, talking of diaphragms, mastectomies, and all manner of amatory aberrations. After 11 P.M., shows like "Saturday Night Live" can get away with spoofing everything from sex-change operations to circumcision. But in the key precinct of prime time, the censors are caught between the networks' apparent decision both to heat things up and to cool the resultant protest. As a result, there is no coherent standard, and the censors' prime-time rulings—at least as the writers and producers see it—are becoming curiouser and curiouser.

In one episode of "Three's Company," centered on an apartment visit by Jack's mother, who did not know about the cohabitation arrangement, the producers had Janet quip: "I did my best . . . I put the toilet seat up." Later, she was supposed to say, "I put the toilet seat down." ABC's standards department permitted the first line and, inexplicably, deleted the second. NBC censor Herminio Traviesas OK'd "79 Park Avenue," a miniseries about a call girl (played by Lesley Ann Warren) that plumbed new depths of sleaze-tease. But the same sensibility recoils in horror from any open-mouth kisses. "We cut one recently where they showed the tongue actually protruding," reports Traviesas. "It was disgusting." CBS's "On Our Own" is permitted to milk guffaws from premarital sex, but a brief, above-the-waist flash of bare female backs was ordered axed. "There's no sense to any of it," grumbles Sam Denoff, the show's producer.

Under the prodding of station operators bent on curtailing vidsex, the National Association of Broadcasters recently stiffened the industry's code of broadcast standards. The NAB, whose membership numbers more than 500 stations, ruled that "subscribers shall not broadcast any material which they determine to be obscene, profane, or indecent." The Catch-22, in addition to broadcasters sitting as their own judges, is that code observance is purely voluntary. "The standards are there as guides," shrugs an NAB spokesman. "There is no authority that can enforce them."

We will not subsidize sexual exploitation. We will not subsidize the vulgarization of life. We will not pay for moral pollution.
—Harry N. Hollis, Jr., Southern Baptist Christian Life Commission

Hollis and virtually every other anti-vidsex crusader insist that it is not the topic per se that is at issue but how it is handled. As part of the Television Awareness Training workshops, for example, a film montage of tasteful prime-time treatments of sex is shown to point up the positive side. Included is a discussion of temporary impotency on "M*A*S*H"—triggered by Hawkeye's battle fatigue—that was 99 and 44/100 percent free of the usual macho bravado. Similarly, an installment of ABC's "Family" dealing with a lesbian schoolteacher achieved a poignant evocation of the many manifestations of love. And Edith Bunker's rape trauma was so sensitively rendered that the episode is being screened—and applauded—at rape-prevention centers around the nation.

What churns up the protesters' moral juices is the fact that TV tends to glorify sexual activity without impressing on viewers, particularly adolescents, the responsibilities that go along with it. "There are nearly 1 million unwanted pregnancies a year among teen-agers in this country," notes the Rev. William Fore of the National Council of Churches. "The problem of sex on TV is that it doesn't deal with the consequences."

That may depend on how one defines "consequences." Consider the recent imbroglio over "James at 15," NBC's bittersweet study of adolescent growing pains. NBC's Paul Klein had asked for an episode in which the series' teenage protagonist would lose his virginity on his sixteenth birthday. Chief writer Dan Wakefield duly put together a script in which James bedded a Swedish exchange student. The treatment, however, failed to meet a key NBC criterion: that the couple must be made to face the possible consequences of their act by having the girl falsely suspect she was pregnant. That was how the episode played last week, under a new title ("James at 16")—but it had Wakefield's credit as writer removed. The critically acclaimed novelist ("Going All the Way") had huffed off his job over NBC's sex-cum-anxiety dictate: "I didn't write what I've written for 20 years to come around to *that*."

On the other hand, ABC managed to fall into its own trap in its promotion of "Soap." To arouse the American libido, ABC previewed the series for the press a full three months before its television première. The resultant spate of articles about the show's below-the-belt fixation so inflamed the heartland that the network was deluged with no fewer than 22,000 letters of protest before the first episode ever appeared. Although the outcry has since waned, this frightened off so many advertisers that ABC was forced to offer sponsors sharply reduced rates. The upshot is that the network, by one estimate, has already lost nearly $1 million in ad revenue, which may help to explain why "Soap" is currently being recast from a heat-generating sexcom into just another whodunit.

The most important outcome of the no-

"Soap" campaign was that it taught the pressure groups just where the industry's Achilles' heel lies—that is, with the people who foot its bills. Accordingly, the major thrust of such protest is now being directed at the advertisers rather than the networks. Perhaps the most relentless sponsor-baiter is the National Federation for Decency, a 5000-member watchdog group founded by a United Methodist minister named Donald Wildmon. Recently, Wildmon's organization disseminated the results of a 15-week monitoring study of "the top sponsors of sex" (American Home Products Corp., Ford Motor Co., and Sears, Roebuck and Co. were cited as the worst offenders). "Networks and sponsors have the right to put out any kind of programs they want," says Wildmon. "But we have an equal right to say we're not going to buy your products."

As some programmers see it, the issue is not that simple. Organized boycotts, in their view, are an infringement of their First Amendment rights. Fred Silverman has compared the boycott efforts to the blacklisting campaign that terrorized the industry during the '50s. "There is no place in an orderly democratic society for such a blunt tool," maintains Silverman.

But that position is not shared by many affiliate-station managers, who must daily decide whether what the network sends down the line should be edited to conform to their audience's sensibilities. "Boycotts are as American as apple pie," declares Stephen Kimatian, a Group W executive at the ABC Baltimore affiliate. "There's no fairer way in a democracy to assert your rights than through economic leverage." All that seems clear is that, through fair means or foul, citizen lobbyists are having an increasing effect on TV's sexual gryoscope —and none more so than the nation's homosexual activists.

Q. Will Jodie go straight on "Soap"? I'm a member of the gay liberation movement and I think his going straight is a false rip-off.
　　　　　　　　　　　　　　　　　　—T.S.

A. In the current story line, Jodie is getting involved with a nymphomaniacal nurse, but that doesn't mean he's gone straight. Time will tell.
　　　　—TV Mailbag column, New York Post

Not only did Jodie remain a resolutely gay spirit but, in one of "Soap's" few moving moments, he was finally accepted by his macho brother Danny for exactly what he was. Both those developments, along with the abandonment of plans to have Jodie undergo a sex-change operation, came about after prolonged pressure from the National Gay Task Force, the New York-based clearinghouse for homosexual protest. In addition, representatives of the task force met with the series' producers and ABC executives to discuss the depiction of Jodie as a mincing neurotic. The network duly promised changes and, as task-force media director Ginny Vida is first to proclaim, "Jodie is now the only sane, sensitive person in the whole show."

Homosexuality finally came out of the prime-time closet about five years ago. In those days, however, gays were almost invariably portrayed as sick. In 1974 alone, Marcus Welby confronted a homosexual child molester, "Police Woman" tracked down some lesbian murderers, and the NBC movie "Born Innocent" featured a horrifyingly graphic scene of lesbian rape in a girls' reformatory. "That year we went from total TV invisibility to total TV abuse," recalls Vida.

Television's overlords have hardly declared a moratorium on limp-wristed portrayals of homosexuals, arguing that many do indeed seem to act that way. Nor is the medium displaying any inclination to shy away from the subject's more sordid aspects. The NBC movie "The Moneychangers" featured a homosexual assault by a gang of prison inmates in which the camera stopped just short of private parts. Even so, gay liberationists have achieved a visible transformation of their video image. On a recent episode of "Maude," a conservative neighbor came in for a fusillade of ridicule when he launched a campaign to close a local gay bar. And NBC's "Alexander: The Other Side of Dawn," a made-for-TV movie about male hustling, offered a sympathetic portrayal of the plight of impoverished young runaways who sell their bodies just to survive.

Groups like Vida's are now regularly consulted by producers planning to deal with homosexual story lines. Gay Media Task Force coordinator Newton Deiter, who spends as many as 20 hours a week going over proposed scripts, reports that Johnny Carson's people are so sensitized that they frequently check with him before allowing Johnny to utter a homosexually oriented gag. Deiter's organization is now concentrating on three objectives: more TV depictions of lesbians; more portrayals of homosexuals as Jewish, Hispanic, and black, instead of pure Wasp; and series in which homosexual characters are given continuing, positive roles as, say, businessmen, lawyers, or even athletes.

Whether the heterosexual audience would quietly sit still for all that is anything but certain. In the survey by Doyle Dane Bernbach, 67 percent of the viewers held that *any* homosexual theme was unsuitable for entertainment programming. Shortly after the poll was released, coincidentally enough, singer Anita Bryant announced that she was forming a watchdog committee to identify and monitor TV shows that present gay lifestyles as "natural and normal." Whatever comes of that, the homosexual backlash against the tube appears as determined as its black counterpart of a decade ago. "We don't expect us all to be portrayed as Bill Cosbys and Diahann Carrolls," sums up Newton Deiter. "All we want to see on TV is a rounding out of gay characters. On that count, we're about halfway home."

When television viewers see unmarried women primarily as victims, married men primarily as fools, and children with "asexual" parents, they are receiving clear messages about "appropriate" sexual conduct.

—Elizabeth Roberts, Project on
Human Sexual Development

Of all the video protest groups, none has a more intriguing—perhaps impossible—mission than the Project on Human Sexual Development based in Cambridge, Mass. In the PHSD's view, the enemy is not the moral tone of the tube but the way it presents male and female relationships. A PHSD study showed that, next to parents, television ranks as the highest authority for teaching children the facts of adult sexual behavior. According to the PHSD, TV is fumbling that educational responsibility as much by the lessons it leaves out as by those it imparts.

"You don't usually see men express affection for each other on TV," complains Roberts, executive director of the foundation-funded group. "You don't usually see women solve their own problems, or even be close friends. These are massive messages TV is putting out and they need to be questioned." To get its own message across, the PHSD has launched a series of consciousness-raising seminars with the industry's creative community. The participants, the people who most shape the product, have discussed everything from the depiction of women as male bait on "Charlie's Angels" to the games played by video kids. "It was a giant sensitivity session," says NBC executive Peter Andrews of one such get-together. "We realized how to be more cognizant of the subliminal content our programs have."

Obviously, the networks will never be able to please everyone on so volatile a subject—nor should they try. Their fundamental concern, and one shared by all the communications media, is to attract the largest audience possible. This requires shrewd advance analysis of imminent market trends. If the public appetite seems to call for a sexier TV diet, it is in the broadcasters' valid interest to provide it. At the same time, it smacks of hypocrisy for the networks to wave the First Amendment as soon as public ire over vidsex scares off sponsors. After all, if they truly have faith in their product, almost nothing can legally prevent them from distributing it. "Networks, like editors, must

HELP FOR TELEVISION VIEWERS

Either you control your TV or your TV will control you. Use these questions to help you make decisions about TV viewing.

BEFORE A PROGRAM

1. Will watching this program represent responsible Christian stewardship for me?
2. Why am I considering watching this program?
3. What has this program been like in the past?
4. Is this a good way to be informed or entertained?
5. Would watching this program together help or hurt my family?

DURING A PROGRAM

1. What moral values are promoted or undermined?
2. Is God's name profaned; is vulgar language used?

3. Is violence glorified; is sex exploited?
4. Are alcohol and other drugs glamorized or taken for granted?
5. Does this program make me more trusting or more suspicious of others?

AFTER A PROGRAM

1. Am I a better person for having watched this program?
2. Was this a program that encouraged morality or immorality?
3. Should I consider watching this program again; why or why not?
4. How can I use this experience to honor God and help others?
5. Should I communicate my convictions about this program to advertisers or television people?

"So each of us shall give account of himself to God" (Romans 14:12)

Southern Baptist pamphlet: When is pressure repressive?

have the courage of their convictions," observes Richard Pinkham, vice-chairman of the Ted Bates advertising agency.

For their part, the forces for cleaner airwaves do not always seem to recognize that, when compared with some of its European counterparts, American TV seems fairly conservative. Stations in Italy are allowed to present hard-core porn flicks, strip-tease exhibitions, and even a demonstration of lovemaking positions. A scene in the British production of "I, Claudius," which stirred almost no protest over there, showed the mad emperor Caligula stabbing his pregnant sister, plucking the fetus from her womb, and eagerly devouring it. Needless to say, this sequence was expurgated from the American public-TV version, although a bare-breasted dance scene was left in.

Perhaps what is most needed is a more effective early-warning system to alert parents to blue-tinged fare. Some want the present wording of network advisories to be made considerably more descriptive. Instead of the standard "Network advises viewer discretion," such warnings might go so far as to caution: "This program contains references to rape, impotency, incest, etc." Of course, such explicit alarums could conceivably stir up as much viewer protest as the shows they refer to. Other proposed alternatives include a PG-style ratings system similar to the one used in the movie industry and an electronic signal that would flash or buzz at the opening of potentially objectionable programs. In France, for example, a small white box appears on the screen to announce such shows.

As for the "proper" depiction of vidsex, the problem inevitably comes down to one of attitude rather than latitude. Only incurable prudes would insist that a medium purporting to portray the human condition should draw a curtain over so integral a part of human activity. What is disturbing, however, is that so much of the sex on TV seems designed to pander to prurience in the most cheaply exploitative manner. With snigger and smirk, the new batch of sitcoms and miniseries flaunt their boldness like prepubescents mouthing dirty words around the schoolyard.

In one of the funnier episodes of "James at 15," James's younger sister—a delightfully precocious tomboy named Sandy—reported that she had finally decided what to write about for a class composition assignment. Her topic, Sandy enthusiastically announced, would be "preteen-age love . . . and how to stamp it out to save energy for sports." Not even the most hard-line pressure group is trying to stamp out sex on the tube. But more and more viewers, from all points on the geo-cultural compass, are raising a legitimate question. When television speaks of sex to the real-life Sandys, is it unreasonable to expect it to sound reasonably grown up?

THE GREAT AMERICAN TEACHING MACHINE— OF VIOLENCE

Harry J. Skornia

If I were to attempt to destroy a nation internally, I would brainwash that nation into accepting violence. I would educate masses to hate and kill and burn and destroy. I would condition people to tolerate violence as an acceptable type of behavior and condone its use as the most effective way to solve problems. I would provide specific lessons in the use of guns and knives and show how cars can be used as instruments of death. I would present this information entertainingly—in the form of television.

Today's most popular television programs provide more teaching than occurs in the home, the church, and the educational system combined. Television provides amazingly effective, absolutely marvelous lessons—the problem is that the lessons capitalize on skills of murder, arson, and robbery. The Mike Hammers, Kojaks, and other television stars rate high as great teachers of American youth who

Reprinted from *Intellect* (April 1977). Copyright 1977 by Society for the Advancement of Education.

learn from what their heroes, their models, do. The fact that youth readily learn what television teaches is substantiated in a 1200 percent increase in juvenile crime during the last 20 years—America's "TV age."

For almost 10 years as head of the National Association of Educational Broadcasters, the parent of public broadcasting, I evaluated the effectiveness of television as an instructional instrument. Based on 2000 research projects in over 100 countries, my findings indicate that television is, indeed, a miracle instrument for teaching. The success of television teaching depends on four factors: the teacher, production techniques, the learner and his readiness or motivation to learn, and the opportunity for utilization or application. The typical commercial television program employs superior teachers who are attractive "personality" actors, uses expensive technology and well-trained personnel to perfect the production, and captures eager and "ready" viewers, according to figures of Nielsen and the networks. Life in a violent society presents the frustrations, temptations, and opportunities to "apply" what is learned from television. Both educators and crime enforcement officers can provide countless examples of the utilization or imitation of violent acts demonstrated on television. Today's programs frequently become tomorrow's crime waves, as hijacking and other crimes of terrorism illustrate.

INVESTIGATING THE EFFECTS OF TV VIOLENCE—THREE SCANDALS

At this point, I am worried about democracy. It is not that democracy has failed, but that it has been usurped by corporate and advertising control and Watergate-type politicians. Commercial television—a dangerous, criminal, and inexcusable threat to America—is responsible for many of the disasters our nation is experiencing. As early as 1969, Sen. John O. Pas-

tore prodded the U.S. Surgeon General to launch a $2 million study of the relationship between violence on television (including televised news, movies, and cartoons) and violence, delinquency, and crime in real life. There are at least three scandals which emerge from this sordid chapter of broadcasting history.

The first scandal was revealed in the makeup of the committee established to administer and direct the Surgeon General's study. For some reason, as yet unknown and uninvestigated, the Surgeon General gave the networks and the broadcasters' trade association (the National Association of Broadcasters) a veto power over who would be named to the committee. The industry, in other words, was allowed to "blackball" those research scholars who had accomplished the most research and who knew the most about the problem. The rationalization was that they were "prejudiced" authorities. If the same practice had been tolerated in the cigarette study, tobacco companies would have been allowed to exclude from the committee those people who had done significant research regarding cigarette smoking and cancer.

The second scandal involves the press release issued when the study was completed. In essence, the release was sufficiently ambiguous to give the impression that there was *no* firm proof that television violence was dangerous to the nation and that a cause-and-effect relationship had *not* been established. This press release became the basis of most headlines and stories across America. For example, the *New York Times'* headline read: "TV Violence Found Unharmful to Youth." This is probably all many people know about the study. The distortion of the press release survives to perpetuate the deliberate concealment of the fact that the study *did* find a cause-and-effect relationship and called for a halt to television violence at once because it *was* causing millions of acts of violence, particularly among youthful offenders and neurotics.

The third scandal concerns the way in which the broadcast industry itself has deceived the American people about the relationship between television violence and crime in America. In March 1972, Sen. Pastore's Subcommittee on Communications of the Senate Committee on Commerce was convened to hear evidence concerned with rigging the committee, distorting the press release, and other related matters. The cameras of the networks were there—but what they recorded has never been revealed to the nation. The committee's hearings, comparable in significance to the Watergate hearings, were never broadcast to the American television audience because they were American television's own Watergate. However, the Canadian Film Board, concerned about the flood of violence exported to Canada by the U.S., also recorded the hearings. Like most other civilized countries, Canada has subsequently begun to erect barriers against the importation of American-made programs of violence. In spite of American network censorship and other tactics of concealment, deceit, and obstructionism, the Canadian Film Board film remains available. The American public needs to know the exposé it records. I have a 56-minute copy of the Canadian Film Board film of the hearings. The film documents Surgeon General Jesse L. Steinfeld, who declares that "the broadcasters should be put on notice." He further warns that, "while the Committee Report is carefully phrased, . . . it is clear . . . that the causal relationship between televised violence and antisocial behavior is sufficient to warrant appropriate and immediate remedial action."

The film also records former FCC Commissioner Nicholas Johnson's declaration to Sen. Howard Baker: "I feel Senator, . . . [that] there are no words too strong to describe the outrage that you ought to feel, as I do, over what [network officials] are doing, and what they are failing to do, with the responsibilities we have given them . . . to serve in the public interest." Dr. Leo Bogart states that "the idea that an industry should not only be represented directly in a scholarly inquiry into its activities, but should also exercise a veto over the membership of the investigating panel, is too stupid and scandalous to escape commentary." FCC Commissioner Rex Lee comments that "the Surgeon General and his committee made it very clear that there was a causal relationship, and that something has to be done."

Because the film has not been aired in the U.S., the "cover-up" continues as the networks dispute the Committee's findings with their most expensive talent and programming. Not only have the Canadian Film Board and other video tapes and film footage been kept off most U.S. television, but the printed copies of the hearings also became strangely unavailable from either the Government Printing Office or the Senate Commerce Committee itself. It was not until a resolution was passed by the Senate in May, 1974, that additional copies of the Pastore Hearings of March, 1972, became available again in July, 1974.

COMBATING TV VIOLENCE

After World War II, I helped to design West German broadcasting. We created *public* corporations in which *all* segments of the nation (labor, industry, agriculture, education, religion, men, women, and youth) were equally involved—no one was able to control, for no *one* segment can serve *all* of society. In the coming revision of television, the United States should adopt the type of controls designed for West Germany—a design which also makes the Japanese and British systems more responsible and respected than the American network system we now have.

All of us who are concerned about the effects of television violence can do something to preclude it. Among the consumer action groups working actively to improve the quality of television, the National Association for Better Broadcasting (NABB), of which I am Second Vice-President, is the best known and most active group. Joining with the NABB in this effort are Action for Children's Television (ACT) of Newton, Mass.; the Office of Communication of the United Church of Christ; *Televisions* magazine, published by the Washington Community Video Center; and numerous local councils emerging in most urban areas to challenge the licenses of stations which fail to serve the public interest. An example of a very active local group is Chicago's Citizens Committee on the Media, which recently notified WGN, one of the largest stations in Chicago, of intent to file formal action against the station.

As consumers, our greatest weapon is to boycott the products sponsoring offensive programs and to inform the manufacturers of the reason for the boycott. The J. Walter Thompson Co., the largest advertising agency in the country, reported that an agency survey of 200 adults found that 10 percent had considered boycotting a product advertised during a violent TV show and that 8 percent had actually refused to buy such a product. The study served as a reason for Thompson's admonition to clients that sponsoring violent TV shows may no longer be a lucrative practice.

President Leo Singer of the Miracle White Co., a television sponsor, has announced that his company will never again sponsor or buy spot announcements on, or adjacent to, programs presenting violence. Following his announcement on October 9, 1973, to the Lions Club International in Chicago, Singer received 125,000 letters commending his action. Other sponsors have joined Singer in his effort. In a press release dated June 17, 1976, the NABB quoted letters to its executive vice-president, Frank Orme, from Procter and Gamble, Gillette, Kinney Shoe Co., Jack-in-the-Box (hamburgers), and the Albertson's Food Centers, who all pledge to cease advertising on horror shows and other violent television programs. Conscientious Americans should support such sponsors and encourage others to take similar positive measures.

A nation respects and imitates the actions of personalities whom the nation's media cast up as models. In today's America, those actions are force, violence, and militarism. The models are show business celebrities, athletes, and nonintellectuals. Hate, violence, and crime dominate American television. The great American teaching machine could just as well teach love, credibility, and compassion.

AGGRESSION ON TV COULD
BE HELPING OUR CHILDREN

Jerome J. Lopiparo

In this age where adults are constantly being told that most of the exotic foods we eat are bad

Reprinted from *Intellect* (April 1977). Copyright 1977 by Society for the Advancement of Education.

for us, anything that intoxicates is harmful, and our government is not as gloriously above reproach as we once believed, it should not come as any surprise that a lot of people are saying that our children's favorite diversion is bad for them too. However, in view of the fact that a child born today will, by the time he or she is 18, have spent more of his or her life watching TV than in any other activity except sleep, the subject of TV aggression deserves a long, hard look.

What kind of TV program offers children the most fascination? Which ones do they sit looking at in excited wonder? It does not take a great deal of expertise to pick either the horror (or monster) movies or the "shoot-em-up" crime shows. This applies not only to television, since violent, aggressive plots are the favorites of children, whether they be in movies, cartoons, or comic books. It seems that, the more gore the program has, the more they like it.

Are these presentations of violence and aggression really hurting our youngsters? The National Commission on the Causes and Prevention of Violence stated in 1969 that:

> It is reasonable to conclude that a constant diet of violent behavior on television has an adverse effect on human character and attitudes. Violence on television encourages violent forms of behavior and fosters moral and social values about violence in daily life which are unacceptable in a civilized society.

This statement is but one example of the highly speculative and naive warnings we have all heard. To attribute to TV the sole responsibility for the unfortunate state our "moral and social values" are in smacks of closed-minded scapegoating.

THE ROOTS OF VIOLENCE

To begin with, let us all agree that we live in very violent times. The Vietnam conflict, the Arab-Israeli wars, and the disastrous murder of the Olympic athletes are only a few examples. Still, can we recall any period in recent history when we were without violence? In the 1960s,

we experienced the tragic assassinations of the Kennedys, while, in the 1950s, we almost became involved in a war in Lebanon, in addition to the horrors of the Korean war. Few of us could foresee the terrible precedent that would be set by the abortive attempt on President Truman's life in that same decade. The 1940s saw us involved in a worldwide holocaust, while the 1920s and 1930s were the setting for Dillinger, the Capone gang, and the emergence of that weapon many foreigners still see as a symbol of mid-America—the machine gun. We could go on and on, but can we say with any degree of validity that one era was any more violent than another? Suffice it to say that everyone has been so busy getting on the bandwagon to ban violence on TV that perhaps, in the confusion, our understanding of children and the basic processes underlying their behavior has become muddled.

It seems that behavioral scientists have been wrestling with the causes and effects of violence forever. Freud believed that man is instinctually aggressive and that within all of us there is a drive leading us either to destroy ourselves or, if the aggression is directed outward, to destroy others. Konrad Lorenz, renowned for his studies of animal behavior, makes an even stronger point. He feels that human aggressiveness is biologically caused, becoming a destructive force through the shaping and molding of our society. He warns that this aggressive energy literally swells within us and, sooner or later, simply explodes in the form of destructive behavior. The frightening implication about Lorenz's theory is that this aggressive energy needs no special stimulus to set it off (although humans usually find no difficulty encountering triggering stimuli), and so its dangerous quality is further enhanced by its unpredictability. A consideration which is most important in terms of our television-viewing child is that *both* of these scientists agree that to fail to express this inborn aggression can have negative effects.

CHILDREN AND AGGRESSIVENESS

If aggression reposes within all of us, whether we choose to believe it to be instinctual or caused by the circumstances of living in our society (as the behaviorists would have us believe), how are we to manage it? To answer this, let us look at the confused way that most parents perceive aggression. A parent soon discovers that aggression is a chauvinistic phenomenon. Boys are allowed—if not openly encouraged—to show anger and to be assertive. Girls—women's liberation notwithstanding—are still being advised by their parents that aggressive behavior is not wholly appropriate for a female. Certainly, when aggression manifests itself in physical violence, it usually becomes an exclusively male prerogative.

Most psychologists working with school-age children will tell you that parents—fathers included—will be quite disturbed when they are told that their son has been exhibiting aggressive behavior. They will generally assure you that they will put a quick stop to it. How? Why they will spank the child, of course. It should not come as a surprise then that the child, in complete innocence and, when you think about it, with complete justification, later explains that his approving authority, his role model for his aggression, is none other than his parents! It becomes analogous to the satirical commentary of the "peaceniks" about our efforts in Vietnam:

"We'll teach them to be peaceful even if we have to fight and destroy every last one of them to do it."

Can a child develop normally if he does not experience aggression? It is generally agreed that some aggression in a child is a desirable thing, since it is one of the most effective ways of expressing independence. When we stifle this behavior, we may be cheating the child out of opportunities to experience his potential as a developing human being.

Another beneficial aspect of a child's expressing aggression is the very fact that he is expressing it, and therefore is not holding his feelings in. A potential danger lies with the child who inhibits his outward displays of aggression in the sense that, if we are not careful, he may direct them inward. The consequences of this may be seen in excessive nail-biting, deliberate pulling out of hair, depression, or self-abasement.

POSITIVE ASPECTS OF AGGRESSION

Earlier, I cited the negative aspects of aggressive-behaving parents, but, if the aggression is toned down a bit and assertiveness is substituted, a very positive situation may take place. The child who perceives his parents as assertive may derive a feeling of security from it, related to a sense that his parents will obviously be well equipped to *protect him* should danger threaten their home. Thus, the hostile world may be a little less frightening for him.

Probably the most important reason aggression must be part of a child's life is that it helps him cope with his feelings of powerlessness. Children do not feel powerful! They do not feel that they can effect change either in their own lives or in the lives of others. If they want to do something, they must ask an adult; if they want something changed, they have to hope adults feel the same way, for that is the only way it is going to happen. It is for this reason that children are drawn to TV violence. Many of the frustrations they feel can be very effectively worked out via the TV screen. It is safe, the person you're attacking cannot retaliate, you can be a hero or a villain with just a flip of the dial, and, most important, you can experience that elusive feeling of *power!*

Closely tied in with the quest for power, aggression has also been linked with what Dr. Gregory Rochlin, a prominent psychiatrist and author of a recent text on aggression, terms our "narcissistic balance." He believes that, when something threatens our accomplishments, our relationships with others, or puts our system of rewards in jeopardy, our self-respect is in danger of being lowered. When self-respect is affected, our "narcissistic balance" may be impaired, and aggression usually is the result. Are any of the foregoing conditions probable in a child's life? There seems little disagreement that they are. We thus uncover another potential source of the aggression we are so ready to lay at the doorstep of violent television programs.

What has been said here is obviously not the last word on the subject of media-depicted aggression. Most psychologists will tell you that there is a small minority of individuals who have a predisposition for violence, and, when they see it portrayed on a TV screen, it may well trigger overt aggressiveness. This is not an area of dispute. What is argued, however, is the fact that most critics have failed to advise the public of the positive aspects of media aggression for the vast majority of children *and* adults who are *not* on the brink of violent behavior, but who, nonetheless, need the vicarious release these programs provide. Perhaps the bulk of the difficulty lies in our unwillingness to accept the premise that within all of us—child and adult alike—there reposes a potential for violence, TV or no TV. Once this is accepted, we may then be more receptive to the notion that the *expression* of this aggression, whether via fantasy or outright overt behavior, is not only normal, but, in many respects, quite beneficial. What we are then left with is the possibility that the aggressiveness our children watch on TV may actually be *reducing* overt expressions of violence, rather than increasing them as the critics would have us believe.

ON NETWORK RESPONSIBILITY
FOR THE EFFECTS
OF VIOLENT PROGRAMMING

DESERET NEWS

Salt Lake City, Utah, April 26, 1978

Can and should broadcasters be held legally responsible when fictional violence is imitated in real life?

This week the U.S. Supreme Court cleared the way for a test of this pivotal question before

Reprinted with permission from *Deseret News*.

a state court in San Francisco.

The case at hand seeks $11 million from NBC and station KRON-TV. The suit was filed on behalf of a 9-year-old girl who was sexually brutalized four days after a nationally televised movie portrayed a similar crime.

It is hard to overestimate the importance of

this suit not only because of its potential impact on TV, but also because of the effect it could have on movies, magazines, newspapers, and books.

Though the trial is unprecedented, the remarkable thing is that such a suit was not filed before. Certainly there have been plenty of opportunities.

Three years ago, a number of skid row derelicts in Los Angeles were killed in a series of slayings that bore a close resemblance to an episode on the "Police Story" TV show.

In Utah, witnesses testified that two of the defendants in Ogden's Hi Fi Shop torture-killings had several times seen a movie in which one victim was forced to drink a caustic substance. The same thing was done to victims at the Hi Fi Shop.

Only last month, two teen-age boys were charged with killing a dealer in the numbers racket. The boys allegedly were hired by a rival gambler. Only a few days before this killing, the TV series "Kojak" aired an episode in which professional criminals hired juveniles as "hit men."

This disturbing pattern ought to give pause to those mass media moguls who insist that mindless violence is the key to higher ratings. So should a study a few years ago by the National Commission on the Causes and Prevention of Violence, which found:

- Violence on TV programs was initiated just as often by characters identified as the "good guys" as by the "bad guys."
- Nearly half of the characters on TV who kill someone and more than half of those performing other acts of violence achieved a happy ending on the programs.
- Arrest and trial followed violence in only two out of 10 TV programs.

Instead, how about portraying violence as illegal and socially unacceptable? How about showing that violence creates problems instead of solving them? In other words, how about getting realistic with violence instead of glamorizing it?

In fact, if TV wants to be starkly realistic, how about bringing back, say, "Perry Mason" or "The Defenders" with an episode showing some broadcasters whose bank accounts are drained by the high court costs of defending one of their more brutal programs even if they end up winning the case?

ST. PETERSBURG TIMES

St. Petersburg, Florida, April 29, 1978

Should a television show be held financially responsible for causing a crime? That's the tough question a San Francisco jury will take up, thanks to recent action by the U.S. Supreme Court.

The court let stand a lower court decision that guarantees of freedom of speech do not automatically protect a television network and station from a lawsuit. So the mother of a 9-year-old girl, charging her daughter was sex-

ually assaulted with a bottle in a reenactment of a television crime, will be able to press a claim for $11 million in damages.

The TV movie, "Born Innocent," was an NBC drama about what happens to a first offender sent to a big city detention center for young girls. It showed the public a forgotten side of juvenile justice, a place where youngsters who tell of drug use and sexual abuse by fellow inmates are seldom heard.

The drama showed several girls apparently raping the main character, portrayed by Linda

Reprinted with permission from *St. Petersburg Times*.

Blair, with a wooden rod. Three days later four teen-age girls did the same thing to a child with a bottle. They told police they had seen the show.

Assuming the movie really did trigger this awful crime, should NBC and the San Francisco television station which carried the movie therefore share responsibility for the assault?

We always thought individuals had to be held accountable for their own behavior. Sadly enough, girls have been raped with objects since before the invention of television. And millions who saw the show did not run out and assault a child. Can the drama itself be held guilty because of those who did?

The four teen-agers who assaulted the girl were convicted and sentenced to probation. In civil cases where minors cause damage, their parents are usually held responsible, and have to pay for it. Shouldn't that standard apply here? Doesn't the blame for this crime fall on the shoulders of those who committed it? And the financial liability on their parents?

No amount of money can really compensate the victim, of course, and part of her mother's reason for pressing the case is to punish NBC and KRON-TV. Yet the drama raised important questions about the treatment of young girls who break the law. It may have influenced the way officials run juvenile detention centers. Perhaps it prevented one or more real life rapes. Should these questions have been squelched because some girls might be prompted to act out the dramatization?

We wonder if NBC could have handled the rape scene differently, and if that would have made any difference. Perhaps that is a possibility all three networks have been exploring since 1974, when the suit forced NBC to begin paying hefty legal fees. The networks do take some care in presenting violence. It wouldn't hurt to take more.

But should a jury force them to do it? The issue of free speech is at stake here, and not necessarily just for the creators of television drama. Fact can be just as provocative as fiction. What if a kidnap victim in Indianapolis can show that he probably was taken hostage because a local looney saw Walter Cronkite describe a kidnaping in Washington?

If CBS had to pay several million dollars as a result, news of kidnapings would probably dwindle. Is that good? Isn't secret crime scarier than known crime? Rumor and fear could easily replace fact, especially if magazines and newspapers became liable to the same damage suits.

In a sense newspapers are instant history, often more dramatic and fresher than the history books. But if the printed word were found liable for crime, the publishers of history books would also have to think twice.

Does the knowledge of Lincoln's assassination prompt some nut to take a shot at a new president? It was certainly a spectacular crime, and the books keep it alive. How do we know Lee Harvey Oswald or Squeaky Fromme hadn't just finished reading about John Wilkes Booth?

What we have outlined is obviously a domino effect, but it is not necessarily a far-fetched one. And it must be taken into account in considering the question of "Born Innocent," because the $11-million damage suit could tip the first domino.

We feel much sympathy for the little girl who was the victim of rape, and we can see how the mother would think her daughter would never have been attacked if the teen-age girls hadn't seen it on TV. People do imitate violence, including suicide.

But to hold NBC and KRON-TV responsible for the imitation puts the blame in the wrong place. And the consequences of attaching a legal and enormous financial price tag to that mistake could harm us all.

SUGGESTIONS FOR FURTHER READING

Chapter 5 Journalism and the Truth

Edward Jay Epstein, *Between Fact and Fiction: The Problem of Journalism* (New York: Vintage, 1975). A collection of his essays analyzing newspaper bias and distortion.

Robert Cirino, *Power to Persuade: Mass Media and the News* (New York: Bantam, 1974). A collection of examples documenting distortion in the choice of words, headlines, captions, photographs, film and story placement.

Chapter 6 Television News

Edward Jay Epstein, *News from Nowhere: Television and the News* (New York: Vintage, 1973). An in-depth study of the evening news of ABC, CBS, and NBC.

Chapter 7 Television Entertainment

Horace Newcomb (ed.), *Television: The Critical View*, 2d ed. (New York: Oxford University Press, 1979). A collection of essays by various media critics examining the effects of television.

Chapter 8 Minorities and Women

Ernest Holsendolph, "TV Cited on Stereotypes," *The New York Times* (January 17, 1979): C21. "The United States Civil Rights Commission said today that minorities and women continued to be cast on television as hackneyed stereotypes and that they were underemployed in the television business."

Chapter 9 Sex and Violence

Geoffrey Cowan, *See No Evil: The Backstage Battle over Sex and Violence in Television* (New York: Simon and Schuster, 1979). An account of Cowan's successful battle over the "family viewing policy." See especially Chapter 12, "From Violence to Sex."

Thomas Elmendorf, "Violence on TV: The Effect on Children," *Vital Speeches of the Day* 43 (October 1, 1976). This speech, given before the House Sub-committee on Communications, clearly outlines the fears many professionals feel about the effects of TV violence.

part III

RIGHTS IN CONFLICT

When the framers of the Constitution wrote the Bill of Rights, it provided for so *many* rights that it was inevitable that some of them would eventually overlap. So they set up a judicial system that could constantly examine those rights to see how their application would change over time.

In recent years the rights claimed by government, the public, and the media have tended to conflict with alarming frequency. The government demands the right to keep secrets and to make journalists testify. The media demand extra privileges for news gathering and protection from privacy laws. And the public wants privacy for themselves and gossip about others. And that's just a sample—the list of overlapping rights goes on and on.

This part of the book examines some of the more important cases of conflicting rights in the media. Chapter 10 looks at the conflict between a defendant's right to a fair trial and the public's "right to know." Chapter 11 looks at the issue of special privileges for news gatherers. Chapter 12 examines the conflict between government secrecy and the public's right to know, and Chapter 13 examines the conflict between that same right to know and personal privacy.

chapter 10

FREE PRESS VS. FAIR TRIAL

The issue of free press/fair trial is one of the most clear-cut media controversies in America today, and therefore one of the most difficult to resolve. The First Amendment to the Constitution guarantees freedom of the press, and the Sixth Amendment guarantees the right of every defendant to a trial by an impartial jury. As some observers have pointed out, "When the mass media set out to report a sensational trial, the two amendments come into inevitable conflict."[1]

The courts have attempted to solve this conflict in various ways, one of the most notable being the use of "gag" orders, which are court orders prohibiting the media from disseminating information that might be prejudicial to the defendant's fair trial. In 1976 the Supreme Court agreed to hear the "Nebraska case," which sought to test the constitutionality of gag orders; in its ruling the Court severely limited the use of these orders and therefore alleviated the controversy somewhat. However, the viewpoints that emerged during that controversy exposed many of the basic issues related to free press/fair trial. In the first reading in this chapter Richard Oliver, city editor of the *New York Daily News*, outlines what he calls "a newsman's view": the courts should find methods of ensuring a fair trial that do not restrict press freedom; he goes on to suggest some of the methods he considers appropriate. In the second part of this reading Burton B. Roberts, a New York State Supreme Court Justice, explains why, in his view, these alternate methods might not be enough.

The Nebraska decision limiting gag orders was hailed as a victory for the press, but a footnote in that decision led to the practice of closure—excluding the press entirely from trials and pretrial hearings—that most reporters find even more damaging than gag orders. In the second reading in this chapter David Rudenstine, an attorney and associate director of the New York Civil Liberties Union, explains why he thinks closure is "worse than a gag." His article appeared in the *Nation* in July of 1978, a year before the Supreme Court announced a decision in support of closure. Rudenstine's article is followed by excerpts from that decision, delivered by Supreme Court Justice Potter Stewart.

The Supreme Court's decision in favor of closure created a great deal of controversy, as seen in the newspaper editorials in this section. Most papers, such as the *Oregon Journal* and the *Philadelphia Inquirer*, came out strongly against the court's ruling. Some, such as the *Salt Lake Tribune*, surprisingly came out in favor of it. The powerful Gannett chain was so incensed by the ruling that they placed paid editorial ads denouncing it in all the major newspapers and newsweeklies in the country. An example of one of these ads follows the editorials mentioned above.

Later rulings by the Supreme Court limited the use of closure; so this controversy, like the "gag order" controversy, has quieted somewhat. But once again, the arguments expressed in these readings provide an excellent summary of this area of free press/fair trial conflict.

Several other issues have surfaced in recent years dealing with the conflict between fair trial and free press. One of these issues hit its peak in 1978 with the arrest of *New York Times* reporter M. A. Farber for his refusal to reveal his sources for a series of articles he wrote on a murder story. Law professor Philip B. Kurland presents his views on this issue in

an interview; a similar interview allows Jack C. Landau, director of the Reporters Committee for Freedom of the Press, to present the opposing view.

A year after the "disclosure of sources" issue hit its peak, the Supreme Court ruled against the press in another matter: it found that reporters may not use the First Amendment to avoid answering questions about their "state of mind" when they have been accused of libeling a public figure. The case arose when an ex-army officer sued the CBS news program "60 Minutes" for libel because of a program episode entitled "The Selling of Colonel Herbert." When the Court ruled that the producer of that episode had to answer questions dealing with his thoughts and intentions while putting the episode together, most newspapers decried the ruling as another infringement of constitutional rights. The editorial in this section from the *Newark Star Ledger* is an example of that point of view. The *Chicago Tribune* took the less popular approach of approving the ruling.

The final issue dealt with in this chapter is that of televising courtroom proceedings. In 1965 the Supreme Court ruled that Billy Sol Estes had not received a fair trial because of the presence of television cameras in the courtroom, but since that time 38 states have either decided to permit such coverage, or have proposals pending to that effect.[2] Several other states are considering such proposals; as they do, arguments on both sides are being heard. In the set of interviews that conclude this chapter, U.S. District Court Judge Jack Weinstein explains why he thinks TV cameras in the courtroom are beneficial, and attorney John Sutro gives an opposing view.

NOTES

1. Peter M. Sandman, David M. Rubin, and David B. Sachsman, *Media: An Introductory Analysis of American Mass Communications*, 2d ed. (Englewood Cliffs, N.J.: Prentice-Hall, 1976), p. 180.
2. "Courtroom TV May Get a N.Y. Channel," *New York Times* (January 27, 1980): 6E.

SHOULD THE PRESS BE GAGGED?

A NEWSMAN'S VIEW

Richard Oliver

Gagging the press is the chic thing these days in courtrooms from New York to California. But in reality the gag order is as old as tyranny itself. And, like tyranny, it is a threat to everyone.

Let's take a closer look at this judicial fad that has been called into use recently in two murder trials—the Sonny Carson murder case in Brooklyn and a Nebraska case now before the U.S. Supreme Court. And the press was barred from the courtroom during jury selection in the Patty Hearst case.

The issue in all these cases is now more than simply the innocence or guilt of the defendants, but whether the public, through its free press, is entitled to know what is happening in its courts. In the Brooklyn and Nebraska cases, the press was ordered not to publish matters of public record, facts, and background material that had come out in open court and had been published previously.

The (appeals) courts struck down the gag order in the Brooklyn case, although that ruling appeared to leave the door open for gag orders under certain circumstances. The Nebraska case has resulted in an appeal to the U.S. Supreme Court by the press.

The judges in these gag-order cases contend

From *New York Sunday News* View Section (February 1, 1976), p. 55. Copyright 1976 New York News Inc. Reprinted by permission.

that publication of certain background information—facts deemed necessary to make news stories understandable to readers—could prejudice the jury and jeopardize the defendant's right to a fair trial. So, without even showing that the forbidden material would actually prejudice a jury, some judges turn to the gag-order gimmick.

Never mind the First Amendment, freedom of the press, and the public's right to know, the advocates of gag orders are really saying. Forget the words of Supreme Court Justice William Brennan: "The First Amendment tolerates absolutely no prior judicial restraint of the press (based on the fear) that untoward consequences might result."

THERE ARE WAYS

Forget about the established tools of the court to keep jurors from being influenced by the press:

- **Admonition**—the judge cautions the jurors that they are bound by law from reading or listening to news accounts.
- **Change of Venue**—shifting the trial to another city or county.
- **Continuance**—delaying the trial until the publicity has worn off.
- **Sequestering**—keeping the jury in private, "locked up," to avoid exposure to the news media.

And there are other ways, such as bringing in a jury panel from another area, or excluding jurors before they are accepted on the panel. The remedies, according to recent studies, are rarely used. Some judges find it easier to gag the press.

Leaving aside for a moment the highfalutin' words and phrases of the continuing conflict between the news media and the legal establishment, let's look at the confrontation itself. The headline on these stories usually says something like: "Free Press vs. Fair Trial." The implication is that you have to take sides—that if you are for one, you must be against the other.

Well, that is hogwash. In truth, you cannot have one without the other. We need both, and we should cherish both.

Those judges who find themselves lured by the gag-order gimmick might well consider the recent admonition of New York's top judge, Chief Judge Charles D. Breitel. He cautioned the courts, the legal profession and the news media not to assume that any single group is the exclusive protector of the public interest.

One thing is clear, however. In the words of another top judge, Warren Burger, the Chief Justice of the United States: "For better or worse, editing is what editors are for."

A JUDGE'S VIEW

Burton B. Roberts

A controversy, which by no means is insoluble, has arisen between the media and the courts. On one hand, there is the constitutional right of the media to print the complete background of a defendant in order to guarantee the public's right to know what is happening during a criminal trial.

On the other hand, the court must, also under the Constitution, guarantee the rights of a defendant to a "public trial by an impartial jury," a jury that cannot be influenced by anything outside the courtroom.

In a few extremely rare and unusual cases, courts have asked the media to use restraint in reporting certain background information in order to protect this Sixth Amendment right of a defendant. The use of that kind of restraint order has to depend on the facts and circumstances of the individual case.

No general rules can be established other than to say it is a remedy of last resort. But I can see why it might become necessary to make such a request to the press in a rare circumstance.

In my opinion, the First Amendment, guaranteeing freedom of speech and press, is the darling of the Constitution's nursery. But the primacy of the First Amendment is not absolute. It was settled long ago that the Constitution does not provide for an unfettered right of expression. One cannot shout "fire," when there is no fire in a crowded theater.

In a criminal case, a defendant is presumed to be innocent until a jury unanimously agrees that his guilt has been established beyond a reasonable doubt. This is a real right, applicable to a "sinner" as well as a "saint." Both are presumed to be innocent. Indeed, both may be innocent.

If a defendant elects not to take the stand, his unsavory past, his criminal record, cannot be brought to the attention of a jury.

Only in the rarest instances will a court direct the media not to write anything either about a case or the defendant's background. For, after all, the court directs the jury not to read anything about the case, or it can even sequester a jury.

The first remedy, practically speaking, however, is often ignored. Jurors are human, and they will read newspapers or have articles brought to their attention.

SEQUESTERING IS COSTLY

The second remedy is rather expensive. Sequestering a jury costs at least $2000 a day; in a month-long trial that means $60,000 in taxpayers' money, and to what avail. In addition to the expense, sequestering a jury can cause great inconvenience to jurors and their families and create imbalances in the pool of jurors due to lack of availability.

In those extremely rare instances that a court directs the media not to publish something in the interest of a fair trial, cannot the press reveal that background after the verdict is in? I do not advocate adopting the British system, which certainly curtails the right of the media to cover trials. But I do advocate that in certain rare instances the court has the right to direct that the media exercise restraint. If the court has abused its discretion, certainly a higher court can correct this in short order.

I believe that guidelines fair to both the defendant and the press can be worked out if the two sides get together. The issue should be resolved in light rather than heat.

CLOSURE IS WORSE
THAN A GAG

David Rudenstine

Courthouse reporters around the country are discussing the current trend among judges who, determined to limit prejudicial pretrial publicity, have taken to banning them from hearings in advance of criminal trial. The New York City judge who presided over the "Son of Sam" case closed the second round of compe-

Reprinted from "Closure Is Worse Than a Gag," by David Rudenstine in *The Nation* (July 8–15, 1978): 41–43. Used by permission from *The Nation* magazine, copyright 1978 The Nation Associates, Inc.

tency hearings to the press on the ground that further publicity would endanger David Berkowitz's right to a fair trial. In another sensational murder case, where both the victim and the defendant were Yale University students, the judge barred the press from a hearing at which the admissibility of an alleged confession was decided. In a third case, a Gannett newspaper reporter was locked out of a rural New York courtroom while the judge considered the admissibility of a confession in a case involving the murder of a local policeman.

Closure of pretrial hearings has been ruled permissible by some lower courts. If the Supreme Court—which agreed to rule on an appeal pressed by the Gannett chain—decides to uphold these lower court rulings, First Amendment values will have been dealt a blow.* The press claims that closure of pretrial hearings violates historic rights grounded in the First Amendment. Judges ordering closure respond that it does not interfere with the press's right to publish what it knows; it only prevents reporters from learning what they would like to know. As will be seen in a moment, the difference between the right to publish and the right of access in this context is not as clear as some courts suggest.

The fair trial/free press debate opposes two competing interests deeply rooted in the U.S. Constitution. The Sixth Amendment guarantees a defendant charged with a crime to trial by an impartial jury; the First Amendment guarantees a free press. Justice Hugo Black once referred to these twin rights as "two of the most cherished policies of our civilization."

When a case attracts lively public interest, hence intense press attention, it is sometimes difficult to impanel an impartial jury. As a result, numerous techniques harmless to First Amendment principles have been developed to curtail the adverse effects of pretrial publicity. In *Nebraska Press Association v. Stuart*, the Court referred with approval to changing the trial location; adjourning the trial until possible pretrial prejudicial publicity faded; carefully questioning prospective jurors at the *voir dire* stage; impressing on jurors their duty to decide a case only on evidence presented at trial; controlling what the attorneys, parties, and court officers say and how they behave before and during trial; sequestering the jury if necessary, and giving stern instructions at the charging

stage that the case must be decided only on the evidence presented in court. Nevertheless, some technique threatening to the First Amendment interests occasionally becomes popular. This happened a few years ago and resulted in a landmark decision by the Supreme Court with a direct bearing on the issues raised by the *Gannett* case.

Nebraska grew out of a crime involving the murdering of six members of one family in a small Nebraska town. Press, TV, and radio coverage was immediate, massive, and national. A few days after the alleged assailant was arrested, a local Nebraska court entered a gag order on the information that the media could release. The order, appealed through the Nebraska courts, eventually reached the Supreme Court which said that the gag order was a "prior restraint"—the "most serious and the least tolerable infringement on First Amendment rights." It invalidated the gag order because it found that a fair trial could be assured by other techniques harmless to First Amendment interests and because it was "far from clear" that the prior restraint would have protected the defendant's rights. The Court did not say that gag orders would never be permissible to assure a fair trial; it did say that it had never reviewed a case in which a gag order was essential to a fair trial.

One technique not approved or discussed in *Nebraska* was the closing of pretrial proceedings to the public and press. However, the Court referred to this procedure in a footnote and indicated that it was not passing on its appropriateness since the *Nebraska* case did not raise it. The *Gannett* case results from that footnote.

Pretrial hearings are critical in criminal cases. At those hearings, for example, courts decide whether a confession by an alleged killer was voluntary; whether the wiretap of a political figure comported with constitutional safeguards; whether a mass murderer is competent to stand trial; or whether a search leading

---

*Editor's note: As Rudenstine feared, the Supreme Court upheld the lower court rulings favoring closure. See next reading for excerpts from this decision.

to physical evidence of a crime was consistent with constitutional protections.

The outcome of these hearings may determine whether a defendant goes to trial, cops a plea, or the case is dismissed. Moreover, because about 90 percent of criminal cases are disposed of prior to trial, preliminary hearings are often the only judicial proceedings in a case other than sentencing. Closing preliminary hearings often means putting the crucial aspect of a criminal case beyond the reach of the press and public.

Although the *Nebraska* decision is relevant to the closure debate in *Gannett*, the circumstances of the two cases are sufficiently different to cause concern as to how the latter will be resolved. A gag order bars the press from publishing things it knows; a closure order bars the press from knowing things to publish. The First Amendment guarantees that the press may publish what it knows, but it doesn't necessarily guarantee the press access to that information. Thus, the closing of pretrial hearings may not be directly barred by the First Amendment. It doesn't follow, however, that closure is permissible, for the Sixth Amendment guarantees not only an impartial jury but a public trial. It is difficult to square the concept of closure with that principle and the First Amendment values it implies. That is the issue which *Gannett* brings before the Supreme Court.

New York's highest court approved closure in an opinion that departs substantially from previous practice. The new rule provides that preliminary hearings should be "presumptively" closed to the press and public whenever press commentary threatens a defendant's right to trial by an impartial jury. If the hearing is to remain open, the burden is on the press to show that a "genuine public interest" outweighs the "risk of premature disclosures." The court did not state that closure should be employed only if other techniques less damaging to First Amendment values were inadequate or that the

margin of benefit that closure might produce must be evaluated before it is authorized. It held in effect that closure was presumptively correct in cases of public interest. This is a sweeping rule and it will be a rare day when the press is able to overcome the presumption.

The Supreme Court may follow its own footsteps and decide *Gannett* as it did *Nebraska*, but that outcome is hardly assured. Neither the First Amendment rights asserted in *Nebraska* nor the public trial right with its implied First Amendment values that are at stake in *Gannett* is absolute—no right is. But core First Amendment rights are traditionally more nearly absolute than any others and attempts to impinge upon them are closely scrutinized. The public trial claim asserted in *Gannett* is surely significant, but its strength is not as thoroughly tested nor its parameters as clearly defined as the First Amendment rights raised in *Nebraska*. Moreover, it is generally accepted that some narrow circumstances, such as the protection of an undercover agent's identity or national security, may justify closing a limited portion of a trial. Hence, while the outcome in *Nebraska* is pertinent to the closure issue, it is not controlling.

Before outlining the reasons closure should be strictly limited, two weak but distracting responses to the objection that closure collides with the public trial requirement deserve mention. First, it might be argued that the right to a public trial belongs to a defendant; if he waives it, the trial or pretrial hearings should be closed. But that is inconsistent with the time-honored notion that the public's valid interest in judicial proceedings is sufficient to compel them to be open, even over a defendant's objection. As the Supreme Court stated: "A trial is a public event. What transpires in the courtroom is public property."

Second, it might be contended that only trials are guaranteed to be public and that hearings before trial may be closed. But that claim makes an arbitrary distinction between a trial and pretrial hearings, whereas the reasons compelling open trials apply with equal force to the earlier proceedings.

Closure is actually worse than a gag order. The latter at least seeks to limit only information prejudicial to a defendant's fair-trial rights; closure deprives the press and public of *all* information revealed at a preliminary hearing, regardless of its effect on a defendant. Closure casts a much broader shadow.

Press coverage of pretrial hearings is necessary to assure the integrity of those proceedings. It is the major way the public learns of police conduct. It is essential if the public is to stay abreast of developments in important cases and be informed of prosecutorial, defense counsel, and judicial conduct (or misconduct). The knowledge that judicial proceedings will be reported is often credited with deterring witnesses from perjury and occasionally with bringing forward key witnesses previously unknown to the parties. News about pretrial discussions may help make an eventual plea bargain more intelligible to the public. Moreover, closure tends to kindle the public distrust that greets any star chamber proceeding.

Public and press access to judicial proceedings helps assure judicial accountability. What Justice Brennan has said of gag orders applies here: "Indeed, the potential for arbitrary and excessive judicial utilization of any such power would be exacerbated by the fact that judges and committing magistrates might in some cases be determining the propriety of publishing information that reflects on their competence, integrity, or general performance on the bench."

Unless closure is restricted by the tightest rules, the practice will grow. Defense counsel in cases drawing press attention will routinely ask that the preliminary hearing be closed. Wishing to protect a possible conviction from reversal, prosecutors will probably acquiesce. Judges, also worried about reversals, will be inclined to approve. The result could well be that the press and public would be routinely barred

from all such hearings. Developments since New York's highest court decided *Gannett* lend substance to this concern.

More speculatively, the ultimate containment problem might be to prevent closure from being applied to trials. If widely used at the preliminary stage, courts may eventually seek to circumvent the strong principles of *Nebraska* by using closure at the trial stage. That result seems unthinkable in light of the forceful opinion in *Nebraska*, but not every court in the land grants the First Amendment the respect the Supreme Court showed in *Nebraska*.

As for the benefits promised by closure, they are indeed uncertain. Unless closure can assure a fair trial with substantial certainty, it is too drastic a technique to be seriously considered. And that benefit seems far from clear. Cases drawing press attention are usually subject to considerable publicity before any hearing is held. More curiously, perhaps, the effectiveness of closure is undercut because the press, though barred, may still report the fact of, and the reason for, the hearing. An example best makes the point. A young man is accused of hammer-bludgeoning to death a young woman while she slept in her parents' home in a New York suburb. The judge closes a preliminary hearing held to determine the admissibility of some apparently damaging statements. The *New York Times*, barred from the courtroom, reports: "At issue in the current hearings is whether statements alleged to have been made by [the defendant], statements that the judge said 'could be characterized as confessions,' will be allowed when the trial starts next week. There are reportedly four separate instances in which the defendant is alleged to have confessed to the killing. . . ." The contribution of closure to fair trial interests is the difference between a report like that and one that would have included the statements themselves. That hardly seems sufficient to justify a remedy as drastic as closure.

Of course, even the techniques mentioned earlier that are harmless to First Amendment interests raise problems of their own. An adjournment to allow the impact of pretrial publicity to fade might conflict with a defendant's right to a speedy trial. A change in trial location might work a hardship on the defendant and defendant's family, counsel, and witnesses. But these consequences are less certain and less weighty than the damage to First Amendment interests that will assuredly flow from a closure order.

If the Supreme Court approves the closing of pretrial hearings by standards less demanding than it requires for gag orders, it will be departing substantially from the importance it placed on First Amendment values in *Nebraska*. If it treats closure as it treated gag orders it will remain loyal to the view that there is no insoluble conflict between the values of a fair trial and a free press. The Court has found this view persuasive in the past and there is nothing new to change its mind. But the Court left the issue open and now has agreed to decide it. Until it does there is an edge of unsettling uncertainty, for the stakes are high.

EXCERPTS FROM
GANNETT V. DEPASQUALE

U.S. SUPREME COURT

Gannett Company, Inc., v. DePasquale, County Court Judge
of Seneca County, N.Y., et al., July 2, 1979

Mr. Justice Stewart delivered the opinion of the Court.

The question presented in this case is whether members of the public have an independent constitutional right to insist upon access to a pretrial judicial proceeding, even though the accused, the prosecutor, and the trial judge all have agreed to the closure of that proceeding in order to assure a fair trial.

Wayne Clapp, aged 42 and residing at Henrietta, a Rochester, N.Y., suburb, disappeared

in July 1976. He was last seen on July 16 when, with two male companions, he went out on his boat to fish in Lake Seneca, about 40 miles from Rochester. The two companions returned in the boat the same day and drove away in Clapp's pickup truck. Clapp was not with them. When he failed to return home by July 19, his family reported his absence to the police. An examination of the boat, laced with bulletholes, seemed to indicate that Clapp had met a violent death aboard it. Police then began an intensive search for the two men. They also began lake dragging operations in an attempt to locate Clapp's body.

The petitioner, Gannett Co., Inc., publishes two Rochester newspapers, the morning *Democrat & Chronicle* and the evening *Times-Union*. On July 20, each paper carried its first story about Clapp's disappearance. Each re-

From *Media Law Reporter*, vol. 5 (July 2, 1979): 1337. Reprinted by special permission from *Media Law Reporter*, copyright 1979 by The Bureau of National Affairs, Inc., Washington, D.C.

ported the few details that were then known and stated that the police were theorizing that Clapp had been shot on his boat and his body dumped overboard. Each stated that the body was missing. The *Times-Union* mentioned the names of respondents Greathouse and Jones and said that Greathouse "was identified as one of the two companions who accompanied Clapp Friday" on the boat; said that the two were aged 16 and 21, respectively; and noted that the police were seeking the two men and Greathouse's wife, also 16. Accompanying the evening story was a 1959 photograph of Clapp. The report also contained an appeal from the state police for assistance.

Michigan police apprehended Greathouse, Jones, and the woman on July 21. This came about when an interstate bulletin describing Clapp's truck led to their discovery in Jackson County, Mich., by police who observed the truck parked at a local motel. The petitioner's two Rochester papers on July 22 reported the details of the capture. The stories recounted how the Michigan police, after having arrested Jones in a park, used a helicopter and dogs and tracked down Greathouse and the woman in some woods. They recited that Clapp's truck was located near the park.

The stories also stated that Seneca County police theorized that Clapp was shot with his own pistol, robbed, and his body thrown into Lake Seneca. The articles provided background on Clapp's life, sketched the events surrounding his disappearance, and said that New York had issued warrants for the arrest of the three persons. One of the articles reported that the Seneca County District Attorney would seek to extradite the suspects and would attempt to carry through with a homicide prosecution even if Clapp's body were not found. The paper also quoted the prosecutor as stating, however, that the evidence was still developing and "the case could change." The other story noted that Greathouse and Jones were from Texas and South Carolina, respectively.

Both papers carried stories on July 23. These revealed that Jones, the adult, had waived extradition and that New York police had traveled to Michigan and were questioning the suspects. The articles referred to police speculation that extradition of Greathouse and the woman might involve "legalities" because they were only 16 and considered juveniles in Michigan. The morning story provided details of an interview with the landlady from whom the suspects had rented a room while staying in Seneca County at the time Clapp disappeared. It also noted that Greathouse, according to state police, was on probation in San Antonio, Tex., but that the police did not know the details of his criminal record.

The *Democrat & Chronicle* carried another story on the morning of July 24. It stated that Greathouse had led the Michigan police to the spot where he had buried a .357 magnum revolver belonging to Clapp and that the gun was being returned to New York with the three suspects. It also stated that the police had found ammunition at the hotel where Greathouse and the woman were believed to have stayed before they were arrested. The story repeated the basic facts known about the disappearance of Clapp and the capture of the three suspects in Michigan. It stated that New York police continued to search Lake Seneca for Clapp's body.

On July 25, the *Democrat & Chronicle* reported that Greathouse and Jones had been arraigned before a Seneca County magistrate on second-degree murder charges shortly after their arrival from Michigan; that they and the woman also had been arraigned on charges of second-degree grand larceny; that the three had been committed to the Seneca County jail; that all three had "appeared calm" during the court session; and that the magistrate had read depositions signed by three witnesses, one of whom testified to having heard "five or six shots" from the lake on the day of the disappearance, just before seeing Clapp's boat "veer sharply" in the water.

Greathouse, Jones, and the woman were indicted by a Seneca County grand jury on August 2. The two men were charged, in several counts, with second-degree murder, robbery, and grand larceny. The woman was indicted on one count of grand larceny. Both the *Democrat & Chronicle* and the *Times-Union* on August 3 reported the filing of the indictments. Each story stated that the murder charges specified that the two men had shot Clapp with his own gun, had weighted his body with anchors and tossed it into the lake, and then had made off with Clapp's credit card, gun, and truck. Each reported that the defendants were held without bail, and each again provided background material with details of Clapp's disappearance. The fact that Clapp's body still had not been recovered was mentioned. One report noted that, according to the prosecutor, if the body were not recovered prior to trial, "it will be the first such trial in New York State history." Each paper on that day also carried a brief notice that a memorial service for Clapp would be held that evening in Henrietta. These notices repeated that Greathouse and Jones had been charged with Clapp's murder and that his body had not been recovered.

On August 6, each paper carried a story reporting the details of the arraignments of Greathouse and Jones the day before. The papers stated that both men had pleaded not guilty to all charges. Once again, each story repeated the basic facts of the accusations against the men and noted that the woman was arraigned on a larceny charge. The stories noted that defense attorneys had been given 90 days in which to file pretrial motions.

During this 90-day period, Greathouse and Jones moved to suppress statements made to the police. The ground they asserted was that those statements had been given involuntarily. They also sought to suppress physical evidence seized as fruits of the allegedly involuntary confessions; the primary physical evidence they sought to suppress was the gun to which,

as petitioner's newspaper had reported, Greathouse had led the Michigan police.

The motions to suppress came before Judge DePasquale on November 4. At this hearing, defense attorneys argued that the unabated buildup of adverse publicity had jeopardized the ability of the defendants to receive a fair trial. They thus requested that the public and the press be excluded from the hearing. The district attorney did not oppose the motion. Although Carol Ritter, a reporter employed by the petitioner, was present in the courtroom, no objection was made at the time of the closure motion. The trial judge granted the motion. . . .

This Court has long recognized that adverse publicity can endanger the ability of a defendant to receive a fair trial. . . . To safeguard the due process rights of the accused, a trial judge has an affirmative constitutional duty to minimize the effects of prejudicial pretrial publicity. . . . And because of the Constitution's pervasive concern for these due process rights, a trial judge may surely take protective measures even when they are not strictly and inescapably necessary.

Publicity concerning pretrial suppression hearings such as the one involved in the present case poses special risks of unfairness. The whole purpose of such hearings is to screen out unreliable or illegally obtained evidence and ensure that this evidence does not become known to the jury. . . . Publicity concerning the proceedings at a pretrial hearing, however, could influence public opinion against a defendant and inform potential jurors of inculpatory information wholly inadmissable at the actual trial.

The danger of publicity concerning pretrial suppression hearings is particularly acute, because it may be difficult to measure with any degree of certainty the effects of such publicity on the fairness of the trial. After the commencement of the trial itself, inadmissible prejudicial information about a defendant can be kept from a jury by a variety of means. When such information is publicized during a pretrial proceeding, however, it may never be altogether kept from potential jurors. Closure of pretrial proceedings is often one of the most effective methods that a trial judge can employ to attempt to ensure that the fairness of a trial will not be jeopardized by the dissemination of such information throughout the community before the trial itself has even begun. . . .

The Sixth Amendment, applicable to the States through the Fourteenth, surrounds a criminal trial with guarantees such as the rights to notice, confrontation, and compulsory process that have as their overriding purpose the protection of the accused from prosecutorial and judicial abuses. Among the guarantees that the Amendment provides to a person charged with the commission of a criminal offense, and to him alone, is the "right to a speedy and public trial, by an impartial jury." The Constitution nowhere mentions any right of access to a criminal trial on the part of the public; its guarantee, like the others enumerated, is personal to the accused. . . .

While the Sixth Amendment guarantees to a defendant in a criminal case the right to a public trial, it does not guarantee the right to compel a private trial. "The ability to waive a constitutional right does not ordinarily carry with it the right to insist upon the opposite of that right." . . . But the issue here is not whether the defendant can compel a private trial. Rather the issue is whether members of the public have an enforceable right to a public trial that can be asserted independently of the parties in the litigation.

There can be no blinking the fact that there is a strong societal interest in public trials. Openness in court proceedings may improve the quality of testimony, induce unknown witnesses to come forward with relevant testimony, cause all trial participants to perform their duties more conscientiously, and generally give the public an opportunity to observe the judicial system. . . . But there is a strong societal interest in other constitutional guarantees extended to the accused as well. The public, for example, has a definite and concrete interest in seeing that justice is swiftly and fairly administered.

We certainly do not disparage the general desirability of open judicial proceedings. But we are not asked here to declare whether open proceedings represent beneficial social policy, or whether there would be a constitutional barrier to a state law that imposed a stricter standard of closure than the one here employed by the New York courts. Rather, we are asked to hold that the Constitution itself gave the petitioner an affirmative right of access to this pretrial proceeding, even though all the participants in the litigation agreed that it should be closed to protect the fair trial rights of the defendants.

For all of the reasons discussed in this opinion, we hold that the Constitution provides no such right. Accordingly, the judgment of the New York Court of Appeals is affirmed.

It is so ordered.

ON CLOSURE

OREGON JOURNAL

Portland, Oregon, July 9, 1979

The U.S. Supreme Court spends its working days in consultation with the Constitution.

But sometimes one has to wonder if the honorable justices read that remarkable document.

The Sixth Amendment says, among other things, that "the accused shall enjoy the right to a speedy and public trial."

Now a five-member majority of the high court says that does not mean that the trial must be public.

What else is a public trial?

Those farsighted framers of the Constitution knew exactly what they had in mind when they drafted the Sixth Amendment.

The constitutional requirement for a public trial would guard against the star chamber proceedings other countries employed.

A public trial would be the accused's ultimate guarantee of a fair trial.

The same is just as true today as it was when the Bill of Rights was being added to the Constitution.

But the Supreme Court now says that trial judges have virtually unlimited discretion to boot public and press out of their courtrooms if they wish.

The decision actually was based on a case involving pretrial proceedings, but the majority opinion goes further and refers to the trial itself. It looks like the first step toward allowing trials to be conducted behind closed doors.

The Supreme Court is supposed to be the ultimate protector of the freedoms guaranteed by the Constitution. But when the Court holds that the Constitution does not say what it says, there is nowhere else to turn.

Human liberties are not in good hands with the Burger court. They took another licking, and a potentially severe one, with the authorization for judges to close their courtroom doors.

Reprinted by permission from *Oregon Journal*. Copyright 1979 Oregon Journal.

THE PHILADELPHIA INQUIRER

Philadelphia, Pennsylvania, July 5, 1979

In 1615, Edward Peacham, accused of treason, was dragged before an English court for what would now be called a pretrial hearing. Later,

Reprinted by permission of The Philadelphia Inquirer, July 5, 1979.

eight Crown officials, headed by none other than Attorney General Sir Francis Bacon, made this report to King James:

"Upon these interrogatories, Peacham this day was examined before torture, in torture, between torture, and after torture: notwithstanding, nothing could be drawn from him, he still persisting in his obstinate and insensible denials and former answers."

The men who wrote the Constitution of the United States knew the name of Edward Peacham and of others who had faced the infamous secret proceedings of the Star Chamber. They knew that unrestrained power of government led to tyranny, and in the Constitution, that web of interlocking protections, they made sure, in the Fifth Amendment, that no person would be required to testify against himself, and in the Sixth, that "in all criminal prosecutions, the accused shall enjoy the right to a speedy and public trial."

Now, by grim coincidence on July 2, which many people consider to be the real Fourth of July, the U.S. Supreme Court, in a 5–4 decision, has ruled that the door of the courtroom, in pretrial proceedings as well as the trial itself, may be shut to the public if the judge, the prosecution, and defense all agree.

The ruling came in a New York case. On the same day, the court refused to hear a challenge (joined by this and other newspapers and journalism organizations) to a Pennsylvania Supreme Court rule barring press and public from the pretrial hearings in the second murder trial of former United Mine Workers president W. A. (Tony) Boyle.

The majority ruling is narrow, abstract, lopsided, and imbued with suspicion, not of the potential of governmental or judicial tyranny, but of the presumed tyranny of the press.

It is narrow in asserting that the Sixth Amendment guarantees are, as Justice Potter Stewart put it for the majority, provided "to a person charged with the commission of a criminal offense, *and to him alone*" (our emphasis). That reading is so narrow as to squeeze the life out of the guarantee. The right to a public trial is also a public right. As Justice Harry A. Blackmun cited in dissenting, "The knowledge that every criminal trial is subject to contempora-

neous review in the forum of public opinion is an effective restraint on possible abuse of judicial power."

The majority ruling simply ignores reality, which is that prosecution and defense may well have a mutual interest, contrary to the public interest, in secrecy. As the American Civil Liberties Union put it, the majority interpretation of the law "would have let the Nixon Justice Department accept a guilty plea from the Watergate burglars behind closed doors" and "erected an iron curtain between the criminal process and the inquiring press."

The decision assumes that the great danger to the fairness of a public trial by an impartial jury is the public trial itself—that is, that "adverse publicity" can so poison the public mind as to make it impossible to convene an impartial jury. This is a dubious proposition. Certainly the press has, on occasion, committed unpardonable excesses—the Lindbergh trial and the case of Dr. Sam Sheppard being notorious examples. Yet these are the exception, not the rule. In the Watergate trials, there was also a great deal of "adverse publicity," generated by the simple reporting of the facts as they developed, but no one seriously argues that the juries in those cases did not produce fair verdicts, some guilty, some not guilty.

There are, as a matter of fact, many methods by which fair trials can be assured in such cases, including the selection of the jurors (as in any case), the sequestration of the jury if necessary, a change of venue, and so on. Secrecy is not one such method. Not in trials. Not in pretrial hearings where, as Justice Blackmun noted, some 90 percent of cases are disposed of, leaving them as "the only opportunity the public has to learn about police and prosecutorial conduct, and about allegations that those responsible to the public for the enforcement of laws themselves are breaking it."

What of the public's right to know what happens in its courts? "Members of the public have no constitutional right under the Sixth and Fourteenth Amendments to attend criminal trials," the majority said. Incredible. The decision turns the two amendments on their heads.

As James Madison once wrote: "Nothing could be more irrational than to give the people power and to withhold from them information without which power is abused."

THE SALT LAKE TRIBUNE

Salt Lake City, Utah, July 6, 1979

The Sixth Amendment provides that "in all criminal prosecutions, the accused shall enjoy the right to a speedy and public trial." The Fourteenth Amendment made this provision binding on the states.

The amendment does not say that the accused must have a speedy and public trial if he or she does not want one. And it does not say, though many think it implies, that the press and public have the same right as the accused.

In holding in a 5–4 decision that judges, with consent of the defendant may close preliminary criminal proceedings to the public, the Supreme Court of the United States Monday chose to hew closely to precise words of the Sixth Amendment. The majority, however, also pointedly recognized the benefits as well as abuses of public access to all steps in a criminal proceeding

Public trials were guaranteed the accused because secret proceedings are more apt to be rigged. The same reasoning extends to pretrial hearings where, according to Justice Harry A. Blackmun, some 90 percent of all criminal proceedings are disposed of before trial.

That protection, however, has come to be a mixed blessing. In some instances publicity generated at public pretrial hearings has made it difficult to assure defendants a fair trial later. In such cases the accused might feel his interests are best served by banning public and press from pretrial proceedings. And that, said the Supreme Court majority, is his right, a right that supersedes the general public's interest in knowing what goes on in its courts.

Although the Monday ruling was mainly a Sixth Amendment public trial issue, the ongoing conflict between that mandate and the First Amendment's promise of a free press was addressed, too, and once more the Sixth Amendment prevailed.

As with so many rulings, critics are quick to conjure up hypothetical worst examples of what could happen. But experience suggests that the terrible possibilities are seldom realized.

Critics see this ruling as the latest in a disturbing series of anti-press action, one which could give judges unlimited power to conduct closed-door proceedings. But in states such as Utah where local laws already condone what the court is now sanctioning, the experience has been anything but devastating.

Encouraging judges to encourage defendants to request secret pretrial proceedings does carry potential danger of declining confidence in the judicial system. But most accused persons, we believe, will for various reasons continue to prefer having their cases heard in the open and nothing much will be changed.

Reprinted by permission from *The Salt Lake Tribune.* Copyright 1979 The Salt Lake Tribune.

THE DOORS OF INJUSTICE

SENECA FALLS, New York—In 1976, an ex-policeman disappeared while fishing on Seneca Lake in Upstate New York. Two men were arrested and accused of his murder, even though the body was never found.

Carol Ritter, court reporter for Gannett Rochester Newspapers, went to cover the pretrial hearing for the accused.

When she arrived at the courtroom, Ritter and other reporters were barred from the hearing on the pretext that the accused would not be able to get a fair trial if the pretrial hearing was covered by the press.

The Gannett Rochester Newspapers strongly disagreed and challenged the judge's right to close the doors of justice to the people, including the press. They took that challenge to the Supreme Court of the United States.

Gannett believes no judge should have the right to shut the people and their free press out of such pretrial hearings, where an overwhelming majority of criminal prosecutions are resolved.

Can you imagine up to 90 percent of all court cases being settled in secret? Gannett could not. But on July 2, 1979, the Supreme Court ruled it could happen.

Gannett protests vigorously this abridgment of the First Amendment. Not only has the Court limited journalists' access to gathering and reporting the news for the public, but it has also trampled on the people's freedom to know, the cornerstone of our rights as a free people in a free society.

The freedoms of the First Amendment must be cherished, not shackled.

At Gannett, we have a commitment to freedom in every business we're in, whether it's newspaper, TV, radio, outdoor advertising or public opinion research.

And so from Burlington to Boise, from Fort Myers to Fort Wayne, every Gannett newspaper, every TV and radio station is free to express its own opinions, free to serve the best interests of its own community in its own way.

Gannett
A World Of Different Voices
Where Freedom Speaks

Reproduced by permission of the Gannett Company, Inc. This ad appeared in several news magazines between July and October 1979.

MUST REPORTERS DISCLOSE SOURCES?

YES—"REPORTERS HAVE TO OBEY THE LAW LIKE EVERYONE ELSE"

NO—"WE HAVE TO HAVE CONFIDENTIALITY OR WE CAN'T DO OUR JOBS"

Interview with Philip B. Kurland

Q: Professor Kurland, why do you believe newsmen do not have the constitutional right to keep sources and information confidential?

A: I feel that way for two reasons: one, because the Supreme Court has said there is no such right. Reporters can live in a dream world and say, "We know what the Constitution says, and the Supreme Court doesn't." But as the law exists today, the press doesn't have that right.

Second, because the right of freedom of speech and press is given to everybody, not just the institutional press. The use of the word *press* at the time it was put into the First Amendment did not denote newspapers or magazines but anybody who was engaged in the printed rather than the spoken word. So there's no reason to say there's a greater privilege for the institutional press than for the individual who seeks to publish his views.

Q: Aren't journalists entitled to have a privilege comparable to lawyers and doctors?

A: The privileges to which you refer, and which the newspapers from time to time speak of as constitutional privileges, are not constitutional privileges. The doctor-patient privilege, the priest-penitent privilege—they're all dependent on statute.

Interview with Jack C. Landau

Q: Mr. Landau, why do you believe newsmen have the constitutional right to keep sources and information confidential?

A: The First Amendment to the Constitution says that the press is supposed to be immune from government. By requiring reporters to disclose sources, government hampers the press from collecting information. If you can't collect it, you can't publish it. This is clearly contrary to the First Amendment.

While the press has always made this First Amendment argument very strongly, it seems to me there's also another First Amendment argument relating to freedom of association. A reporter should be free to circulate through the community. He should be free to talk with people and to have those people have the assurance that their identities aren't going to be disclosed.

Q: What will happen to the press if the courts continue to try to force reporters to reveal confidential information?

A: People will not provide information to the press in sensitive cases if they think their identities are going to be made public.

The highly publicized case of *New York Times* reporter M. A. Farber is a perfect exam-

Reprinted from *U.S. News & World Report* (October 9, 1978): 71–72.

Kurland interview continued

There's nothing in the Constitution that forbids either state governments or the national government from effecting a statute which would create this kind of privilege for the press.

Q: Isn't the public well served by enabling reporters to protect their sources?

A: Not under all circumstances. What you've got is a problem of balancing. The courts recognize this. There is an obligation on the part of anybody who seeks information from reporters to justify access to the information. In the case of *New York Times* reporter M. A. Farber, there's some question whether access to secure his private notes has been justified.

Q: Do you contend that news reporters are acting above the law when they refuse to turn over confidential information to the courts?

A: Not long ago, the press maintained that even the President of the United States can't be a judge in his own case. The same thing holds true for the press. Reporters have to obey the law like everyone else.

Q: Don't reporters run the risk of being used as an arm of the state, as an investigative tool of government?

A: No more than any witness to an event whose testimony is necessary for a trial. I don't become an agent for the government because I've witnessed a crime and am called on to give testimony.

Q: Critics say that some lawyers use the press as a ploy, actually preferring that reporters refuse to give information so the lawyers can claim that their clients have been denied fair trials—

A: I don't think the courts have been stringent enough in imposing ethical standards on either prosecution or defendants in the abuse of these matters—either the abuse of trying their

Landau interview continued

ple of what could happen. If the courts force Farber to disclose confidential information and sources, the next newspaper reporter that comes across a situation where there may have been a crime committed may not be able to disclose it to the people in New Jersey or New York.

Q: Don't the First Amendment claims of the press collide with other constitutional rights, such as a defendant's right to a fair trial?

A: I'm not sure there is a conflict. Furthermore, there are lawyers all over the country who have in their files information which would clearly acquit or convict people. But those lawyers have an attorney-client privilege. No one has argued that the country is going to fall apart because of that privilege. I don't understand why, when it comes to the press, all of a sudden it becomes a cosmic disaster for society to protect sources.

Q: Critics contend that the press is trying to put itself above the law by protecting confidentiality—

A: We are not putting ourselves above the law any more than a major law firm is putting itself above the law when it asserts its attorney-client privilege.

The lawyers say, "We have to have a confidentiality privilege or else we can't do our job." The press says, "We have to have a confidentiality privilege or we can't do our jobs."

If you want to look at the social impact, the lawyer is protecting only a single individual. But in a case like Watergate, the reporters may be protecting thousands, maybe millions, of individuals.

Q: Hasn't the U.S. Supreme Court said there is no such privilege for the press?

A: This Supreme Court has said that. And the Supreme Court a hundred years ago said that

Kurland interview continued

cases in the newspapers or of abusing subpoenas. There are cases in which lawyers don't
really want witnesses' testimony but only want
to make a public issue of it.

**Q: Do judges often order reporters to turn
over information without first determining
that the information is essential to the outcome
of the case?**

A: There may be some cases like that. The
rules should be clear that judges should not
issue such orders unless good cause is shown
that the reporter is in possession of unique information of importance or relevance to the
processes of the criminal law and not elsewhere
available. That kind of judgment is dependent
on the discretion of the person who's making
the judgment, obviously. Whether the judges
have made that judgment correctly in most
cases, or incorrectly in most cases, I can't say.

**Q: Are there ways that reporters could pro-
tect sources while not impairing the right of an
individual to a fair trial?**

A: An individual's interest in a fair trial is not
abused or violated unless the reporter's data are
proved to have a likelihood of weightiness and
there's a necessity for them. If those items are
shown to be not only relevant but substantial, I
do not see a way for the reporter to avoid meeting the command of the court.

**Q: Is there a way around many of these con-
frontations between the courts and the press?**

A: There's a clear way around it—and it's
one that the press has obviously recognized.
And that's to go to Congress and ask for the creation of a legal privilege, often called a "shield
law." I'm a great believer in the notion that
public policy is primarily to be made by our
legislatures and not by our courts. I think that's
the forum to which the press will have to go if
it's going to get the kind of relief that it wants.

Landau interview continued

blacks could be discriminated against, and that
women were nonpeople.

**Q: Doesn't the press already have protection
in many states by "shield laws" that are designed to protect reporters from revealing
sources or confidential information?**

A: So far, 26 states have such laws. In California, New Jersey, and New York, judges have
pretty well ripped them up through their rulings. But, in general, they are working. There is
a question, however, as to whether perhaps we
need a national shield law that would override
any state constitutional bounds.

Then, of course, there comes the next question: Would the Supreme Court uphold such a
federal law? That I don't know.

**Q: Are the courts riding on a wave of press
unpopularity with the public?**

A: Yes. The attitude of the courts is pretty
reflective of what one might call the moderate,
conservative business establishment. In 1970,
Vice-President Spiro T. Agnew came along and
touched a very sensitive nerve all over the
country. He made attacks against the press politically respectable.

Corporations started going out and being
more aggressive. The bar started serving more
subpoenas. The judges started upholding more
subpoenas. The critics of the press became
more popular. I think it was a whole movement
of which the courts are only one part.

**Q: Are you saying that there is a broad trend
to penalize the press?**

A: There's a broad trend to try to use the
press as an important information resource.
The state wants to use the press as an investigative arm, or the defense wants to use the
press as an investigative arm, or the judge
wants to use the press as an investigative arm.
It's a general movement to try to take away the

Kurland interview continued

Q: Is there growing hostility toward the press by the courts?

A: In the last Supreme Court term, the press lost a substantial number of cases. They're not used to that. None of the issues decided against the press were reversals of a prior position by the Court. These were new questions, not a change of position with regard to the old ones. I see great sensitivity on the part of the press. The notion of the press as the ombudsman for American government—which the press continues to repeat—is not necessarily shared by all the citizenry, and not even by the courts.

I think the question that has to be asked is: What are the responsibilities of the press to the government and to society? It is not a question whether the press has a right to be free of restraints by government and society.

Copyright 1978 U.S. News & World Report.

Landau interview continued

independent standing of the press and really make it an appendage of the government.

As a result of recent court decisions, I think editorial independence and privacy are in terrific danger. They can take all your files. They can march into your office. They can seize your telephone records. So I don't think that we are exaggerating the danger that these cases are posing.

Q: Will the press continue to fight these decisions?

A: Reporters are willing to go to jail, and publishers are willing to pay extraordinary amounts to defend the First Amendment. The press is not used to being unpopular—not with the courts, not with politicians, and not with the local business community. But we may have to become unpopular for a while and take the heat in order to defend something which is really crucial.

MUST REPORTERS REVEAL THEIR "STATE OF MIND"?

THE STAR-LEDGER

Newark, New Jersey, April 20, 1979

The U.S. Supreme Court, which has been cutting deeply into press freedom with a series of decisions, has inflicted another grave blow

Reprinted by permission from *The Star-Ledger*. Copyright 1979 The Star-Ledger.

with an Orwellian ruling concerning the "state of mind" of newsmen involved in libel litigation.

This is an extension, albeit a curious one, of the court's ruling last year that police have the right to invade a newspaper office and undertake wide-ranging searches of files, drawers, and even wastebaskets . . . without prior announcement.

Not content with that serious incursion of First Amendment press guarantees, the Supreme Court—by a 5–4 vote—has now chosen to delve even deeper into the newsgathering process, probing the psyche of reporters.

There's an element of absurdity—if not sheer ludicrousness—in the latest ruling by the Supreme Court that newsmen may be compelled to answer questions regarding their mental processes during the preparation of an article that later became the subject of a libel suit.

A jury must deal in evidentiary material, the actual, known facts in cases where it is required to make judgments. Under the new ruling involving press rights in libel proceedings, a jury will be called on to make an intelligent determination on what a reporter or editor had been thinking about when the article was being prepared months or even years before.

A reporter or editor is primarily concerned in the preparation of an article with accuracy and a consciously balanced presentation that treats principals in a fair, equitable manner. These are professional processes that are removed from such subjective aspects as opinions, intents, conclusions, and beliefs.

The court does not appear to be concerned with press responsibility for objectivity; it now wants an accounting of what's going on in a newsman's mind when he or she is writing a story.

This is a murky area, the deep recesses of the mental process, the subconscious thoughts of reporters and editors to ferret out the possibility of malice that could be crucial in a libel action. This appears to be the main thrust of the badly conceived court ruling.

In a landmark ruling by the Supreme Court in 1964—a decision upheld in a number of subsequent challenges—plaintiffs in libel cases were required to show "actual malice" or "reckless disregard" of the truth. The practical effect of this decision was to minimize frivolous suits against newspapers . . . legal harrassments that would have a chilling effect on news gathering.

The new high court ruling will have a diametrically opposite implication; it would, in effect, encourage even marginal libel actions that are bound to have a critically inhibiting impact on the press.

It will no doubt lead to critical abuses in the future by severely limiting the constitutional flexibility of the press to investigate and criticize officials. The ultimate loser in the unwarranted restricting of press responsibility will be the public.

It is most unfortunate, therefore, that the public may never know the "state of mind" of the five justices as they reached their anti-public, anti-press decision.

CHICAGO TRIBUNE

Chicago, Illinois, April 20, 1979

Despite the strong words of protest from some journalists over the Supreme Court's latest libel ruling, it does not represent a retreat

Reprinted, courtesy of the Chicago Tribune. All rights reserved.

from First Amendment protections of the free press.

The centerpiece of the Constitution's protection of the press in libel cases is a doctrine first stated by the Supreme Court in 1964. Under that doctrine, as it has developed in the years since, a reporter is liable for damages involving a public figure only if he publishes false material, knowing it to be false or recklessly disregarding whether it is accurate or not. This is not an unfair burden on the press.

The technical name of this doctrine has caused confusion ever since. The Supreme Court called knowing falsehood or reckless disregard of the truth "actual malice," but those words in the legal context do not carry the dictionary definition. Malice in libel law does not mean ill will or bad motive.

The legal definition of "actual malice" does call into question the subjective knowledge or beliefs of the journalist. What did he know? Did he doubt the truth of what he reported?

The recent Supreme Court decision merely requires journalists to answer pretrial questions about their own subjective feelings as they gathered and wrote the challenged report.

The case involved a "60 Minutes" broadcast about former Army Lt. Col. Anthony Herbert. He charged that it was false and damaging to his reputation. CBS producer Barry Lando, claiming protection under the First Amendment, refused to answer questions about his opinions concerning the truthfulness of what sources had told him and about his intentions in developing the Herbert report.

The majority of the Supreme Court's justices refused to accord Mr. Lando such a privilege. Even the press's staunchest and most articulate defender on the Court—Justice William Brennan—did not feel an absolute privilege would be proper.

Justice Lewis Powell wisely noted that the Supreme Court was not saying that First Amendment concerns will never arise in pretrial questioning, but only that trial judges should take these into account on a case-by-case basis. No special rule need be engraved into the Constitution.

For the Court to have granted the sort of privilege Mr. Lando and others demanded, it would either have had to scrap the useful doctrine of "actual malice" [since it necessarily involves an assessment of the subjective judgments of the journalist] or effectively eliminate defamation actions by public figures.

Neither choice would have been acceptable —even from the press's point of view. Doing away with the "actual malice" doctrine would likely have led to the introduction of something less protective of the press's right to report vigorously on the conduct of public officials. If subjective information about journalists' beliefs and intentions were held privileged, trial courts might well have begun to refuse to allow reporters to give any testimony about their motives and sense of professional duty. Often this kind of testimony can provide the best defense in a libel case.

The other alternative—giving journalists the privilege without changing the "actual malice" doctrine—would have worked a hardship on people who have genuinely been damaged by reckless or consciously false reporting. The press does not deserve a license to lie—even about public officials. Not only would such a license be unfair, it would in the end jeopardize the credibility of the press.

TV CAMERAS
IN THE COURTROOM?

YES—LETTING PUBLIC SEE WHAT'S GOING ON "MAY IMPROVE THE COURTS"

Interview with Judge Jack Weinstein

Q: Judge Weinstein, why do you favor allowing television news coverage of trials?

A: Because the people are entitled to know what goes on in this important segment of their government.

The courts are one of the three great branches of government. The court system serves an educational function in deterring criminals. In their work in civil rights, courts attempt to educate the people on what the Constitution and our ideals require.

In short, I don't think the public is getting the information it needs through the written media alone.

Q: But wouldn't TV cameras affect what goes on in court?

A: Yes, they would. I think television would improve matters. Putting the eye of the public into courtrooms, so to speak, may improve the work of courts at every level—even the U.S. Supreme Court, where I think it's perfectly clear that arguments ought to be televised.

Many of the arguments before the Supreme Court are substandard. A city or state official who wants the publicity and prestige of arguing a case before the Supreme Court when he's not competent to do so would be seen on television. People back home would see what's going

NO—"TRIALS ARE NOT FOR PUBLIC ENTERTAINMENT"

Interview with John Sutro

Q: Mr. Sutro, why do you oppose television coverage of trials?

A: Because the purpose of trials is to provide a forum for the administration of justice. Trials are not for public entertainment. They aren't a drama to be played for the public, but are held to ascertain the truth.

Q: But wouldn't television, by showing what goes on in court, thereby educate the public?

A: No. There isn't a television station that would show a court proceeding from the moment the judge takes the bench until the jury is discharged. That could take from a day or two to a matter of weeks.

The only portions that are going to be televised are those that are dramatic—where the accused takes the stand or where the principal witness testifies or when some lawyer is making a big speech.

If you're going to educate the public with respect to how justice is administered, the public must know exactly what transpires from the moment the judge takes the bench until the jury is dismissed.

Q: The public doesn't see that now, does it?

A: Courtrooms are open to the public. A person attending a trial sees exactly what goes on

---

Reprinted from *U.S. News & World Report* (April 17, 1978): 51–52.

Weinstein interview continued

on, and there would be pressure to let the best-qualified make arguments at the Court.

Q: Is there a danger that judges, witnesses, and lawyers might be tempted to ham it up before the cameras?

A: Yes, and that possibility has to be guarded against. But the experience we have had in the six states that permit televised trials—Alabama, Colorado, Florida, Georgia, Texas, and Washington—indicates that this is not a substantial problem. [In a seventh state—Montana—new rules allowing TV in courtrooms took effect on April 1.]

Cameras today are very small. Very quickly in a trial you forget about everything else and concentrate on the trial itself. There are incompetents who would use television for publicity, but I think they can be dealt with.

Q: How about claims that television would broadcast only the most sensational court news?

A: There is that danger, but we have public broadcasting systems that would tend to give the courts more time. And I think that the media, over time, tend to give the average citizen a fair idea of what's going on.

Take the Bakke appeal on so-called reverse discrimination: You had people from all over the country standing out in the street trying to get a seat for the arguments before the Supreme Court. These were young people interested in a major issue and the future of the country. It seems to me that there was so much interest in the Bakke case that televising the full argument, even with some editing, would have given the public a much better appreciation of what was really involved.

Q: Should the defendant be permitted to veto TV coverage of his trial?

A: Yes. The defendant should have this right—at least at the outset—until we acquire experience.

Sutro interview continued

in the courtroom. If you're looking at TV, you see only what the camera pictured, and there's no camera that can show you everything that goes on in court.

Q: Don't newspapers summarize what happens in a trial, and often distill the dramatic aspects?

A: Yes. But the newspaper reader knows he is reading only the reporter's appraisal of what happened. If you look at a television program, you're purportedly looking at what actually took place. By televising only a part, however, the picture is distorted.

Q: Why not allow televising of Supreme Court arguments, at least in important cases?

A: I agree with Chief Justice Burger, who I understand disapproves of televising appellate arguments. I don't think arguments on technical legal points are appealing to the public generally. If there were a murder of a well-known person and there were a trial, that's what would interest the television viewer.

Q: Would trial participants be affected by television?

A: Yes. It would upset witnesses; it would upset jurors; lawyers wouldn't act like themselves, and judges would be placed in an undesirable position. If a witness has to be subpoenaed to testify because he is unwilling to volunteer, then the presence of television would scare him to death.

The judge's job is to do whatever is necessary to see that a trial is handled properly. If the judge is conscious he is being televised, his attention might be diverted from that task. Also, judges are human; some would inevitably ham it up.

As for the lawyers, a lot of them would conduct themselves differently if they were on television. They may try to create a public image for themselves.

Weinstein interview continued

Q: Should the judge have veto power, too?

A: Again, I think I'd tend to move slowly and give any of the three parties involved—defendant, prosecutor, and judge—the right to veto television. I think that ultimately we would reach the point where we are now in the case of print media, where certain fixed rights are involved in covering trials. But initially, since there is so much objection—ill-founded objection, in my view—it would be politic and sensible to limit use of TV.

Q: Should the camera be required to always focus on whoever is speaking, or could it pan the courtroom at will?

A: I wouldn't be too tight about restricting the camera. Trials get awfully dull. Everything that goes on in the courtroom is part of the total scene, and the reaction of a defendant or juror sometimes is quite revealing.

But there are a myriad of those kinds of details that must be worked out. Given good will and good sense, which I think exist in both the media and the law, I see no reason why they couldn't be worked out.

I have a lot of confidence in television people, just as I have in the press. I think generally they're very sensible and they appreciate the problems of the courts. They don't want to complicate our ability to give people due process of law.

Q: Should any court procedures be excluded from television coverage?

A: Deliberations by the jury would have to be excluded. I would not have them open to anyone. You want the jurors to feel perfectly free to say anything they want so they can be candid with each other.

Q: When could televising start?

A: As to appeals hearings, I think television coverage of them ought to start forthwith. I just can't see any valid objections to that. Rules will have to be developed for trial coverage.

Sutro interview continued

Q: Don't lawyers dramatize the case for the jury anyway?

A: Sure, there are some lawyers who are actors. They are the ones who get written up in books and articles. But there are an awful lot of lawyers whose demeanor is very calm and not a bit that of an actor. It would be very unfortunate to have the public evaluate the capability of lawyers based on the way they appear on television.

Q: Why not let the judge decide whether he wants TV in his courtroom?

A: That would be terrible. Most state judges have to stand for election. If a judge turned down television, he'd be as popular with the TV stations and the press as a case of the measles. The judge would be placed in a most undesirable position.

Q: Would federal judges, appointed to lifetime terms, be subject to pressures, too?

A: If you were a federal district judge and you turned down the televising of a criminal case of great public interest, I don't think that either the TV stations or the press would give you any kudos.

Q: Some broadcasters argue that the First Amendment's guarantee of freedom of the press gives them a right to televise courtroom proceedings—

A: There is nothing in the First Amendment that does that.

Under the Constitution, anybody connected with a television station is as welcome in the court as any newspaper reporter. The television editor or newsman can sit in court and observe what goes on and get on the air that night to say whatever he wants—within the area of reasonableness.

Q: As technology becomes more pervasive in our daily lives, isn't it almost inevitable that television will come into the courtroom?

Weinstein interview continued

Q: Chief Justice Warren Burger opposes TV in the courtroom. Will federal courts allow television as long as this is so?

A: No. The Judicial Conference makes the rules for federal courts, and the Chief Justice pretty well dominates the Judicial Conference for very good hierarchical reasons. But the Chief Justice is a very sensible, flexible person, and now the American Bar Association is starting to take a positive view toward televising trials.

The states where television is allowed have encountered no serious problems.

At the very least, trials should now be videotaped for use in the training of trial lawyers. That's something that might appeal to the Chief Justice, who is critical of the quality of trial work by many lawyers.

As it became clear there was no more to fear from this modern device than from the telephone, we would be more sensible and expand the use of TV.

Sutro interview continued

A: Definitely not. A television news program is entertainment in the broad sense. It isn't like looking at a comedy program, but the news show does aim to entertain.

But a trial's most important goal is to determine if a person accused of a crime did or didn't do it. Television has no place in that.

Copyright 1978 U.S. News & World Report.

chapter 11

SPECIAL PRIVILEGES FOR NEWS GATHERERS

The issue of special privileges for news gatherers overlaps, to a certain extent, the issue of free press/fair trial, but it is a broader issue. It deals with more than privileges that might conflict with a defendant's right to a fair trial. It deals with a reporter's general access to places or events that are off limits to the general public, such as prisons, mental health facilities, crime scenes, and so on—many of which have no relation to ongoing trials.

The first reading, "Reporters, Keep Out!" by David M. Rubin, delineates the problem from a professional journalist's point of view. Rubin's article was written as a warning to reporters that test cases for "special privileges" must be good ones, or the press will stand to lose privileges it already has. Although Rubin goes out of his way to present examples in which special privileges have been abused (or obtained illegally), we have little doubt that his sympathies lie with preserving special privileges for news gatherers.

In the second reading Robert M. Kaus, a lawyer and writer for the *Washington Monthly*, presents the other point of view. Kaus does not believe that the press deserves—or needs—special privileges.

Editorial comment on the "special privileges"

issue has, understandably, run heavily in favor of such privileges. This is exemplified in the third reading in this section, an editorial from the the *Saginaw (Michigan) News*, which appeared following the Supreme Court's decision that the press has no constitutional right of access to jails or other government institutions greater than the access granted to the general public. The *Providence Journal*'s editorial, which follows it, is much less critical of the Court's decision.

REPORTERS, KEEP OUT!

David M. Rubin

David Berkowitz, the "Son of Sam" killer, lived in a small apartment on the top floor of a seven-story building in Yonkers, New York. During the morning of August 11, 1977, shortly after Berkowitz was arrested, New York City detectives and Yonkers police sealed off that apartment and, under authority of a warrant, sifted through papers, pictures, and other belongings in search of evidence. Outside the apartment they posted a notice reading, "Crime Scene, Do Not Enter."

Down below, on the street in front of the building, a dozen reporters and photographers swapped stories with curious locals and waited for tidbits from the police. Among the journalists were David Berliner, a seasoned reporter now stringing for the *Washington Post*, and Robert Kalfus, a photographer for Rupert Murdoch's *New York Post*, the tabloid which had helped to fuel the hysteria over Son of Sam.

As the day slipped by and his deadline approached, Berliner frequently asked the police when he might get a look at the apartment; each time he was turned away. Kalfus, however, was more enterprising. Earlier in the day he had

ridden the elevator to the Berkowitz apartment, only to be met by a Yonkers policeman who told him to "get the hell off the floor." Undaunted, Kalfus discovered that he could reach the roof of the building through an unguarded garage entrance. From the roof he climbed down a fire escape to Berkowitz's apartment window. Peering through the glass, Kalfus saw police hats, but no policemen. Hastily, he shot a few pictures from his outside perch. Then, worried that the police might return, he retreated to the roof and down to the street, where he joined the others waiting to get into the apartment.

At about 3 P.M., a group of New York City detectives came out of the building carrying boxes. Berliner says he heard one of them say, "Okay, boys, we're finished. It's all yours." He interpreted this to mean that the search had been completed and that the journalists would now be allowed inside—a courtesy Berliner had come to expect in police-press relations.

Without waiting for another invitation, Berliner, Kalfus, Leonard Detrick (a photographer for the New York *Daily News*), and Theodore Cowell (a stringer for *Time*) walked into the building and rode the elevator to the seventh floor.

Reprinted from the *Columbia Journalism Review*, March–April 1979.

What they found surprised them. A group of neighborhood children was trying to pry the number off Berkowitz's apartment door as a souvenir. The warning sign—"Crime Scene, Do Not Enter"—was still in place. They found the door locked; but there was no guard.

Kalfus volunteered to try entering through the outside window. He and Cowell retraced the fire-escape route and found the window secured with only a hook and eye. A little jiggling of the frame loosened the hook, permitting them to raise the window without damaging the frame. Once inside, they let in Berliner and Detrick, who had been interviewing a woman down the hall.

For the next 20 minutes the quartet took pictures and made notes; Berliner saved time by speaking into his tape recorder. Then, heralded by a terrific pounding on the door, Yonkers police came crashing in "like Kojaks on a rampage," according to Berliner. The journalists were handcuffed and whisked off to police headquarters, where they were charged with obstruction of governmental administration and criminal trespass, the penalty for which is up to one year in jail and a $1000 fine, or both. Had they damaged the apartment, the four could also have been charged with criminal mischief, but the police found no damage and were never able to establish how they had gotten in.

Police demanded that the photographers turn over their exposed film. Detrick's was found bunched up in his sock when he crossed his legs at the wrong moment. Kalfus was cleverer. He palmed his exposed rolls and gave the police some unexposed ones. His pictures were printed the next day in a *Post* centerspread headlined "Inside the Killer's Lair." His pluck was widely applauded by *Post* editors, and Kalfus says he thought he might even receive a bonus. Berliner's story appeared on page one of the *Washington Post*.

The case resulting from the quartet's journalistic initiative—*People v. Berliner et al.*—received remarkably little press attention, given the intriguing issues of newsgathering rights it raises. Here were four reporters out to get the story. They behaved in a clever way that has often been sanctioned and rewarded in the past. Two major papers published their work. Yet they found themselves defendants in a criminal trespass case and, had Berkowitz not had other concerns, they might well have found themselves defendants in a civil privacy action brought by the Son of Sam.

Did the public have a right to know what was in Berkowitz's apartment? If it did, should the journalists have entered through the window? Does it matter that the door was unguarded, or that a sign was still posted? Is prosecution for trespass the appropriate legal remedy in such cases? If it is, will it be used to deny the press access to other newsworthy places where journalists may not be welcome?

Fortunately for the press, *Berliner* did not produce a conviction. Judge Aldo A. Nastasi of Yonkers dismissed the charges because the police had finished their search and had executed the warrant. They were not, therefore, in possession of the apartment when the journalists entered it; the appropriate party to have brought the trespass action would have been Berkowitz himself. But as Westchester County Assistant District Attorney John Falussy says, "I was not about to bring Berkowitz back to Yonkers from jail to prosecute a misdemeanor trespass."

Had Judge Nastasi been forced to rule on a First Amendment right of access, however, there is little doubt about what his verdict would have been. The journalists' conduct "can best be described as reprehensible," he wrote at the end of his opinion, "and cannot be justified as legitimate in pursuit of a news story."

Berliner is only one of a number of access cases that have come to trial recently. Such cases are a product of what one unsympathetic New York State Court of Appeals judge calls the "overly aggressive" manner of much journalism at the moment. Reporters make news by pounding on the locked doors of nursing homes or by being ejected from restaurants and locker rooms; their attempts to get in, or stay in, are behind the development of access as a significant First Amendment controversy.

Chris Little, counsel to the *Washington Post*, calls access "a problem of continuing, day-to-day concern." "Invariably," says Bruce Sanford, a Cleveland attorney who runs seminars on First Amendment questions for Scripps-Howard and UPI, "after we have discussed libel and privacy, reporters and editors bring up questions about how far the press can legally go in pursuing or dramatizing a story. What *are* the legal boundaries of news gathering?"

"Access" is a concept that has come up before in other First Amendment contexts. In a thoroughly different usage, it is often meant to refer to the "right" of the public to seek representation of its views in the media. Cases concerning protection of confidential sources are access cases in another sense, since the press has claimed the need for such confidentiality to protect the flow of information. Cases in which courts interpret open-record and open-meeting laws are also related cases, since the freedom of information movement is directly concerned with access to official government meetings and documents. Cases contesting the right of the press to *receive* information also raise the access issue. Finally, access to trials, including pretrial hearings, evidence, names of juveniles, and names of jurors, is an important First Amendment concern. In its current term the Supreme Court will rule on the right of a newspaper to publish the name of a juvenile defendant (*Smith* v. *Daily Mail*) and on the right of the press to attend a pretrial hearing (*Gannett* v. *DePasquale*).*

But the law concerning journalistic right of access to *nonjudicial news settings* is at an earlier stage of development and may be even

more critical in the long run. It is at a point much like protection of sources before *Branzburg* v. *Hayes* (in which the press was told it does not have a First Amendment right to protect confidential sources) and the integrity of newsrooms before *Zurcher* v. *Stanford Daily* (in which the press learned that newsrooms are subject to searches by police officials in possession of warrants). In the present judicial climate, moreover, there is growing potential for an access case that will be equally damaging to the press.

Little and Sanford agree that clashes occur most often when police and fire officials bar access to crime scenes or stop photographers from shooting pictures in public places. But cases have also tested the press's right of access to restaurants guilty of health-code violations, children's homes in which the quality of care is suspect, fire scenes, public schools, prisons in which the treatment of inmates is an issue, locker rooms, migrant-worker camps, legislative press facilities, and private living rooms. Some of these cases were called trespass, some invasion of privacy, and in others the news source sought prior restraint on publication based on the manner in which the information was gathered. As yet the courts have answered very few of the questions raised by news gathering, but what they have said is cause for concern.

On only a few occasions have the courts acknowledged that the freedom to publish is of little value if the freedom to gather information is curtailed. Justice Musmanno of the Pennsylvania Supreme Court put it most forcefully in 1956 when he wrote that "A print shop without material to print would be as meaningless as a vineyard without grapes, an orchard without trees, or a lawn without verdure. Freedom of the press means freedom to gather news, write it, publish it, and circulate it." Similarly, softening the blow of the majority opinion in *Branzburg*, Justice White denied the decision suggested "that news gathering does not qualify for First Amendment protection; without

---

*Editor's note: The Supreme Court decided in favor of the Daily Mail but against Gannett. (See the Gannett editorial ad reproduced in Chapter 10.)

some protection for seeking out the news, freedom of the press could be eviscerated." Despite such sentiments, however, the courts have thus far been unwilling to grant the press a protected position in information gathering.

The few important Supreme Court cases in this area have developed around the question of access to prisons and prisoners. In three opinions—*Pell* v. *Procunier* (1974), *Saxbe* v. *Washington Post* (1974), and *Houchins* v. *KQED* (1978)—the Court has held that reporters do not have a right to interview specific prisoners, visit specific parts of a prison, or bring cameras inside. The access rights of the press are coextensive with those of the public, the Court has said, and where the public is excluded the press may also be forbidden to go. Wrote Chief Justice Burger in *Houchins*: "We . . . reject the . . . assertion that the public and the media have a First Amendment right to government information regarding the conditions of jails and their inmates and presumably all other public facilities such as hospitals and mental institutions. . . . The First Amendment is 'neither a Freedom of Information Act nor an Official Secrets Act.'"

Diane Zimmerman, who teaches press law at New York University law school, suggests that in *Houchins* Burger has already come close to saying there is *no* right of access to information under the First Amendment. Justice Douglas saw this coming in his dissent in *Pell*. There he argued that if the press's right of access is no greater than the public's, the government will be able to deny access to the press by simply denying it to the public as well.

Along with holdings in related cases, these unfavorable prison decisions have established at least this much about a right of press access:

- The judiciary looks with skepticism on claims to a First Amendment right of access.
- The press is not protected by the First Amendment for any crimes or civil offenses it commits in the course of news gathering.
- The press has no greater right of access than the public.

There have been a few victories broadening access. Attempts to discriminate among journalists have been stopped by the courts. For example, without a compelling governmental interest, the mayor of Honolulu could not bar a journalist from attending regular press conferences open to the rest of the press corps. Nor could the New York Yankee baseball team bar a female reporter from the locker room at the conclusion of a game if male reporters had been admitted.

Two recent decisions in Florida indicate that if journalists are customarily *invited* by police onto private property to view a police raid or the victim of a fire, a trespass or privacy action against the press is not likely to stand. But in one of these cases—*Green Valley School* v. *Cowles Florida Broadcasting* (1977)—Chief Judge Rawls of the First District Court of Appeals in Florida said that the presence of broadcast reporters during a police raid ". . . could well bring to the citizenry of this state the hobnail boots of a Nazi stormtrooper equipped with glaring lights invading a couple's bedroom at midnight with the wife hovering in her nightgown in an attempt to shield herself from the scanning TV camera."

Pushing for access on First Amendment grounds is dangerous for the press precisely because many judges are simply ignorant of news-gathering procedures and requirements, or are hostile to the press's methods. Reporters know that, in fact, the press *does* receive preferential treatment. Press cards permit journalists to cross police and fire lines and, at the invitation of officials, to examine crime scenes. Almost all legislative bodies have press facilities. Reporters can usually arrange to tour military installations and other institutions off limits to the public. And, as long as they don't bring their cameras, journalists in Texas can attend executions. How many such privileges might journalists lose by litigating access cases in the present climate?

An answer may be forthcoming in the case of *Le Mistral* v. *CBS*, which was decided at trial in

1976 and is now on appeal.* If not a case of *Branzburg* proportions, it is nevertheless potentially a very dangerous one for the press.

On the afternoon of July 6, 1972, WCBS-TV reporter Lucille Rich entered a fashionable French restaurant, Le Mistral, in Manhattan, with cameras rolling, to interview owner Jean Larriaga. That day the restaurant had appeared for the second time on a list of health-code violators prepared by city inspectors. What happened next is a matter of dispute. CBS claims that Rich and her crew behaved with decorum, did not upset patrons, and left when asked to by the owner.

Larriaga tells a different story, one which New York State Supreme Court Justice Martin B. Stecher told the trial jury it was entitled to accept. CBS employees, Stecher said, "burst into plaintiff's restaurant in noisy and obtrusive fashion and following the loud commands of the reporter, Rich, to photograph the patrons dining, turned their lights and camera upon the dining room. Consternation followed. Patrons

---

*Editor's note: As this book went to press, *Le Mistral* v. *CBS* was still in the process of being appealed.

THE SETTINGS AND THE CASES

The courts have been asked to decide on access rights to a variety of nonjudicial news settings. Some of the more important cases:

Crime Scenes, *Florida Publishing Co.* v. *Fletcher,* 340 So. 2d 914 (Fla. 1976): The *Florida Times-Union* is not guilty of trespass or invasion of privacy for publishing a picture of a fire victim taken in a private dwelling without permission of the victim's mother. *Schnell* v. *City of Chicago,* 407 F. 2d 1084 (1969): Photographers obtained a temporary restraining order enjoining Chicago police from interfering with their activities during the 1968 Democratic convention.

Foreign Countries. *Zemel* v. *Rusk,* 381 U.S. 1 (1965): A U.S. citizen does not have a First Amendment right to travel to Cuba.

Locker Rooms. *Ludtke* v. *Kuhn,* 4 Med. L. Rptr. p. 1625 (U.S. District Court, So. District of N.Y., 1978): Women reporters, here Melissa Ludtke of *Sports Illustrated,* cannot be banned from New York Yankee locker rooms if male reporters are allowed inside; such exclusion denies Ludtke equal-protection and due-process rights.

Migrant-Worker Camps. *Freedman* v. *New Jersey State Police,* 135 N.J. Super. 297 (1975): *Daily Princetonian* journalists must be allowed to visit a migrant family living on the property of a farmer; but the latter can dictate terms of access.

Press Conferences. *Borreca* v. *Fasi,* 369 F.Supp. 906 (1974): The mayor of Honolulu cannot exclude a reporter from his press conferences without compelling governmental interest.

Press Galleries. *Consumers Union* v. *Periodical Correspondents Association,* reversed on other grounds, 515 F.2d 1341, cert. denied, 423 U.S.

waiting to be seated left the restaurant. Others who had finished eating left without waiting for their checks. Still others hid their faces behind napkins or tablecloths or hid themselves beneath tables. . . . Mr. Larriaga . . . refused to be interviewed and as the camera continued to 'roll' he pushed the protesting Miss Rich and her crew from his premises." Larriaga sued for, among other things, trespass, and a sympathetic jury awarded the restaurant $1200 in compensatory damages and a chilling $250,000 in punitive damages.

The case frames important access questions in an interesting way. Under what cir-

cumstances can the press enter a restaurant? Should CBS have asked for permission from Larriaga before bringing in camera equipment? Before sending in Rich alone? Does the intent of Rich and her crew matter—that is, could they be found guilty of trespass because they did not intend to order something? If a member of the public can enter a restaurant without passing an "intent" test, shouldn't a journalist be able to as well? Is the notion of trespass different for broadcast media? Would a print reporter have encountered the same resistance from Larriaga, or the same trespass action? The example of *Le Mistral*, says Professor Zimmer-

---

1051 (1973): Exclusion of *Consumer Reports* writers from congressional periodical galleries violates the magazine's First Amendment, due-process, and equal-protection rights. *Kovach* v. *Maddux,* 238 F.Supp. 835 (1965): The Tennessee State Senate cannot punish the Nashville *Tennessean* for refusing to leave a closed senate meeting by banning its reporters from the senate floor and adjacent press facilities. *Lewis* v. *Baxley,* 368 F.Supp. 768 (1973): Alabama cannot require that journalists file a "statement of economic interest" before permitting customary access to state facilities.

Prisons. *Garrett* v. *Estelle,* 556 F.2d 1274, cert. denied, 46 U.S.L.W. 3800 (1978): Texas may deny reporters the right to bring audio or visual recording equipment to executions. *Houchins* v. *KQED,* 98 S. Ct. 2588: The press has no greater right of access to California's Santa Rita prison than the public. *Kearns-Tribune* v. *Utah Board of Corrections,* 2 Med. L. Rptr. 1353 (1977): Utah may exclude both the press and the public from executions. *Pell* v. *Procunier,* 417 U.S. 817 (1974): By regulation, California prisons may prohibit interviews with specific inmates. *Saxbe* v. *Washington Post,* 417 U.S. 843 (1974): Federal Bureau of Prisons regulations may pre-

vent the interviewing of specific inmates in medium- and maximum-security prisons.

Private Dwellings. *Dietemann* v. *Time Inc.,* 449 F.2d 245 (1971): The First Amendment does not accord *Life* reporters immunity from a privacy invasion committed while news gathering.

Restaurants. *Le Mistral* v. *CBS,* 3 Med. L. Rptr. 1913 (N.Y. Supreme Ct., Appellate Division, 1978): CBS is guilty of a trespass for going into a restaurant uninvited and shooting film of the owner and patrons.

Schools. *Green Valley School* v. *Cowles Florida Broadcasting,* Fla. App., 327 So. 2d 810 (1977): Privacy and trespass actions brought by a private school against WESH-TV after it aired film of a police raid were dismissed because the newsman was invited onto the property by police. *Quinn* v. *Johnson,* 51 App. Div. 2d 391 (1976): When trespass was alleged, WABC-TV in New York was restrained from showing compromising film shot at a children's home. The station was allowed to air the film after faces were blurred and a reply by the home was included.

man, could lead to the use of threats of trespass action to bar *all* reporters on a story from restaurants and other places that serve the public. "If CBS loses," she says, "even a *Times* reporter could have trouble."

It is not difficult to imagine other, similar situations that could be troublesome for the press. Can a school principal refuse access to the school after it has been the scene of violence against teachers? Can a military-base commander bar the press so that it has difficulty investigating charges of recruit mistreatment? Cases have already occurred in which WABC-TV was restrained from showing film about the mistreatment of residents by the staff of a children's home; a judge felt the reporter was trespassing at the home when the film was shot. And a reporter's access to migrant workers was contested in New Jersey when the owner of the land on which the migrants lived charged him with trespassing.

The anti-press mood on the matter of access is clear. Justice Stecher, who tried *Le Mistral*, said that CBS had no more right to enter the restaurant than he had to "just barge into somebody else's premises and bring in a rock band . . . to rehearse." This is a mood that the press challenges at its peril. When the *Birmingham News* failed to get access to local birth records in a recent freedom of information request, it took the county to court. The U.S. District court for the Northern District of Alabama ruled, however, that the county could seal not only its birth records, but its *death* records as

well. The paper thereby lost information it had been receiving for at least a dozen years.

What can the press do in the face of such hostility? Zimmerman suggests that the objective must be "to constitutionalize the right of access to government information, at least, so that access will be guaranteed to press and public."

This will require changing the mood of the judiciary. Sanford recommends a vigorous effort by journalists at the local level to educate judges and police officials about the news-gathering process. In Denver, for example (where Sanford's client is the *Rocky Mountain News*), this has meant lunches, seminars, and informal contacts between press and bench over a period of years. In this climate, says Sanford, litigation over access comes up less often than in cities where the judiciary is more hostile.

At the *Washington Post*, Little tells journalists in the field to argue for their rights of access, but not to break the law. Little is not afraid to litigate for access, but, he says, "in choosing when to litigate, the fact situation should be such that it is possible to argue the press's side in the best possible light," (Both *Berliner* and *Le Mistral*, on the other hand, presented less than such ideal fact situations.)

It is just a matter of time, nevertheless, before a Farber-like case catches the fancy of the public and puts news-gathering access to a significant First Amendment test. The press will be fortunate to come out of that test with its privileges intact.

THE GOVERNMENT
AND THE PRESS

Robert M. Kaus

Maybe it's best to start from personal experience. Every now and then over the past few years I have turned on my television to see an earnest reporter, standing on the steps of a courthouse, explaining his determination to go to jail rather than to reveal a confidential source. My feelings in this situation are inevitably mixed. On the one hand, it is impressive to see anybody standing up for principle at some personal cost. Having a fondness for journalistic types, I would rather identify with them than the judges and prosecutors trying to coerce their testimony. Yet, probably for that very reason, I am also a bit resentful—because, in explaining their role as news gatherers, these reporters invariably emphasize how different they are from me. It is their constitutional function, I am told, to risk official wrath, snoop out information, and disclose it to the public. As a member of that public, all I presumably must do is stay tuned. The legal distinctions the reporters draw seem to grow into a social gulf between them and me. I begin to wonder, why can't I be a glamorous and privileged investigator? Who chooses these people? After all, these are constitutional rights they're talking about. Don't I have the same right to be a reporter as they do?

Reprinted with permission from *The Washington Monthly*. Copyright 1978 by The Washington Monthly Co., 1611 Connecticut Ave., N.W., Washington, D.C. 20009.

I felt these pangs of jealousy most recently while watching Myron Farber—the *New York Times* reporter who refused to show his notes to the judge in a murder trial—stoically puffing a pipe behind the bars of a New Jersey jail. But the Farber case, I was told, was only the climax of a very bad year for the ideal of a free press, particularly in the Supreme Court. As Lyle Denniston of the *Washington Star* reported in a funereal postmortem, "Six major decisions came out, and the press clearly lost, or seemed to, in five." Those five included one that was "beyond understanding" (Ben Bradlee)—"the most dangerous ruling the Court has made in memory" (Howard K. Smith).

"The Court's view," wrote Charles Seib in the *Washington Post*, "seems to be that the First Amendment's guarantee of a free press is little more than a nod by the framers of the Constitution in the direction of the idea that a free flow of information is vital to self-government." While licking their wounds, newsmen knew who to blame: they were victims of "Mr. Nixon's Revenge" (Tom Wicker), of the "Hohenzollern mentality of the Burger court which surfaced in a reflex hostility to every attempt to hold the government to account or question its motives" (Jack Anderson). And, looking ahead, journalists saw nothing but trouble. There are a host of First Amendment cases on the Supreme Court's docket—cases as important, as significant, as those decided last spring.

It is hard to disagree with some of the press's charges. Last spring's decisions contained several potentially disastrous interpretations of the Bill of Rights. But if those decisions had a unifying theme, it was in a series of attacks—as yet inconclusive—on the idea that the press, and the people who work in the press, enjoy constitutional protections unavailable to ordinary citizens. As an ordinary citizen, I appreciated that sentiment, and it seemed to me that much of the outcry was only journalists' anger at being stripped of their pretensions to special treatment. The issue that most of the press ignored, or at least repressed, was the elitist nature of many of its own arguments. That issue is worth a closer look, since the current Supreme Court term will see a continuation, and possibly a resolution, of the conflict over the press's claims of special privileges.

THE CORPORATE VISION

During the past decade, it seems that every time reporters have felt threatened by the courts, their response has been to say, in effect, "You can't do this to us, we're reporters." The "journalist's privilege"—the right to refuse to testify before grand juries and courts—is only the most prominent of the special rights reporters have claimed. Newsmen have also argued for special rights of access to sources of government information, special protection from libel suits, and special freedom from police searches and wiretapping.

What all these press arguments have in common is the claim that a distinct class of people called "the press" have rights not enjoyed by the general populace. The arguments share a particular vision of both the First Amendment and American society. It is a corporate vision, in the sense that it views society as a single organism in which different citizens play different roles and have different legal needs. Academics (who at times seek their own

special rights) would be the brains in this social corpus and reporters the "eyes and ears," leaving the rest of us to fight for the positions below the neck.

As social visions go, this corporate ideal is nothing new. Students of feudalism may find it depressingly familiar. But its application to the First Amendment is an innovation. The Constitution traditionally has evoked a vision of citizens undifferentiated in their political roles and possessing equal measures of constitutional protection. The rule of "one man, one vote" provides the classic example of the traditional "universal" approach. Newsmen, in that view, are merely citizens who use their rights every working day.

The clash between the corporate and universalist theories may be heard in the background of most of the dramatic judicial confrontations over press rights. In these battles the corporate view has a lot going for it. In particular, it responds to a currently popular perception of media power. Let's face it, the corporate theory says, the average Joe has little opportunity either to gather information or to express his view. This ability is concentrated in a few institutions, called the press, who alone can keep people informed. Rather than clinging to a nineteenth century ideal of a participative society, in which every citizen is part journalist and part scholar, we should face up to modern reality and give the press the legal tools it needs to get its job done.

STEWART'S FAMOUS SPEECH

The corporate view received its biggest boost in late 1974, when Supreme Court Justice Potter Stewart delivered a now famous speech at Yale Law School. First Amendment cases, Stewart argued, had concentrated excessively on the "rights of isolated individuals"—"the soapbox orator, the nonconformist pamphleteer, the religious evangelist." If the framers of the Constitution had meant to grant the "organized press" no more rights than those individuals, Stewart continued, they would not have written separate phrases into the Bill of Rights protecting freedom "of the press" as well as "freedom of speech." Stewart concluded that the First Amendment confers special status on the press as an institution: "The publishing business is, in short, the only organized private business that is given explicit constitutional protection."

It was an indication of the press's attitude toward this theme when the *Washington Post*—a member of the "organized press" if there ever was one—took the unusual step of reprinting Stewart's speech on its editorial page. The *Post* called it "a more substantial contribution to the public understanding of the government-press conflict than almost anything else that has been said by a government official in the recent past."

In the three years following Stewart's speech, the corporate theory faded from public view; yet its influence spread among the legal and journalistic establishments. Student-run law reviews published articles endorsing Stewart's analysis. Lawyers nodded knowingly when Justice Powell, a darling of many established constitutional pundits, endorsed special rights of press access to prisons. It seemed, as respected First Amendment scholar Melville Nimmer proclaimed, that the corporate theory was "an idea whose time is past due."

But the hope that the corporate view would sweep the Supreme Court without a fight was dashed in the waning months of last spring's term. Chief Justice Burger fired the first salvo in a concurring opinion tacked onto a decision on corporate political expenditures. "The Court has not yet squarely resolved," Burger accurately asserted, "whether the Press Clause confers upon the 'institutional press' any freedom from government restraint not enjoyed by all others." He also pointed out that even the most ardent defenders of special press rights, such as

Nimmer, concede the historical evidence indicates "the framers" added the Press Clause merely to make sure written speech was covered along with oral speech.

Had Burger's blast been written by another justice, it might have set off more shock waves than it did. However, the tendency to explain it away as the idiosyncratic raving of a press-hater did not disappear until the Court dropped the real bombshell of the season a month later in the form of *Stanford Daily* v. *Zurcher*. In the *Stanford* decision the Court authorized police to obtain warrants to search the homes and offices of persons not suspected of criminal activity. The decision broke new ground in allowing such searches for all evidence relating to a crime, rather than just for weapons or contraband. Moreover, the Court declined an open invitation to single out newsrooms as having any categorical right to less intrusive procedures. In other words, the Court treated the privacy rights of the public and the press shabbily, but at least it mistreated both groups equally.

The last of the "series of blows against the press" (Seib) fell when the Court ruled that the general public has no right of access to any particular information about prison conditions—and that the press has no greater right than the public.

What Role of Special Privileges?

Even these setbacks, however, will probably not be enough to deter journalists who have latched onto the idea of special privileges. Editorial doomsaying to the contrary, a count of the ballots of the justices shows that they fell one vote short of conclusively rejecting the corporate theory. Neither Powell nor Justice Stevens have committed themselves on the issue. The prospect that they will adopt Stewart's view is real enough to attract a good supply of test cases from embattled reporters.

The *Farber* case is one indication that journalists haven't abandoned broad privilege claims. In another area, libel—where the Burger Court has already raised the possibility of special protection for the media—we may expect to find lawyers for the *Post* and *Times* in court bending every nuance in the direction of special privileges.

If the press can't get privileges from the courts, there's always the Congress. Several bills have been introduced that would exempt press offices from the type of search approved in *Stanford Daily*. As of now, the major press organizations are officially backing the approach of Senator Birch Bayh, which would protect everybody, not just newspapers. But this tactical alliance with the man-on-the-street already shows signs of weakness. It may be easier for Congress to help out only the group yelling the loudest—the press—rather than risk the ire of law enforcement officials by enacting broader protection.

A SMALL PROFESSIONAL CASTE

It is too bad that so much civil libertarian effort will continue to be spent trying to establish press rights as the rights of a small professional caste. By supporting constitutional preference for reporters, these efforts will inflate the influence of the established press while inevitably discriminating against the inquiring citizen, the sparetime scholar, and the community activist—the individuals whose speech rights Stewart belittles. In practice, Stewart's theory is to the established press what the "captial crisis" is to Wall Street—a fancy-sounding rationale for the pursuit of special interests. It is not the only way to read the First Amendment. We could work instead to fashion a definition of the "press" that includes both wage-earning reporters and anyone else who chooses, in his own way, to tell the public his discoveries or views. The privileges given this broad class of "press" would be more limited than those reporters now demand, but like the traditional

rights of free speech, they would be available to each and every citizen. And in all the areas of current First Amendment conflict, it is this universal approach, and not the corporate approach, which consistently focuses our attention on the real issues.

The Farber Case

The "journalist's privilege" question, and the *New York Times'* Farber case, provide a good illustration of the impact of these different approaches. Farber claimed that the First Amendment and New Jersey's shield law protected all the notes and information he accumulated while investigating 13 suspicious deaths at a New Jersey hospital. If he were required to give up his notes, he argues, future journalists would find it harder to locate sources and hence to investigate important stories. Sounds good so far. But the privileges journalists like Farber have claimed are so sweeping that they could not be extended to nonjournalists without opening the door to the destruction of our system of judicial fact-finding, depending as it does on the general obligation to testify. Indeed, the more immunity from testimony journalists demand, the more they must search for a narrow definition of "the press" in order to limit the potential impact of the privilege. So a fledgling freelance writer who looked into the New Jersey deaths would probably not get the same protection Farber would get. As for an intern at the New Jersey hospital who simply grew suspicious of the deaths and decided to check into them—forget it. He is not a "journalist" under any workable standard, and he would have to either reveal his contacts and notes or go directly to jail.

But, the *Times* might argue, our hypothetical intern could save himself this hassle simply by phoning up Farber instead of investigating his suspicions himself. In this perverse fashion, a broad journalist's privilege could force citizens to leak to reporters rather than make inquiries on their own. The professional news media would be granted a constitutional franchise to conduct investigations. Of course, as we are constantly reminded, journalists are professionals and they usually do a pretty good job of getting out the facts. But wouldn't we prefer a rule encouraging the curious probings of millions of private citizens who might sense something fishy at their jobs, or in their governments?

So, while requiring the testimony of reporters raises problems, they are not problems only reporters have. There is something offensive about prying secrets out of *anyone's* brain. For example, antiwar campaigns in the 1960s probably were hurt by prosecutorial attempts to force those who attended clandestine meetings to testify about what they saw and heard. One federal prosecutor, Guy Goodwin, made a career of hauling suspected radicals before grand juries and then jailing them when they refused to testify about their lives and their friends. To prevent this sort of abuse, we should define more carefully the circumstances under which judges can compel testimony, or authorize those methods only in investigations of the gravest offenses. In his 1972 "journalist's privilege" case, *New York Times* reporter Earl Caldwell argued for an immunity that would evaporate if the information sought by a court was both relevant to a legitimate inquiry and unobtainable by less intrusive means. Yet these seem like fair precautions to take before any citizen—journalist or not—is hauled in front of a judge under threat of contempt.

WHAT ACCESS TO GOVERNMENT INFORMATION?

In another field of First Amendment conflict —that of access to government information—a fixation on press rights once more obscures the basic issue: how much of what information should be kept secret? The Freedom of Infor-

mation Act provides a simple model for resolving this problem—legitimate secrets are to be kept secret from both press and public; information that need not be secret is available for universal view. You can argue about which files to throw open, but does anybody doubt that is the right question to ask? The corporate approach, emphasizing the rights of the press to documents and information, would tend to create a new category of confidential data—"For Journalists' Eyes Only"—and then impose on newsmen a blind professional obligation to pass along whatever other secrets they could lay their hands on. It doesn't take much time to realize that this solution simply appeases the press without accommodating the broader public interest.

Libel cases are a third important area in which special protection for the press is unjustified and unnecessary. In a libel suit against CBS producer Barry Lando, which the Supreme Court will decide this term, an appellate court ruled that "reporters and broadcasters" may refuse to answer questions concerning the thought processes that guide their investigations.* But why restrict the rule to "reporters and broadcasters"? Is their speech so much more deserving of protection than that of an angry homeowner who attacks corruption at a city council meeting, a radical group that distributes leaflets door-to-door, or a businessman who criticizes the illegal practices of a competitor? Libel suits can "chill" anyone's urge to speak freely—and the crucial line can be drawn without granting reporters greater freedom to defame than others.

How to Avoid the Corporate Theory

In the long run, the corporate theory probably serves the group it seeks to protect—the es-

---

*Editor's note: The Supreme Court decided against CBS in this case. (See two editorials in response to this decision reprinted in Chapter 10.)

tablished press—worst of all. The reason is simple: with special privileges comes the justification for imposing special responsibilities. The more the press paints itself as a small occupational group straddling the only meaningful channels of communication, the greater the pressure will be to make sure that its power is used wisely. In the past, this pressure has appeared in the form of proposals like "right to reply" statutes in which a newspaper would be forced to print rebuttals to editorial criticism. Waiting in the wings are even more ambitious schemes of state-enforced public "access" to the pages of private journals. Such "reforms" will be difficult to resist if the press officially acknowledges and subsidizes its dominant position by obtaining grants of exceptional rights. The corporate theory is more than the self-serving image of the professional reporter. It is

the theory that, in broadcasting, brought us the FCC and the fairness doctrine. The press must choose the ground on which it will stand—and the danger of state regulation of the print media, whether through public "access" or broad FCC-style oversight, is too great to risk.

A universal approach to press rights won't give the institutional press all the privileges it might want. In particular, no egalitarian version of the "newsman's privilege" will remove the possibility that reporters will on occasion have to go to jail if they want to protect confidential sources. For those journalists who insist they must make absolute promises of confidentiality in order to do their jobs, reporting will inevitably be a risky occupation. Let their badge of professionalism be a willingness to take those risks, rather than a willingness to seek special legal privileges.

ON PRESS ACCESS TO INSTITUTIONS

THE SAGINAW NEWS

Saginaw, Michigan, July 3, 1978

The U.S. Supreme Court has erected another barrier impeding the nation's media in performing its role as public surrogate with the people's government.

You may have missed it. It went by pretty fast

Reprinted from *The Saginaw News.* Copyright 1978 The Saginaw News. Used by permission.

in the outpouring of decisions traditionally preceding the court's summer recess.

What we refer to is a 4–3 decision—mind you a 4–3 decision with two justices not participating—denying print and broadcast journalists "any special right of access to prisons and jails."

Get that again.

The high court, Chief Justice Warren Burger writing the fragile majority opinion, has said the Constitution grants the press no right to enter such facilities beyond those normally accorded the general public.

Granted, the ruling came out of an Alameda County, California, case involving a TV station's suit against the county sheriff. The station was investigating conditions in the jail. The sheriff denied camera crews access.

A lower federal court upheld the TV station. The majesty of the highest court shot down the lower court.

Burger's conclusion on this case sends another chill.

The Constitution, he said, "does not mandate a right of access to government information or sources of information within the government's control. [Thus] the media has no special right of access to the Alameda County Jail different from or greater than that accorded the public generally."

The thrust of this decision leaves little doubt four members of the nine-member Court are backing across-the-board limitations on all media—not just camera crews.

We perpetually remind ourselves in this business that press freedom is not to be confused with "license" or undue "liberty" to do just as we please. Sometimes gross mistakes are made.

We do not pant to get into jails or prisons just looking for scandal. But when serious charges are made, we do feel an obligation to investigate.

Since jails and prisons are bought and paid for by the public—only run by the government—we have the cockeyed notion that the public is entitled to know from time to time how this one or that one is being run. We think that is our function—or at least one of them.

We think we also know another body blow at First Amendment guarantees of press freedom when we feel one. And one more rightward drift by this high court.

THE PROVIDENCE JOURNAL

Providence, Rhode Island, July 1, 1978

The U.S. Supreme Court ruled this week that the press has no greater right of access than the public generally to government institutions. So be it. But that should not be taken as license by government agencies here or elsewhere in the nation to limit media coverage of their activities.

The press doesn't need any special privilege of its own in claiming the right to report freely and effectively on what public officials are doing in the people's name. This is a role that it

Reprinted from *The Providence Journal.* Copyright 1978 Providence Journal Co. Used by permission.

undertakes on behalf of the public—not its publisher or owner. When it asserts the right to cover legislative, executive, or judicial affairs, it is doing so as the agent of the people, not of a profit-making entity. Since the people en masse can't be accommodated at such events, the press is their legitimate surrogate, deserving admission to let them know what is taking place.

Associate Justice Potter Stewart made this point, while joining in the 4-to-3 majority's opinion against a California television station's demand to interview inmates in an Alameda County jail. Judge Stewart considered that de-

mand "overbroad" in the particular circumstances. But, in a separate concurrence, he
emphasized the press's constitutional right of
"effective access" to government agencies—
even perhaps more so than the public at large.

"In short," he declared, "terms of access that
are reasonably imposed on individual members
of the public may, if they impede effective reporting without sufficient justification, be unreasonable as applied to journalists who are
there to convey to the general public what the
visitors see."

It is in this spirit that government officials
should view the Supreme Court ruling. It ought
not to be considered at all as permission to
undo any of the open-government reforms
which the press has utilized more than the public. These have given Rhode Islanders and
Americans generally a clearer insight than ever
before, or than anywhere else in the world, into
the workings of their government. This has
been a healthy development. There is nothing
in the high court's decision that warrants its reversal.

chapter 12

GOVERNMENT SECRECY

One of the basic conflicts in rights arises when the government wants to keep a secret and the media wants to make the secret known to the public. Former CIA director William Colby sums up the government's position when he says:

> President Ford once said he would gladly share our government's secrets with all 212 million Americans if such information would go no further .... Some secrets, after all, do protect the nation. Secret technology to locate and shoot down foreign nuclear missiles could be jammed if known in detail by a potential enemy. Confidential give-and-take in diplomatic negotiations would be impossible under klieg lights. And disclosure of the intelligence purpose behind an apparently commercial venture can enable a foreign nation to thwart the operation.[1]

Ramsey Clark, the former U.S. Attorney General, does not share Colby's point of view. He states:

> Democratic institutions are founded on assumptions, among them being the belief in the possibility of an informed public. That is why education

has always been a major component in democratic theory. So, at the threshold, we see some conflict between secrecy in government and the idea of democracy. Secrecy in government deprives the public of essential information on important governmental matters .... I have come to the conclusion—I came to it some time back—that there should be no acceptance of secrecy in government, that the risks of secrecy in government far exceed any possible benefits .... It usually involves the need, or the desire, of authority to deceive the citizens whom it serves.[2]

Colby and Clark's points of view clashed in an unprecedented manner in 1979 when the *Progressive* magazine sought to publish an article entitled "The H-Bomb Secret; How We Got It, Why We're Telling It." The U.S. District Court in Wisconsin issued an injunction restraining the publication of the article, and the media exploded with arguments on both sides. The government dropped its case several months later when a newspaper, the *Madison (Wisconsin) Press Connection*, printed a long letter from an amateur researcher who had uncovered basically the same information that was contained in the *Progressive* article. Although the case

thus ended undramatically, the issues it raised remain controversial, as seen in the first three readings in this chapter, which are samples of newspaper editorials that highlight the controversy of the *Progressive* case: the *Dayton Daily News* and the *Pittsburgh Press* believed that national security was most important; the *New York Times* believed that First Amendment guarantees were most important. This is a complex issue, and the best way to analyze it is to examine some of the actual court records. The fourth reading, therefore, is an excerpt from the judge's decision to issue the original restraining order, and the fifth reading is an excerpt from the *Progressive*'s brief appealing that order. These readings provide an interesting look into the way our legal system approaches a problem of this magnitude.

NOTES

1. William E. Colby, "How Can the Government Keep a Secret?" *TV Guide* (February 12, 1977): 2.
2. Ramsey Clark, "The Case against All Forms of Government Secrecy," *Center Magazine* (January–February 1978): 70.

ON THE *PROGRESSIVE* H-BOMB CASE

DAYTON DAILY NEWS

Dayton, Ohio, September 19, 1979

In the name of protesting censorship, a few newspapers have won a victory for the right to

Reprinted from *Dayton Daily News*. Copyright 1979 Dayton Daily News. Used by permission.

act foolishly and dangerously, to no good public purpose.

The *Madison (Wisconsin) Press Connection* got itself so wrapped up in its own conception of the First Amendment that it published a lengthy letter with accurate information about how to make a hydrogen bomb. This caused the Justice Department to give up court actions to prevent other publications from printing similar material.

What was the point in publishing it? That such information can be collected from various public sources? Anyone with enough brains to hear or read the news in the past year knows that situation exists. Why worsen the situation by putting that information together and throwing it into the public?

The editors warmed in the glory of their own publicity may argue that anyone who is determined to find out how to make an H-bomb can already do it, but that sophistry doesn't carry much solace with it. There are all kinds of crazies loose in the world, and there is no point in making it easier for them to find out how to even begin putting together weapons of mass destruction.

Another excuse that the editors are using is that the H-bomb information isn't all that sophisticated, that the U.S. government is just being bad for trying to stop publication of this stuff.

The U.S. government was trying to be responsible by containing, as best it could, even general knowledge about making an H-bomb, and there is nothing sinister about that motive.

It is reprehensible that newspapers had to fight "censorship," in a society where the press has such free reign, by an act so irresponsible that it nearly makes the odious case *for* censorship.

THE PITTSBURGH PRESS

Pittsburgh, Pennsylvania, September 22, 1979

The simple printing of a letter in the *Madison* (Wisconsin) *Press Connection*, a nondescript tabloid with a circulation of about 11,000, has torpedoed the U.S. government's celebrated prior-censorship case against the *Progressive* magazine, another journalistic gnat, and prompted the Justice Department to abandon efforts to suppress publication of technical information about the hydrogen bomb.

The *Press Connection* was one of a number of newspapers around the country that were sent copies of an open letter to Illinois Senator Charles H. Percy by a computer programmer named Charles R. Hansen.

Because the letter "substantially exposed" the essential secrets of H-bomb construction which the government had been trying to prevent the *Progressive* from publishing since last

Reprinted from *The Pittsburgh Press*. Copyright 1979 The Pittsburgh Press. Used by permission.

March, the Justice Department also dropped its case against the *Daily Californian*, a student newspaper in Berkeley which was planning to print its copy of Mr. Hansen's letter.

As far as is known, Mr. Hansen and the author of the *Progressive* article, free-lance writer Howard Morland, worked independently of each other. However, both indicated they had the same goal—"to dramatically illustrate . . . that the ultimate secret is no secret," as Mr. Morland put it in a court affidavit.

If, as they claim, they used only unclassified information from encyclopedias, open library shelves, and government publications, they certainly proved their point.

But it remains to be seen how this can possibly contribute to more informed public debate of nuclear-weapons policy, as both men contend.

Citizens do not have to know exactly how an H-bomb is put together in order to discuss nuclear weapons intelligently. Just as they don't have to know exactly how an auto is put together in order to discuss highway safety intelligently.

This whole issue seems to have been sparked by people more interested in gaining publicity than in advancing national security.

THE NEW YORK TIMES

New York, New York, September 19, 1979

No grave danger to national security justified the unprecedented six-month suppression of the *Progressive* magazine's article about H-bomb design. That, at last, will be proved with its publication. If the Government had really lost a valuable secret, it plainly would—or should—have stood mute instead of alerting technicians the world over. As was quickly apparent, the feared damage lay mainly in the demonstration of how much weapons information can be collected and deduced from public sources. And that meant there was—or should have been—no basis for restraining an American publication.

This case was in fact a political contest for both sides. The Government raised dark fears about alleged instructions on "how to build" an H-bomb so as to dupe a federal judge into suppressing the article. But even the judge found no how-to manual, only untested conclusions by Cabinet officials and famous scientists that the article "could possibly" help some nations already possessing an A-bomb to build an H-bomb too. Which nations? Had he asked, he would have been told India, or Israel, or South Africa—none that would need to add H-bombs to A-bombs and none that would need the *Progressive*'s help. The Government's concern was more with power at home than abroad. It wanted to use this sensational-sounding case to have the courts declare it the sole arbiter of who may receive and disseminate nuclear weapons data, no matter how innocent their source.

For its part, the *Progressive* hardly expected its liberal readers to value a dreary technical treatise on H-bomb concepts. Nor did it want to proliferate thermonuclear weapons. The magazine was out to prove that many nuclear secrets are not in fact secret. It thus wanted to show that the government's elaborate classification system exists not so much to protect the nation as to confine discussion of nuclear policies, both military and civilian, to a small and certified group of experts.

One need not share the magazine's opinions to recognize its right to promote them as it did. One need not deny the Government's right and duty to protect some weapons secrets to deplore the resort to prior restraint against such an insubstantial threat. The Government again cried wolf at the sight of a mouse, thus offending and damaging true national security.

We congratulate the *Progressive* and the American Civil Liberties Union for resisting, against the advice even of some customary defenders of a free press. The Government's case simply collapsed when other publications began to print similar H-bomb information, found by other amateur students in public sources, including Government libraries,

From *The New York Times* (September 19, 1979). © 1979 by The New York Times Company. Reprinted by permission.

museums and a journal for model-airplane builders. But vindication for the defendants does not automatically bring satisfaction of their constitutional rights.

Before suffering a technical knockout, the Government had created some pernicious legal theory. Lacking evidence that anyone had stolen H-bomb secrets, it claimed the right to suppress all nuclear weapons information on the ground that it is "born classified"—even if born in the minds of free men. And lest this reading of the law fail, it then proclaimed that "technical" information—allegedly distinguishable from "political" ideas—was never entitled to the free speech and press guarantees of the First Amendment. If the courts now avoid ruling on them, these doctrines would lie around, in Justice Jackson's phrase, like loaded pistols. It would be wiser to unload them while they lie within reach.

EXCERPTS FROM UNITED STATES
OF AMERICA, PLAINTIFF,

V.

THE PROGRESSIVE, INC.,
ERWIN KNOLL, SAMUEL DAY, JR.,
AND HOWARD MORLAND, DEFENDANTS

United States District Court, W. D. Wisconsin March 26, 1979

Findings of fact and conclusions of law, March 28, 1979

The United States sought a temporary restraining order to enjoin the publishers of a magazine from publishing or otherwise communicating or disclosing allegedly restricted data contained in an article entitled "The H-Bomb Secret; How We Got It, Why We're Telling It." The District Court, Warren, J., held that publication of the article would likely constitute a violation of the Atomic Energy Act and endanger national security, and that a preliminary injunction should therefore issue despite the fact that it would result in a prior restraint of the publisher's First Amendment rights.

Preliminary injunction issued. . . .

MEMORANDUM AND ORDER

Warren, District Judge.

On March 9, 1979, this Court, at the request of the government, but after hearing from both

Reprinted with permission from 467 F.Supp. 990. Copyright © 1979 By West Publishing Co.

parties, issued a temporary restraining order enjoining defendants, their employees, and agents from publishing or otherwise communicating or disclosing in any manner any restricted data contained in the article "The H-Bomb Secret: How We Got It, Why We're Telling It."

From the founding days of this nation, the rights to freedom of speech and of the press have held an honored place in our constitutional scheme. The establishment and nurturing of these rights is one of the true achievements of our form of government.

Because of the importance of these rights, any prior restraint on publication comes into court under a heavy presumption against its constitutional validity. . . .

However, First Amendment rights are not absolute. They are not boundless.

Justice Frankfurter dissenting in *Bridges* v. *California* . . . (1941) stated it in this fashion: "Free speech is not so absolute or irrational a conception as to imply paralysis of the means for effective protection of all the freedoms secured by the Bill of Rights." In the *Schenck* case, Justice Holmes recognized: "The character of every act depends upon the circumstances in which it is done." . . .

In *Near* v. *Minnesota* . . . (1931), the Supreme Court specifically recognized an extremely narrow area, involving national security, in which interference with First Amendment rights might be tolerated and a prior restraint on publication might be appropriate. The Court stated:

"When a nation is at war many things that might be said in time of peace are such a hindrance to its effort that their utterance will not be endured so long as men fight and that no court could regard them as protected by any constitutional right." No one would question but that a government might prevent actual obstruction to its recruiting service or the publication of the sailing dates of transports or the number and location of troops. . . .

Thus, it is clear that few things, save grave national security concerns, are sufficient to override First Amendment interests. A court is well admonished to approach any requested prior restraint with a great deal of skepticism.

Juxtaposed against the right to freedom of expression is the government's contention that the national security of this country could be jeopardized by publication of the article.

The Court is convinced that the government has a right to classify certain sensitive documents to protect its national security. The problem is with the scope of the classification system.

Defendants contend that the projected article merely contains data already in the public domain and readily available to any diligent seeker. They say other nations already have the same information or the opportunity to obtain it. How then, they argue, can they be in violation of 42 U.S.C. §§ 2274(b) and 2280, which purport to authorize injunctive relief against one who would disclose restricted data "with reason to believe such data will be utilized to injure the United States or to secure an advantage to any foreign nation . . ."?

Although the government states that some of the information is in the public domain, it contends that much of the data is not, and that the Morland article contains a core of information that has never before been published.

Furthermore, the government's position is that whether or not specific information is "in the public domain" or has been "declassified" at some point is not determinative. The government states that a court must look at the nature and context of prior disclosures and analyze what the practical impact of the prior disclosures are as contrasted to that of the present revelation.

The government feels that the mere fact that the author, Howard Morland, could prepare an article explaining the technical processes of thermonuclear weapons does not mean that those processes are available to everyone. They lay heavy emphasis on the argument that the danger lies in the exposition of certain concepts never heretofore disclosed in conjunction with one another. . . .

The Court has grappled with this difficult problem and has read and studied the affidavits and other documents on file. After all this, the Court finds concepts within the article that it does not find in the public realm—concepts that are vital to the operation of the hydrogen bomb.

Even if some of the information is in the public domain, due recognition must be given to the human skills and expertise involved in writing this article. The author needed sufficient expertise to recognize relevant, as opposed to irrelevant, information and to assimilate the information obtained. The right questions had to be asked or the correct educated guesses had to be made.

The ability of G. I. Taylor to calculate the yield of the first nuclear explosion from a *Life* magazine photo demonstates that certain individuals with some knowledge, ability to reason, and extraordinary perseverance may acquire additional knowledge without access to classified information, even though the information thus acquired may not be obvious to others not so equipped or motivated. All of this must be considered in resolving the issues before the Court.

Does the article provide a "do-it yourself" guide for the hydrogen bomb? Probably not. A number of affidavits make quite clear that a sine qua non to thermonuclear capability is a large, sophisticated industrial capability coupled with a coterie of imaginative, resourceful scientists and technicians. One does not build a hydrogen bomb in the basement. However, the article could possibly provide sufficient inforcation to allow a medium-size nation to move faster in developing a hydrogen weapon. It could provide a ticket to bypass blind alleys.

The Morland piece could accelerate the membership of a candidate nation in the thermonuclear club. Pursuit of blind alleys or failure to grasp seemingly basic concepts have been the cause of many inventive failures.

For example, in one of the articles submitted to the Court, the author described how, in the late 1930s, physicists in various countries were simultaneously, but independently, working on the idea of a nuclear chain reaction. The French physicists in their equation neglected to take full account of the fact that the neutrons produced by fission could go on to provoke further fissions in a many-step process—which is the essence of a chain reaction. Even though this idea seems so elementary, the concept of neutron multiplication was so novel that no nuclear physicists saw through the French team's oversight for about a year.

Thus, once basic concepts are learned, the remainder of the process may easily follow.

Although the defendants state that the information contained in the article is relatively easy to obtain, only five countries now have a hydrogen bomb. Yet the United States first successfully exploded the hydrogen bomb some 26 years ago.

The point has also been made that it is only a question of time before other countries will have the hydrogen bomb. That may be true. However, there are times in the course of human history when time itself may be very important. This time factor becomes critical when considering mass annihilation weaponry—witness the failure of Hitler to get his V-1 and V-2 bombs operational quickly enough to materially affect the outcome of World War II.

Defendants have stated that publication of the article will alert the people of this country to the false illusion of security created by the government's futile efforts at secrecy. They believe publication will provide the people with needed information to make informed decisions on an urgent issue of public concern.

However, this Court can find no plausible reason why the public needs to know the technical details about hydrogen bomb construction to carry on an informed debate on this issue. Furthermore, the Court believes that the defendants' position in favor of nuclear nonproliferation would be harmed, not aided, by the publication of this article.

The defendants have also relied on the decision in the *New York Times* case. In that case, the Supreme Court refused to enjoin the *New York Times* and the *Washington Post* from publishing the contents of a classified historical study of United States decision making in Vietnam, the so-called "Pentagon Papers."

This case is different in several important respects. In the first place, the study involved in the *New York Times* case contained historical data relating to events that occurred some three to 20 years previously. Secondly, the Supreme Court agreed with the lower court that no cogent reasons were advanced by the government as to why the article affected national security except that publication might cause some embarrassment to the United States. . . .

The Court is of the opinion that the government has shown that the defendants had reason to believe that the data in the article, if published, would injure the United States or give an advantage to a foreign nation. Extensive reading and studying of the documents on file lead to the conclusion that not all the data is available in the public realm in the same fashion, if it is available at all.

What is involved here is information dealing with the most destructive weapon in the history of mankind, information of sufficient destructive potential to nullify the right to free speech and to endanger the right to life itself.

Stripped to its essence then, the question before the Court is a basic confrontation between the First Amendment right to freedom of the press and national security.

Our Founding Fathers believed, as we do, that one is born with certain inalienable rights which, as the Declaration of Independence intones, include the right to life, liberty, and the pursuit of happiness. The Constitution, including the Bill of Rights, was enacted to make those rights operable in everyday life.

The Court believes that each of us is born seized of a panoply of basic rights, that we institute governments to secure these rights and that there is a hierarchy of values attached to these rights which is helpful in deciding the clash now before us.

Certain of these rights have an aspect of imperativeness or centrality that make them transcend other rights. Somehow it does not seem that the right to life and the right to not have soldiers quartered in your home can be of equal import in the grand scheme of things. While it may be true in the long run, as Patrick Henry instructs us, that one would prefer death to life without liberty, nonetheless, in the short run, one cannot enjoy freedom of speech, freedom to worship, or freedom of the press unless one first enjoys the freedom to live.

Faced with a stark choice between upholding the right to continued life and the right to freedom of the press, most jurists would have no difficulty in opting for the chance to continue to breathe and function as they work to achieve perfect freedom of expression.

Is the choice here so stark? Only time can give us a definitive answer. But considering another aspect of this panoply of rights we all have is helpful in answering the question now before us. This aspect is the disparity of the risk involved.

The destruction of various human rights can come about in differing ways and at varying speeds. Freedom of the press can be obliterated overnight by some dictator's imposition of censorship or by the slow nibbling away at a free press through successive bits of repressive legislation enacted by a nation's lawmakers. Yet, even in the most drastic of such situations, it is always possible for a dictator to be overthrown, for a bad law to be repealed, or for a judge's error to be subsequently rectified. Only when human life is at stake are such corrections impossible.

The case at the bar is so difficult precisely because the consequences of error involve human life itself and on such an awesome scale.

The Secretary of State states that publication will increase thermonuclear proliferation and that this would "irreparably impair the national security of the United States." The Secretary of Defense says that dissemination of the Morland paper will mean a substantial increase in the risk of thermonuclear proliferation and lead to use or threats that would "adversely affect the national security of the United States."

Howard Morland asserts that "if the information in my article were not in the public domain, it should be put there . . . so that ordinary citizens may have informed opinions about nuclear weapons." . . .

The Court is faced with the difficult task of weighing and resolving these divergent views.

A mistake in ruling against the *Progressive* will seriously infringe cherished First Amendment rights. If a preliminary injunction is issued, it will constitute the first instance of prior restraint against a publication in this fashion in the history of this country, to this Court's knowledge. Such notoriety is not to be sought. It will curtail defendants' First Amendment rights in a drastic and substantial fashion. It will infringe upon our right to know and to be informed as well.

A mistake in ruling against the United States could pave the way for thermonuclear annihilation for us all. In that event, our right to life is extinguished and the right to publish becomes moot.

EXCERPTS FROM THE
PROGRESSIVE'S APPEALS BRIEF

"Defendants have stated that publication of the article will alert the people of this country to the false illusion of security created by the government's futile efforts at secrecy. They believe publication will provide the people with needed information to make informed decisions on an urgent issue of public concern.

"However, this Court can find no plausible reason why the public needs to know the technical details about hydrogen bomb construction to carry on an informed debate on this issue."

Reprinted from *The Progressive* (September 1979): 45–46.

In a few words, Judge [Robert] Warren has explained the basis for his decision to issue a preliminary injunction in this case. The First Amendment, however, was not drafted to enable any branch of government to determine what information the public "needs to know." That was a responsibility left—for better or worse—to a free press and a free people.

Although there may be an extremely rare instance when government can restrain free speech in the name of national security, at the heart of the First Amendment lies the almost insuperable presumption against such restraint. To determine whether the government has overcome this barrier, this Court must conduct an independent, *de novo* review of the entire record.

The government brought this action under the Atomic Energy Act, which prohibits the dissemination of "restricted data" (information concerning nuclear material or nuclear weapons), and under the inherent power of the Executive Branch. It claims that the Morland article describes three principal concepts of the hydrogen bomb, concepts which together can be simply stated in a single short sentence. The district court restrained publication even though each of the concepts is known to thousands and can be found or readily derived from information already in the public domain—in encyclopedias, college textbooks, magazines, newspapers, and government publications, all available in public libraries.

Far from being a blueprint for the production of a nuclear weapon, the article discusses the important political issues of nuclear proliferation and government secrecy. "Knowledge of the basic principles of hydrogen weapon design," as the article says, "provides insight into the purposes of continued nuclear testing . . . and the devastating effects of nuclear war." "[W]e have less to fear from knowing than from not knowing. What we do with the knowledge may be the key to our survival." That is precisely the kind of political speech sheltered from government censorship by the First Amendment.

Defendants submitted the affidavits of numerous physicists, including several from the government's Livermore and Argonne laboratories, stating that the basic concepts of thermonuclear weapons are not secret but available to all who seek them. The government has offered affidavits to the contrary and contends that publication of the article would "undermine" the government's nonproliferation policy. The government bases its case on specula-

tive and conclusory affidavits which fail on their face to establish the "sure," "inevitable," "grave," "direct," "immediate," and "irreparable" harm to the nation required to justify prior restraint. They clash with the many affidavits of eminent scientists submitted by the defendants, a strong difference of views which in and of itself demonstrates that the government has failed to meet the rigorous standards of the First Amendment.

Besides meeting the constitutional test for prior restraint, the government also must demonstrate that publication would violate the Atomic Energy Act. It cannot do so because the defendants had no "reason to believe" that publication of information already in the public domain would violate the Act. The Act, moreover, cannot be used to enjoin protected speech and conduct because its provisions are vague and overbroad, constitutionally invalid.

The preliminary injunction was issued even though there is no allegation or proof that any of the information was unlawfully acquired. To the contrary, the government contends that regardless of the fact the information was lawfully acquired by a journalist, the information became "classified at birth" the moment it was learned or understood, and from that moment it was a felony to communicate that product of his public research and private thought. The sweep of the statute is automatic and boundless, encompassing all information as defined above, regardless of its source or purpose. That concept would create a system of thought control and peacetime censorship without parallel in our history. Unless construed to avoid constitutional vagueness and overbreadth, the statute's breadth and uncertainty violate due process and First Amendment rights. . . .

No constitutional principle is more firmly established than the "heavy presumption" against the constitutionality of "[a]ny system" that imposes prior restraint on expression. The Supreme Court has consistently held that the government bears a "heavy burden" in attempting to overcome that presumption. As Chief Justice Burger has noted, every member of the Supreme Court agrees that prior restraints are presumptively unconstitutional.

The Court long ago recognized that the constitutional presumption against prior restraint lies at the very core of the First Amendment: "[I]t has been generally, if not universally, considered that it is the chief purpose of the [First Amendment's] guaranty to prevent previous restraints upon publication." Prior restraints are presumptively unconstitutional because the primary function of the First Amendment is to ensure "the widest possible dissemination of information from diverse and antagonistic sources," and the "unfettered interchange of ideas."

In repeatedly and firmly enforcing the rule against prior restraint, the Court has established an extraordinarily demanding *substantive* standard which must be met before protected speech can even conceivably be restrained. The Court has also established strict *procedural* requirements far more rigorous than in ordinary cases. Together, they create an "almost insuperable presumption" against such restraint.

In light of the substantive standards that must be applied, the district court's findings of fact are insufficient on their face to warrant prior restraint. . . .

chapter 13

PRIVACY VS. THE "RIGHT TO KNOW"

The reporter's traditional belief in the public's "right to know" has figured prominently in each of the "rights in conflict" mentioned so far. As seen in the previous readings, the right to know can cause conflicts with a trial defendant, a local government, or a national government. This chapter examines a conflict between the right to know and individual rights.

In the first reading Floyd Abrams, a constitutional lawyer, expresses his fear that privacy laws will inhibit a free press. Arthur Miller, a law professor, presents the opposing view in the second reading. The final reading in this chapter concerns a choice that had to be made by a news photographer—a choice between what he saw as his personal and professional conscience about privacy. It is included here to stress the fact that privacy is a personal issue as well as a legal one.

THE PRESS, PRIVACY, AND THE CONSTITUTION

Floyd Abrams

A swift move jostles a would-be assassin's arm. The shot misses President Gerald Ford. Sara Jane Moore receives a life sentence. But what of Oliver Sipple, the ex-Marine who deflected her aim? He becomes an instant hero, but national publicity also reveals that he is a member of San Francisco's gay community. Now, almost two years after the assassination attempt, Sipple's suit against several newspapers for invading his privacy proceeds through the California courts.*

The Sipple case has broad implications. It is one of a growing number brought against the press by people who claim that even true statements about themselves may not be published. And it exemplifies what has become the single most ominous threat to the First Amendment's guarantee of press freedom—the explosion of privacy law.

For the press, recent years have seen a general easing of a variety of legal threats. When it appeared that sky-high libel judgments against national newspapers and magazines by local juries might inhibit—and ultimately prohibit —coverage of the civil rights movement of the 1950s, libel law was all but rewritten by the Supreme Court. The press was provided with constitutional protection even for the publication of false statements about public officials, so long as the press had not deliberately falsified or printed the statements with serious doubts as to their truth.

When an effort was made to prohibit publication of the Pentagon Papers, the Supreme Court speedily rejected it. When lower court judges issued a flood of gag orders against publication of material about pending criminal cases, the Supreme Court made it all but impossible for any such orders to be entered in the future. And when a state attempted to force newspapers to publish material they chose not to print, the Supreme Court unanimously rebuffed that effort.

Not all recent decisions involving the press have been in its favor. In the case of *New York Times* reporter Earl Caldwell, the Supreme Court declined to grant journalists a right to refuse to testify with respect to their confidential sources. And in cases involving the press's right to enter prisons to interview inmates, the Court rejected the argument that the First Amendment provided special rights of access for the press. But neither of these areas, important as they are, approach that of privacy in terms of the risks they pose.

Discussions of those risks have become the staple of conversation at gatherings of editors and those of lawyers familiar with the field. When editors of newspapers meet to discuss the current state of the American press, the growth of privacy law is invariably high on the agenda. And at an American Bar Association

*Editor's note: To date, Sipple's suits have been unsuccessful.

From *The New York Times Magazine* (August 21, 1977): 11–13. © 1977 by The New York Times Company. Reprinted by permission.

meeting of a committee on free speech and free press held earlier this month, all the lawyers present agreed that the expansion of privacy law posed more of a threat to the press than any other.

One threat involves the possible substitution of an official governmental view—of legislators or judges—for the judgment of editors as to what is "newsworthy." Another is that the more privacy cases are decided against the press, the more the press will be inhibited in gathering news; as a consequence, much important news gathering may become all but impossible.

In the end, the press is the surrogate for the American public. Because that public today absorbs more news than ever before, its dependence on journalists and broadcasters is unprecedented. Thus, any balancing of the right of privacy against the right of the press to report—and the public's need to know—is not merely a journalistic dilemma, but an American dilemma.

Before 1890, there was no such concept in American jurisprudence as privacy law. In that year, two young Boston lawyers, who had been roommates at the Harvard Law School and then law partners, published an article on privacy in the *Harvard Law Review*. One was Louis Brandeis, whose lustrous career on the United States Supreme Court began 26 years later; the other was Samuel Warren, a wealthy and socially prominent Bostonian.

The background of the article—probably the single most important one in all American legal history—is remarkable for its pettiness. Warren, not Brandeis, spurred its drafting. Married in 1883 to the daughter of a Massachusetts senator, Warren had become increasingly irritated by the descriptions in the Boston "yellow press" of parties given by the socially prominent couple. The article faithfully reflects the irritation of the upper classes at their social inferiors.

Gossip is published, so the article says, "to occupy the indolent." One effect of gossip is to "belittle" by "inverting the relative importance of things, thus dwarfing the thoughts and aspirations of a people." Since the very publication of gossip "crowds the space available for matters of real interest to the community, what wonder that the ignorant and thoughtless mistake its relative importance. Easy of comprehension, appealing to that weak side of human nature which is never wholly cast down by the misfortunes and frailties of our neighbors, no one can be surprised that it usurps the place of interest in brains capable of other things."

Out of such nineteenth century condescension, the law of privacy was born. But what, specifically, would it protect against? Brandeis and Warren had complained of the "obvious bounds of propriety and decency" being overstepped and of "idle or prurient curiosity" being served. They had urged that individuals be permitted to recover money damages for such publications, that injunctions be issued in some cases, and that it would "doubtless be desirable" for criminal statutes to be adopted to punish invasions of privacy. But what is "propriety"? And how is one to tell "idle" curiosity from news?

The law was slow in its efforts to answer these questions. Brandeis and Warren had published their article in 1890. By 1941, only eight states had recognized a right to sue for what was characterized as invasion of privacy; by 1964, the number of states was 31; now it is 47 (excluding only Rhode Island, Nebraska, and Wisconsin).

Some privacy claims are, quite literally, laughable. There is the suit by a former boxer against Groucho Marx: Groucho, during a "You Bet Your Life" show of the late 1940s, had said, "I once managed a fighter named Canvasback Cohen. I brought him here, he got knocked out, and I made him walk back to Cleveland." The real Cohen sued, alleging that Groucho's joke was an invasion of his privacy. Like Groucho, the court sent Cohen walking.

Other claims, however, raise more serious

questions as to the scope and nature of privacy protection. Four types of privacy cases have arisen through the years. One relates to the truthful disclosure of "private" facts; this is illustrated by the example of Oliver Sipple, the ex-Marine who saved President Ford. Another involves what are claimed to be physical intrusions or trespasses by the press in the course of its news gathering; this is exemplified by the case of a medical quack named A. A. Dietemann, who sued *Life* magazine for the manner in which it gathered facts in order to expose him. The third type of privacy action has to do with the right to sell one's own name or likeness; an example of this is that of Human Cannonball Hugo Zacchini, who sued a television station for broadcasting his act. The fourth category arises when the press is said to have placed someone in a "false light" in the course of describing him; this is illustrated by the so-called "Desperate Hours" case, in which James Hill claimed a magazine article misrepresented his family's experience while being held hostage by criminals.

"PRIVATE" FACTS

The day after the assassination attempt on President Ford, members of San Francisco's gay community mentioned to *San Francisco Chronicle* columnist Herb Caen that they were "proud—maybe this will help break the stereotype." Caen's article of September 24, 1975, contained such a reference to Sipple. Then, when Sipple was pressed on the subject, he disclosed that he had been one of the "court" of an elected "emperor" of the gay community. Believing that reporting on Sipple's activities in San Francisco's thriving gay community was newsworthy, California newspapers published articles referring to those activities. Sipple's suit, in turn, claims that because of the articles about him, his parents and brothers and sisters in Ohio learned for the first time

of his homosexual affiliations and, as a result, abandoned him.

Sipple's lawyer, John Eshleman Wahl, has rhetorically inquired whether, if Sipple had known "that saving the life of the President would subject his sex life to the speculation and scrutiny of the national news media," he would have chosen to save the President's life at all. "How, in the name of logic and justice," Wahl has urged, "does a discussion of Mr. Sipple's private sexual orientation have anything to do with his saving of the President's life? Obviously and clearly it does not—but it sells papers."

In reply to this, *Los Angeles Times* attorney Robert S. Warren and journalists on that newspaper have pointed to the newsworthiness of Sipple's affiliation with San Francisco's gay community—both because Sipple's act was so contrary to the stereotyped (now Anita Bryant-ized) view of homosexuals, and because it seemed for a time that President Ford might not publicly thank Sipple because he was gay. (Ford did.) Warren also points to Sipple's own disclosures of his participation in San Francisco's gay community, disclosures Sipple claims were made on some kind of off-the-record basis.

As the law has thus far developed, it is difficult to envisage the *Los Angeles Times* losing the Sipple suit. A recent case involving yet another Californian, who had asserted a privacy claim arising out of an article about him in *Sports Illustrated*, seems to assure this result. That case was brought by a champion body surfer named Michael Virgil whose hobbies (which he disclosed to a *Sports Illustrated* reporter) included eating spiders, putting out lighted cigarettes in his mouth, and diving down flights of stairs to impress women. When *Sports Illustrated* published an article containing that information, Virgil sued. And lost.

In its opinion the U.S. Court of Appeals spelled out its view as to the law, a view which appears to reflect that of most other lower courts, but which the U.S. Supreme Court has not yet ruled upon. So long as a truthful description of private facts about a person in the news is "newsworthy," the Court of Appeals said, a newspaper may not be found liabile for publishing them. What is not newsworthy? According to the court, "the line is to be drawn when the publicity ceases to be the giving of information to which the public is entitled and becomes a morbid and sensational prying into private lives for its own sake, with which a reasonable member of the public, with decent standards, would say that he had no concern." Concluding that the disclosures published in *Sports Illustrated* about Virgil could not meet such a test, the District Court (to which the case was returned) dismissed Virgil's suit. As will happen, one may guess, to Sipple's suit because of the newsworthiness—whatever the taste—of the revelations about him.

But the dismissal of the Sipple suit, even if it occurs, will not diminish the risks posed by other such privacy suits and other findings by other judges or jurors as to what is—and what is not—newsworthy. The Sipple suit, like that of Virgil before it, raises a more critical issue than that of what is newsworthy: it is who should decide what is newsworthy.

There are some in the press and the bar who consider the victory of *Sports Illustrated* in the Virgil case a major one, precisely because of its conclusion that the revelations about Virgil were newsworthy. But it is far from that. For one thing, the test set forth by the court in the Virgil case contains language so vague ("morbid and sensational prying"), so open-ended ("a reasonable member of the public"), and so subjective ("decent standards") that it makes it all but impossible to determine in advance what may be published and what not. What would a member of the public with "decent standards" say, for example, about publishing information about President Kennedy's amorous meanderings? Or about Margaret Trudeau's walks on the wild side? Or about the fact that

Frank Hogan, when he ran for District Attorney of New York County, had cancer and was likely not to live out the entirety of his term? Or even about accurate reports of Samuel Warren's nineteenth-century cocktail parties?

Historically, decisions as to what is and is not "newsworthy" are precisely the ones made by editors, not judges. They are not always made well or responsibly. But, as Chief Justice Warren E. Burger (whose record in First Amendment cases involving the press is far more supportive than is generally recognized) has written: "For better or worse, editing is what editors are for; and editing is the selection and choice of material. That editors— newspapers or broadcast—can and do abuse this power is beyond doubt, but . . . calculated risks of abuse are taken in order to preserve higher values."

Judges are, as well, government officials, and it is generally taken as one of the great gifts of the First Amendment that it puts all such officials out of the newsrooms, not in them. One New York columnist, for example, while denouncing a federal judge for a widely publicized recent decision affecting middle- and lower-income people, mentioned the judge's Park Avenue address. As a result, the judge received a torrent of angry and sometimes threatening mail. Should the journalist have printed the judge's address? The argument against printing it is strong. But should a judge—any judge—be permitted to make such a decision?

In libel law—that body of law relating to the publication of defamatory falsehoods—it has historically and constitutionally been the case that so long as what was published was true there could be no recovery against the press for its publication. But in the branch of privacy law involved in Sipple's case, what the offended party in effect says is not that false things have been said about him, but that true things have been said which should have gone unsaid. To a high degree, all such claims thus involve delicate and difficult questions of taste, an area in which journalists hardly can claim to have any better judgment than the rest of us and in which they sometimes have far worse. Yet to permit judicial tastes—or those of other governmental officials with "decent standards"— to determine what may be printed is surely far more dangerous. That, if anything, is the lesson of our history.

PHYSICAL INTRUSIONS

A. A. Dietemann was a disabled veteran who—as a court would later phrase it—"was engaged in the practice of dealing with clay, minerals, and herbs . . . simple quackery." On September 20, 1963, two *Life* magazine reporters visited Dietemann in his home—which was also the office for his quackery. One of the reporters, acting as if she were a patient, described imaginary cancer symptoms to Dietemann, who promptly responded by advising that the reporter had eaten some rancid butter 11 years, 9 months, and 7 days prior to the examination. While Dietemann (who carried a wandlike object in his hand) spoke with his "patient," his words were carried by a small radio transmitter in the reporter's purse to a parked car outside the Dietemann home where another *Life* reporter, an assistant district attorney, and an investigator for the California Department of Public Health listened. The second reporter in Dietemann's house also took photographs without Dietemann's knowledge.

As a result of this journalistic effort, Dietemann was arrested for practicing medicine without a license. *Life* photographers took pictures of the arrest, and two weeks later *Life* published an article entitled "Crackdown on Quackery," containing a photograph surreptitiously taken at Dietemann's home.

Dietemann pleaded nolo contendere to the charge. He then sued *Life* for invasion of privacy.

Dietemann's claims, of course, raised far different problems from Sipple's. The legal result in the case was written in 1971 by the distinguished federal judge Shirley Hufstedler. Her opinion, for herself and other members of the United States Court of Appeals, concluded that Dietemann could recover for the invasion of his house by the *Life* reporters and that a $1000 verdict rendered in his favor by a jury (for injury to his "feelings and peace of mind") was constitutionally permissible. According to the court, Dietemann's "den was a sphere from which he could reasonably expect to exclude eavesdropping newsmen." As for the argument of *Life* that the First Amendment protected its kind of investigative journalism, Judge Hufstedler sharply responded that "the First Amendment has never been construed to accord newsmen immunity from torts [civil wrongs] or crimes committed during the course of news gathering."

Yet the result in the case remains troubling. It is one thing to say that as a general matter one's home is sacrosanct from invasion by outsiders and that journalists are as responsible as the rest of us for illegal or improper eavesdropping, just as they are for speeding or even jaywalking. It is quite another to conclude that when a person passes himself off as a doctor and uses his home as his office, journalists may not act as prospective patients and record the illegal activities that occur there.

Professor Alfred Hill, of Columbia Law School, has recently highlighted the difficulty raised by the Dietemann verdict with the following hypothetical question. Suppose that reporters infiltrate the highest Mafia councils, employ hidden cameras and other surreptitious devices, and, as a result, obtain and publish conclusive proof of major criminal activity of the Mafia, the police, prosecutors, and other officials at the highest government levels. If all that were so, Hill asks, can it be that the exposed Mafiosi could recover for breach of their *privacy*?

One solution to this issue might be for American law to borrow one aspect of British law and permit a jury to conclude that, even though a physical intrusion by the press had occurred, the publication so benefited the public that no recovery should be permitted. This would permit newspapers willing to do so to risk some physical intrusion or deception of quacks or of Mafiosi while knowing that a jury might well reject the defense. (Most newspapers, in fact, do not engage, as a journalistic matter, in the kind of deception involved in the Dietemann case.)

This is hardly a tidy solution, since it leaves open the possibility of different jury verdicts in all but identical cases, and jury decisions based on the success or failure of the alleged intrusion by the press. But if cases such as Dietemann's are to continue to be heard at all, such an approach seems to strike a better balance than did the court in the Dietemann case itself.

SELF-PROMOTION

At the county fair in Burton, Ohio, on September 1, 1972, the audience saw a renewed version of an old American tradition: a human cannonball who was projected out of a cannon-like object into a net 200 feet away. A local television station filmed the 15-second spectacle and broadcast it on its 11 P.M. news program. While the film was being shown, the newscaster described the act as follows:

> This . . . now . . . is the story of a true *spectator* sport . . . the sport of human cannonballing. . . . In fact, the great Zacchini is about the only human cannonball around, these days. . . . Believe me, although it's not a *long* act, it's a thriller . . . and you really need to see it *in person* . . . to appreciate it . . .

Ten months later, Hugo Zacchini—the cannonball himself—filed suit in the Ohio courts.

He alleged that the right to show the film of his act belonged to him and that the television station, by showing the film, had invaded his privacy.

The kind of privacy law involved in Zacchini's case protects an entirely different interest from that involved in both the Sipple and Dietemann cases—the right of self-promotion or publicity, of selling one's own talent. Yet Zacchini's act was broadcast on a regularly scheduled news program, with no effort by the station at any commercial exploitation of the act. Who wins?

So far, Zacchini. In a 5–to–4 decision rendered on June 28, 1977, the Supreme Court, in an opinion written by Justice Byron R. White, concluded that the First Amendment does not "immunize the media when they broadcast a performer's entire act without his consent." Although states may decline to permit recovery in such cases if they wish, the White opinion concluded that there is no constitutional compulsion that they do so. The case was thus returned to the Ohio courts for them to decide whether Zacchini should recover anything.

Like so many decisions in the field of privacy, the Zacchini ruling raises about as many questions as it answers. As Justice Lewis F. Powell's dissent inquires, what is an "entire act" anyway? Just the shooting of Zacchini through the air? Or the fanfare, possibly stretching over several minutes, "all accompanied by suitably ominous commentary from the master of ceremonies"? What will the effect of the opinion be, Powell asks, on the reporting on television of events at local fairs, of sports competitions, such as a winning ski jump, or of showing a short—but whole—skit from a theatrical revue?

More broadly, Justice Powell's dissent contends that far from focusing on whether an "entire act" was broadcast, the appropriate question is what use the station made of the film footage. If the use is "for a routine portion of a regular news program," Powell urges that the

First Amendment should protect a broadcaster from a Zacchini-type of suit in the absence of proof by the plaintiff that the broadcast was a "subterfuge or cover for private or commercial exploitation." Otherwise, he argues, the public will simply be left uninformed about information it is entitled to know.

Justice Powell's dissent highlights the difficulty now posed with respect to the broadcasting of certain newsworthy events. It is true that "entire" acts have rarely been broadcast as news anyway; they rarely are newsworthy and to that extent the Zacchini decision may have limited future effect. But the question remains whether the public is well served by any notion of privacy that prevents them from observing events as newsworthy, if trivial, as that of Hugo Zacchini's flights.

"FALSE LIGHT"

In September 1952, three escaped convicts entered the suburban Pennsylvania home of Mr. and Mrs. James J. Hill and their five children. For the 19 much publicized hours that followed, the Hills were held captive in their own home. They were treated courteously and not molested or otherwise treated violently. Two of the three convicts were killed a few days later by the police in a wild shoot-out.

Based on the experiences of the Hills, Joseph Hayes wrote a best-selling novel, *The Desperate Hours*. The book added to the actual tribulations of the Hills certain incidents which had not occurred. It told of beatings of the father and son by the convicts and a verbal sexual insult to the daughter. When *The Desperate Hours* was made into a play, *Life* magazine transported some of the actors to the home where the Hills had been held hostage to take pictures.

One was of the son being manhandled by a convict; it was captioned "brutish convict." Another was of the daughter biting the hand of one of the convicts to force him to drop a gun; it was captioned "daring daughter." A third showed the father throwing his gun through the door after his "brave try" to free his family failed.

Hill (represented in the Supreme Court by Richard Nixon) sued *Life* under a New York privacy statute, claiming that the *Life* article had given the impression that the play mirrored the Hills' experience, something *Life* knew "was false and untrue." In its opinion, written by Justice William J. Brennan, Jr., the Supreme Court rejected the argument that liability for this kind of invasion of privacy could ever be imposed, even for false statements, "unless actual malice—knowledge that the statements are false or in reckless disregard of the truth—is alleged and proved. . . ." It was a major press victory, but it appears to be one which will be limited to cases—like Hill's—in which individuals were portrayed in a "false light," and not to cases such as that of Sipple, Dietemann, or Zacchini.

Cases such as those described illustrate some, but hardly all, of the mileposts which privacy has passed. But the risks of the rapid growth of privacy law are not limited to such cases. They include, as well, a wide range of state statutes adopted to protect privacy. These also directly threaten the ability of the public to learn significant facts which even Brandeis and Warren would have agreed do not constitute "gossip." In Rhode Island, for example, a statute has been adopted permitting destruction of misdemeanor records after completion of a sentence or probation and following a specified period of time with no convictions. In California and New Jersey, records of marijuana-law violators may be destroyed. In New York and Missouri, authorities will not release information about arrests that do not result in conviction. And in South Carolina, a bill is now under consideration which would require destruction of records when a person found guilty is pardoned.

All these laws are well intended. They reflect serious societal judgments that in many cases criminal records should be destroyed in order to avoid further harming those accused and not convicted, those convicted of minor crimes or those whose convictions have been expunged by pardons. These laws are supported by organizations usually sensitive to First Amendment concerns, such as the American Civil Liberties Union.

But the rapid spread of such laws is among the most troublesome developments of the privacy explosion. Not the least problem posed by such statutes is their interference with any ability of the press to scrutinize criminal justice agencies. Cases which are not pursued by the prosecution for political reasons or dismissed by the courts—either because of corruption or incompetence—could not be followed if arrest records were not available. Exposés in the press, such as the 1972 St. Louis Globe-Democrat series which disclosed traffic-ticket fixing in the city courts and which led to the removal of two judges and the chief clerk and to criminal indictments, would be all but impossible to develop.

Similarly, scrutiny of a multiple arrest record of an individual who was not later convicted of any crimes may lead to the conclusion that he had been unjustly persecuted, or, perhaps, that some kind of favoritism had led to a failure to convict an obviously culpable party. In either event, society would benefit from exposure of the very information such statutes seek to destroy.

The case against destruction of conviction records is, if anything, even stronger. Courtrooms, after all, are public property; trials, as the Supreme Court has observed, are public events; and convictions are matters of the greatest public consequence. The notion that an individual may be duly accused, tried, and convicted of a crime and that no record may lawfully be kept on his conviction is Orwellian in its implications. It involves the destruction of history, of truth, in the name of privacy. It would even prohibit citizens from learning if a candidate for school-board president—

or United States President—had committed crimes which bear directly on his capacity to serve in office.

In Britain, the situation is even more forbidding: There, it is a crime to publish the fact of a prior conviction if an individual has not served more than 30 months in prison and has not been arrested again within seven years. Thus, if an English equivalent of Spiro Agnew (if that can be imagined) should run for Parliament eight years after his felony conviction, no mention could be made of the conviction in the British press.

(A striking example of the differences between the British and American legal systems may be seen in the fact that, because of its references to the Sipple case, this very article would, under British law, constitute a contempt of court, thus subjecting its author and the editor and publisher of this newspaper to fines or jail sentences. Under British law, all such references would have been illegal, since that case is still before the courts—where it may remain for years. Through American eyes, it surely seems a strange way for a free nation to function.)

There is another side to the rapid development of privacy law in recent years, one that is far more appealing and surely less threatening than that involving the press. It stems from the conclusion of the Supreme Court that, against abuses by the government itself, the Constitution affords significant privacy protection.

Once again, Brandeis is most to be credited—this time, more affirmatively—with the development of this body of law. In a stirring and subsequently much quoted 1928 dissenting opinion in a case involving government wiretapping, he observed that the makers of our Constitution had "conferred, as against the government, the right to be let alone—the most comprehensive of rights and the right most valued by civilized men."

The Constitution itself was later held to afford privacy not only from direct government surveillance and intrusion but from governmental intrusions into a wide range of deeply personal decisions. These included the right to marry regardless of the race of one's spouse, the right to purchase contraceptives, the right to an abortion, and other decisions relating to family relationships and child rearing. In one recent decision of this type, Justice Brennan concluded: "If the right of privacy means anything, it is the right of the individual, married or single, to be free from unwanted governmental intrusions into matters so fundamentally affecting a person as the decision whether to bear or beget a child." In other areas, it is surprising that protection against government interference into deeply private decisions has not been extended still further. It remains inexplicable that the courts can continue to rule, as they have, that homosexuals may be subjected to criminal prosecution for sexual practices in private between consenting adults.

If anything, expansion rather than contraction of privacy law may be expected in the future. To the extent any such expansion relates to the protection of the individual from the government, Brandeis's eloquent 1928 formulation remains the last word: To protect the "right to be left alone," he wrote, "every unjustifiable intrusion by the government upon the privacy of the individual, whatever the means employed, must be deemed a violation of the [Constitution]." To the extent privacy law is expanded so as to make it still riskier or more difficult for the press to publish the truth, a quite different conclusion may be drawn. It is now 87 years—four score and seven—since Brandeis and Warren drafted their article. Is it too late to say they were wrong?

THE PRESS AND PRIVACY

Arthur R. Miller

OVERZEALOUS REPORTERS VS. THE RIGHT TO PRIVACY

During the past few years, Americans have become increasingly sensitive to the right of individual privacy. Popular concern over the computerization of personal information, governmental surveillance of citizens, the excessive zeal of the FBI and CIA, and the abuses of Watergate has led to a remarkable series of statutes, administrative regulations, and judicial decisions designed to limit data collection, to extend the rights of those on whom files are

Reprinted from *Los Angeles Times* (April 16, 1978). © 1978 Arthur R. Miller. Used by permission.

kept, and prevent access to dossiers by those with no legitimate need to know their contents.

The nation's press has begun to argue that it needs immunity from these new rules. But I believe the media have it backward; it is the public's right to privacy that needs increased protection against the press.

Although I appreciate that the nation's journalists have served as a bastion against abuse of governmental power, as in the case of Watergate, I reject the suggestion that the media have such a paramount status that the judgment of editors as to what is newsworthy need not be balanced against other social considerations.

After all, as Justice William O. Douglas once observed, "The right to be let alone is indeed the beginning of all freedom." The U.S. Supreme Court has protected the privacy of personal association, ideology, the home, the marital relationship, and the body. Similarly, an individual's desire to control the dissemination of information about himself is a natural part of personal autonomy and should not be dismissed as some kind of eccentric Greta Garbo-Howard Hughes syndrome.

Many people feel embarrassed or demeaned when information about them is disclosed or exchanged, even though it may be accurate and not professionally or socially damaging. To some, loss of privacy equals loss of dignity. Lewis Carroll put it well in *Alice's Adventures in Wonderland*: "Oh, 'tis love, 'tis love, that makes the world go round!" the Duchess remarks, prompting Alice to whisper, "It's done by everybody minding their own business!"

We live in a crowded, complex world, one in which a host of decisions affecting our daily lives—whether we are insurable, creditworthy, employable, or eligible for government benefits—are made by people we never see, using information over which we have no control. The individual is increasingly at the mercy of information brokers who covet, collect, and abuse personal information on other people.

Ironically, while the media decry these developments, they assert their right to investigate our private lives—an act which surely contributes to the erosion of privacy and emphasizes the need for protection. An excessively zealous newspaper, television network, or radio station poses a significant threat to our right to be let alone. Indeed, disclosures in the public press about one's private life can be more devastating than dissemination of the same information by a credit bureau.

Recent Court Victories

With the help of the courts, we must protect our right of privacy by balancing it against the legitimate needs and First Amendment rights of America's media. The courts, after all, have accorded extraordinary protection to journalists in recent years, thereby creating the contemporary imbalance between individual rights and press prerogatives. The media's liability for defamation has been limited, the scope of executive privilege has been contained, and publication restrictions based on national security have been overcome. The courts have done these things by expansively interpreting the First Amendment and striking down countless attempts to intimidate journalists by repressive agency regulations or governmental practices.

Despite these court victories, the press now claims that it is threatened by America's growing social sensitivity to privacy. Journalists apparently think they are engaged in a never-ending series of life-and-death cliffhangers. Challenged by one Goliath after another, media Davids must repeatedly sally forth to slay the enemy. This strikes me as a highly distorted and egocentric view of the universe. Spiro Agnew notwithstanding, not everyone is out to get the media.

I am not persuaded that press freedom will come tumbling down like a house of cards unless every competing social interest is subordinated to this one right. However fragile the condition of newspapers at the time of the American Revolution, the present economic power of the broadcast networks and publishing giants casts serious doubt on any suggestion of media vulnerability.

WHY DOES THE PRESS WORRY?

Why do journalists insist on pressing their prerogatives to the limits? Why is it that the press reacts like a terrified hemophiliac to the slightest pinprick of criticism? Apparently, it fears that recognizing the importance of any other public interest may inhibit news gathering and is the first step toward erosion of the media's special status. But the nation's press can remain vibrant without a license to intrude on our privacy. The law already affords the media so much protection that tempering journalistic zeal by requiring a modicum of respect for people's privacy poses no real risk that anything of news value will be lost.

Moreover, other, profound human values are at stake. People involuntarily thrust into the glare of publicity pay a terrible price when they lose their right to be let alone. Oliver Sipple, who lunged at Sara Jane Moore and deflected her revolver as she fired at President Ford, paid that price in 1975, when the media revealed his membership in San Francisco's gay community.

Unless reporters are deterred from excessive and unwarranted curiosity, many of us may be inhibited from participating in society's affairs. Any risk of dampening press enthusiasm for news gathering must be measured against creating a public fear, what George Orwell called "the assumption that every sound you made was overheard, and, except in darkness, every move was scrutinized."

Despite this specter, the press begrudges us some of the measures recently taken to protect our privacy. For example, it demands immunity from laws that deny unfettered access to certain criminal records—typically those of juveniles and of people who have been rehabilitated.

Monitoring the Criminal Justice System

Vigorous and diligent reporters can effectively monitor the criminal justice system without examining the records of individuals who have paid their debt to society, who have met the stringent prerequisites for having their records sealed, and who deserve a second chance. Why should society not draw a protective curtain over the record of a youthful peccadillo that has never been repeated? It is inexcusably self-serving for the press to say that those who are protected by such curtains must be sacrificed on the altar of the First Amendment's absolute primacy.

The media ask for prerogatives unavailable to anyone else. For example, some journalists argue that a reporter who trespasses or uses false pretenses to enter someone's home should not be accountable if the resulting story "benefited the public." In short, where the press is concerned, the end justifies the means. Yet if a police officer entered a private home without a lawful warrant, we would be outraged by his violations of the rules against intruding on a citizen's private domain—even if the officer believed his entry would "benefit the public."

To permit the press to justify intrusive conduct because it "benefited the public" is an open-ended invitation to arbitrary and capricious actions. It could encourage certain elements of the press to invade the privacy of people and institutions with whom it disagrees. The media understand this risk, having reacted with shock to the revelation that various governmental intelligence organizations have spied on political dissidents and infiltrated various liberal organizations.

Should we not react with comparable shock if ultraconservative and right-wing journalists engage in similar conduct? And how could we condone violation of the privacy and associational freedoms of the members of the American Independent Party, the John Birch Society, or even the American Nazi Party, by liberal elements of America's press?

Accepting the notion that the end justifies the means compromises the rule of law. Higher "justification" was precisely the defense employed by the Nixon administration. The press argues that there is a difference between surveillance by a governmental agent and by a reporter. True, but it happens to be one of degree, not principle. Our fear of official surveillance reflects a healthy apprehension about the oppressive use of governmental power. But in mid–twentieth century America, the power of media institutions has become such that, as a practical matter, the ramifications of intrusive behavior by the government, the media—or any other powerful social institution—are much the same.

The First Amendment and the Press

Insisting on increased media sensitivity to privacy may be a modest incursion on editors. But the First Amendment does not give the press unfettered discretion. In various contexts, courts have decided that certain other values are worth protecting, even if it means second-guessing the journalist. The Supreme Court's recent conclusion that the Constitution does not give a television station immunity to broadcast the Human Cannonball's entire theatrical performance shows that our respect for property rights allows people to exploit their talents without fear of appropriation by the media. In the libel field, the courts have tried to achieve a principled accommodation between free speech and the integrity of an individual's reputation. And under certain circumstances, the law gives a rape victim's name a privacy-type protection.

To be sure, the courts are extremely reluctant to substitute their judgment for that of the media in determining what is "newsworthy." But, by exercising this restraint, judges have made journalists unaccountable and, in some cases, have abandoned the lambs to the wolves. In some contexts, particularly in gossip and "where are they now" columns, the media rationale underlying a decision of newsworthiness is circular: "When we publish it, people read and find it interesting; that makes it newsworthy and gives us the right to acquire and print it."

WHAT IS NEWSWORTHY?

"Interesting" is not synonymous with "newsworthy." What is "newsworthy" about the activities of someone unconnected with the events of the day, especially a person who has been seeking anonymity for years? Even our "interest" in Jacqueline Kennedy Onassis doesn't make her every movement "newsworthy" and justify photographers following her day in and day out. Nor does our "interest" in the drug difficulty of a teen-age child of a senator or governor make it "newsworthy." The drug problem can be reported upon without identifying individuals; their relation to prominent citizens is irrelevant.

The apparently unauthorized entry into the locked apartment of David R. Berkowitz, accused of the "Son of Sam" murders, shows how far some journalists may go in quest of "a story," a real problem during this post-Watergate period of media euphoria and muscle-flexing.

The press claims that it is accountable to its readership. I doubt that. Americans are captivated by gossip. We revel in the latest pratfalls of celebrities of every description and derive vicarious pleasure from the intimate discussions of Dear Abby and the like.

No one disputes the public's "right to know." But like any platitude, it is only a generalization. The deeper questions are: "Know what?" and "What practices may the press employ to gather information?" As things now stand:

- The press may publish demonstrable falsehoods, subject only to remote threat of liability.
- The media claim the right to publish any "truth," no matter how private it may be or how prurient the interest to which it caters.
- Some journalists justify using improper and intrusive techniques in terms of the "benefit" produced by their stories.

In our complex society, rights frequently collide. Thus, it is imperative that no institution press its special prerogatives to the utmost. I believe that the press would further its own long-term interests if it more equitably balanced individual privacy against the public's right to know, and if it developed principles that would stay the typesetter's hands when the former seemed paramount.

THE PERFECT PICTURE

James Alexander Thom

It was early in the spring about 15 years ago—a day of pale sunlight and trees just beginning to bud. I was a young police reporter, driving to a scene I didn't want to see. A man, the police-dispatcher's broadcast said, had accidentally backed his pickup truck over his baby granddaughter in the driveway of the family home. It was a fatality.

As I parked among police cars and TV-news cruisers, I saw a stocky, white-haired man in cotton work clothes standing near a pickup. Cameras were trained on him, and reporters were sticking microphones in his face. Looking totally bewildered, he was trying to answer their questions. Mostly he was only moving his lips, blinking and choking up.

After a while the reporters gave up on him and followed the police into the small white house. I can still see in my mind's eye that devastated old man looking down at the place in the driveway where the child had been. Beside the house was a freshly spaded flower bed, and nearby a pile of dark, rich earth.

"I was just backing up there to spread that good dirt," he said to me, though I had not asked him anything. "I didn't even know she was outdoors." He stretched his hand toward the flower bed, then let it flop to his side. He lapsed back into his thoughts, and I, like a good reporter, went into the house to find someone who could provide a recent photo of the toddler.

A few minutes later, with all the details in my notebook and a three-by-five studio portrait of the cherubic child tucked in my jacket pocket, I went toward the kitchen where the police had said the body was.

I had brought a camera in with me—the big, bulky Speed Graphic which used to be the newspaper reporter's trademark. Everybody had drifted back out of the house together—family, police, reporters, and photographers. Entering the kitchen, I came upon this scene:

On a Formica-topped table, backlighted by a frilly curtained window, lay the tiny body, wrapped in a clean white sheet. Somehow the grandfather had managed to stay away from the crowd. He was sitting on a chair beside the table, in profile to me and unaware of my presence, looking uncomprehendingly at the swaddled corpse.

The house was very quiet. A clock ticked. As I watched, the grandfather slowly leaned forward, curved his arms like parentheses around the head and feet of the little form, then pressed his face to the shroud and remained motionless.

In that hushed moment I recognized the makings of a prize-winning news photograph. I appraised the light, adjusted the lens setting and distance, locked a bulb in the flashgun, raised the camera, and composed the scene in the viewfinder.

Every element of the picture was perfect: the grandfather in his plain work clothes, his white hair backlighted by sunshine, the child's form wrapped in the sheet, the atmosphere of the simple home suggested by black iron trivets and World's Fair souvenir plates on the walls

Reprinted with permission from the August 1978 *Reader's Digest*. Copyright © 1978 by the Reader's Digest Assn., Inc.

flanking the window. Outside, the police could be seen inspecting the fatal rear wheel of the pickup while the child's mother and father leaned in each other's arms.

I don't know how many seconds I stood there, unable to snap that shutter. I was keenly aware of the powerful story-telling value that photo would have, and my professional conscience told me to take it. Yet I couldn't make my hand fire that flashbulb and intrude on the poor man's island of grief.

At length I lowered the camera and crept away, shaken with doubt about my suitability for the journalistic profession. Of course I never told the city editor or any fellow reporters about that missed opportunity for a perfect news picture.

Every day, on the newscasts and in the papers, we see pictures of people in extreme conditions of grief and despair. Human suffering has become a spectator sport. And sometimes, as I'm watching news film, I remember that day.

I still feel right about what I did.

SUGGESTIONS FOR FURTHER READING

Chapter 10 Free Press vs. Fair Trial

Bruce W. Sanford, "No Quarter from This Court," *Columbia Journalism Review* (September–October 1979): 59. Outlines anti-press actions by the current Supreme Court. "The Supreme Court landed the blows—but some of the wounds were self-inflicted."

"A Right to Rummage? Police Can Frisk Newsrooms Says the Court," *Time* (June 12, 1978): 101. One of many articles written after the Supreme Court ruled that police may search newsrooms unannounced.

Chapter 11 Special Privileges for News Gatherers

Justice William J. Brennan, Jr., "Why Protect the Press?" *Columbia Journalism Review* (January–February 1980). A Supreme Court justice proposes a philosophical model that would explain and allow special privileges for the press.

Chapter 12 Government Secrecy vs. the "Right to Know"

Robert Friedman, *"The United States v. The Progressive,"* *Columbia Journalism Review* (July–August 1979): 27. A review of the *Progressive* case.

Chapter 13 Privacy vs. the "Right to Know"

David Shaw, "Public Figures, Private Lives," in *Journalism Today: A Changing Press for a Changing America* (New York: Harper and Row, 1977), p. 18. An analysis of the implications of the newspaper axiom "names make news."

NASA

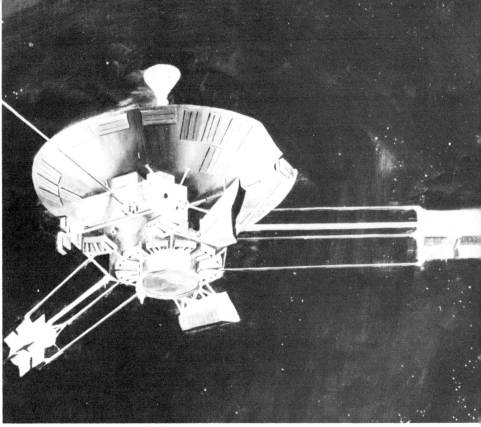

NASA

part IV

SOME ISSUES FOR THE EIGHTIES

In a way, all the issues dealt with in this book are "issues for the eighties," since they will all be active controversies during this decade. But some controversies will eventually *define* the eighties, at least in terms of the mass media. Someday historians will look back on the eighties as a decade of new technology and new relationships between the government, the media, and the public.

This part of the book concentrates on things that will happen in American media rather than things that have happened. Chapter 14 deals with issues arising out of new technology, such as computers, electronic news gathering, cable television, and satellite transmission. Chapter 15 deals with the debate about broadcast deregulation, and Chapter 16 deals with the issue of media access.

chapter 14

ISSUES ARISING FROM NEW TECHNOLOGY

New technology is causing a revolution in all communications media. New media devices are being introduced faster than people can learn how to use them; that is the theme of the first reading in this chapter, in which Robert C. Maynard of the *Washington Post* examines the effects of the computer on the newspaper industry. The article reminds us that technological capability alone is not enough to bring technology to common use; first, the technology must be made amenable to the quirks of people. Until a technological innovation satisfies the people who must work with it, its costs might prove prohibitive.

New media technology causes some other problems too—problems that do not directly affect the people who operate the devices. For example, the use of a minicam in television news causes few problems for the person behind the camera, but it does tend to change the news that is presented. Eric Levin of *TV Guide* examines this issue in the second reading in this chapter. Levin's conclusion is that although minicams might initially encourage television reporters to trivialize and sensationalize the news, they are not dangerous in the long run. Other critics might disagree.

There is also disagreement about the consequences of another new media technology: two-way cable television. A two-way cable system is now in use in Columbus, Ohio, and similar systems are being planned for other communities across the country. This technology has been hailed by some as the perfection of democracy and criticized by others as the death of that same form of government. In the third reading in this chapter John Wicklein, a journalist and educator, examines the workings and possible consequences of two-way cable.

In the final reading in this chapter Les Brown, media critic for the *New York Times*, outlines some other new technologies (such as satellite transmission) and explains some of the issues that arise because of them. The main issue, as far as Brown is concerned, is that of broadcast deregulation. He gives us a background on the 1978 Van Deerlin bill (now defunct), which fanned the flames of a long-lasting broadcast deregulation controversy. That controversy will be considered in more depth in the next chapter.

THE COMING OF THE COMPUTER

Robert C. Maynard

The late Norbert Wiener, frequently referred to as the father of the computer, made an observation once that is pertinent to the current ferment in the newspaper business over the use of technology. Wiener said that science is like a candy store, and if you have enough money, you may buy anything you want.

It would have been inconceivable to a lawyer practicing a generation ago that a time would come when he could merely press a few typewriter keys and have, within seconds, all the case law relevant to a particularly complicated area flash before him on a video screen. Yet, such information retrieval systems are becoming increasingly commonplace.

Journalism, like the law, has often been thought of as being tied to tradition in doing its business: slow to change, wedded to the past.

Now a series of technological developments threatens to bring the news business along quicker than many had ever imagined, indeed quicker than many journalists believe wise.

Most of the emphasis of the new technology has been on the production aspects of the business. The publishers and the craft unions are in protracted discussions all across the land over the loss of jobs to machinery and the problem of which unions will have jurisdiction over which aspects of the new technology.

Those arguments have been going on for some years and will only be solved through long and difficult bargaining and discussion. Technology might be able to eliminate jobs, but it doesn't replace the obligation of human beings to solve their problems with each other.

Reprinted from *Of the Press, By the Press, For the Press (and Others, Too)* edited by Laura Balib. Copyright 1974 The Washington Post Writers Group. Used by permission.

While those discussions go on, other aspects of journalism are increasingly affected by the potential capabilities of the computer. We are discovering we have a long way to go and much to learn before a smooth relationship between news and the computer becomes possible.

As in the law, research is indispensable to journalism. When an important news event occurs, whether a major fire or some dramatic political development, the reporter attempting to cover the event or the issue must first learn as much as possible of what has gone before.

The journalist's repository of the past, the morgue or library, is a place in which tons of yellowed newspaper clippings are stored. Orderly morgues are a blessing to a journalist in a hurry. Poorly organized ones have been known to drive otherwise stable souls to strong drink.

A small-town editor once was writing an editorial about Abraham Lincoln and attempted to put his hand on the pertinent clippings. He found nothing filed under what seemed to him to be the logical categories. "Lincoln"? No. "Presidents"? No. "Assassinations"? No. In exasperation he summoned his librarian back from lunch. "Deceased" was the right answer.

So, now the inheritors of Norbert Wiener's philosophy have come to the rescue of the journalist in a hurry. But, as the old mathematician warned, it hasn't been cheap.

For an expenditure so far of several million dollars, you can learn the date and subject of every clipping mentioning Abraham Lincoln in the library of the New York Times. And you can do it without shuffling through a single pile of yellowing, fading clippings.

Spotted around the newsroom are video display terminals. A reporter can ask the computer some very sophisticated questions, such as the dates of all the stories in which, for one example, the names of Willy Brandt, Richard Nixon, and Alexei Kosygin appear together. The terminal will light up with the stories by date and give a few key words of what each story is about.

Any number of instances occur in which the ability to cross-reference public figures in a hurry would prove very useful to a journalist. The computer can make that possible, but the cost so far is nearly astronomical.

Besides, the system has a flaw that many reporters at the Times find vexing, to say the least. If you found that Brandt, Nixon, and Kosygin have been mentioned in 12 stories, by looking at the dates and the two or three word digest, you might conclude that one story in particular is precisely what you need to make a good story better.

At that point, you press the button that ordinarily would cause the selected story to be displayed on the screen. As you sit there rubbing your palms in anticipation, the machine tells you the equivalent of "wait until tomorrow."

The reason is simple and human—too human for the taste of some reporters. The machine can tell the reporter all or most of what is available in the library, but if the reporter actually wants to see the story, a human being has to fetch it and lay it down before the camera's eye. If that human being is out to lunch, off for the day or otherwise occupied, you have to go to the morgue and fetch it, just as in olden days. For some time to come, it is fair to guess that much of the merging of journalism and computer technology will face flaws of that sort and of an even higher order of magnitude.

Newspapers are rushing around to the "hardware" manufacturers buying millions of dollars of research and equipment that either doesn't work at all or only works for part of the time, doing less than Norbert Wiener's minions promise for their machinery.

In a recent bulletin, the American Newspaper Publishers Association warned its members against paying cash for the new machinery. Always hold back some of the total sale price, the association warned, so that you can have time to make certain the equipment works before you pay for it.

While that is probably sound advice to anyone making a major purchase in this Nader-conscious age, it is especially good advice to newspapers. Some journalists, in fact, are openly debunking the new technology.

Eventually, the marriage between journalism and technology will probably work about as well as the rest of our gadgetry. Computer technicians will get the hang of journalism and tomorrow's journalist will have a better grasp of what makes computers work and therefore how to make them work for the news. But as the *Times* experience suggests, it isn't going to replace jobs nearly as quickly as some publishers hope—or as some workers fear.

SENSATIONAL—BUT IS IT NEWS?

Eric Levin

The wells had run dry, the crops were shriveled, the ground was parched and dusty. Farms in North Carolina last summer were dying of lack of rain, and of the punishing effects of the sun. After the fifteenth consecutive day of 90-degree heat, WRAL-TV in Raleigh decided to dramatize the crisis by anchoring its 6 P.M. newscast on Monday, July 18, live from a brittle cornfield owned by Charles King, a farmer in hard-hit Garner.

King took Charlie Gaddy, the anchorman, for a walk through his field, uprooting wizened cornstalks with one hand as he went. Later, other reporters fed in additional on-the-scene stories on the drought's crippling effect.

"I don't think we got across to the people the scope of what was happening until we went out to the King farm," Gaddy said later. "The impact was tremendous. Audiences don't usually respond to news shows, but we got letters for weeks afterward."

WRAL's brand of live-from-the-field journalism is a pure product of the age of the minicam—a small, lightweight, expensive but highly portable TV camera. This latest period in the development of television news dawned about four years ago and is now approaching, in one sense, its zenith. Minicams, according to a recent survey, are being used to gather some or all of the news at more than 500 of the nation's roughly 650 commercial TV stations with news operations. No longer a novelty, the minicam—and the array of advanced recording, transmitting, and editing equipment that goes with it—is here to stay. The question now is: what have minicams done for, or to, the news?

"One of the biggest things," says Ed Godfrey, news director of WSB-TV in Atlanta, "is that it gives us at least an hour more reporting time per day." Besides sending live pictures to their stations via microwave transmitters, minicams

Reprinted with permission from *TV Guide*® Magazine. Copyright © by Triangle Publications, Inc. Radnor, Pennsylvania.

can be used to record their pictures on video-tape cassettes, which, unlike film, require no processing. So reporters can stay out later.

The ability to televise live from the scene of any story almost at will is, more than anything else, the feature that makes minicams so attractive to TV stations. In city after city, a pattern repeated itself. "The first station in a market to get the equipment always promoted the hell out of it," says Gene Strul, news director of WCKT in Miami. "In this market, it was WTVJ. They launched a big campaign saying, 'You'll see it when it happens!' This overplayed the value of a lot of the stories they covered."

In Boston, WCVB-TV was first to acquire minicams, and news director Jim Thistle admits, "We went through a silly season, doing stories that really didn't justify the live mode. We once went live at 6 P.M. from outside a courtroom where the verdict had been delivered two hours earlier."

The period of rampant promotion and trivialization usually ended when all stations in a given market—or at least the three network affiliates—acquired minicams. "As soon as everybody has it," says Ron Becker, assistant news director at WXIA-TV in Atlanta, "nobody has the edge. So you all go back to journalism."

But it's not that simple. "The real problem with the technology is not promotion and trivialization," says Marc Doyle, news director of Atlanta's WAGA-TV. "The problem is in breaking news, in making more out of an event than it's worth." As an example, he cites the hijacking of a Frontier Air Lines jet last October. The jet was commandeered to Atlanta, where it landed at noon at Hartsfield International Airport. WAGA and (to a greater extent) WSB reported live on the hijacking through the day and evening by breaking into programming for feeds of roughly two-to-five minutes' duration.

But WXIA focused its live cameras on the hijacked plane continuously from noon to 7 P.M. and—with time out for network news—on

through the end of the incident (the hijacker's suicide) at about half past 10. Doyle calls it "a flagrant abuse of the live capability. Their reporters ran out of things to say and were forced to resort to speculation."

WXIA news director Dick Williams accepts some of that criticism. "We did go on too long," he says. But he argues that during the daytime hours, at least, "It was really fun. People were digging it." And the daytime ratings, as he notes, bear him out. They were higher than normal, and the 6 P.M. news ratings at the traditionally third-place station were the highest in its history (topping perennial leader WSB).

Ratings, however, are an unsatisfactory measure of news value and ethics. On June 24, 1975, for instance, when an Eastern Airlines jet crashed near Kennedy Airport in New York, killing 113 of the 124 people aboard, WNBC-TV got to the scene first with its minicams and garnered the highest ratings in town that night. Anthony Prisendorf, the reporter who stood in front of those live cameras, remembers the crash as "the worst story I ever covered." By sheer accident he happened to be near the airport when the jet went down. When his crew set up—in the record time of seven minutes—he found himself "close, much too close" to the action. "It was horribly grim," he recalls. "Bodies were writhing right in front of us. Once you set up the live feed, you're rooted to the spot. All I could do was tell the cameraman to keep the shot wide. Meanwhile, in my walkie-talkie I could hear the control room saying, 'Beautiful. Keep it coming.'"

Roger Higle, now with WNEW-TV, who was on the assignment desk, recalls, "Because of the rush to go live, Tony had no opportunity to go around and do a normal reporting job."

Giving the reporter time to investigate before he turns to the camera—and time to update the story away from the camera later on—is one of the crucial factors in live newscasting. Dick Williams says he tried to spell his reporters during the long Frontier hijacking and tried constantly to bring in FBI officials and other experts for interviews. "Live TV, by itself," he admits, "is not journalism. It's play-by-play."

A valid question is whether minicams, by their nature, tend to trivialize and sensationalize the news. Prisendorf thinks not. The people in charge, he says, "tended to trivialize the news to begin with." A recent survey conducted for the Radio-Television News Directors Association found that minicam technology "does not appear to have brought the upswing in police-call news and soft features which some critics predicted."

"Anyone who is interested in sensationalizing the news will find that minicams make it easier to do," observes WAGA's Marc Doyle. "But it doesn't have to be that way. On the whole, I think the viewing audience is probably better off than before. Stations are able to provide a better, faster, more substantial service today because of the flexibility of the minicam."

WIRED CITY, U.S.A.

THE CHARMS AND DANGERS OF TWO-WAY TV

John Wicklein

"Go in," said my host. I stepped through the door into what appeared to be a carpeted inner office lighted from above by fluorescent panels. "Take three steps." I did as he told me. From across the hall, I heard the clatter of a teleprinter springing into operation. "The room has sensed your presence—it sent the alarm to our computer," my host informed me. "The computer activated our printer across the hall, but it could have activated one at police headquarters as well."

My host was Miklos Korodi, general manager of QUBE, a two-way interactive cable system that Warner Cable Corporation has installed in Columbus, Ohio. The motion-sensing burglar alarm is one of several home-security services

Reprinted from *The Atlantic Monthly* (February 1979). Copyright 1979 John Wicklein. Used by permission.

that QUBE plans to offer its subscribers this spring.

"Here, watch this." Korodi held a piece of burning rope up to a smoke detector in the ceiling. A raucous buzzer alarm sounded in the room, and the computer printer became active again. In a real installation, information on the location of the house, on flamables inside it, and on the position of the nearest fire hydrant would be printed out at the firehouse while the alarm was rousing sleepers in the burning home.

QUBE has announced that it will also offer a "duress" button so that a subscriber may call police when a threatening situation exists, and a medical emergency button for use when an ambulance is needed. A personal security medallion will be an optional extra; an elderly woman, for instance, could wear the medallion around her neck so that she could press it if she should slip and fall on the ice while putting out the garbage. The alarm, relayed by radio through a black box inside the house, activates the computer to provide the ambulance crew with her medical history as well as information about what medication she is taking and any medicines she must avoid.

The black box, designed by QUBE's engineers, is a microprocessor about a foot and a half long, six inches wide, and four inches deep. It is filled with miniature circuits encased in small silicon chips that can duplicate the operation of a room-sized computer of the 1960s. The Data General computer at QUBE's "head end" queries the box continually, asking, in effect, "Is everything all right there?" If it isn't, the microprocessor spells out the problem so the city's emergency forces can respond.

The security services, the general manager told me, will be sold in modular units or combined packages. A basic fire-alarm package, including duress and medical emergency buttons, would cost about $100 for installation and $12 a month for monitoring.

Korodi, an outgoing, enthusiastic man in his early forties, seems delighted by the things the new two-way cable system can do. So are members of his staff; the ones I talked to obviously believe that they are inventing the wheel of the new communications. To help them make the invention pay off, they have behind them the megadollar financing of the cable company's parent, Warner Communications Inc. This conglomerate, which grew out of and owns Warner Brothers, also owns, among other things, Panavision, Atlantic Records, Warner Brothers Television, Warner Books, and Atari, Inc., maker of video games.

Both Korodi and the Warner Cable management in New York think that the sale of multiple services will make this cable system, technologically the most advanced in the country, a commercial success. QUBE (a trade name that stands for nothing in particular) is never referred to by its developers as cable television. They speak of two-way cable: one line carries signals from the head end out to the customer, one line relays customer responses back to the head end. Or, better yet, two-way *interactive* cable.

There are reasons for the precise terminology. After all, a burglar is interacting with the system when he takes three steps into a home and sets off an alarm. Most of the television services of QUBE's multiservice offering are built around its two-way interactive capability. This permits subscribers at home to make decisions about what the system is offering them and then, through the adapter on their standard TV sets, to tell the computer what those decisions are. On the interactive channels, it allows them to "talk back" to their televisions.

"They like to play the system," says one Warner executive, and, indeed, they are being programmed to do that by QUBE's promotional campaign. "Touch the button," says the large, four-color, slick paper brochure, "and enter the era of two-way participation in the infinite, unfolding, never-ending worlds of QUBE."

These worlds include thirty channels controlled by touch buttons on a keypad console about the size of a plug-in electronic calculator. Ten channels provide the commercial and public television stations, a public access channel (required by the Federal Communications Commission), and a program guide channel. Another ten supply "premium" selections—primarily movies, such as *Julia* and *Equus*, that have not yet appeared on commercial television. Premium channel 10 supplies something else you don't see on commercial television: for $3.50 a selection, you get soft porno (to use the QUBE staff's reference, "hard-R") films with predictable titles such as *Dr. Feelgood* and *Hot Times*. The soft-core channel is fed into the home only if a subscriber orders it. In addition, it and all other premium channels can be locked by removing a key that presumably can be kept out of the hands of the children. Premiums also include entertainment specials produced or purchased by QUBE, such self-help courses as "Shorthand" and "How to Prepare for College Entrance Examinations," and local college sports.

Unlike Home Box Office, which charges subscribers a fixed fee for each month of pay-TV programs, QUBE's computer bills viewers for each selection, at prices that range from 75¢ for "Shorthand" to $9.00 (in football-maniacal Columbus) for a live telecast of an Ohio State football game.[1] This is in addition to the $10.95 monthly charge for basic service. You are not a passive viewer when you push a premium channel button, and since the computer is solicitous about your having to make the decision, it allows a two-minute grace period before it enters your selection into its memory.

Even greater participation is demanded by the system in the third group of ten channels—the community channels, where viewers are solicited to "interact" with their sets. Most of the interaction centers on the "Columbus Alive" channel, which every weekday offers programs produced at QUBE's studio building on the Olentangy River Road. This building, the head end, has been reconstructed from a large-appliance warehouse. It has three television studios equipped with color minicams that double as cameras in mobile units on assignments around Columbus. And here is housed the heart of the interactive system, the "polling" computer, which gathers billing and response data from subscribers. The computer scans all subscribers' homes at six-second intervals, asking: Is the set turned on? What channel has been punched up? What was the last response button touched?

The home console has five "response buttons" in addition to the channel-selection buttons. The first two can be used as "yes" and "no" buttons; all five can be used to answer multiple-choice questions or to punch up number codes to indicate, for example, a selection of products displayed on the screen.

Each evening the production staff of "Columbus Alive" gathers at the Olentangy studio to begin two-way communication with 29,000 subscribers in QUBE's franchise area, which encompasses 104,000 households. I watched the production one night in the office of Ron Giles, one of the program hosts. Giles is chubby and bald, and he clearly enjoyed what he was doing on the tube: conducting a variation of the original "Today" show. Formerly a network executive and now a TV consultant, Mike Dann, who designed the old "Today," designed this variation to give subscribers a mix of interviews, reports from remote locations, and good-natured banter between Giles and his co-host, Susan Goldwater. The night I saw the show, Goldwater, an attractive, articulate person (now separated from Representative Barry Goldwater, Jr.), was interviewing a priest and a former nun on the question "What is it like to be homosexual in Columbus?" Goldwater told the audience that an estimated 80,000 homosexuals live in the Columbus "metro" area, which has more than a million people. "Let's find out how many of you know homosexuals," she said.

A statement, superimposed on the living-room furniture of the set, appeared on the screen: *I have a friend, relative, or acquaintance whom I know is homosexual.*

"If you do know a homosexual," said Goldwater, "push button no. 1 for yes; if you do not, press button no. 2 for no. Touch in now."

Within seconds, the computer supplied a result to the studio's character generator, which printed it out on the screen: Yes—65%; No—35%.

Goldwater continued the interview, with interruptions to throw similar questions to the audience and get their responses. When the show got slow, I used the keypad to do some channel switching. I punched up the porn channel to find out if it was really there. It was. On another channel, I found a young, bearded instructor from a local college presenting a three-credit course on basic English composition. He took attendance by asking individual members of the class (who had paid tuition directly to the college) to "touch in." Electronically updating the Socratic method, he salted his lecture with question-and-answer segments, asking students to use the response buttons to answer "true" or "false," or pick the correct answer from five choices flashed on their screens. (In some "QUBE Campus" classes, if an enrolled student gets the answer correct, the red "message light" on his keypad lights up—instant reward.)

Back at "Columbus Alive," I found Giles seated beside a man in a dark gray suit who looked like a bookstore clerk. Indeed, he was a representative of Readmor Bookstores in Columbus, and had come to talk to us about hardcover versus paperback books. After a short exchange with his guest, Giles asked the audience a series of questions about their reading habits. The computer reported back that more people bought paperbacks than hardcovers, and the surprising information that 41 percent said they bought more than ten paperbacks a month. This may reflect the fact that QUBE's franchise area is on the affluent western side of Columbus and its suburbs, and encompasses the Ohio State University campus. (Three other cable companies cover the rest of the city. Columbus, which has complete jurisdiction over franchising provisions, formed four service areas so that they might all be wired for cable in a relatively short time. The practice is fairly common in larger cities.) As the segment was ending, the titles of four books mentioned on the program, numbered 1 through 4, were posted on the screen. "If you would like to order one of these books," said Giles, "touch the corresponding buttons. The computer will gather your name and address, and Readmor will send you the book."

I was surprised to learn that this "book interview" was a commercial, paid for by Readmor Bookstores; at no time was it identified as such to the audience. When I asked one of the show's producers why, she said they wanted the show

"to flow into informal commercials so it won't interrupt the rest of the content." QUBE sells this eight-minute segment as an "Informercial," charging the advertiser about $75 in the "Columbus Alive" slot. A two-minute version, called a "Qubit," sells for half that rate.

Informercials and Qubits have also been used for test marketing. Advertisers and market-research firms have long used Columbus, with its 600,000 Middle Americans, as Test City, U.S.A. *Us* magazine asked QUBE viewers to touch in their judgments on five proposed magazine covers and then printed the two that rated top: John Wayne and the Incredible Hulk. Judging by their willingness to respond, subscribers apparently enjoyed being part of the commercial process. Korodi sees advertisers asking viewers to choose between pilot commercials, or to rate their interest level at 10-second intervals as they watch sitcom pilots.

Computerized two-way systems, if they catch on, can make Nielsen and Arbitron rating obsolete. They involve no sampling guesswork— the QUBE computer knows down to the last household how many sets are tuned to one of its channels. Says Korodi, "We can give the advertiser demographics he never had before— how many people in the $20,000 to $30,000 bracket are watching this commercial, that sort of thing." The computer, he went on, can cross-refer answers to opinion questions with income groups, to tell which economic class wants what.

The computer is capable of charging an order for a book or other merchandise to the subscriber's credit card or to a charge account at a department store, if the subscriber provides the number to be fed into its memory. This is only a step from another service called electronic funds transfer, or EFT, which Korodi expects to test in a year or so. In this, subscribers could select products and pay for them immediately by transferring funds from their bank accounts to the accounts of businesses that advertise goods and services. Each subscriber would have a confidential "personal identification number" that only he could punch into the system, which would tell the computer that he, and not an electronic embezzler, was ordering the money to be transferred.

"This is all possible today," Korodi told me, "but on each service we have to ask, Is it a business? We are addressing ourselves to people's needs, then looking at it to see if it is economically justifiable. Then we will market it."

After more than a year of experience with QUBE (the system went into operation on December 1, 1977), Warner is convinced that some form of two-way cable is economically viable. The company has put at least $20 million into QUBE to find this out. To recoup its investment and begin realizing a profit, Warner wants to expand two-way service to others of its 138 cable systems around the country. It intends to apply for a franchise to wire all of Pittsburgh for two-way cable, and is drafting a plan to refit its one-way system in Akron. Warner now has eight franchises in the suburbs of Boston and expects to make an application in that city as soon as it opens the bidding for franchises. New York City recently granted a cable franchise for Queens to Knickerbocker Communications Corporation on the promise that the system installed will be two-way. Other companies have experimented with this form of service in a limited way, but so far only Warner has staked a lot of money on the idea that two-way cable may be the wave of the future.

Since Warner hopes to amortize the start-up costs of QUBE by extending two-way cable to its other systems, a logical question is whether the prototype in Columbus can make a profit in its day-to-day operations. When I put that question to Gustave M. Hauser, president and chairman of Warner Cable, he said, "The answer is yes."

In December Warner announced that it had agreed to buy out Coaxial Communications,

Inc., a 32,000-subscriber system adjacent to QUBE. The acquisition, Hauser said, will enable the company to offer QUBE services to a new franchise area encompassing 72,000 additional homes. "Obviously, from the fact that we have acquired the system next door, we must think things are going quite well now, or we wouldn't be doing it," he said.

Cable industry leaders say they are watching QUBE closely, on the chance that interactive cable may provide the new element that will enable the industry to achieve the "critical mass" of 30 percent saturation of American homes—agreed by many to be the magic figure for major economic success—by the early 1980s. Cable now reaches into 19 percent, or about 14 million, of the 72 million homes with TV.

Growth of cable has been steady, but was slow until pay-TV movies and entertainment programs were offered nationally several years ago to systems by HBO and Showtime. These companies distribute their packages to local cable systems by domestic satellite. Warner Cable offers its own package of films and shows, called Star Channel, via satellite. It has announced that this month it will begin using the satellite to present thirteen hours of children's programs of a nonviolent nature daily to local systems that pay for the service. The programs are an outgrowth of QUBE's children's shows, and will be produced in QUBE's studios.

The attractiveness to subscribers of nationally distributed pay-TV shows helped cable grow from 3000 systems serving 5400 communities in 1974 to 4000 systems serving 9200 communities today. Gross revenues are estimated at something over $1 billion for 1978, up more than $100 million from the year before. In cable, profitability grows with economies of scale, as exemplified by the multiple system operators (MSOs). In 1977, Warner Cable, whose 600,000 subscribers make it the fourth largest MSO, reported a return of $15.7 million on gross revenues of $55.7 million in its basic cable operations. Teleprompter Corporation, which has 1.15 million subscribers in 110 systems and which is the largest MSO, earned $19.6 million on a gross of $99.6 million.

Financial analysts are looking at cable TV as a growth industry, bearing in mind the forecast by Arthur D. Little Company, the research firm in Cambridge, Massachusetts, that movies seen and paid for in the home will put movie theaters out of business by 1985. Promoting the use of two-way cable TV to charge subscribers only for the specific films and shows they watch may make this form of home entertainment big business. It is two-way cable's capability of selective billing for entertainment and consumer services that intrigues cable executives responsible for profit and loss. As one Teleprompter official put it, "We feel definitely that two-way will be here ultimately; it just has to be economically viable."

Supplying only those services that can produce a profit makes sound business sense, but it leaves something to be desired from the standpoint of giving people the services they need, some of which will never turn a profit. A channel whereby a city clinic could conduct a medical diagnosis, with responses, of a person who is housebound is a sure money-loser. So are channels that could be used during a local disaster for two-way communication between city security forces and people in their homes. Two-way system operators may find that they have to provide some nonprofit services in return for gaining the franchise to make a profit from the community.

QUBE has already acknowledged this obligation by offering channel facilities, at no cost to the community, for participatory town meetings and government hearings. One such meeting was held in Upper Arlington, a prosperous suburb in QUBE's franchise area. Using multiple-choice questions, the Upper Ar-

lington Planning Commission asked QUBE subscribers to comment on a draft plan for renewing an older part of the city. The computer was programmed to "narrowcast" the hearing only to those subscribers who lived within the suburb. Two previous public meetings on the issue drew about 125 citizens each. The meeting held by two-way cable TV, the computer reported, attracted 2000 residents during its two and a half hours. "The point of doing this was to involve the people of the community in their own future," said Patricia Ritter, an Upper Arlington administrator who coproduced the event for the city. In that, she said, the televised hearing was a success.

Among its questions, the commission asked, "Should a building maintenance code be adopted?" The computer, knowing where each response was coming from, reported that sentiment in favor of such a code ran about 12 percent higher in the older section, which contains a number of apartment houses, than in the newer areas of town, where single-family homes abound. Residents who touched in their responses knew immediately whether they were among friends or in the minority, because results were displayed seconds after they pressed the buttons. To make subscribers feel free to express their views, the QUBE hosts assured them that the computer was set in a way that would not identify answers as coming from specific homes. If it had been set differently, it could have pinpointed the answers supplied by each household and produced a profile of each subscriber's participation for the evening. The participants apparently had no qualms about feeding their opinions into the system. When asked if they wanted to do it again, 96 percent pressed the "yes" button, and within ten seconds the computer, having worked out that percentage, relayed it to the home screen.

As in other parts of the system, the people of Upper Arlington took part enthusiastically

in the interactive programming. They had previously been asked to give preferences on
products, opinions on political issues, and
suggestions for social issues to be discussed on
"Columbus Alive." Some had been hooked on
the audience-participation game shows presented by QUBE. In one program that is similar
to the national "Gong Show," viewers can direct the show by pressing the "yes" and "no"
buttons to say whether an amateur act should
continue. When a majority of those watching
press "no," the act is dumped in mid-
performance. Now, that kind of power gives a
person satisfaction. It is fun. Two-way cable is
fun. Playing the system, subscribers are only
vaguely aware that the preferences they state,
the products they select, the personal opinions
they express can all be stored in the computer's
memory and tallied, analyzed, and cross-
referenced with demographic and financial information that is known about them. Several
subscribers I interviewed said that they were
not concerned by this. One young working
woman told me, "I don't feel that I have any
reason to be afraid—I may be naive, but I don't
care if my opinions are recorded." Their attitudes seemed to be, Who would *want* that
stuff, anyway? Who could profit by it?

Someone might. Since the QUBE system was
installed and its capabilities have become
known, reporters, city officials, and others in
the community have considered the possibility
that two-way cable TV might prove to be a
method of invading subscribers' privacy. When
I discussed this with QUBE executives, they
replied, in effect, "Yes, it *could* happen, but it
won't happen here."

Dr. Vivian Horner, vice-president in charge
of educational and children's programming,
expressed it this way: "People don't think of
the telephone as an invasion of privacy. Yet
each call you make is recorded. When people
get as used to two-way cable as to the telephone, they will take it much as a matter of fact.

If people feel threatened by it, they will drop
it—the economic base will keep it honest." A
QUBE sales executive echoed this idea: "We
have a time bomb here. We have to be extremely careful and set up very strict rules. If
we abuse them, we're fools."

The Warner Cable management, aware that
the issue of privacy would inevitably be raised,
drew tight security around the system's polling
computer. Access to the computer's records,
Warner says, is restricted to three top-level
executives; entrance to the master control
room, which houses the computer, is restricted
to those who work there.

At a recent meeting of the Communication
Commission of the National Council of
Churches in New York, Dr. Gerry Jordan,
QUBE's director of educational development,
said that moderators of public-affairs programs
always warn viewers whenever the computer is
set to retrieve and print out the names and addresses of subscribers who push the response
buttons. QUBE does not warn subscribers when
they push the buttons to make purchases, on
the ground that viewers must realize that their
names have to be recorded in order for them to
receive the product or service and to be billed.

When commission members pressed Dr. Jordan on what safeguards had been built in to
protect the individual's right to privacy, he
said, "I think we at QUBE are more concerned
than the subscribers are. We expected it to be
much more of an issue with the public than it
has turned out to be." The *New York Times*
asked Hauser the same question. "People who
buy the service will simply have to accept that
they give up a bit of their privacy for it," he
replied. "Beyond that, we'll try to protect their
privacy all we can."

When I interviewed Hauser at the company's
headquarters in New York, he said he felt the
issue of privacy was "a serious one for the
whole society." The amount of personal information QUBE collects is trivial compared to the

total amount that the computers of government and business are amassing, he added. "For us, it is a question of responsibility and using the system properly."

Let's assume the good faith—and business sense—of the present Warner management, which I do. Could not some future management see it as good business to make commercial and political use of the information derived from two-way cable? Let's build a scenario on that idea.

The Place: San Serra, a city of 150,000, in Southern California.

The Time: 1984, when two-way interactive cable has spread to hundreds of cities across the country.

The Scenario: Colbert Paxton, San Serra's mayor, is running for reelection on a law-and-order platform. In a comfortable home on a hill overlooking the city, Martha Johnson, Mayor Paxton's opponent, has just pushed in a response button to order a book—displayed in a department store's information commercial— that advocates abolition of laws restricting sexual activity between consenting adults. She pays for it by punching in the number on her department-store charge card. Next she takes a look at a shopping channel that features personal products for women and punches in an order for an aerosol spray deodorant.

Martha leaves for a nighttime political rally and Arnold, her husband, takes over the controls of the two-way set. Punching up a public-affairs channel, he finds the cable company quizzing its subscribers on their attitudes toward homosexuals:

> Lesbians should be allowed to teach
> in the public schools.
> Yes: Button no. 1
> No: Button no. 2

Without hesitation, Arnold touches no. 2. Then, making sure that their two small children are in bed, Arnold settles into a chair and

selects a premium film entitled *The Professional Cheerleaders*. Fifteen minutes later, the message light on the keypad flashes on, telling Arnold that the cable company or one of its clients has a message for the subscriber. Arnold dials the message light number, and is switched by the computer directly to the department store. In a recording, the store's credit manager points out that the Johnsons are in arrears on their credit payments and says that the book that Mrs. Johnson has just ordered cannot be sent until the Johnsons transfer $15.95 directly from their bank account to the store's account. Angry, Arnold punches in the necessary funds transfer, using the Johnsons' personal identification number, and goes back to his movie.

At the cable-company headquarters, the information sales department, which works around the clock, is compiling for its confidential clients data the computer has collected concerning subscribers who have been interacting with their sets. Several clients have indicated interest in the Johnsons' interactions and have ordered computer profiles from the system.

Client 1, Mayor Paxton's campaign manager, is delighted to learn that Arnold, whose wife is a feminist and a supporter of legislation to eliminate legal restrictions concerning sex, has expressed an opinion against one of her campaign stands. He chuckles at the use he can make of the fact that Arnold also watched a porno movie while his wife was out. He knew what time Martha left the house because the cable company, at the mayor's request, has installed a motion sensor to monitor the Johnsons' doorway from outside the house. It relays information about comings and goings which are then checked out by a police surveillance car parked unobtrusively down the darkened street.

Client 2, a publisher of skin magazines, also gets notification of the porno-film selection, and sends the Johnsons a sales brochure in a plain manila envelope.

Client 3, a local environmental group trying to decide whether to work for Mrs. Johnson, is disappointed to learn that she would unthinkingly order an aerosol that is dangerous to the ozone layer.

Client 4, a national credit-rating company, finds that the department store has rejected Mrs. Johnson's purchase on credit and puts that datum into her dossier for the next customer who purchases credit-rating information on her. It also enters a correction regarding the Johnsons' bank balance, which the computer obtained when Arnold paid for his wife's book.

Is all this possible? It is entirely possible, today, using a two-way cable system no more sophisticated than the one now operating in Columbus, Ohio. And the information-gathering activity described in the scenario is not illegal.

Will people drop out of a two-way system if they discover that their interactions are being monitored? First of all, they do not have to be told that they are being monitored: no law requires the cable operator to tell them. But beyond that, people will probably get used to it. Once the services provided by two-way cable TV become almost indispensable, people won't worry about them. They won't, that is, unless objections are raised by consumer protection groups and by legislators concerned with two-way cable's implications for civil liberties. Federal, state, and local legislation is nonexistent in this area. Most systems are franchised by local municipalities, using guidelines set by the Federal Communications Commission (FCC). The guidelines say nothing about restrictions on two-way cable. . . .

. . . The mood in Congress seems to favor less regulation, not more. Unless state legislatures act—and they don't seem much concerned— the task of protecting subscribers from invasion of privacy is going to fall on community cable-advisory groups and on council members whose local ordinances set the conditions concerning cable franchises. They have the right to do this because the FCC decided that cable franchising should be the province of local jurisdiction, usually municipalities. Thus, a city government may decide to grant a franchise for its entire territory, or, as in Columbus, may divide the area into several sections and grant exclusive or competitive franchises for each. In most states, the local body can approve rates, determine the number of channels to be provided, and decide what those channels will be used for. Often, for example, a municipality will require that channels be set aside for use by government bodies, the school system, community groups, or individual citizens. All this is in contrast to the licensing of local television and radio stations, which is handled exclusively by the FCC.

In Columbus, a member of the Public Cable Advisory Commission, a citizens' group appointed by the mayor, said the commission had been considering the problem of privacy, but as yet had made no recommendation for regulation.

Bob Kindred, who publishes *Cable TV Programs*, a guide to what can be found on local cable-television systems in the Midwest, would like to see two-way cable thrive. But he is afraid that sometime in the future people will rebel against two-way cable, unless restraints are placed on how it uses the information that its computer collects. "A number of questions they ask, I don't answer," he said. (A vice-president of a Columbus bank had the same thought: "I won't put anything in there I don't want people to know.") People are going to want protection built in by law, Kindred added, "and this will probably help cable."

When I asked Hauser what he thought about that, he said, "This is a national problem that is being looked into now—there is no particular onus on our business. What we don't need is local regulation in the name of privacy that will inhibit the growth of this business totally, but which may be all wrong. If there is to be regulation, it should be part of a comprehensive scheme of regulation."

Clearly, federal law concerning privacy would be preferable to thousands of varying local laws. But just as clearly, some law is needed. Otherwise, the privacy of all two-way cable subscribers is potentially for sale.

1. Last July, Warner Cable and the American Broadcasting Company reached an out-of-court agreement to allow QUBE to broadcast five OSU games each season for two years. Warner had filed suit against ABC, contending that its exclusive four-year contract with the National Collegiate Athletic Association (NCAA) to broadcast games of any member college was a violation of the antitrust laws. Under the agreement, QUBE's cablecasts were viewed as a "limited experiment." QUBE agreed to make research data compiled by its computer available to ABC and NCAA so that they could study how cable coverage affected attendance at the games.

COMES THE REVOLUTION

Les Brown

Dazzling new kinds of television are entering the picture, the gifts of an exploding technology. Individually or in combination, the electronic marvels that are now bidding for a place in the scheme of national and global communications could touch off a second television revolution, one that might deal a severe jolt to the existing commercial television system and profoundly affect the ways consumers use the medium.

Through these new delivery systems, with their special components and antennas, the ordinary television set may take the place of the bygone neighborhood movie house and could become, as well, an extension of the opera house, football stadium, library, university,

classroom, church, town council, and hospital emergency room. And we can foresee the set serving as a burglar- and fire-alarm system, a home computer, and a receiving unit for electronic mail.

The promises of the new media are intoxicating, but so also was the promise of conventional television in the 1940s. It is not too early to begin the watch on the emerging media, while public policy for them is still being formed. Here are the principal new technological developments:

■ *Pay cable* is pay television by means of cable TV, which results in the consumer paying first for basic cable service and then an additional monthly fee for the premium fare, usually a channel of movies, sports events, and special entertainments. The growing consumer demand for pay cable is highly significant, since it has been spurring the expansion of cable TV to the densely populated areas of the country. Modern cable systems typically offer 30 active

Reprinted by permission of The Pilgrim Press from Les Brown, *Keeping Your Eye on Television*. Copyright © 1979 Office of Communication, United Church of Christ. All rights reserved.

channels of television, although some provide up to 36. It follows that more channels open the way to more varied forms of programming and greater public access. By the fall of 1978, approximately 18 percent of U.S. households subscribed to cable TV. Media experts predict that when the penetration reaches 30 percent, cable TV will become a national advertising medium and a true competitor to conventional television.

■ *Communications satellites* are the space-age alternative to telephone land lines as a means of interconnecting television stations or cable-TV systems for the distribution of programs nationwide. Two separate commercial systems—Western Union's Westar and RCA's Satcom, each with two satellites aloft—operate as common carriers, making their transponders available to all comers on a first-come-first-served basis. The Public Broadcasting Service already distributes all its national programming by satellite, as do the various burgeoning cable networks and such special program services as the Christian Broadcasting Network and the Hughes Sports Network. The key to the expansion of satellite transmission is the proliferation of the special receiving antennas known as earth stations. Their increase is assured by the rapidly dropping prices for the compact 4.5-meter models to serve local TV stations and cable systems. The combination of new cable channels and easy, economical national distribution by satellite will inevitably add up to new networks.

■ *Satellite-to-home broadcasting* is a development that permits households to receive programming directly from a satellite, without its being relayed by a local station, through the use of a small parabolic antenna that might be mounted on a rooftop or hung outside a window. Direct-to-home satellite transmission is in limited use in Japan and has been demonstrated successfully in this country, but the FCC is not likely to authorize it for the United States because of the political pressures that would be brought to bear. Broadcasters fear the competition and have already effectively argued that local stations might be killed off and that the doctrine of localism would therefore be jeopardized.

■ *Fiber optics* is the technology that converts electronic signals to lightwaves, transmitting them over thin glass fibers with the use of a laser beam. Optical fibers are so thin that a small bundle of them can carry more than 1000 channels of television. They are likely in time to take the place of telephone wires and cable TV's coaxial cable; in fact, a single "wire" of optical fibers can provide both telephone and cable-TV service.

■ *Electronic data transmission systems* permit viewers to call up on the screen a wide range of printed material from an information bank through the use of special decoders. Some forms operate through cable and some through conventional television in conjunction with the telephone. Initially their application is in the retrieval of news, stock reports, and other current information, but ultimately they may be tied in with computer data banks.

■ *Home video recorders* are mass-marketed videotape consoles that permit consumers to record up to four hours of programs off the air to be watched at the viewer's discretion. These units can also play prerecorded tapes purchased in a store.

■ *Video disk players* are the video counterparts of the phonograph, whose program material comes on 12-inch metallized records. One type uses a stylus and a grooved disk, another a laser beam and a smooth disk. The disks contain 30 minutes of programming on each side.

■ *Two-way cable* is cable TV with a return wire that permits interactive communication. The viewer at home, equipped with a unit containing response buttons, may send digital signals back to the transmission center. When a computer is joined to the system, the interactive mode becomes useful for public-opinion polls, purchases of specific pay-television fare, viewer participation in game shows, the ordering of merchandise advertised on television, and burglar- and fire-alarm protection for the home.

Late in 1977, in the test market of Columbus, Ohio, Warner Communications began operation of a remarkable two-way cable system to which it gave the trade name QUBE (pronounced *cube*). The significance of the name is that the system is multifaceted, involving the use by viewers of a hand-held console with four sets of buttons.

Ten buttons in one column serve as the controls for over-the-air television. These buttons can bring forth on the screen any of 10 conventional television stations, those of the immediate locale and others imported from distant cities. A second row of 10 buttons is for pay programs—movies ranging in price from $1.50 to $3.50 each, sports events, college courses, and cultural events—each priced on a per-viewing basis.

The third row of 10 buttons provides special channels programmed by Warner, each channel dedicated to a single type of fare—for example, high-grade children's shows (many of which are imported from abroad), news, sports, religion, and culture. The principal channel in this row offers continuous live local programming, all of it designed to elicit viewer responses.

These responses are implemented by the last row of five buttons, which are larger than the others. By pressing the appropriate buttons, people at home may vote on performances in an amateur variety show and answer questions in quiz programs. They may also purchase products from the screen advertised by local retailers or bid on merchandise being auctioned. Of greatest consequence, however, is the use of the response buttons to poll viewers on local and national issues, with the results tabulated by the computer in less than a minute. On occasion, during an interview with a public figure, viewers have been asked whether they believed what the subject was saying. The response from the audience can put the interviewee on the spot in a way that does not happen in conventional television.

Many people have a tendency to look to this new panoply of electronic miracles for the solutions to the problems presented by conventional television. Indeed, a number of government policymakers have been doing just that. They reason that a great proliferation of channels as promised by cable and fiber optics relieves the problem of spectrum scarcity. New networks via the satellite figure to break the competitive lockstep of ABC, CBS, and NBC and end their creative stagnation. Video re-

corders, the video disk, and pay television liberate the consumer from the agendas set by the networks and local stations and let the viewer become the programmer. Interactive television permits instant feedback and direct viewer participation.

All this is true—technology does come to the rescue—but there are caveats. The timetable for the next television revolution (if, indeed, there should be one) is highly uncertain. The present system should not be deregulated, as some in Washington propose, purely on an assumption that technology will change everything tomorrow.

The new media have yet to prove themselves in the marketplace, and there is every chance that some will fall into the technological backwash, along with the Picturephone, 3-D movies, and facsimile—all of which held great promise in the 1950s but failed to become thriving businesses.

Moreover, these media come freighted with an array of new public problems that may themselves beg for regulatory solutions. QUBE, for example, gives viewers the power to answer back, but it is still Warner Communications, a giant media and entertainment conglomerate, that controls the questions. And all the new television delivery systems will be in the hands of business concerns anxious to improve their profit status every year. So there are no guarantees that the promised cultural and educational fare, and the programs of social significance, will last any longer in these new media than they did in commercial broadcasting.

In Washington the sentiment is strong to open the doors wide to these new technological developments, to remove all regulatory obstructions so that they can have every opportunity to compete with each other and with conventional television in the marketplace. This desire, in part, grows from the knowledge that for almost 30 years the FCC, responding to the commercial broadcast lobby, had stifled the development of over-the-air pay television and slowed the growth of cable TV with burden-some regulations for nearly as long.

But there is another reason for the wish to turn the new technology loose. A number of key figures in government have become disillusioned with the broadcasting system spawned by the Communications Act of 1934, and they see no point in trying to preserve it in its present form. Recognizing that a sham has been made of the principle of licensing and that the ideals of the act have never been realized, these officials are prepared to write the whole thing off as a failure and to let market forces decide what shape American television is to take.

Representative Lionel Van Deerlin, Democrat of California and chairman of the House Communications Subcommittee, introduced in 1978 a radical bill to revise the Communications Act from top to bottom. The bill envisioned a wide-open marketplace for all the various forms of electronic communications—including conventional television and radio—so that all might compete evenly for survival, in the spirit of free enterprise. This meant taking virtually all the regulatory wraps off radio and, after a 10-year period, television as well. Conspicuously absent from the proposed new version of the Communications Act was the phrase "public interest, convenience and necessity." The public-interest standard that had been the foundation of American broadcasting for half a century was to be junked.

The bill was not a piece of mischief by friends of the commercial broadcasting establishment. It was born of realistic appraisals and honest concerns about the existing system, chiefly by political liberals. The position of the bill's proponents, gained from interviews with them, may be summarized in this manner:

> Let's do away with the pretense that we can have a system of broadcasting in the public interest, and let's be coldly realistic. Broadcasters are businesspeople whose natural drive is to maximize profits. Isn't it pointless, and wasteful of

energies, to ask them to act against their true nature? Isn't it an exercise in futility to try to convince them that they are public trustees who have to serve the public interest ahead of their own economic interests? Why not let market forces come into play, as they do with the print media, ultimately providing something for every taste and need? Why not let the marketplace (i.e., the consumers) and not the government decide how these media should perform and which ones should prevail? Competition is in the public interest, and this is the surest way to achieve diversity and public service.

Congressman Van Deerlin's proposal found adherents among influential persons in government who were staunch upholders of the First Amendment. These officials had always been uneasy about broadcast regulation. In their view the awarding of broadcast licenses by a government agency, the withholding of licenses, and the stipulation of conditions under which such licenses are granted are all abridgments of the freedom of expression guaranteed by the First Amendment. The print media are free from all such regulation. When different standards of freedom are applied to different media performing similar services, they concluded, the First Amendment itself is in jeopardy. The idea of a new Communications Act that would do away with license renewals appealed to them because they could see no reason why the free-speech amendment should be so dangerously compromised for a public-interest standard that is largely myth.

But the Van Deerlin bill's detractors far outnumbered its supporters. The freeing of commercial broadcasting from the public-interest standard alarmed leaders of the broadcast reform movement and galvanized all the various citizens groups into a single opposing force. Everett C. Parker, director of the Office of Communication, United Church of Christ, condemned the bill as "the greatest giveaway of the public's rights since Teapot Dome." In his testimony at the subcommittee hearings on the bill, Dr. Parker stated:

In stripping away all the requirements for licensees to account for how they serve the public, the bill grants television, radio, and other telecommunications monopolies the right to determine, unilaterally, what political, economic, cultural, and educational ideas shall be disseminated to the American public. Such a privilege has never before been conceded in our society to a monopoly. It is the exact power that the Declaration of Independence denied to the King of England.

Others pointed out that the bill ignored all the progress that had been made within the system during the previous decade, the period since the public began to play an active part in broadcast affairs. The fact that the present system had failed, they argued, did not necessarily mean it was a failure. Semantically, a failure is a concluded flop, but to say something has failed is still to allow for the chance that it can be made to work. The achievements of the citizens movement, they contended, were evidence that the system can be made to work and that the ideals of the 1934 Communications Act could still be realized.

Among opponents of the bill were commercial television broadcasters, which made this one of the rare times that they and the consumer groups were on the same side of an issue. Most broadcasters objected to the bill because it proposed to charge them fees for the use of the electromagnetic spectrum in exchange for relieving them of their public-interest responsibilities; it was the fee that bothered them, not the principle. But a considerable number of broadcasters were also seriously troubled by the prospect of being freed from the public-interest standard, since it was clear to them how that would affect their industry.

Some predicted privately that deregulated television stations would drift fairly quickly into pornography. It was a certainty, they said, that the station most desperate for an audience in its community would turn to explicit sex. If that station succeeded, the rival stations would eventually have to follow. Something like that

has been happening to motion picture theaters.

Television in Italy provides the example to illustrate that theory. After years of having only a state-run network on the air, the Italian government in 1976 permitted local commercial stations to go on the air as unregulated entities. To gain attention, one began showing hardcore adult movies like *Deep Throat*. Another instituted a game show on which a housewife removed articles of her clothing when contestants gave wrong answers and put them back on, one at a time, when the contestants' answers were correct. Inspired by the popularity of that program, another station eliminated the game-show gimmick and just brought on women who performed amateur stripteases. Very soon the commercial stations made nudity and pornography an everyday part of Italian television.

Aside from the likelihood of that happening here in an unregulated system, American television stations with no accountability to the public would be free to run violent cartoon programs directed at children, programs offensive to minorities, and editorials that are extreme or even bigoted in their views. They might even elect to provide no service whatever to persons over the age of 50, since the older adults carry a low priority with advertisers.

The Van Deerlin bill never made it to the floor of Congress in its original form but instead was withdrawn for extensive revision, thanks partly to the lobbying efforts of citizens groups with individual members of the subcommittee. Nevertheless, the bill in retrospect had considerable value. For one thing, it illuminated the need for an enlightened, updated national policy to embrace all forms of electronic communications. For another, it charged up the citizens-action movement, making those groups and others more appreciative of the public-interest standard and more conscious of the need to preserve it. Finally, it brought forward some new assumptions for thoughtful examination.

Early in 1979 Congressman Van Deerlin introduced a new version of his bill with "sweeteners" to make it more palatable to broadcasters and common carriers such as the Telephone Company, and even less attractive to the public-at-large. In the Senate, Senator Ernest F. Hollings, who chairs the Senate Communications Subcommittee, has submitted a bill aimed mostly at reform of common carrier regulation, but which would provide for substantially less regulatory oversight for radio and for a five-year license term for television.

One central assumption of the Van Deerlin proposal is that two-way cable TV, the video disk, and the other new media will be as pervasive in this century as commercial broadcasting and that they will all be able to compete in the marketplace on an equal footing. This assumption overlooks the fact that the existing television system has had a long head start on the new developments, is firmly entrenched with a large and generally satisfied audience, and therefore will have a decided advantage in an open market.

No matter how many new channels and networks come into being through cable TV and satellites, the existing commercial stations will continue to dominate viewing for a long time for two principal reasons: First, they are the established Main Streets of television and have conditioned viewers to believe they are where the action is; second, they involve what most people regard as a "free" service, while the newer channels will be charging fees. (It should be noted that people do pay for socalled free television through increased prices for the advertised products.)

The competition, therefore, will be between new media drawing many thousands of viewers, and conventional television drawing tens of millions of viewers.

Another assumption of the Van Deerlin bill is that the vigorous competition among the various electronic media will make for a vast,

groaning board of fare, just as competition in the print media has produced a wide range of books, magazines, and periodicals. What is more likely, however, is that most of the entrepreneurs will take aim at the most lucrative markets to exploit, and for the most part these markets will be penetrated by entertainment rather than by information. An indication of that is pay cable's concentration on movies and sports, types of fare already offered abundantly by commercial television.

Advocates of deregulation believe that by granting full First Amendment protection to broadcasters and cable operators the cause of robust, wide-open debate on major issues will be served. They anticipate a renaissance of hard-hitting investigative journalism. But there is more reason to believe that those who control the television signals, relieved of the public trustee obligations, will concentrate on programs that have the greatest profit potential and will shun low-rated public affairs programming. Investigative journalism is expensive— more expensive for the size of the audience it delivers than a situation comedy.

As attractive as the new media may be, they were not developed on huge amounts of venture capital for eleemosynary purposes. Already it is evident that there is a lively market in the video-cassette field and in the QUBE system in Columbus for what euphemistically are called erotic movies, while no such lively consumer market has as yet developed for instructional programming. Like other corporations, those that are marketing the new electronic developments have a mandate to increase their profits every year, and this inevitably means that their initial good intentions with educational and cultural programming will give way steadily to more lucrative software.

Moreover, if today the local television or radio broadcaster is considered to be a powerful media figure in a community, the operators of cable systems may become 30 times more powerful, since they will control the flow of signals on 30 channels and not just one.

Because there is the potential for such extraordinary control of mass communications in cable TV, many public-interest advocates have been campaigning for a national policy that would designate cable systems as common carriers. A common carrier, exemplified by telephone and telegraph, is a medium that is open to use by the entire public on a nondiscriminatory basis and at posted rates. This would mean that cable operators would control the wires and the transmitting mechanism but would have no involvement whatsoever with the programming. Under such an arrangement, anyone who wished to broadcast would have the opportunity to buy a portion of television time for his or her own programs and would be able to sell advertising in those shows just as television stations do.

The cable industry opposes common-carrier status if for no other reason than that it would involve federal supervision of the rate structures and a ceiling on profits. Cable entrepreneurs point out that Warner Communications would never have risked $20 million on a futuristic system such as QUBE—indeed would not have bothered to invent the system—if it were so divorced from programming that it could not determine what would be offered.

It is impossible not to be impressed with QUBE and with its potential to provide programming for every taste and need in a community. Beyond that, the great cultural change that is likely to occur when people are able to use television interactively, instead of merely watching the screen passively, is altogether desirable. Yet, at the same time, it is difficult not to be concerned about the possible social consequences of this new form of television. A computer checking out television households every six seconds and making records of how people vote in polls, or of what programs they

choose to watch, clearly invades privacy. This is the Big Brotherism that had been prophesied by George Orwell in his famous novel 1984.

Charles D. Ferris, the chairman of the FCC, once remarked that he feared the implications for politics of QUBE's ability to conduct instantaneous public-opinion polls, for although it is good for legislative representatives of a community to know where their constitutents stand on an issue, there is also a danger that the polls may be conducted before the public is fully informed on the issues. Elected officials might endanger their careers if their votes on legislation did not follow the mandate of the QUBE poll, even though their own clear understanding of the issues might dictate a different vote.

While the viewer may take comfort in having the ability to interact with television by sending forward his or her responses on issues, the fact remains that the cable company controls the questions and may shape them according to its own political or ideological purposes. Further, in a cable-computer opinion poll the viewer is left to take it on faith that the result flashed on the screen will be the result shown by the computer. Like a sighted person playing heads-or-tails with a blind person, the cable company is free to deceive by reporting a false tally on issues in which it has an interest and thus may influence legislation as it chooses.

But of all the reservations about the new media, the most serious one concerns ownership. Satellites, pay-cable networks, and sophisticated interactive systems such as QUBE are big businesses, far too big for independent entrepreneurs or small groups of local investors. Knowledgeable observers predict that if QUBE proves hugely successful in Columbus, and if Warner begins to expand it around the country, other entertainment and media conglomerates will quickly enter the field by gobbling up existing cable systems across the country and converting them to systems resembling QUBE. As the game gets richer, it will require the capital investment that can be made by companies like Gulf & Western, Time Inc., MCA Inc., and General Electric. Thus, the powerful in the media stand to become more powerful still.

Along with this prospective development is the possibility of American Telephone & Telegraph Inc. extending its telephone monopoly to cable TV. This could happen because the technologies of television, telephone, and computers have all converged into a single technology, and because AT&T has already begun conversion of its installations from copper wire to fiber optics. Since the same bundle of optical fibers that provides telephone service may also provide cable-TV service, it becomes unnecessary to have two separate wires entering the home.

Under present regulations telephone companies are prohibited from owning cable-TV systems. But there is talk in Washington of lifting the ban, because telephone companies could solve the problem of bringing adequate television service to remote rural areas of the country where cable companies cannot afford to build systems. In fact, the Van Deerlin bill proposes to give telephone companies the freedom to enter the cable field.

So in a time when a concerned public is calling for more diversified ownership that is more broadly representative of all segments of the society, the looming trend is for more concentrated ownership. It is a mistake, then, to trust the emerging electronic media, as Representative Van Deerlin does, to bring about the reforms in conventional broadcasting that citizens groups have been working toward. If anything, these media are raising new issues and posing new threats to the public interest.

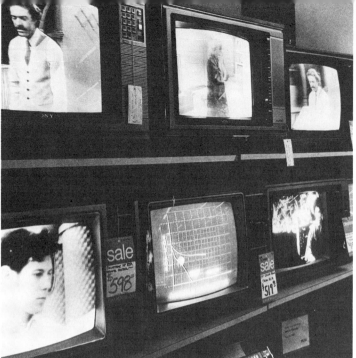

chapter 15

BROADCAST
DEREGULATION

The Van Deerlin bill, outlined by Les Brown in the final reading of the preceding chapter, is now defunct. Yet the very appearance of that bill fanned a controversy on broadcast regulation that had been simmering since the beginning of American broadcasting. The controversy continues to generate heat today, due in part to the fact that the FCC decided to follow through on many of Van Deerlin's proposals after the bill was abandoned by Congress.

The following articles will put this debate into historical perspective. First there is the 1978 debate and series of rebuttals between Nicholas Johnson, former FCC commissioner and chairman of the National Citizen's Communications Lobby, and Karl Meyer, the television critic for *Saturday Review*. This debate centers on the deregulation of television as proposed by Van Deerlin.

The next readings deal with the subsequent FCC proposal to deregulate radio. The literature on this proposal is voluminous; we will have to content ourselves here with three summary statements. The first is a news analysis of the issue by Ernest Holsendolph of the *New York Times*. The next is the policy statement of the Telecommunications Consumer Coalition, an organization that opposes deregulation, and the last is the policy statement of the National Association of Broadcasters, which favors deregulation.

GIVEAWAY OR BREAKTHROUGH: A DEBATE ON TV LICENSING

Nicholas Johnson

A "giveaway"? I think that a modest characterization. The broadcasting industry's profits average about 100 percent a year of depreciated capital investment. Its net profit, as a proportion of gross, is four times that of the oil industry. These profits are made possible by the government-created and -protected monopoly that comes with an FCC license. Any attempt at "marketplace competition" on a broadcaster's channel is flirtation with the federal penitentiary. The only inhibition on the broadcaster's "license to print money" is the FCC's renewal process, every three years—and the public rights attendant to the monopoly.

H.R. 13015, the Van Deerlin bill, now proposes to keep the monopoly, keep the government protection, but remove all the public's rights and broadcasters' obligations. It grants licenses in perpetuity. If it seems a little outrageous that $600,000 worth of studios, cameras, and transmitters can be worth $75 million today because of a three-year license, consider the joy in executive suites at the prospect of doubling or trebling that value.

It is hard to imagine the arguments in favor of

Reprinted from "Giveaway or Breakthrough: A Debate on TV Licensing," by Nicholas Johnson and Karl E. Meyer in *The Nation* (September 30, 1978): 298–302. Used by permission from *The Nation* magazine, copyright 1978 The Nation Associates, Inc.

the bill. Needless to say, network television has not given the American people much analysis of it. So the *Nation* has scheduled this exchange, and a subsequent rebuttal, to see if Karl Meyer can find any justification for the bill. At this point, not having seen his piece for this issue, I will start with fundamentals.

In a democratic society it is essential that the mass media be open, diverse, responsive, and legally accountable to the public. Why? The answers seem obvious; it's like trying to explain why the right to vote in elections is thought important. or the presumption of innocence in criminal trials. And yet, extraordinary as it may seem, those are the kinds of fundamental issues raised by the Van Deerlin bill.

The current law provides that broadcasters are public trustees with no right of property in their frequencies or channels. They must provide news and public affairs programs regardless of profitability. They have special fair-employment responsibilities to minorities and women. They cannot use their awesome political power to silence candidates, or views on controversial issues, with which they disagree. The law does not permit the federal government to dictate specific program content (as distinguished from program categories) and the FCC has shown no inclination to do so.

The law gives the public legal rights. Broadcasters must make their public files available at all times. They must conduct a "community ascertainment" of their audience. Candidates can insist on "equal time." Anybody can file a "fairness complaint" with the FCC. And all can participate in the license renewal process every three years—and, therefore, conduct a *meaningful* dialogue with stations' management at any time.

Why do these public rights, and broadcaster limitations, make any difference in a democracy? Why can't we just let big business totally dominate the nation's communications system as it does other areas of our lives?

Put in its most fundamental terms, it is because a democracy rests on two principles of faith: (1) the common people, once adequately educated and informed, are capable of governing themselves; (2) the wisest public opinion and policy will emerge from an uncensored dialogue (a "marketplace of ideas") in which every citizen has an equal opportunity both to speak and to hear all views.

Both principles may be utter nonsense, but on them, to paraphrase Learned Hand, we have "staked our all." Unless Lionel Van Deerlin and Karl Meyer really want to argue for an alternative form of government, we can go on to address how radio and television can best serve these two presumptions of a democratic society.

By the time the average television viewer is 65 years of age, he or she will have devoted nine full years to watching TV. Today, democracy's dialogue is going to take place on radio and television or it's not going to take place at all. Conversations after Sunday services, debates in the town hall, and occasional handbill campaigns just don't have the impact on society that they did 200 years ago.

Van Deerlin wants to substitute "marketplace forces" for government regulation. It's a goal I have often espoused, and even tried to imple-

ment, for other industries during my 10 years as U.S. Maritime Administrator and FCC Commissioner. There are only two problems with attempts to apply it to broadcasting.

We do not now have a marketplace in broadcasting. Broadcasters and elected officials (who owe their political lives to broadcasters) have opposed all attempts to create a real marketplace (cable and pay TV, paid and free access to the airwaves, additional VHF stations, and so forth). Moreover, however well marketplace forces may be thought to regulate economic abuses, there is no reason to believe them effective in providing a free society with the full range of art, information, and opinion necessary to its self-governing.

"Deregulating" a protected monopoly, while continuing the monopoly and the protection, does not create competition. It just creates an unregulated monopoly. We don't leave protection from contaminated water, or unsafe drugs, to "marketplace forces," and there's no reason to suspect better results from doing so in broadcasting.

The ideas of television's marketplace are ideas about the odors of mouths and armpits—and praises sung to the politics and lifestyles of transnational conglomerate corporations. No, the ideas of the marketplace do not make a marketplace of ideas.

Big business has access to the airwaves—and it should. But if similar access is to be available to labor, education, religion, agriculture—in short, to the common people who are supposed to be governing this country—the Van Deerlin bill is, in a quite literal sense, one of the most un-American pieces of proposed legislation to be seen in a long time.

Of course it's an economic giveaway. That's obvious. But that's also the least of its faults. If this bill passes we'll lose far more from the Capitol than the gold on its dome. We'll have lost much of its foundation as well.

Karl E. Meyer

I take it as a truism that American commercial television is still juvenile and embarrassingly delinquent, and that the prime concern of broadcasters is the packaging of audiences for delivery to advertisers. Our networks have been an unequivocal success in only one respect: coining money. In 1977 the three networks enjoyed pretax profits of $406 million, an increase of 37.4 percent over the previous year. (See *Broadcasting*, August 14, 1978.)

By contrast, public television, our best hope for assuring program diversity, subsists in the slums. In the current fiscal year, the Corporation for Public Broadcasting will spend about $15 million on national television programming. This is why PTV stations must beg for handouts from viewers and business underwriters.

The overriding merit of the proposed Communications Act of 1978 (H.R. 13015) is that it would narrow the gap between private affluence and public squalor. As drafted by the House Communications Subcommittee, of which Lionel Van Deerlin is chairman, the legislation would, for the first time, compel commercial broadcasters to yield up some of their profits to the public system. It is this point that is obscured in misleading and pietistic attacks on the Van Deerlin measure as an unconscionable giveaway.

The true giveaway was perpetrated in 1934 when the original Federal Communications Act turned over the public airwaves to commercial broadcasters without charging a penny. It was the equivalent of giving away oil-drilling rights on public property—in Great Britain, for example, commercial TV pays a substantial annual levy for use of the air. Under the Van Deerlin reform, a VHF TV station in New York would be subject to an annual fee of around $7.74 million and a UHF station would write a

check for $2.063 million. (The figures are from a fee schedule compiled for discussion purposes by the House subcommittee. See *Broadcasting*, July 24, 1978.) Total annual revenues from all fees could rise as high as $700 million, and would be earmarked for public broadcasting, and for special funds to encourage minority station ownership and the expansion of services to rural areas.

To win passage of this basic reform, Van Deerlin has offered what I believe is a token concession to broadcasters—his bill envisions the eventual elimination of license renewal procedures for both radio and TV, and would modify troubling censorship formulas that give federal regulators the questionable right to meddle in program content. The public-spirited Nicholas Johnson, who once clerked for Mr. Justice Black, has some curious allies in his recent vehement attacks on Van Deerlin. Echoing Johnson, the Rev. Everett C. Parker, director of the United Church of Christ Office of Communications, calls the Van Deerlin rewrite "a bigger giveaway of public rights and property than Teapot Dome." It is certainly true that the proposed legislation would make it harder for inquisitorial watchdog groups to enroll the FCC in their censorship campaigns.

For example, no sooner had the Supreme Court upheld the right of the FCC to punish the broadcasting of four-letter words by Pacifica's WBAI-FM in New York than a Massachusetts outfit called Morality in Media filed a complaint with the FCC alleging that a Boston public television station was airing obscene and offensive material in [sic] Masterpiece Theatre and Monty Python's Flying Circus. (See *Broadcasting*, July 24, 1978.)

Anyone who takes the First Amendment seriously must be troubled by federal oversight of broadcasting. The peculiar status of radio and television was initially justified on the ground of scarcity, since technology imposed limits on the number of broadcasting frequencies. But today in every major city there are many more radio stations than newspapers, and new developments in television (satellite transmission, cable TV, and improved tuners) promise a comparable proliferation of channels. The scarcity argument is increasingly hollow and untenable.

True enough, the Van Deerlin legislation would give radio stations permanent licenses and after a decade do the same for television. But what is being given away? In practice, the three-year renewal ritual is a charade, of benefit chiefly to the 800-odd lawyers accredited to the FCC bar. (Even an unchallenged TV license renewal can involve $90,000 in legal fees.) In 1976, a typical year, out of 2995 renewal applications, 2964 were promptly granted, and only one-fourth of 1 percent were denied. Denials have invariably arisen from fraudulent business practices, not from failure to meet standards of public service. (For details, see the admirable analysis in *Reluctant Regulators*, by Barry Cole and Mal Oettinger; Addison-Wesley, 1978.)

In theory. the FCC is supposed to uphold the public interest against the broadcasting industry; in practice, it has generally been the other way around, despite valiant reforming efforts by outstanding commissioners such as Frieda Hennock, Newton Minow, and Nicholas John-son. Perhaps the most visible contribution of the FCC has been to train two generations of lawyers as advocates for the broadcasting industry. (See Cole and Oettinger, *passim*.)

Under the Van Deerlin measure, the concept of public stewardship of television is preserved and citizen challenge of gross abuse by a station is possible at any time. Existing equal time and fairness doctrine formulas are replaced by a more general requirement of equitable treatment, and by the narrowing of equal time restrictions on TV to candidates for local office. No doubt these and many other features of an omnibus bill deserve rigorous discussion and may need improving amendments.

I am appalled, however, by the intemperate tone of liberal attacks on Van Deerlin. It is surely high time, in Dr. Johnson's words, to clear our minds of cant. The new legislation is "giving away" powers that have demonstrably failed to achieve their lofty purposes. These powers, moreover, open a quagmire of First Amendment questions, as in the Pacifica case. I cannot believe the Republic will be imperiled if we treat broadcasters more nearly like publishers of newspapers, books, and magazines. With this proviso: that profits earned from junk television should help to underwrite a public system that may yet evolve into an American counterpart of the BBC. To give away the fiction of regulation for the actuality of real money for quality programming is no mean bargain.

Johnson in Rebuttal

Having seen Karl Meyer's statement, this available space for response can scarcely do it justice. It is riddled with what are, to me, misstatements and faulty conclusions. Here's an example:

Mr. Meyer implies that Dr. Parker and I lead "inquisitorial watchdog groups ... in censorship campaigns." I resent that and believe my record unblemished in support of public access, freedom for the creative community, and opposition to government and corporate censorship of program content. As Chairman of the NCCB I even urged that the "family viewing hour" was unconstitutional and won in the courts. It was the broadcasters who supported it.

That's personal. The rest misreads the bill.

Meyer cites the Supreme Court's recent *Carlin-WBAI* decision (banning seven dirty words) as argument for Van Deerlin's reform. Great. Has he read the bill? Section 417(a)(6) expressly makes "obscene, indecent, or profane language" grounds for the *revocation* of one of those licenses in perpetuity! Neither the drafters of the 1934 Communications Act nor the modern-day "inquisitorial watchdogs" had urged that drastic a remedy. That's typical of Meyer's analysis.

What about the fee system? Meyer says it has been "obscured in misleading and pietistic attacks." Not from me it hasn't. I didn't mention it. Now that he has raised it, I will.

When I was an FCC Commissioner we instituted the broadcast industry's first significant fee system. We didn't have to rewrite the entire Communications Act to do it.

For Meyer to suggest the Van Deerlin fees will support the programs the bill describes is either a bad joke or deliberately misleading. The fees are for the new FCC, public broadcasting, providing rural America with cable TV, and minorities with funds to acquire stations! Such programs require multibillion-dollar budgets, not millions. Even a 100 percent confiscatory tax on broadcasting couldn't make a down payment on, let alone complete, such programs.

Given the unsurpassed political power of broadcasters, it is unrealistic to think that they will not set the fees they will be paying to support public broadcasting. They already have an incentive to hold down appropriations. What chance would public broadcasting have for adequate funding if its budgets came directly from the profits of its commercial competitors?

And what are we being asked to give up for these trifling coins? What Meyer has the gall to call "a token concession." Well, this token concession happens to involve the total abandonment of broadcasters' public responsibility, repeal of the "public interests." That's quite a price.

Meyer says FCC regulations haven't produced much. Dozens of citizen-broadcaster agreements prove him wrong. It's not the *use* of the license renewal hearings; it's the *availability* of that process. Negotiated progress has been significant in employment, children's programming, public-service announcements, public affairs, format changes, and fair treatment of issues. Earlier this month a children's programming agreement was announced by a group called "WATCH" in Washington. This agreement alone is reason enough for keeping these rights. One would think, if the FCC and public-interest standards were not performing adequately, the remedy would be to strengthen them, not abandon them. If that's too much to hope, let's at least hang on to what we have. To sell me on even more broadcasting power in exchange for a handful of inflated dollars, and the remote hope of some other technological solution 10 or 20 years from now, is going to require a more persuasive carnival barker than I have as yet encountered.

Meyer in Rebuttal

It is with despair and bafflement that I read Nicholas Johnson's cantankerous assault on the Van Deerlin bill. He wants more diversity in broadcasting. So does everyone else. But he totally ignores the license fee that the bill would impose on commercial broadcasting, thereby providing revenues that would encourage diversity without relying on regulatory doctrines that have proven feeble in practice and risky in theory.

I suggest that Johnson have a chat with one of his erstwhile allies, Henry Geller, who worked for 14 years at the FCC, most of that time as general counsel. Geller has changed his mind about the benefits of the regulations that he for years tried earnestly to enforce. In a *New York Times* interview (July 18, 1978), Geller put it this way to Les Brown:

> If our goals are for more cultural, educational, and more minority services, we surely are not going to get them from commercial broadcasting. So why not let commercial broadcasters do what they do best, take the money from the licensing fee and apply it to the betterment of the public broadcasting system? That's one answer, and it also carries a First Amendment bonus.

Geller is frankly concerned with the First Amendment implication of federal regulation, which clearly does impinge upon program content. How can Johnson possibly argue that the FCC has shown no inclination to meddle in the wake of the Pacifica decision? Just what does Johnson mean by saying that all media should be legally accountable to the public? Is he proposing that the post office should license the *Nation* and create a Bureau of Magazine Standards to assure that William F. Buckley is given equal time in each issue? In reality, existing regulations provide a weapon for zealots as well as the high-minded to engage in shakedown maneuvers against radio and TV stations. Even when the high-minded triumph, the agreement may entail a questionable payoff to citizens' advocates—as was the case in New York City, when a $90,000 reimbursement was paid to those who campaigned against changing the classical music format of WNCN-FM. The cause was noble (I pledged $25 to help save WNCN) but the legal fee was outrageous. One of Johnson's most dubious votes as FCC Commissioner was in support of such reimbursement of petitioning groups. (See *Reluctant Regulators*, pp. 240–41.) And what the PTA does today the National Rifle Association, you may be sure, will do tomorrow. With large fees to lawyers.

Like Henry Geller, I believe that the Van Deerlin bill is a solid first step, though I am sure that it can be improved. Unlike Johnson, I do not believe that the incantation of populist slogans constitutes a real debate. We need to hear a case against the new communications act, but I'm afraid Nicholas Johnson has not even begun to make it.

VAN DEERLIN, ROUND 2:
JOHNSON AND MEYER
CONTINUE THEIR TV DISPUTE

Nicholas Johnson

Karl Meyer and I have had our debate, and rebuttal, over the proposed new Communications Act (*The Nation*, September 30). I'm prepared to refer readers to that exchange, and stand by it. Mr. Meyer wants another round. Can't say as I blame him. It really was his burden to make the case for this bill. He couldn't do it. In fact, he hasn't even addressed the fundamentals with which I opened.

We haven't seen each other's further statements in this issue. For all I know he's saved his only valid arguments for last. But I doubt it. Failing that miracle, it seemed most appropriate to summarize the case.

Representatives Lionel Van Deerlin and Louis Frey and advocate Karl Meyer believe that radio and television should not be subject to public accountability—neither directly (through currently existing public legal rights) nor indirectly (through FCC regulation). They would give stations licenses in perpetuity, and repeal virtually all public rights (including FCC enforcement of equal employment opportunity for minorities and women).

They argue that (1) abolishing government regulation is a good in its own right; (2) gov-

Reprinted from "Van Deerlin, Round 2: Johnson and Meyer Continue Their TV Dispute," by Nicholas Johnson and Karl E. Meyer in *The Nation* (October 21, 1978): 406–407. Used by permission from *The Nation* magazine, copyright 1978 The Nation Associates, Inc.

ernment regulation of broadcasting has been at best ineffective and at worst a First Amendment threat; (3) the "marketplace" will serve adequately any legitimate "public interest" in broadcasting, and (4) fees to be paid by broadcasters will more than make up for lost public rights.

Opponents of the Van Deerlin bill (H.R. 13015) argue that the bill is, at best, an ill-considered, naive, balancing act involving the most politically powerful vested interests. At worst it is a fraudulent, virtually secret giveaway of public rights essential to the functioning of our democratic society.

For 50 years Presidents, Supreme Court Justices, Senators and Members of Congress, academics, members of the audience, and even some broadcasters, have urged that broadcasting carries special obligations and responsibilities. They have been joined in this view by their counterparts around the world.

Those of us who oppose the Van Deerlin bill side with that half-century of human judgment. We do not argue that the 1934 Communications Act cannot be improved. It can. We have endorsed the Ottinger bill (H.R. 11951) to that end. We do not argue that the FCC's regulation cannot be made less onerous. It can. We do not oppose innovation in broadcast regulation. We encourage it. We do not oppose marketplace mechanisms where they work. We have argued *for* fewer restraints on cable and pay broadcasting (over broadcasters' successful opposition).

We answer the proponents' four arguments by saying (1) government regulation is neither good nor ill in its own right. It depends on why and how it is done. (2) However ineffective the FCC has been, it has many commendable decisions to its credit. Moreover, the existence of a regulatory scheme has given pause to irresponsible broadcasters and power to the concerned public in negotiating its own settlements with them. Genuine First Amendment threats from the FCC are few, and easily redressed by the courts. Without regulation, threats by broadcasters to the *public's* First Amendment rights (which the Supreme Court has said are "paramount") are seriously jeopardized. (3) There is no "marketplace" in broadcasting. Congress and broadcasters oppose creating one. Even if it existed it wouldn't be adequate to provide programming diversity. (4) The proposed "fees" are so grossly inadequate as to be either laughable or fraudulent.

Any *one* of the following would be grounds for some regulation of broadcasting: (1) its creation and protection from competition by government, (2) the monopoly status each broadcaster enjoys on the occupied frequency, (3) its pervasive presence in our lives, (4) the limited number of available frequencies. and (5) its impact upon the values and functioning of a democratic society—in politics and government, education, religion, economics, art and culture, the perception of the elderly, minorities, women, and a thousand other ways.

Not just one, but *all* are present here.

Nonetheless, the arguments of Meyer and the broadcasters are being heard by Van Deerlin and others in Congress. The public has not even been informed, let alone heard from. The threat is real.

We need to hear from you if this outrageous bill is not to become law. Please write: National Citizens Communications Lobby, 1028 Connecticut Ave., Washington, D.C. 20036.

Karl E. Meyer

On rereading my exchange with Nicholas Johnson on the merits, or lack of them, of the Van Deerlin bill, I felt we were firing compressed pellets at very different targets. Since the matter is of importance, I ask indulgence for this attempt to raise the sights by restating what I believe to be at issue.

What really divides us is the definition of progress in television programming. My criterion is prime time. When I turn on the tube, I see the same vast wasteland that Newton Minow memorably deplored in 1961—a mindless procession of kiddie sitcoms, jiggly shows, and "action" dramas, interspersed with interminable commercials. Only on occasion do we get anything superior on the networks, and even the recent modest gains in adult comedy (as in

the Norman Lear and MTM programs) seem in jeopardy.

It was entirely typical that not one of the three networks was willing to take up Joseph Papp and Norman Lear on their proposal last year to produce a weekly series of American dramas. Without public television, whatever its inadequacies, most viewers would lack any alternative to the prepackaged *dreck* that engulfs us.

Nicholas Johnson, by contrast, places high value on citizen-broadcaster agreements made possible by the present system of FCC licensing of TV and radio stations. I would not deny that these agreements have yielded some benefits in terms of equal employment, public service announcements, etc. However, too often these agreements are token concessions that enable broadcasters to justify their outpouring of prime-time drivel. Furthermore, when they threaten stations with costly challenges, citizen groups are employing a weapon that any organized minority can use to chill controversy and impose its taste on all of us.

I am prepared to accept that the Van Deerlin proposal is imperfect. As Johnson argues, the license fees it contemplates may not be high enough for adequate financing of public broadcasting. Let us, then, urge higher fees. It also may be, as Martin Mayer maintains, that the proposed deregulation of cable TV is risky, and that instead of abandoning TV licensing, the term should be extended from three to 20 years. (Mayer's temperate appraisal of Van Deerlin appears in the October issue of *American Film*, along with a reflective interview on Van Deerlin with FCC Chairman Charles Ferris.)

But Nicholas Johnson is not analyzing, he is castigating. I cannot accept his premise that the existing system has worked, or can be made to work. And some of his statements warrant these Parthian pellets:

■ True enough, when Johnson was a commissioner the FCC did impose a token tax on broadcasters, but the amount involved was peanuts. Between 1970 and 1975, a grand total of $31.9 million was collected from broadcasters—but the fee was ruled to be illegal by the courts, and the FCC has been ordered to return all moneys collected (see *Broadcasting*, May 23, 1977).

■ True enough, and to his credit Johnson did challenge the introduction of "family viewing hour," as concocted by the FCC in collaboration with the National Association of Broadcasters. But as much as the merits, what exercised citizen groups was the fact that they had been left out of policy formulation (see Cole and Oettinger, *Reluctant Regulators*, pp. 276–88). I wish that Johnson would address himself forthrightly to the censorship implications of organized boycott threats against sponsors of such shows as "Charlie's Angels"—tactics reminiscent of the blacklisting era. I do not mean to impute to Johnson the narrow-mindedness of some of his allies in the assault on Van Deerlin. But he might recall the sentiment attributed to the Duke of Wellington during the Peninsular campaign: "I don't know if my troops will scare the enemy, but they sure as hell scare me."

FCC AND LAISSEZ-FAIRE
BROADCASTING PLANS

Ernest Holsendolph

The Federal Communications Commission formally proposed last week to free the radio industry of significant control by the government, but a number of issues divide the commissioners and must be resolved before a new policy can be adopted.

All seven commissioners believe, in varying degrees, that less regulation is better and that the marketplace can govern an industry better than the government. They note that the broad-

From *The New York Times* (September 10, 1979): D11. © 1979 by The New York Times Company. Reprinted by permission.

casting industry has matured and that radio stations have proliferated. Forty-five years ago, when there were only 583 radio stations, individual communities might have been dependent on one or two stations, but many communities now had a dozen or more.

One element of the board, led by its chairman, Charles D. Ferris, believes that this new abundance of radio "voices" can be freed from government controls because public tastes and demands can be depended on to provide them with a healthy range of entertainment, news, and special-interest programs, and that public resistance would keep them from overcommercializing.

In its action last week, the commissioners proposed that radio stations no longer be held individually responsible for keeping commercials to a maximum of 18-and-a-half minutes an hour. Nor should the stations be required to devote a minimum of 6 percent of their airtime to news or other nonentertainment programs, or keep detailed logs on how airtime is used, or survey their markets and public leaders to determine the needs of the community.

SKEPTICISM OVER NEW POLICY

What emerged from the commission's discussion of these proposals last Thursday, however, was that a majority of the commissioners have yet to be fully convinced that the new policy would not backfire—that the broadcasting industry would not lapse into a cacophony of commercials, or that it would move toward more entertainment at the expense of informational programs, or tend to overlook the needs of members of minority groups.

An FCC staff report supporting the proposals said that, with the growth in the number of stations, all-news stations and stations oriented toward blacks and Hispanic persons have come into existence and are flourishing.

There are now 118 all-news stations, the commission said, and 270 stations in 173 localities regularly schedule programs in Spanish; 44 of them are full-time Spanish stations. Programs in 63 other foreign languages or dialects are also broadcast.

The commission said that records submitted by radio stations in Alabama and Georgia show the stations consistently broadcast less than the 18-and-a-half minutes of commercials per hour allowed by the FCC and that they seemed to broadcast more news and public affairs programs than required, indicating that this was the marketplace at work.

CONCERN FOR MINORITY GROUPS

Consumer groups have yet to be convinced, however, that such programming was caused by market demands and not by fears that if they failed to "play it safe" they would jeopardize their licenses when they sought renewals. They also want to know what the commission plans to do if all the stations in one market attempt to capture a share of the mass audience and ignore ethnic groups, the poor, or other groups that lack the economic influence or the skills to make their demands known.

Commissioner Tyrone Brown and other critics assert that, in the final analysis, advertisers are the most significant radio consumers, and listeners merely the products of the industry. If that is correct, they ask, what would compel broadcasters to pay attention to programs of interest to minority audiences?

In addition, an economist on the commission's staff acknowledged that it could not be determined from the Georgia and Alabama surveys whether the stations' failure to reach the maximum number of minutes allowed for advertising per hour represented restraint among the broadcasters or a lack of demand for advertising time.

At last week's meeting, Commissioner Abbott Washburn said: "I can't go along with any move that diminishes our interest in overcommercialization in broadcasting."

Commissioner Joseph Fogarty wondered whether the commission had compiled an adequate record on which to base its proposed changes, including an argument persuasive enough to prevent a federal court from overturning the policy change.

The commission will try to explain its proposals to the public through a series of local workshops, with the first scheduled for next Friday in Boston under the auspices of the Consumer Affairs Office.

Everett Parker, an official to the United Church of Christ who opposes the proposed rules changes, has already criticized the workshops as an unfair propagandizing effort. It was only the opening shot in what could be a bitter contest between the commission and some consumer groups.

FCC PROPOSALS TO DEREGULATE RADIO

Telecommunications Consumer Coalition

Radio is the chief target of Washington's relentless "deregulators." This year's congressional bills to write consumers out of the Communications Act of 1934 appear stalemated. Now the Federal Communications Commission has launched its own scheme to deregulate radio.

On September 6, the FCC announced that it wanted to:

■ Drop FCC policies limiting the number of commercials on radio.
■ Remove all requirements for radio stations to carry news, public affairs programming, public service announcements, and all other community service programming on radio.

■ Abolish ascertainment—the FCC-required consultation with community leaders about local needs and problems.
■ Eliminate program logs—the radio station's public record of its service to the community.

The commission has substituted economic "marketplaces" for the communities radio stations have traditionally served. It has confused "consumer wants" with what consumers will tolerate. The FCC admits that, in broadcasting, audiences are sold by the station to the advertiser. The tastes, needs, and problems of specialized audiences, such as consumer interests are likely to be ignored, according to the commission. Public affairs programs and public service announcements will no longer be

Courtesy of the Telecommunications Consumer Coalition.

required and are likely to disappear. Under "marketplace forces" news and informational programs will continue, if profitable; but the absence of market interest will doom these kinds of programs. Doomed, too, will be the jobs of people who plan, produce, and air such programs. The station's economic viability is the sine qua non of the FCC proposals.

The FCC deregulation is also an open invitation to stations to automate. As the tapes start rolling in, the jobs of local announcers, interviewers, dj's, women's specialists, news staffs, and program and production personnel will be eliminated. But nobody should have to go.

These radical proposals are a threat to *all* local groups who use radio to reach the public. They challenge hard-won citizen rights in broadcasting. They destroy effective public participation in the radio license renewal process. If we allow the FCC to toss radio completely to the marketplace, deregulation of television and cable TV, elimination of the fairness doctrine and equal opportunities for political candidates aren't far behind.

RADIO DEREGULATION

National Association of Broadcasters

The marketplace has replaced the FCC as the regulator of the radio industry. The 1000 pages of commission rules for broadcasting that now appear in the Code of Federal Regulation have become virtually obsolete.

Radio stations broadcast what the public wants to hear. If they didn't, they would sacrifice listeners to another one of the 8000 radio stations now operating in the United States. The sheer number of stations guarantees that the public interest is served. Even in the most complex marketplace, almost every segment of the population is served.

With a deregulated radio industry, the amount of nonentertainment programming would, if anything, increase. Studies conducted by the NAB and the FCC's own Office of

Plans and Policy come to the same conclusion—stations, especially in the smallest markets, offer far more news and public service programming than required by the FCC itself. With the Commission currently setting an 8 percent minimum on nonentertainment programming for AM stations, 6 percent for FM stations, those studies show that a significant percentage of stations in all markets offer at least 10 to 25 percent of that type programming (25 percent average in smallest markets).

There are critics of radio deregulation that demand a lengthy experiment be conducted, and only in the largest markets, before the commission implements this proposal. With these programming statistics at hand, such an experiment would be nothing more than a waste of time and money for the commission, the public, and for broadcasters.

Courtesy of the National Association of Broadcasters.

The trend in government today is toward deregulation. President Jimmy Carter made it clear at the March, 1979 NAB convention that he expects this commission to dismantle and discard any unnecessary and outdated rules regulating the broadcasting industry. And for good reason. Radio deregulation has proved successful at the commission in the past and will in the future.

Over the last 10 years, the FCC has dropped more than 700 technical rules involving radio. Technological improvements in station operation have allowed a less rigid regulatory approach with no loss of performance or public service. The adoption of this proposal would have the same result—less time and money spent in fulfilling needless rules and more of both channeled in the direction of service to the public.

chapter 16

ACCESS TO
THE MEDIA

One of the reasons broadcast deregulation looms as an important issue of the eighties is that consumer groups, minorities, and various other special-interest groups fear they will lose their access to mass media if that access is not required by law. These groups feel that they do not have enough access now, and that any further infringement would be intolerable. Program suppliers, corporations, politicians, and many individual members of the public have similar fears.

But how is public access possible in a society of over 200 million people? In the first reading in this chapter, Phil Jacklin, a professor and media activist, proposes a radical answer to that question. Jacklin's proposal deals with all media. In the second reading, a wide range of spokesmen on all sides of this issue discuss their opinions of access proposals for television.

ACCESS TO THE MEDIA

A NEW FAIRNESS DOCTRINE

Phil Jacklin

Government regulation of broadcasting is under attack. This is nothing new. Like all industries, the broadcast industry resists regulation. Unfortunately, only the industry point of view is heard and good people are persuaded by it. Thus, in the May, 1973, issue of *Civil Liberties*, Nat Hentoff argues against the Federal Communication Commission's fairness doctrine. He understands the fairness doctrine in the conventional way as the obligation imposed on broadcasters to balance their presentation of controversial issues. More generally, the broadcaster faces an obligation to present programming in the public interest; this general obligation is particularized by the fairness doctrine, which requires the broadcaster to balance discussion of controversial issues *and* to cover and present issues of public importance.

The standard argument against regulation of broadcast programming goes as follows:

- There is an asymmetry in the regulation of radio and television on the one hand and the print media on the other. We have government regulation of radio and television under the fairness doctrine; but the First Amendment is understood to prohibit government regulation of newspapers under any comparable fairness doctrine.

From *The Center Magazine* (May–June 1975): 46–50. *The Center Magazine* is a publication of the Center for the Study of Democratic Institutions, Santa Barbara, California.

- There is no longer a justification for this asymmetry. The rationale of the fairness doctrine (and of all regulation of broadcast content) is the scarcity of usable broadcast frequencies. But there are now far fewer daily newspapers than there are radio and television stations (1749 to 7458). Few cities (5 percent) have competitive daily newspapers, but most are served by several television stations and plenty of radio.
- Therefore, in order to be consistent, we should defend freedom of the electric press and oppose the fairness doctrine.

Hentoff does not affirm this conclusion. He offers it for discussion. As he says, it is "new ground" for him. His argument is all too familiar to those who read *Broadcasting* magazine and follow industry attempts to expropriate the First Amendment. On the strength of it, Senator William Proxmire has recently filed a bill to end regulation of broadcast programming.

The two premises of the above argument are correct. There is an asymmetry and there is no basis for it. Still, the conclusion of the argument is a non sequitur. We need not achieve consistency by changing broadcast law and giving up the fairness doctrine. We can also achieve it by extending the fairness doctrine from broadcasting to the print media. We can do this using the media-scarcity rationale as in broadcasting. If daily newspapers are more scarce than broadcast frequencies, it does not follow that frequencies are not scarce. There is scarcity when demand exceeds supply; in the media case there is scarcity when more people want access to the public than can have it.

We have a choice. Should we extend the fairness doctrine to newspapers which have no competitors and risk further government involvement? Or should we adopt the same laissez-faire policy for broadcasting that is traditional in the print media? I submit that there is a third and better alternative. If we believe in an open society and political equality, if we want to avoid the domination of mass communications by a few big corporations, then we must regulate any preponderant message-source in any medium. But, there is available to us a regulatory strategy which is fundamentally different from that involved in the fairness doctrine as presently understood and is wholly consistent with the First Amendment. We can choose to regulate access rather than content, to ensure fairness about who is heard rather than fairness in what is said.

When, if ever, is there a need (justification or rationale) for government regulation of media? If there is media scarcity, does that justify regulation? Is there a way to regulate media without abridging freedom of the press? Answers to these questions are suggested by a model well known to political economy. Consider the following principles—all applicable to the problems of media law:

■ That a free (unregulated) and competitive marketplace is preferable to a government-regulated or planned economy.
■ That when there exists an economic monopoly or a concentration of economic power, the government must regulate that power to prevent abuses and protect the public interest. As Adam Smith explained, laissez-faire or the absence of regulation is desirable only in a condition of natural competition. When merchants must compete for their customers, the competition ensures that people will be well served. But when economic power is monopolized or concentrated in a few hands, then competition ends and

the government must protect the public interest. This takes us to a third and less familiar principle.
■ That, in the absence of natural competition, it is better to regulate so as to guarantee a competitive marketplace by limiting the extent to which power can be concentrated (e.g., to establish antitrust laws) than to attempt to regulate the behavior of monopoly powers (e.g., by setting production quotas and standards of quality, and administering prices and wages).

I take the traditional view that democracy absolutely requires the kind of communications generated in a competitive marketplace of ideas.

The problem is that in a society of millions dependent on the technology of mass communications, most messages that reach any substantial number of people are transmitted by means of a very limited number of media. In general, the scarcity of access to substantial audiences exists, not because there is a physical scarcity of communications channels, but for economic and sociological reasons. There is no shortage of "channels" in the print media, no shortage of presses or paper; but most dailies enjoy absolute monopolies. And, although there are weekly papers and periodicals, the publisher of the daily newspaper controls 80 percent of all print communications on local and state issues.

In most big cities, there are at the present time 15 to 20 usable television frequencies (VHF and UHF)—the same number as will be provided in a standard cable system. But the three network-associated stations control the programming viewed by 85 percent of the total television audience. (Cable television and future technology will not solve our problem.)

Each of the channels with a substantial audience—print or broadcast—is wholly controlled by a single large message-source. Thus, in a typical city, control of mass communications is concentrated in the hands of a single daily newspaper and three television stations, with the addition in some places of an all-news radio station. The power of a message-source is a function both of the number of messages produced (as counted roughly by measuring the space and time they fill) and of the number of people actually reached by those messages.

It is at this point that the battle is joined by the newspaper and broadcasting industries, which argue thus: "Suppose, as is claimed, that media regulation *is* necessary when a concentration of the power to communicate reduces competition in a marketplace of ideas. There is indeed a limited number of important communicators, but there has been no showing at all that these communicators have abused their powers or refrained from a competition of ideas. The press is doing its job. Our Watergate experience proves that the system works. It is unnecessary and foolish to run the risk of government regulation of communications."

What, then, is the performance of the media? What, if anything, is left out? National media coverage is issue-oriented and admirable in that way. But "Presidential television" and dominance of the media generally led us in the late 1960s to the brink of disaster and over. Denied regular television exposure, neither congressional leaders nor the opposition party could check Presidential power. The Chief Executive dominates national attention. He is the only one with enough continuity of access to exercise national leadership. On state issues, and especially on local issues, there is virtually no one with the access appropriate to leadership except perhaps the press itself.

What ideas are left out? Ask those moved by a conception of the public interest, those who would seek access to their brothers and sisters in the media marketplace of ideas. Ask elected officials, consumer advocates, reformers, ecologists, socialists, the would-be vocal poor, church people, feminists, et al.

On both the national and local levels, the restraints on the competition of ideas are most apparent in the absence of day-to-day political competition. Political competition is the competition of leaders and their programs for public support as expressed in the formation of public opinion. No one except the President has long-term visibility or the concomitant ability to engage in the long-term communications essential to leadership.

Why? Part of the answer lies in the fact that the most powerful media are commercial and business-oriented. There is competition, but it is a competition for the advertiser's dollar and not a competition of ideas. We ignore this because we have been taught to identify the media with the press and to understand the press on the old model of precommercial, crusading journalism. In the good old days, the newspaper publisher wrote and edited his own stories and even ran the press himself. He was a political activist, a Sentinel, an Observer vigilant in behalf of his subscribers, an Advocate with the courage to set himself and his paper against the powerful few. Things have changed. The publisher's source of revenues has shifted from subscribers to advertisers and this has changed the newspaper business in two ways. Advertisers are more interested in circulation than in editorial policy. As a result, in almost every city the largest daily has slowly achieved a monopoly position, not because of the superiority of its editorial policy but because it is the first choice of advertisers. Second, the shift of revenues has changed editorial policy. It has shifted the editor's attention from the problems of the many to the ambitions of a few. As a monopoly message-source on local issues, the paper becomes, in a technical sense, propaganda. On one hand, there is the propaganda of boosterism and Chamber of Commerce public relations (e.g., in San Jose, a new sports arena before new schools, airport expansion before noise abatement). On the other hand, with respect to the problems of ordinary people and especially the poor, there is silence, the propaganda of the status quo. Most big city dailies do not by themselves sustain a marketplace of ideas on local issues.

What, then, is added by the multiplicity of

broadcasters? Broadcasters are typically large corporations, not crusading journalists, not people at all. Corporate broadcasters program so as to generate the largest possible audiences. Then they rent these audiences to advertisers at the rate of $4 per thousand per minute. The lawyers and public relations men who represent them try to identify the electronic medium with the electronic press. But does the corporation have a First Amendment right to program exclusively for profit? (The fairness doctrine prohibits it.) In fact, only about 5 percent of the electronic medium is occupied with the traditional journalistic function—news, documentaries, and public affairs—the rest is electronic theater. Audience-profit maximization leaves very little place for authentic journalism. Television journalists go unprotected while the First Amendment is interpreted as the right of the broadcasting corporation to edit in order to maximize profits, and even to make the local news a form of entertainment, to make of the news itself just another format for stories of sex and violence. What these corporations seek is not freedom for journalism but freedom from journalism. (They have succeeded very well. In point of fact, the FCC's fairness obligation to cover issues has been enforced in only one case.)

There is nothing wrong with an electronic circus as long as the medium also delivers the kind of communications required for democracy. We owe very much to the journalism of the last five years. Still, even the best journalism is no substitute for free speech. There is a profound reason why this is so. Journalists are supposed to be objective and nonpartisan. They themselves are not supposed to participate in the competition of ideas, or to lead people to action. The press sustains a competition of ideas only to the extent that it provides access to spokesmen who are not themselves journalists.

The question then arises: How can a journalist decide in a disinterested way what issues and spokesmen to present? There is no solution to this problem. Indeed, the question is unintelligible. Message-choice, like all choice, presupposes the chooser's interests and needs. Journalists usually avoid the problem by reporting new events relative to something that is already in the news. But in a mass society, the news is identical with what is reported; and what has not been reported is not yet news.

How, then, can the journalist decide what *new* issues and spokesmen should gain access to the public? He can decide only because he does have values and interests; hopefully only by making a judgment about what people want and need to know. Authentic journalism is public-interest journalism. But when businessmen-publishers and corporations do the hiring and the firing, there is no guarantee that we will have authentic journalism. Spiro Agnew's concern was not misplaced: "A small group of men decide what 40 to 50 million Americans will learn of the day's events. . . . We would never trust such power in the hands of an elected government; it is time we questioned it in the hands of a small and unelected elite."

There is another consideration here which is decisive all by itself. Even if there were a competition of ideas between five or ten powerful sources, that would not be good enough for democracy. A society is democratic to the extent that all its citizens have an equal opportunity to influence the decision-making process. Clearly, communication is essential to this process—just as essential as voting itself. (Imagine a society of 1000 in which everyone votes, and all are free to say what they please, but only five people have the technology and power to reach *all* the others. Each of the other 995, except at overwhelming expense, can communicate only with a small circle of friends. Suppose the "five" are wealthy businessmen.)

The media must be regulated, not only to ensure a competition of ideas, but so that all citizens have an equal opportunity to influence and shape this competition. "Fine, but is democracy possible in a society of 200 million people?" Representative democracy is possible. As voters, we are represented in city hall, at the state capitol, and in the Congress by people who, to some extent at least, vote on our behalf and answer to us. These people are supported at public expense and use public facilities. All right, we need to establish parallel institutions which give us representation in public debate, i.e., representation in the media marketplace.

There are many possibilities. Our elected representatives and their ballot opponents and/or prospective opponents—leaders all—might be provided free media time and space on a regular basis. But we should not limit representation in the media marketplace to elected officials and party leaders. There are other ways in which spokesmen representative of whole groups can be identified. Formally organized nonprofit groups like the Sierra Club and the Methodist Church can select spokesmen, and membership rolls will demonstrate that these spokesmen are representatives. Small, informally organized groups of the type characteristic of much citizen activity could achieve short-term access by demonstrating by petition that a substantial number of people supported their efforts (as in the access-by-petition procedure in Holland). A plan for a system of representative access recognizing these four kinds of access has been drawn up by the Committee for Open Media. The details establish the feasibility of the general proposal. The FCC could establish some such system of access in broadcasting under its present authority, or Congress could do it. But what about the monopolistic daily newspapers?

It is useful to imagine what a new communications act would be like if we sought to develop a new strategy for media regulation oriented to regulation of access. We could regulate monopolistic or dominant message-sources in order to protect a competition of ideas in which all have some opportunity to participate or be represented. We could create a system of representative access of the sort sketched above or, alternatively, a new communications act might have the four following provisions:

- *The one-tenth concentration rule.* Any dominant message-source (one which controls over one-tenth of the message reaching any population of over 100,000) in any medium—be it print or broadcast—shall recognize an affirmative obligation to provide access to the public.
- *The tithe in the public interest.* Each dominant message-source shall make available 10 percent of all message capacity (time and/or space) for citizen access. Message capacity shall be defined in terms of time and space and also audience availability to that time and space. Since in broadcasting there is a fundamental difference between the function of full-length programs and spot messages, 10 percent of each would be made available. (Perhaps there should also be a tithe or tax of 10 percent on all profits to pay for production of citizen messages.)
- *The allocation of access by lot.* Access to time and space shall be allocated by lot among registered citizens. Every registered voter is, in virtue of this act, a registered communicator.
- *The access-contribution mechanism.* It shall be permissible for individuals to make access contributions to designated representative persons or groups. It will be permissible for the citizen to designate a representative person or group to use his or her access spot. Individual organizations will be permitted and encouraged to solicit contributions of access time and space.
- The access-contribution mechanism makes possible effective grass-roots support for various organizations at low cost (in time and money) and may lead to individual identification with the groups supported. It is a communications institution which generates community and community organization.

Access designations will, in effect, be votes—expressions of concerns and priorities—with respect to what is communicated. Everyone will participate in message-selection. Communication will reflect the needs, values, and priorities of all citizens.

The great advantage of the access approach is that it provides a strategy for media regulation which is in the spirit of the First Amendment and wholly consistent with it. The decisive difference between the regulatory strategy of the old law and the proposed new law is the distinction between the regulation of message content and the regulation of access. Or, to put the difference another way, it is the difference between the prohibition of certain message-content and the prohibition of monopolization of access by any message-source or group of sources.

The First Amendment prohibits government censorship; it prohibits laws regulating message content. But regulation of access does not entail regulation of content. Whatever source gains access is free to express any message whatever in the sole discretion of that source. While it is arguable that total denial of access is a form of censorship, surely it is not censorship to tell someone who talks all the time to stop talking for a bit so that others may speak. In contrast, the present law requires a regulation of content (broadcast programming). It requires "government censorship" in order to protect "the public interest" and especially to prevent an imbalance of programming that is not "fair" to some points of view. The tension between the Communications Act of 1934 and the First Amendment generates a choice between finding a way to regulate program content which does not risk government control of mass communications, and not regulating broadcast programming out of respect for the First Amendment. Given the preferences and power of the broadcast industry, the government has usually opted for no regulation. The fairness doctrine is rarely enforced. Unfortunately laissez-faire—*de jure* or *de facto*—is morally unacceptable in any context in which power is concentrated.

This returns us to the three principles of political economy and the general theory of regulation. Consider the third principle once more: that, in the absence of natural competition, it is better to limit the size and power of large entities, so as to protect competition, than it is to regulate the behavior of these powers. Thus, it is better for the government to use antitrust laws to force, say, Standard Oil to divest than for the government to mandate production quotas, set product standards, and administer prices. Surely, in such a sensitive field as communication, it is better to regulate access than to rely on government paternalism in the regulation of message-content. As always, free speech in a marketplace of ideas is our best hope.

SHOULD MORE PEOPLE
HAVE A VOICE IN TV?

To persons wishing to have their special-interest programs, concerns, advertising, ideologies, and candidacies disseminated

From *The New York Times* (November 19, 1978): D1, D37–38. © 1978 by The New York Times Company. Reprinted by permission.

through television, the medium is becoming increasingly frustrating. Some major program suppliers in Hollywood, as well as independent producers, argue that with only three commercial networks, the marketplace is too restricted, and that public television, with its limited financial resources, does little to expand the field. Interest groups complain that there is a lack of genuine diversity of viewpoints and that extreme and perhaps unpopular viewpoints rarely get an airing. Political figures, particularly minor-party candidates, contend there is seldom a sufficient forum afforded them. And members of the general public, in letters and telephone calls to stations, often cite the lack of opportunity to "talk back" and have their opinions aired.

The three commercial networks as well as public television stations have made at least token responses to these charges, launching such programs as "Your Turn: Letters to CBS News," replies to local stations' editorials, and WNET's "Independent Focus." But still the complaints are commonly heard. Accordingly, the *Times* asked a number of spokesmen for the industry, minority viewpoints, and the public at large whether or not "access" to television should be expanded, and, if so, how. Their answers follow.

Nicholas Johnson

FCC Commissioner 1966–73 and now head of the National Citizens Communications Lobby in Washington

---

"Access" to radio and television is the essence of modern-day democracy. That's not cheap rhetoric, it's a fact.

Radio and television constitute our society's cerebral cortex. They are how we identify and think through our public policy issues, evaluate our candidates, formulate public opinion, govern ourselves. We do this, not alone through news and public affairs programs, but with situation comedies and popular music as well. (Even the most vapid programs shape our perception of ourselves and our world. Lulling us to sleep is, in a democracy, a political act.)

Television is, by definition, a one-way communications system. Our TV sets have a speaker and picture tube, but no microphone jack. It is also, by American experience, tightly controlled by four enormous corporations—ABC, CBS, NBC, and PBS.

A society with a communications and governing system that is both (1) one-way only and (2) tightly controlled by a few is, by definition, an authoritarian, dictatorial, antidemocratic system. It is no more possible for everyone to get access to the airwaves whenever they want to than it is for every voter personally to participate in every action of Congress. That's what elected "representatives" are for.

On the other hand, there must be some measure of popular control of broadcasting.

- One Southern TV station for years had a policy of excluding all blacks from the screen.
- Fourteen U.S. senators found themselves unable to answer President Nixon's series of prime-time, all-network speeches. No network would let them have the free access Mr. Nixon had enjoyed. None would even sell them time.
- A station in Ohio refused any free or paid coverage of the retail clerks' side of a labor dispute with a department store. The store's commercials, meanwhile, continued to run.
- Both Frank Church and Ronald Reagan found themselves unable to get access for their presidential campaigns during a period in 1976.
- Corporations willing to sponsor quality programming on television find the networks unwilling to accept their money.
- Innovative Hollywood TV producers confront network executives' insistence on formula shows.

Nor are the problems limited to commercial broadcasting. Our public broadcasting stations are becoming equally insular and resistant to public participation.

There are dozens of other examples. Consequently, what we need in this country is not a totally new law repealing the public's right to broadcasting but a reaffirmation that broadcasters are public trustees, that there is—in the words of the Supreme Court—"no right of private censorship in a medium not open to all." In that particular case the Court ruled that the fairness doctrine was constitutional. The fairness doctrine isn't much help for the public or much hindrance for responsible broadcasters. But it is decidedly better than nothing. It assures that stations deal with controversial issues, and that they not be brazenly propagandistic in doing so. It gives no *individual* a right of access.

A public service announcement or reply to a station's editorial can be a form of access. Guests on talk shows are enjoying a measure of access, and so are those covered on the evening news. The fringe-time public affairs programs afford some access to individuals not employed by the stations and networks. Such "access" is, of course, totally random and not a matter of legal right.

The FCC's so-called "equal time" and "personal attack" rules do provide legal rights. Stations may attack individuals—but that gives those attacked a right personally to reply. Stations can promote whichever candidates for public office they choose, but doing so creates a legal right for the opponents to have an equal opportunity at reaching the audience.

Corporations can buy access for their commercial messages—messages that sometimes are dripping with political content—and their programs (which carry express or implied political and economic points of view). Buying access is beyond the reach of most of us (at $225,000 per minute) and is no legal *right* anyway. Stations can simply refuse to accept your money if they don't like your message.

Citizens groups have proposed a rule to the FCC that would require that a certain number of public service spots be devoted to genuine local groups on an uncensored basis. At present, such announcements have to pass censorship by the same advertisers (the Advertising Council) as prepare the commercials—with predictable consequences.

The Congress or FCC could require that a certain proportion of prime time be available on a first-come, first-served basis to all comers—some free, some for pay.

There are more policies that indirectly affect control of the airwaves. Restricting ownership to fewer stations per licensee, increasing the number of stations, reducing station power, shared time systems (one licensee operating during some days, another the rest of the week, as in London), making leased and public access channels available on cable television, and pay cable are all ways of addressing the problem.

Access need not be viewed as an attack on commercial or public broadcasting. Public protections are possible that need not interfere with the operation of broadcast stations for fun and profit. But something must be done to provide the electronic equivalent of the handbill.

We need for the marketplace of ideas something similar to what the antitrust laws do for the marketplace of business. That's all. What could be more American than that?

Fred Silverman
President, NBC

Access is alive and well in television.

Last year, on NBC's facilities alone, more than 25,000 men and women gave their views on virtually every conceivable aspect of every major public issue. Some defended the status quo; many wanted to change it. Their positions ranged from establishment to radical and included everything in between. They ranged from the well known to the not so well known.

The issue, therefore, is not whether access should be permitted but what kind of access best serves the public.

The 25,000 spokesmen appeared on a wide variety of NBC programs, network and local, that were planned and executed by professional journalists. We believe that the journalistic process leads to a responsible use of access which best serves the public interest. At NBC, this process involves careful research to determine what issues are of genuine concern to the community—local or national—and to identify the spokesmen best qualified to present the various aspects of these issues.

We think this approach provides a far better service to the public than one in which the public rostrum of broadcasting could be taken over by anyone who feels like talking, even if he has nothing to say and even if no one wants to listen. That would be an irresponsible use of access and an abdication by the broadcast licensee of his responsibility to serve the public.

Yet, that is exactly what proponents of the "first-come, first-served" system of access are urging. By simply reserving airtime in advance, anyone seeking personal publicity could go on television and get it. There would be no effort to determine what issues are of interest and importance to the community, and every spokesman would be self-selected. That is a way of squandering a precious resource instead of using it effectively for the public.

The Supreme Court has recognized this difference in its ruling that no one has a constitutional right to speak over broadcast facilities. It is the right of the public to hear a wide range of views—not any claimed right of an individual to go on the air—that should be protected.

Everett C. Parker
Director, Office of Communication,
United Church of Christ

Television and radio by their power have preempted all other media of communication. They have become the agenda-setters for our nation. Broadcasters have always operated solely on marketplace promptings. They decide what few issues of public importance are to be discussed, and who shall discuss them. Unacceptable issues and unacceptable ethnic, racial, and political minorities have little chance for access to the air. Frustration and outrage are generated in the people who are locked out. The inherent baseness of this lockout and the danger it poses to democratic processes and societal intercourse are readily apparent.

Since marketplace forces are deficient, regulation is clearly in order to remedy their deficiencies. More time and opportunity must be made available for discourse, less for entertainment. Broadcasters will argue that such change in programming practices will erode their economic base. Since government is not disposed to restrict their profits, regulatory policy may have to provide incentives for broadcasters to open their schedules for the discussion of important and controversial issues, and for a wide spectrum of citizenry to air their views. The essential policy may have to be tax reductions or some other form of premium that will make it profitable for broadcasters to provide greater access to their facilities. Continued domination of broadcasting by marketplace forces is too dangerous to our national interest to be tolerated.

Frederick S. Pierce
President, ABC Television

The issue comes down to whether access should be mandated for those individuals or special-interest groups who now believe they are not adequately represented on television. At ABC, we believe mandatory access would be unworkable to administer and less effective than present policies in informing the public on important issues.

Today, there is substantial access to television locally and nationally. Through public affairs and news programming, talk shows, and local editorials and responses there is significant opportunity for the airing of divergent views. In politics, the fairness doctrine gives broadcasters the responsibility to present the issues and candidates equitably.

The current policy places responsibility on broadcasters to deal with issues reflecting the broad public interest. With mandatory access, the emphasis would shift from accountability to timekeeping. There is no doubt that there are more individuals who want access to the airwaves than there is time or frequencies to accommodate them. No matter what the formula, mandatory access would be virtually impossible to administer, because of such questions as how to select the spokesperson, how to allot time, and how to judge the issues in order of importance.

Reed Irvine
Chairman of the Board
Accuracy in Media, Inc.

For a few years AIM made an effort to utilize the FCC's fairness doctrine to try to get access for points of view that we felt were being unfairly ignored in television public affairs programming. Out of some 16 fairness complaints that AIM filed with the FCC, we were able to get an FCC ruling in our favor in only one. This involved the issue of the performance of private pension plans. NBC had aired a documentary called "Pensions: The Broken Promise," which had discussed the subject from the point of view of the flaws and failures. We took the position that they should have shown that the evils they discussed applied to only a very small number of the private pension plans in effect, rather than giving the impression that these plans as a rule were riddled with fraud and deception. For once the FCC agreed and suggested that NBC had an obligation to correct the false impression that their program had created.

NBC could have satisfied the FCC by giving a defender of private pension plans a few minutes on the "Today Show." But NBC refused to take this simple and fair approach. Instead, they appealed the FCC ruling to the courts and ended up spending an estimated $250,000 in legal fees to defend their right not to tell their viewers the other side of the story.

Public television has proved to be even more arrogant than the commercial networks in its refusal to provide opportunities for the airing of views that it has slighted or ignored in treating controversial issues. Officials of PBS openly flout Section 396 (g)(1)(A) of the Communications Act, which requires that programs of a controversial nature that are funded with public money be produced with "strict adherence to objectivity and balance." The FCC has refused to enforce that provision, and the courts have backed them up in their refusal. PBS takes the view that it is not accountable to Congress, and, of course, they don't have to worry about the reactions of sponsors or viewers.

We would like to see the broadcasters demonstrate their dedication to fairness and accuracy, which they profess, by employing ombudsmen to represent the viewers within the corporate structure. We have proposed this in shareholder resolutions to CBS, ABC, and RCA, but the managements have stubbornly refused to consider this simple reform. The obvious alternative to self-discipline is the strengthening of external regulation.

Gene F. Jankowski
President, CBS

I am sure that every newspaper editor on many occasions has been made aware of the understandable frustrations of those contributors whose materials have been edited or rejected outright. Such frustrations are inevitable, since neither the *Times*, CBS, nor any other journalistic medium can accept and publish everything submitted to it for publication. The process of editorial selection of issues, spokesmen, and formats cannot be avoided, whether applied to news or to entertainment. This editorial function can be performed either by a private publisher or, as it is in some countries, by the government. The choice, under our system, is clear.

As the U.S. Supreme Court stated in 1973, in the landmark case of *CBS* v. *Democratic National Committee*, when it rejected the argument that the Constitution requires public access: "For better or worse, editing is what editors are for; and editing is selection and choice of material. That editors—newspaper or broadcast—can and do abuse this power is beyond doubt, but that is not reason to deny the discretion Congress provided. Calculated risks of abuse are taken in order to preserve higher values."

I believe that tradition, experience, and Supreme Court interpretations of the U.S. Constitution all reflect the wisdom of leaving editorial decisions to publishers and broadcasters. Any other choice would destroy the First Amendment, for broadcasters and for the print media as well. As Justice Stewart stated in the CBS case, in reflecting on the values inherent in the First Amendment, "If these values mean anything, they should mean at least this: If we must choose whether editorial decisions are to be made in the free judgment of individual broadcasters or imposed by bureaucratic fiat, the choice must be for freedom."

Norman Lear
Independent producer

The only ideas that have access to network television these days are those ideas that pro-

gram executives believe will clobber the opposition networks in a given time slot. Motivated solely by the need to win ratings, a paraphrase of any current success will have easier access than an original or innovative idea.

Network anxiety in the blistering war of the ratings is centered solely on being number one and it will adhere to the old, unfortunate adage: You don't fool with success. Joseph Papp and I learned this lesson firsthand a year ago. We went to CBS and NBC, at the time ranked two and three respectively, with a proposal to do 24 two-hour dramas, based on the works of America's best playwrights: Williams, O'Neil, Simon, etc. CBS never "took a meeting." NBC did and came to this conclusion: Since the viewers had not shown an interest in such plays produced for television recently (no steady series of this kind had ever before been offered to the public), NBC felt that they, as the number-three network, should not make such a high risk commitment. They suggested that ABC, the current kingpin, was the logical network to be offered our "lofty" proposal. When ABC heard the idea, their response was: "We're number one. Why should we take chances? Take it to NBC, they're number three."

This thinking, which denies access to ideas that have not already been proved successful, will obtain in television until we all address ourselves to modifying the chillingly competitive business climate in which most American executives are currently forced to live—or die.

As long as being number one in sales is our primary goal, we will see no more innovation or concern for the public interest in television programs than we see in automobile design or processed foods.

Lawrence K. Grossman
President, Public Broadcasting Service

Public television believes in the greatest possible access to its broadcast schedule by the widest and most diversified range of interests, institutions, candidates for public office, program-makers—and plain people.

We not only believe in it. We provide it. And we not only provide it, we are always seeking ways to increase it.

PBS was the only national television program service, for example, to carry the debates of the pre-convention presidential candidates in 1976, and the only one to provide a regular forum for minor-party candidates during the ensuing campaign. PBS alone regularly broadcasts documentaries and current affairs specials by independent filmmakers. And not just programs dealing with controversial issues: fully 30 percent of *all* of public television's original broadcast hours last year represented the work of independents.

Having said as much, however, it must also be said that there are limits to the access public television stations can provide or *should* reasonably provide. The independent local broadcast licensee, commercial or public, must in the end make the hard editorial decisions about *what* issues are covered, *how* they are covered, and *whose* voices should be heard.

Susan and Alan Raymond
*Independent documentary producers
affiliated with WNET/13*

A history of the telecasting of our documentary "The Police Tapes" will serve to illustrate the serious problems inherent in PBS's system of disseminating public affairs programming.

In 1976, we suggested and New York's PBS station WNET/13 agreed to our producing a documentary for them about the highest-crime police precinct in New York City.

"The Police Tapes" was broadcast by Channel 13 in New York initially on January 3, 1977. This was a local telecast only; the rest of America was seeing other PBS programming that evening. "Police Tapes" met with favorable reviews. Nielsen ratings revealed the New York audience for it to be sizable; it had attracted the second largest audience in history for a public affairs program on WNET/13.

Later, "Police Tapes" received a Columbia University DuPont Award for excellence in broadcast journalism. (The program was also to receive a Peabody Award as well as an Emmy Award for outstanding documentary program.)

It seemed inconceivable to us that PBS would reject the show. But they did. When the documentary came up during the Station Program Cooperative voting—the principal mechanism by which PBS stations choose their national programs—less than half of the stations voted in favor of "Police Tapes."

When individual program managers were asked why they didn't vote for "Police Tapes," many answered that they felt the documentary was only of local interest to a New York audience and that it had no relevance to their communities. When it was pointed out to them that the program had been aired in Great Britain, France, Australia, and Sweden, they still refused to acknowledge its newsworthiness.

The story does have a happy ending, however. Because we are independents and retained the rights to our work, we were able to sell "The Police Tapes" to ABC for broadcast as an "ABC Close-up." The acquisition of the program by ABC is a landmark event inasmuch as the three commercial networks have all had a long-standing rigid policy of excluding documentaries produced outside their own news gathering organizations.

We hope the example of ABC's opening the door will inspire more such acquisitions by the networks.

Emma Bowen
*President
Black Citizens for a Fair Media*

Black Citizens for a Fair Media strongly feels that the images of blacks, women, and other minorities are conceived and controlled by white males. Television programming still re-

flects stereotypes and prejudices that perpetuate feelings of inferiority in blacks and
superiority in whites. Until minorities gain access in policymaking positions in programming, in both radio and television, shows like
ABC's "Youth Terror: View from Behind the
Gun," CBS's "Baby I'm Back," and others like
them will continue to poison the minds of
viewers.

The FCC must begin to establish and uphold
policies that conform to a basic right of all of
us: the airwaves belong to *all* the people.

Jean O'Leary and Bruce Voeller
Co-Executive Directors
National Gay Task Force

To viewers seeing gays on television for the
first time during the past few seasons, it may
seem that gays have made giant strides in our
campaign for access. Indeed, we have made
progress. In recent seasons, there have been
some excellent shows about gay men as victims
of prejudice, and a few programs that acknowledged the existence of lesbians. Occasionally,
gay representatives have been interviewed on
talk shows and the network news. But we still
do not have lesbian and gay portrayals in proportion to our numbers. There is still a prepon-
derance of stereotypes and nothing close to an
accurate representation of our lives.

We think the FCC, and a new Communications Act, should require that a station's programming actually reflect the interests and
lifestyles of *all significant community groups*.
But government action isn't the real answer.
Access rights for this nation's minorities will
only come when the broadcasters themselves
stop playing the ratings game and the politics
of fear, when they recognize their own power to
decide what's an "important community prob-

lem," and when they acknowledge that, in our
pluralistic society, all TV viewers deserve access to the broadest possible range of lifestyles
and ideas.

Herbert Schmertz
Vice-President
Mobil Oil Corporation

Just prior to the 1973–74 oil crisis, Mobil
sought to buy time to air commercials warning
of this country's overdependence on foreign
oil. To our astonishment, we were refused.
When the crisis then arrived, TV news coverage of the complex factors involved proved
hopelessly inadequate. Shallow and inadequate television reporting contributed to the
public's confusion and bewilderment about the
energy issue, not infrequently offering naive
and misleading conclusions.

In an attempt to shed some light on a vital
issue, we approached the three networks to
purchase time for a series of paid messages on
energy questions. Our request was unanimously refused. We were told that it is network
policy not to sell time for discussion of "controversial issues of public importance."

Our patience finally gave way in 1976 when
WNBC, the network's New York anchor station, preferred a five-part "exposé" of the oil industry that proved a rehash of tired distortions
and factual errors. Mobil felt obligated to respond in order to correct public misunderstanding, but we had to go to the print media to
do so.

In a pluralistic society, there is no persuasive
rationale for network television's closed door,
nor for its monopoly control over the ideas and
information broadcast to the American public.
Eventually, I believe this door will be forced
open by public opinion.

SUGGESTIONS FOR FURTHER READING

Chapter 14 Issues Arising from the New Technology

Jon Bradshaw, "The Shape of Media Things to Come," *New York Magazine* (April 19, 1976): 63. "A science fiction story that's all true," this article examines some of the possible effects of today's technology on the people of the future.

Chapter 15 Broadcast Deregulation

Barry Cole and Mal Oettinger, *Reluctant Regulators:* *The FCC and the Broadcast Audience* (Reading, Mass.: Addison-Wesley Publishing Co., 1978). "An inside look at the conflicts and compromises that temper the FCC's broadcasting decisions."

Chapter 16 Access to the Media

Ernest Holsendolph, "Access Rules for Networks," *New York Times* (November 23, 1979): A25. A news analysis dealing with recent examples of access fights between politicians and TV networks.

INDEX